THE ULTIMATE PISTON FIGHTERS OF THE LUFTWAFFE

THE ULTIMATE PISTON FIGHTERS OF THE LUFTWAFFE

JUSTO MIRANDA

FONTHILL

Fonthill Media Limited
Fonthill Media LLC
www.fonthillmedia.com
office@fonthillmedia.com

First published in the United Kingdom and the Unites States of America 2014
Reprinted 2015 and 2021

British Library Cataloguing in Publication Data:
A catalogue record for this book is available from the British Library

ISBN 978-1-78155-249-0

Typeset in 11pt on 15pt Mrs Eaves XL Serif Narrow
Printed and bound in England

Contents

Introduction

During little more than five years of the Second World War, the power of engines and speed of aircraft increased as much as it did during twenty years of peacetime.

Conventional aircraft and engines reached the limits marked in their original design and even surpassed them, very quickly. The basis for this huge achievement was exotic fuels, short-lived artificially overpowered engines, propellers with four, five and even six blades and thinner wings with special sections of laminar flow.

Some pilots even ordered the paint on their aircraft polished to gain speed. The limit had been reached and the industry was ready for the arrival of the turbojet and the arrowed wing.

And then aviation science discovered the existence of the demon that lived in the air...

On the morning of 6 September 1942, radar positioned along Britain's east coast detected several airplanes coming in from the southeast.

They were six Messerschmitt Me 210 A-1 Zerstörer of the 16./KG6 that had taken off an hour before in a *Frei Jagd* mission from the Dutch base of Soesterburg. The Me 210 was the most modern of the Luftwaffe fighters. Their crews, coming from units of Bf 110, had just one month experience with the new model and were on their first operational sortie.

Several Hawker Typhoon IB of the RAF No. 1 Squadron (code JX) went out to intercept them. The unit, based in Acklington, had exchanged their Hurricanes for Typhoons in July and this was also their first combat with the new Hawker model. The Zerstörer was very fast – 350 mph at 17,820 ft; the Typhoons flew at 412 mph at the same altitude.

It was a difficult interception with the British starting a steep dive at 30,000 ft to gain speed. In the rarefied air, the 7-ton machines accelerated violently and, when reaching 25,000 ft, with the instruments reading 450 mph, the aircraft were actually flying at 675 mph (Mach 0.64). At this point, the Typhoons suddenly went out of control. The ailerons did not respond properly, the horizontal tailplane suffered a violent flutter and the control column jumped in the pilots' hands as if alive.

The whole structure was under a high frequency vibration, transferring to the pilot a feeling similar to an electric current, and the air that circulated through the radiator went in the opposite direction to usual!

At Mach 0.75, a shockwave was formed above the wings and the air around the cockpit went white. At 20,000 ft, the denser air started to restrain the airplanes; upon reaching 18,000 ft, most puzzlingly, the controls were again working fine.

Even after such a terrifying experience, the British pilots still had the courage to reach two of the Messerschmitts (2H+HA and 2N+CA) that had fallen behind and shot them down over Yorkshire.

Back in Acklington, they reported the deficiencies and the pilot notes had to be rewritten. After suffering twenty-eight deathly accidents, the aircraft had to be used as low altitude bomber, abandoning the primary task for which it had been designed. Its German opponent was no more fortunate and was also taken out of service within that same year.

Twin-engined fighters like the Me 210 and Me 262, designed before 1942, were not suitable for high-altitude combat. The reasons were their great mass and the turbulence generated between the lower face of the wing and the engine nacelles.

The same fate was suffered by the British high-altitude interceptor the Westland Welkin in November, and the naval fighter the Firebrand, which had to be converted into a torpedo-strike fighter airplane due to its control problems at high altitude, in March 1943.

Around the same time, the new American fighters P.38 Lightning and P.47 Thunderbolt – based in England – started suffering strange accidents when diving from high altitude.

Something was definitely wrong with the second generation of war fighters...

The odd phenomenon was called compressibility and different types of aircraft suffered it at different speeds, and it manifested itself in different ways, usually defined under the term *compressibility buffeting*. The cause of all this was an odd physical phenomenon known by aerodynamicists as the *Coanda effect*. It states that any fluid running above a curve surface tends to adhere to it and increase its speed proportionally to its curvature.

The wing of the Typhoon was very thick (18 per cent thickness/chord ratio) and in the superior curvature the air flux made itself locally supersonic at 0.64 Mach, producing a shockwave and, therefore, huge structural charges in the tail and in the rear section of the fuselage.

The problem with the Lightning manifested itself at 0.675 Mach as turbulence generated in the junction between the pilot nacelle and the wing. At 0.73 Mach, the disturbance reached the tailplane, pressing down the control surface so that it could not be operated by the pilot to get the airplane out of the dive.

In the Thunderbolt, the disturbance was generated by the cowling of the engine and tended to jam the tailplane at 0.805 Mach. Both airplanes were equipped with an electrically driven dive flap that opened up to 35 degrees in less than one second. Its purpose was not to act as an airbrake, given that, at 25,000 ft, it would not have produced a significant loss of speed. Rather, the turbulence generated when opening the dive flap raised the nose of the machine and effectively took it out of the dive.

The Welkin was designed with an even thicker wing than the Typhoon (19.15 per cent), and suffered such vibrations during the flight test that it was forbidden to take this machine up to its design height when in combat. Its operational career was a symbolic one, never being attached to a squadron.

It is an accepted fact nowadays that the Allied designers never understood the true causes of the compressibility phenomenon. At the end of the war – when they had access to the research conducted by the Germans on the areas of swept wings, the transonic flux, the Mach critical number of the air intakes with an air-flow separator for the boundary layer – the cultural shock was similar to that produced in the Newtonian world with the introduction of the relativistic physics.

The difficulty in understanding these problems during the 1940s was due to the lack of tunnels for testing aerodynamic designs with supersonic capabilities. The only way of studying the supersonic performance of a scale model was to install it over the wing of a fast airplane and film it during a high speed dive. Doing so, the air reached local supersonic speed over the wing, but the airplane did not enter into the uncontrolled phase of the flight – something similar to the few seconds effect of zero gravity that astronauts experience aboard a fast plane in a parabolic flight during training.

This type of research was dangerous and difficult to perform, producing results that were either distorted by the vibrations of the carrier plane, or by unclear films, due to the loss of transparency of the air caused by the turbulence.

The jump seemed too big, however. The engineers never liked to face several innovations within the same project. It was therefore inevitable that some transition models appeared partially based on what had been done up to that point.

Some variants of conventional aircraft were designed with a jet engine replacing the piston engine (Yakovlev Yak-15, Lavockin La 174 Tk). Others had the solid nose housing the armament and two jet engines hanging under the wings (Hawker P.1048, Sukhoi Su-9).

In other cases, the conventional engine was retained and a turbojet, or a just a burner, was installed at the tail, to increase the performance (Ryan FR-1 Fireball, Mikoyan I-250/N, Sukhoi Su-5, Vultee XP-81).

Some fighters were designed with a pusher airscrew using either the twin boom configuration and straight wing (Gloster P 18/37, SAAB J21a, De Schelde S.21, Vultee XP-54) or arrowed wings with empennages mounted over them.

To avoid length instability, some of them had a Canard-type empennage on the nose (Curtiss XP-55 Ascender) although the most advanced ones (Northrop XP-56) did not use them. These two American aircraft reached the flying stage, benefitting from the manufacturer's wide experience in the design of flying wings. Control was achieved by means of vertical tailfins and rudder control aero-boost ducts on the wingtips.

And meanwhile, what were the Germans doing?

They had their own problems, of supply, caused by the naval blockade.

German industry was not able to produce the specially heat and stress-resistant metallic alloys that were required. They lacked metals like the chromium and molybdenum that were essential to harden the steel. Germany had exhausted their stocks and could not import them during the war, as also happened with rubber and oil.

The chemists produced silicones to replace the rubber and made synthetic oil of low quality from coal, but the ceramic materials for the compressor blades of the turbojets would not be ready on time and everyone knew it.

The lack of oil suffered by Germany during the last year of the war induced scientists and engineers to experiment with alternative fuels.

The most refined gasoline was used for conventional piston engines. The BMW 003 turbojets worked with B.4 (87 octane petrol). The J2 and K1 burnt by the Jumo 004 and Heinkel HeS 011 turbojets were heavy kerosenes. The Argus pulsejet of the V-1 worked with crude oil. The Peenemünde engineers designed a V-2 that worked with diesel oil and S-Stoff. Dr Pabst, from the Gas Dynamics section of the Focke Wulf company, suggested that the ramjets of the future Triebflügel fighter burn even less volatile fuels, such as pitch oil or lignite tar. To that end, they had to design a compact evaporating plant that could be installed onboard.

This situation particularly affected the conventional piston engines. The poor ratings of the 87 octane B4 fuel and the poor quality of Schmiertoff lubricant, which obliged engines to be run at high revolutions to deliver the required horsepower, were the cause of numerous problems, while deficient Kühlsotff (50 per cent glycol, 50 per cent water) cooling, vibration fractures and disintegration of bearings, due to shortage of tin during its manufacturing, caused corrosion and piston seizure.

To avoid these deficiencies, some engines were redesigned with bigger cylinders and twin (three-speed) superchargers, due to the poor performance (just thirty minutes) of the one-stage superchargers of first generation.

Attempts were also made to improve performance using two new power boost injection systems, the GM-1 (liquid nitrous oxide) for altitudes over 10,000 metres and the MW-50 (50 per cent methanol, 49.5 per cent water and 0.5 per cent Schutzöl 39 anticorrosion fluid) for emergency power boost at medium altitude.

In spite of all these issues, the reliability of the new BMW 003 and Jumo 004 turbojets, and the HWK 109 rocket engine was so low that the Oberkommando der Luftwaffe allowed the development of some piston engines to continue until February 1945.

As NASA did in the 1960s, the German aeronautical industry was forced to compensate the lack of power of their engines with high technology solutions – in the 1960s it was microelectronics to save weight, in the 1940s, it was aerodynamics.

The research sites of the Luftwaffe were the most magnificent and fully-equipped that the world had ever seen. The most important was the Luftfahrtforschungsanstalt Herman Göring (LFA) located near Braunschweig. By the end of the war, the LFA had five wind tunnels (two of them were supersonic for 1.8 Mach and 4 Mach), a low pressure tunnel for armament testing at high altitude (0.02 atmosphere), and a 10 G centrifugal machine to simulate combat manoeuvres. In the LFA, Dr Zobel used Zeiss interferometers and high-speed moving pictures to measure the pressure distribution around airfoils in the wind tunnels at supersonic speed, and Dr Buseman developed the swept-wing theory for high speed flight.

In Stuttgart, the Luftfahrtforschungsanstalt Graf Zeppelin (LGZ) was equipped with six wind tunnels and dedicated to subsonic ballistics.

In Kochel, the Wasserbau Versuchsanstalt Kochelsee (WVA) had a 4.4 Mach wind tunnel dedicated to the study of the aerondynamics of the A4 rockets.

The Technische Akademie der Luftwaffe (TAL) in Berlin-Gatow, developed a system to study the shockwaves using the Röntgenblitz (flash radiographic device).

In Berlin, the Deutsche Versuchsanstalt für Luftfahrt (DVL) was an organisation tasked with researching the security of military and civil airplanes while in flight. They developed the *area rule* theory and the boundary-layer fences.

The Luftfahrt Forschungsanstalt München (LFM) located in Munich, was dedicated to aeronautical medicine.

In Göttingen, the Aerodynamische Versuchsantalt für Segelflug (DFS) studied gliders and rocket propelled airplanes.

In Stuttgart, the Institut für Kraftfahrtzeuge und Flugmotoren (FKFS) specialised in aircraft engines.

The Flugfunk Forschungsanstalt (FFA) dedicated itself to electronics in Oberpfaffenhofen.

And there also were the organisations of theoretical scientists, DMW, ZWB, LGL and RFR, that coordinated the data coming from all the other research centres.

By the end of the war, a wind tunnel with a diameter of 3.5 metres and capacity for 10 Mach was being built in Kochel. Another of 8 metres and 1 Mach, with the capacity for real size models, was also being built in Otztal.

The theoretical studies about the compressibility were finished by 1941 and there were five different programs to build several types of supersonic airplanes running by the end of the war.

It is interesting to follow the evolution of the German piston fighters as they were incorporating into their design the aerodynamic refinements recommended by the LFA: in the Focke Wulf fighter with Jumo 222, of 22 October 1942, with the propeller still positioned on the nose, but the engine on the centre of the fuselage and the wing moderately swept in the leading edge only; the Blohm un Voss P.192.01 of February 1944, the propeller positioned behind the cockpit; the Daimler Benz Hochleistungsflugzeugh with DB 609 of 5 March 1942, with the propeller back to the mid of the fuselage. The Blohm und Voss P.193, of February 1944, with the engine still in the central section of the fuselage while the propeller is installed behind the tail surfaces. The Dornier P.252/3, of March 1945, with propellers bent backwards as if trying to leave the airplane, in an effort to reduce the drag

The evolution of wings and tail surfaces shows similar change, gradually bending towards the rear of the airplane, while the engine was installed at each new stage in a position more towards the rear.

The radiators were moved to inside the airplane, receiving the refrigeration air through the lateral air intakes located at the wing roots, in the Dornier P.247 and Focke Wulf Hochleistungsjäger of March 1945. By the end of the war, we see the shape of these fighters practically the same as that of the postwar jets. All that remained was the small step of replacing the piston engine with a turbojet and removing the radiators.

Actually, there was never an explosive mutation between the Bf 109 of the early war and the Me P.1110 of January 1945. The designers created a whole series of intermediate steps, following the conservative principles of good engineering.

The specialised authors' fascination for the great variety of futuristic German designs, powered by turbojets has left in the background the research on those last fighters driven by piston engines. The purpose of this book is to present them to the public, for its notable interest.

Justo Miranda
Madrid, December 2012

Chapter 1

Blohm und Voss BV 155 Karawanken

One of the golden rules of strategy states that he who holds the highest position gets a natural advantage over the adversary. He can see at a greater distance and has gravity on his side. This is the reason behind the great fortresses of the past, the observation balloons of yesterday, and the reconnaissance satellites of today. In the aviation world, altitude was the most important thing until anti-aircraft missiles came into scene.

The British Wellingtons that made raids into Europe during the Second World War suffered a remarkably low percentage of losses, compared to the more powerful and modern Lancasters and Halifaxes. The reason behind this being that they flew at higher altitude.

In the Far East, the American Curtiss P-40 fighters could only shoot down the formidable Mitsubishi Zero using their superior ceiling, which allowed them to dive and get away at a high speed.

Many Air Forces at that time had specially modified their airplanes to be used for photographic reconnaissance at high altitude and, at the same time, as fighters to target those enemy reconnaissance airplanes.

Equipment and weapons, sometimes even the paint, were removed to allow aircraft to get ever lighter, and thus ever higher than the enemy. Engines were modified to increase the admission pressure, which in turn decreased the useful life of the machine. This measure was necessary for the engines to get oxygen enough in the thinner air in which they had to fly. Engineers and physiologists cooperated to improve the flying suits and the oxygen regulators to be used at high altitude.

The men responsible for aeronautical production resisted the idea of stopping the already overloaded assembly lines and making short series of special airplanes to the detriment of conventional ones. The recommendation to the manufacturers was that, instead of designing specific models for high-altitude flight, they should focus on modifying existing airplanes. The objective was to use as many common pieces as possible.

In June 1943, the Germans flew the Messerschmitt Bf 109H Höhenjäger. It was a version derived from Bf 109 F-4 for high-altitude flight. This was achieved by increasing the wingspan through the addition of a central rectangular section of 336 cm. The wings and the landing gear of an F-4 were fitted to both sides of this addition.

The small number of modified airplanes were named Bf 109 H-0 and were part of the preproduction series with DB 601 E-1 engines. Some cells of the Bf 109 G-5 were modified using the engine DB 605 A and a pressure cabin. The result was the Bf 109 H-1. Several units of this version were concentrated in the French airbase of Guyancourt for operational evaluation at the beginning of 1944. They flew over the British Isles in photographic reconnaissance missions at an altitude of 13,500 m with big fuel tanks slung under the wings. One of them was shot down over the British naval base of Scapa Flow by one of the optimised for high-altitude Spitfire Mk VIII fighters on 21 February 1944.

Three more versions were planned: The Bf 109 H-2 (Schwerer Höhenjäger) with heavy armament, the H-3 (Leichter Höhenjäger) with light armament, and the H-4 for photographic reconnaissance. None of them were ever manufactured after the H-1 flying tests revealed a too weak wing structure.

This was the end of the Sofort Programm, the objective of which was to immediately achieve results using the airplanes available at the time. The Vorrücken Programm, which was developed in parallel from 1942 and was based on new designs and high technology, was to replace the Sofort Programm.

The RLM published a specification, on 20 May 1942, for the design of the Spezial Höhenjäger that should be able to fly at an altitude above 14,000 metres.

In response, Messerschmitt proposed to adapt the failed Me 209, in the same line of the Bf 109 H. They even built a prototype (Me 209 H V1) with a central section added to the wingspan and an increased tail surface area. The engine to be used (DB 627) was never built and the airplane was finished with a DB 603 G.

Focke Wulf presented three designs: Höhenjäger 1, Höhenjäger 2 and Ta 152 H, the last being the winner in the contest due to the ease of exchanging parts with the FW 190 D-9, already in production.

Meanwhile, the Messerschmitt technicians worked on two more programs: The Me 155 Ausführung B and Me P 1091 Extremer Höhenjäger. The former profited from all the experience derived from the design of the Me 155 Ausführung A naval fighter and was to be used over the *Graf Zeppelin* aircraft carrier. It was cancelled on January 1943. The second program was used to research the construction of wings of greater span and the integration of a turbosupercharger TKL15 in a fighter airframe.

The Me 155 B – optimised variant for high-altitude flight – still had the extended wing and the Fw 190-style landing gear of its predecessor, adding a pressurised cockpit and a two-stage turbosupercharger DB 628 engine.

The Me P1091 Stage II was centred on the design of a 20.5 metre wing. It was designed for high structural resistance containing the landing gear, fuel, two radiators and two Mk 108 guns.

The Me P1091 Stage III had a new, widened fuselage, containing the TKL15, and was to be driven by a DB 632 with contra-rotating airscrews.

All this research resulted in the Me 155 B-1, with a new design of the wing, more fuel and aerodynamic fairing for the new landing gear, which was longer and heavier. It kept the blade system of the P1091 Stage III and the TKL15, but the engine was replaced by the DB 603 U with 1,810 hp.

In August 1943, it was made evident that the Messerschmitt Company, suffering an overload of wartime orders, lacked the right staff to start the production of the Me 155. The RLM decided that a team of technicians and engineers of the Blohm und Voss Company – underemployed due to the low demand for seaplanes – were to be translated to the Augsburg site to support the Me 155 project.

Messerschmitt policy was to manufacture a hybrid using as many common components as possible from the models in production at the time. It was decided that Me 155 B-1 should use the wingtips, tail and landing gear from the Bf 109 G series, and the tailfin and engine bearers from the Me 209.

This hasty style of work, characteristic of wartime, was not well accepted by the Blohm und Voss team. They were used to building reliable and sturdy machines and found many structural errors, requesting a new design. The result was that the new fighter never became operational during the war.

After studying the case, the RLM decided to translate the whole project to Blohm und Voss (as BV 155 A). They took the rest of 1943 to redesign the wing, increasing lift and fuel capacity, mounting two big radiators over the landing gear housing, replacing the latest with one from the Junkers Ju 87 D-6 and increasing the structural stiffness and the area of the tail surfaces.

The engine attachment and integration of the TKL were also reviewed and, to reduce weight, only a four-bladed propeller was kept. The wind tunnel tests revealed that the coolers stayed in the vacuum area generated by the wing during the take-off and that the aerodynamic fineness of the model was still far from perfect.

As a consequence, the design of the BV 155 B included purer lines, a cantilever tailplane, and coolers (with four lowered slats) under the wing.

There was a new requirement to reduce the armament to two guns of 20 mm and one of 30 mm. This resulted on the BV 155 B-1 variant, considered the final production version, in June 1944.

The first model was the BV 155 V1 (W. Nr. 360051). It was finished on 22 December 1944 and flew for the first time on 8 February 1945. At the end of the war, the manufacturing of the V2 (W. Nr. 360052) and V3 (W. Nr. 360053) was not complete.

The mechanisms that proved problematic during the BV 155 V1 tests were suppressed from the design of the BV 155 C. The landing gear track proved to be too wide, the shock absorbers suffered with the landing impact and the coolers handicapped the aerodynamic performance, subjecting the wing structure to undesirable loads.

Two coolers were installed under the engine of the BV 155 C, in the same position as in the British Tempest, and a more conventional landing gear was adopted that was retractable under the fuselage.

From the four planned prototypes, the manufacturing of just the first (V4) started before the end of the war. The BV 155 C-1 would have been the production version.

Connected to the No. 155 program, the Blohm und Voss company produced two more designs. The first one was a conventional model (P.205), which might be considered as a transition airplane between the BV 155 B and the BV 155 C. The second design was a jet model (P.198) created to profit from the great power of the projected turbojet BMW 018.

Messerschmitt Me 155 B Technical Data

Stage	Design (December 1942).
Type	High-altitude interceptor.
Wings	Metallic structure and cladding (with two coolers).
Fuselage	Same as Bf 109 G-5, with pressurised cockpit.
Empennages	Also the same as in the BF 109 G-5, built from wood.
Landing gear	Retractable towards the inside. Retractable tail wheel unit.
Engine	A Daimler Benz DB 628 of 12 cylinders in inverted-V, liquid cooled, with a two-stages turbosupercharger mechanically operated and an induction heat exchanger. It had an estimated power of 1,475 hp at 11,000 m
Propeller	Three-bladed, metallic, 3,370 mm in diameter.
Fuel tanks	Three tanks in wings and fuselage
Armament	Three MG 151/20 guns, one shooting through the propeller axis and two installed at the wing roots.
Wingspan	12.67 m
Length	9.65 m
Height	3.74 m
Ceiling	14,000 m

Messerschmitt Me 155 B-1 Technical Data

Stage	Design (9 September 1943).
Type	High-altitude interceptor.
Wings	Metallic structure and cladding (with four or eight coolers).
Fuselage	Metallic structure and cladding (pressurised cockpit).
Empennages	Built from wood.
Landing gear	Retractable outboard. It went into a special housing located at the leading edge. Wheels of 740 x 290 mm. Retractable tail wheel unit of 380 x 150 mm
Engine	A Daimler Benz DB 603 U of 12 cylinders in inverted-V, liquid cooled, with a Heinkel-Hirth TKL 15 turbosupercharger in addition to the normalised two-stage turbosupercharger, mechanically driven. It had an estimated power of 1,810 hp at take-off and of 12,500 hp at 13,533 m
Propeller	VDM 9 with two contra-rotating devices of four blades each and a diameter of 3,400 mm
Fuel tanks	In the version with four coolers, it was planned one of 410 litres in the fuselage together with four of 160 litres and two of 80 litres in the wings. In the eight coolers version, one of 410 litres in the fuselage and two of 450 litres in the wings.
Armament	Three Mk 108 guns of 30 mm, one of them shooting through the propeller axis and the other two on the wings, shooting outside the circle swept by the propeller.
Wingspan	21 m
Length	11.65 m
Height	3.80 m
Wing area	39 sq m
Empty weight	4,870 kg

Loaded weight	5,530 kg
Max. speed	690 km/h at 16,000 m
Ceiling	16,950 m
Range	1,500 km
Electronics	A Lorenz FuG 16 transmitter/receiver (38.5-42.3 MHz).

Messerschmitt Me P1091 (Stage II) Technical Data

Stage	Design (June 1943).
Type	High-altitude interceptor.
Wings	Metallic structure and cladding (with two coolers).
Fuselage	Metallic structure and cladding (pressurised cockpit).
Empennages	Built from wood.
Landing gear	One from the Bf 109 G-5. Retractable tail wheel unit.
Engine	A Daimler Benz DB 628 of 12 cylinders in inverted-V, liquid cooled, with a two-stage turbosupercharger (mechanically driven) and a heat exchanger by induction. It had an estimated power of 1,475 hp at 11,000 m
Propeller	A metallic three-bladed VDM with a diameter of 2,965 mm
Fuel tanks	Two on the wings and two on the fuselage.
Armament	Three Mk 108 guns of 30 mm, one of them shooting through the propeller axis and the other two shooting outside the circle swept by the propeller, from the wings.
Wingspan	20 m
Length	11.95 m
Height	3.92 m

Messerschmitt Me P1091a (Stage III) Technical Data

Stage	Design (second half of 1943).
Type	High-altitude interceptor.
Wings	Metallic structure and cladding (with two coolers).
Fuselage	Metallic structure and cladding (pressurised cockpit).
Empennages	Built from wood.
Landing gear	The same than in a Bf 109 G-5. Retractable tail wheel unit.
Engine	A Daimler Benz DB 632 of 12 cylinders in inverted-V, liquid cooled, with a Heinkel-Hirth TKL 15 turbosupercharger in addition to the normalised two-stage turbosupercharger, mechanically driven. It had an estimated power of 2,400 hp.
Propeller	Two contra-prop devices with four blades each and a diameter of 3,960 mm
Fuel tanks	Two on the wings and one on the fuselage.
Armament	Three Mk 108 guns off 30 mm, one of them shooting through the propeller axis and the other two shooting outside the circle swept by the propeller, from the wings.
Wingspan	20.50 m
Length	11.952 m
Height	3.90 m

Blohm und Voss BV 155 A Technical Data	
Stage	Design (1943).
Type	High-altitude interceptor.
Wings	Metallic structure and cladding with two big housings for the coolers, where the landing gear also lodged.
Fuselage	Metallic structure and cladding (pressurised cockpit).
Empennages	Built from wood with lower struts.
Landing gear	One from the Junkers Ju 87 D-6. Retractable tail wheel unit.
Engine	A Daimler Benz DB 603 U of 12 cylinders in inverted-V, liquid cooled, with a Heinkel-Hirth TKL 15 turbosupercharger in addition to the normalised two-stage turbosupercharger, mechanically driven. It had an estimated power was of 1,810 hp at take-off and of 1,225 hp at 13,533 m
Propeller	Four-bladed VDM with a diameter of 3,600 mm
Fuel tanks	Two on the wings and one on the fuselage.
Armament	Three Mk 108 guns of 30 mm, one of them shooting through the propeller axis and the other two shooting outside the circle swept by the propeller, from the wings.
Wingspan	20.80 m
Length	12 m
Height	4.10 m

Blohm und Voss BV 155 B-1 Technical Data	
Stage	Flight tests (February 1945).
Type	High-altitude interceptor.
Wings	Metallic structure and cladding housing seven fuel tanks – one of 114 litres two of 193 litres and four of 250 litres These contained the landing gear, the coolers and part of the armament. Two auxiliary tanks of 300 litres – to be launched – or two Mk 103 guns of 30 mm that could be suspended under the external sections of the wings.
Fuselage	Metallic structure and cladding, armoured and pressurised cockpit with ejectable canopy – by means of explosive bolts. Armoured seat.
Empennages	Cantilever type, built from wood.
Landing gear	One from a Ju 87 D-6 with retractable tail wheel .
Engine	A Daimler Benz DB 603 U of 12 cylinders in inverted-V, liquid cooled, equipped with a Heinkel-Hirth TKL 15 turbosupercharger in addition to the normalised two-stage turbosupercharger, mechanically driven. It had an estimated power of 1,810 hp at take-off and of 1,225 hp at 13,533 m
Propeller	Four-bladed VDM built from wood and a diameter of 3,700 mm
Fuel tanks	The seven already described in the wings and another of 410 litres in the fuselage.
Armament	One Mk 108 gun of 30 mm with 75 cartridges, shooting through the propeller axis. Two MG 151/20 shooting outside the circle swept by the propeller, on the wings, each with 200 cartridges.
Electronics	Reflex gun sight Revi 16 B or Askania EZ-42, telescopic gun sight ZFR-3, reconnaissance camera Rb 75/30, radio transmitter/receiver FuG 16 ZY, I.F.F. FuG 25a.

Wingspan	20.33 m
Length	12.10 m
Height	4.02 m
Wing area	38.50 sq m
Empty weight	5,199 kg
Loaded weight	6,037 kg
Max. speed	690 km/h at 16,000 m
Landing speed	170 km/h
Ceiling	16,950 m
Range	1,440 km

Blohm und Voss BV 155 C-1 Technical Data

Stage	Prototype building (May 1945).
Type	High-altitude interceptor.
Wings	Metallic structure and cladding housing seven fuel tanks – one of 114 litres, two of 193 litres, and four of 250 litres These contained the landing gear and two guns of 20 mm. The installation of two auxiliary and launch tanks was planned. Two additional guns of the Mk 103 or Mk 108 type could also be installed.
Fuselage	Metallic structure and cladding, armoured and pressurised cockpit with ejectable canopy – by means of explosive bolts.
Empennages	Cantilever type, built from wood.
Landing gear	Retractable inboard, leaving the wheels (840 x 300 mm) housed in the fuselage, behind the cooler. Retractable tail wheel unit of 380 x 150 mm
Engine	A Daimler Benz DB 603 U of 12 cylinders in inverted-V, liquid cooled, equipped with a Heinkel-Hirth TKL 15 turbosupercharger in addition to the normalised two-stage turbosupercharger, mechanically driven. It had an MW50 power boosting injection system, using methanol-water. Its estimated power was of 1,810 hp at take-off and of 1,225 hp at 13,533 m
Propeller	Four-bladed VDM built from wood and a diameter of 3,700 mm
Fuel tanks	The seven already described in the wings and another of 410 litres in the fuselage.
Armament	One Mk 108 gun of 30 mm with 75 cartridges, shooting through the propeller axis. Two MG 151/20 shooting outside the circle swept by the propeller, on the wings, each with 200 cartridges.
Electronics	Reflex gun sight Askania EZ-42 Adler, two reconnaissance cameras Rb 75/30, radio transmitter/receiver FuG 15, I.F.F. FuG 25.
Wingspan	19.05 m
Length	12.10 m
Height	4.17 m
Wing area	35.80 sq m
Empty weight	5,682 kg
Loaded weight	6,384 kg
Max. speed	690 km/h at 15,000 m
Landing speed	180 km/h
Ceiling	16,830 m

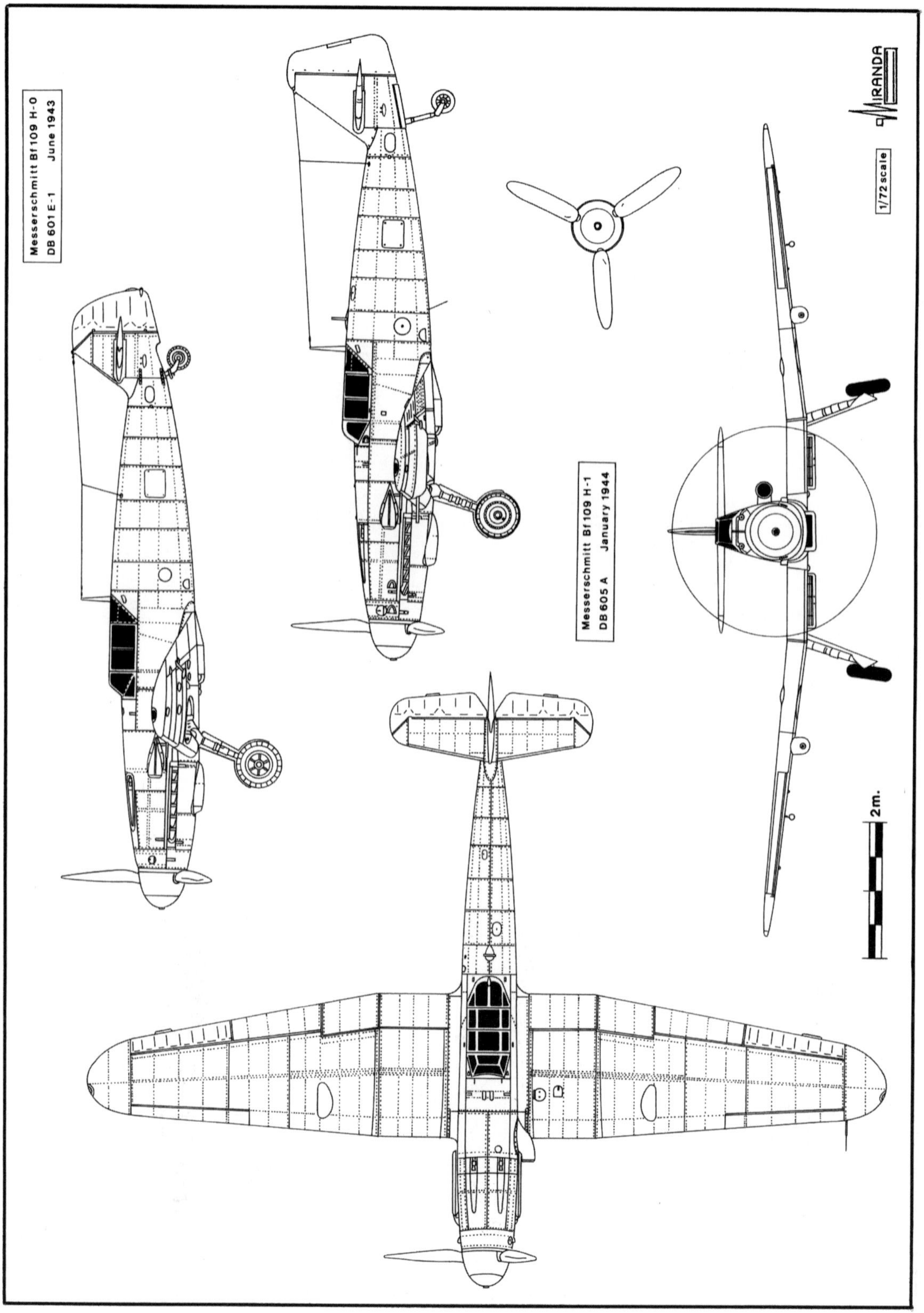
Messerschmitt Bf109 H-0
DB 601 E-1 June 1943
Messerschmitt Bf109 H-1
DB 605 A January 1944
1/72 scale
MIRANDA
2m.

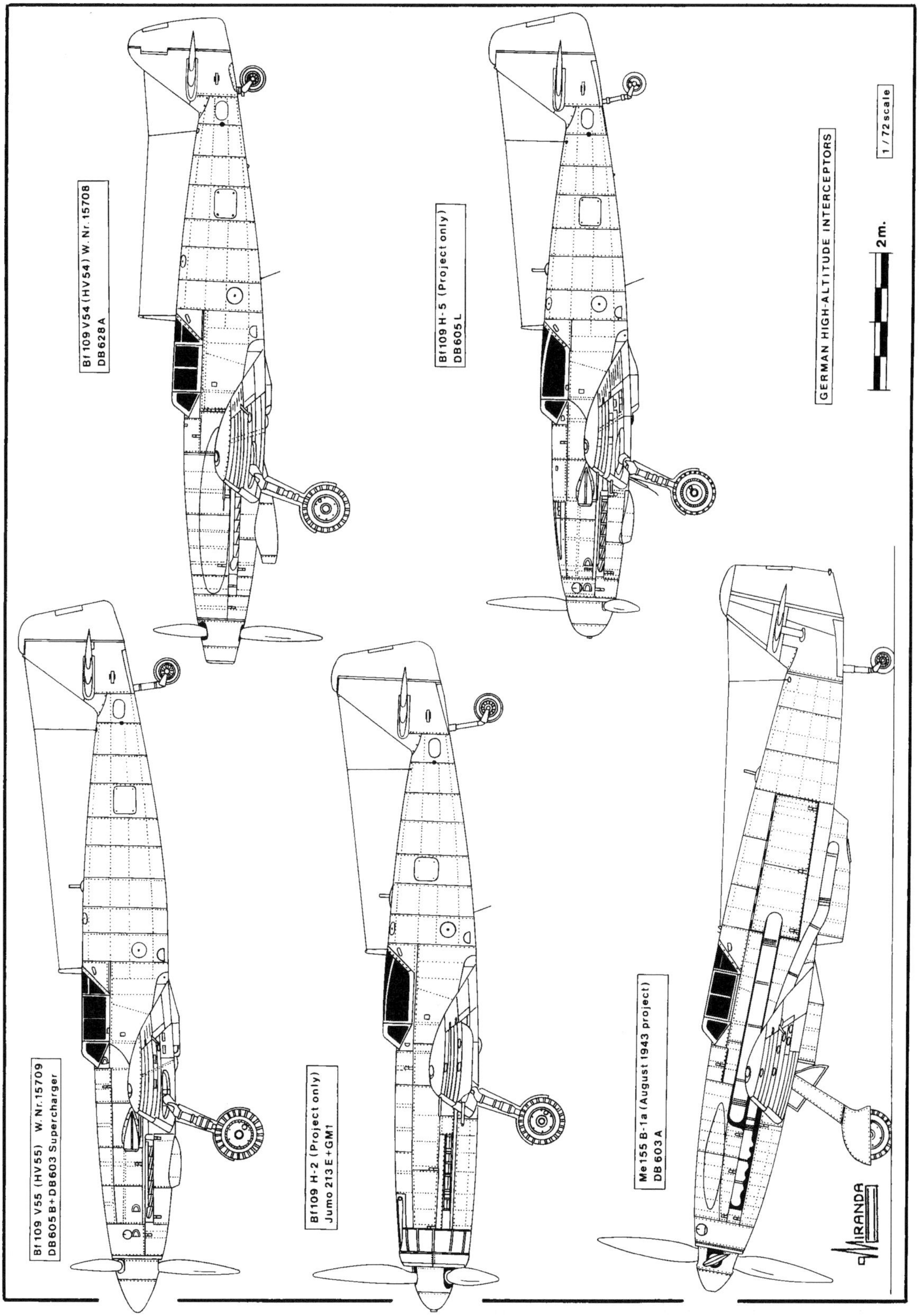
Bf 109 V54 (HV54) W. Nr. 15708
DB 628 A
Bf 109 H-5 (Project only)
DB 605 L
GERMAN HIGH-ALTITUDE INTERCEPTORS
1 / 72 scale
2 m.
Bf 109 V55 (HV55) W. Nr. 15709
DB 605 B + DB 603 Supercharger
Bf 109 H-2 (Project only)
Jumo 213 E + GM1
Me 155 B-1a (August 1943 project)
DB 603 A
MIRANDA

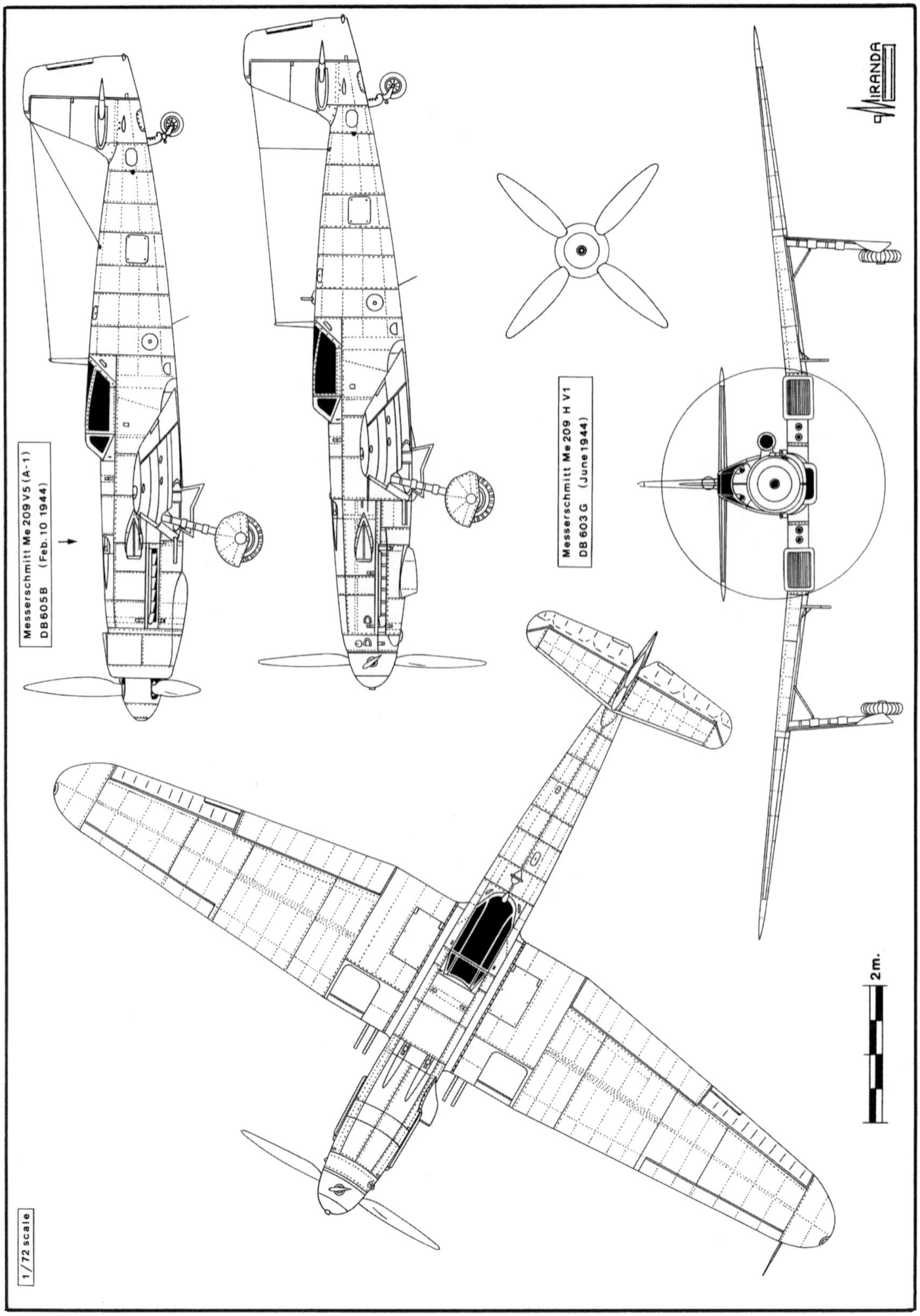
Messerschmitt Me 209 V5 (A-1)
DB605B (Feb.10 1944)
Messerschmitt Me 209 H V1
DB 603 G (June 1944)
2m.
1/72 scale

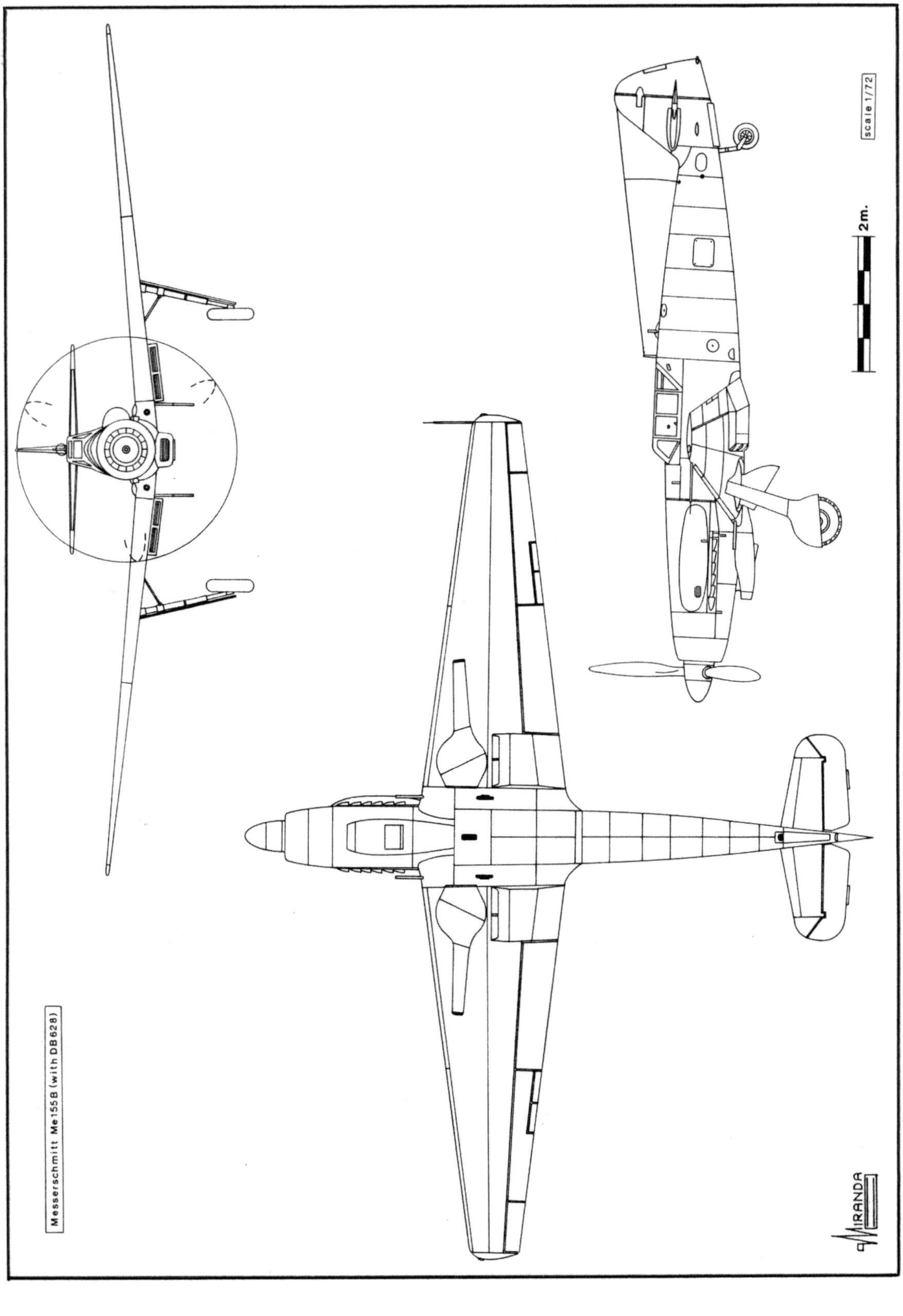
Messerschmitt Me155B (with DB628)
scale 1/72
2m.
MIRANDA

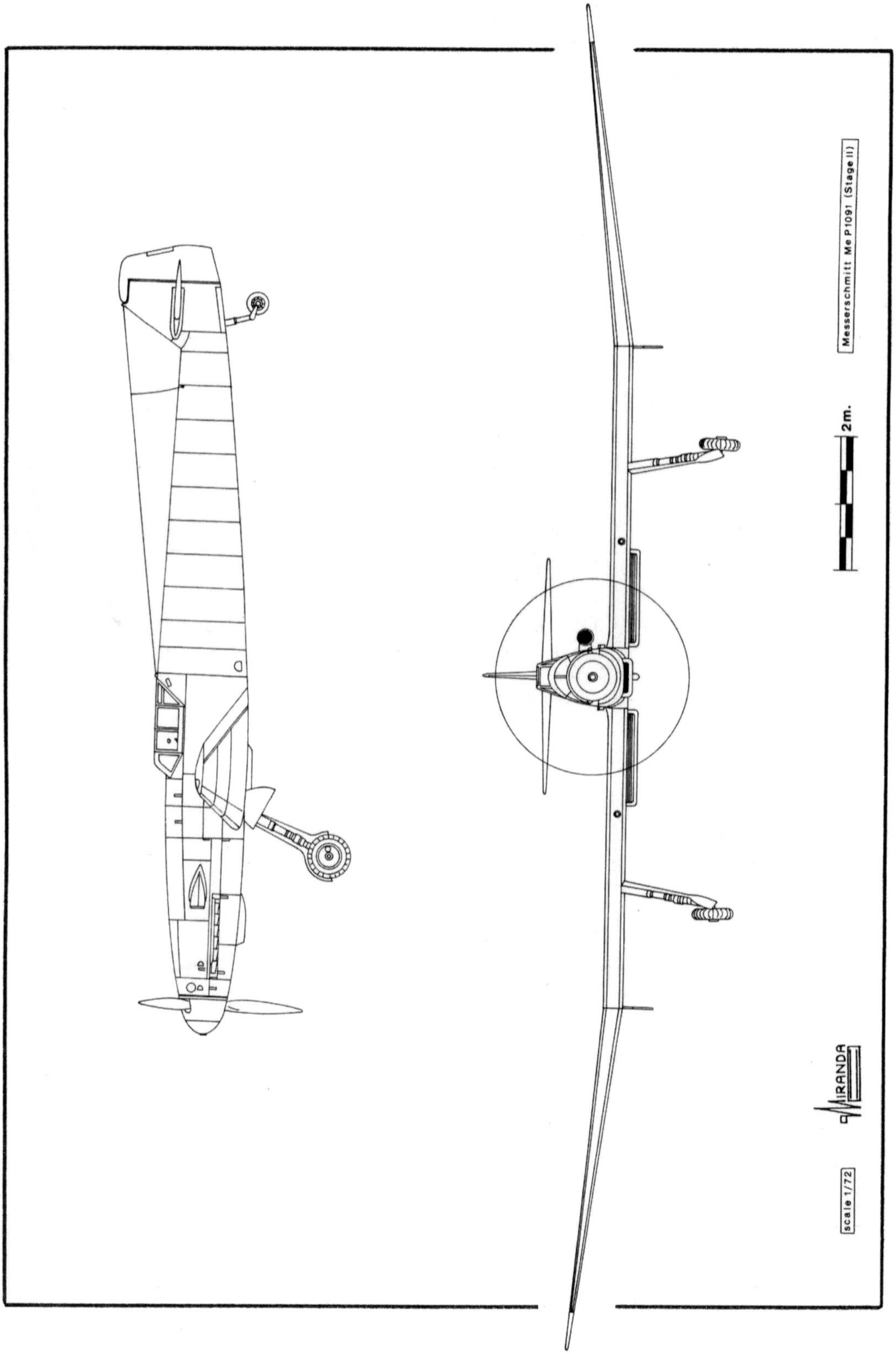
Messerschmitt Me P1091 (Stage II)
2m.
MIRANDA
scale 1/72

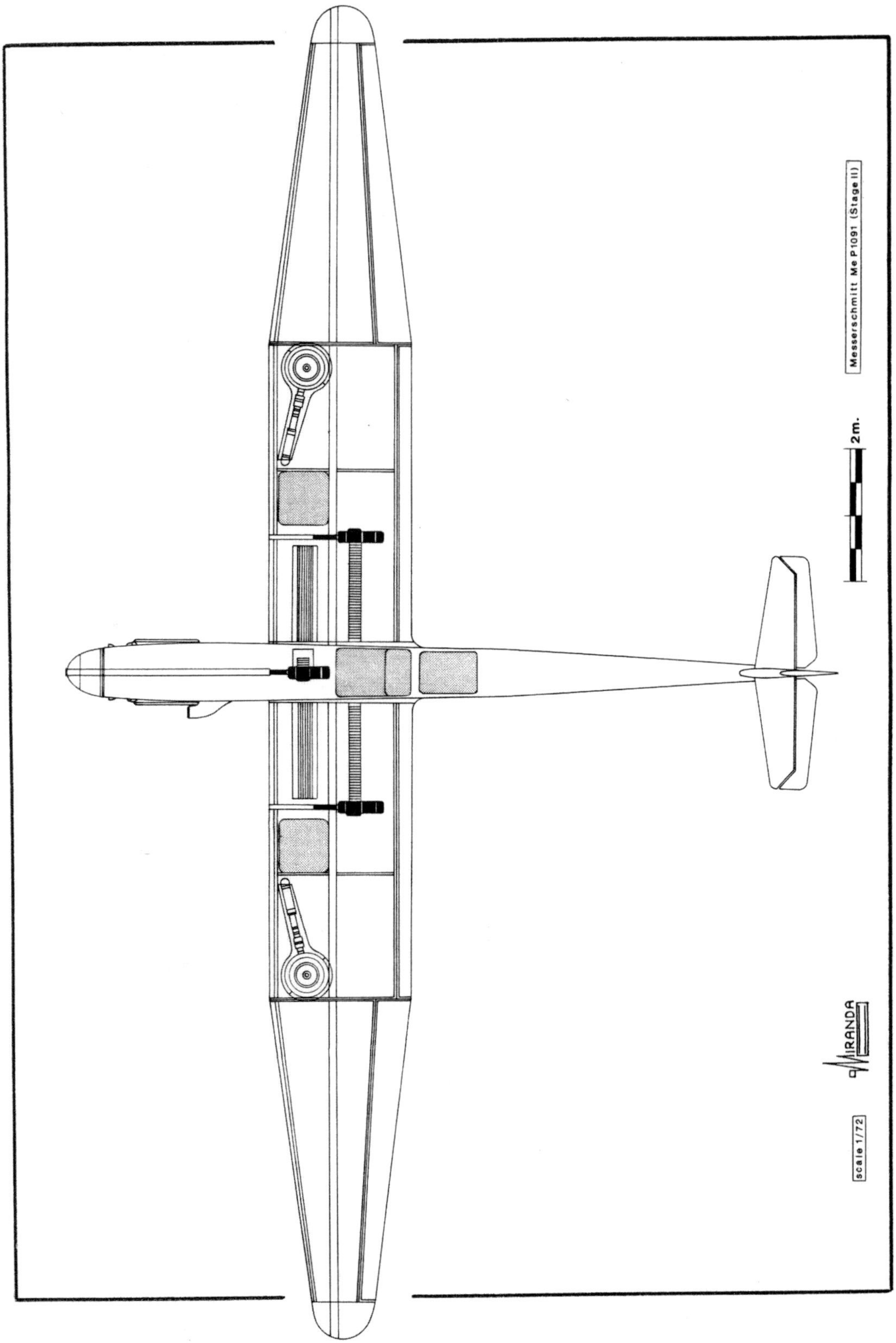
Messerschmitt Me P1091 (Stage II)
2m.
scale 1/72

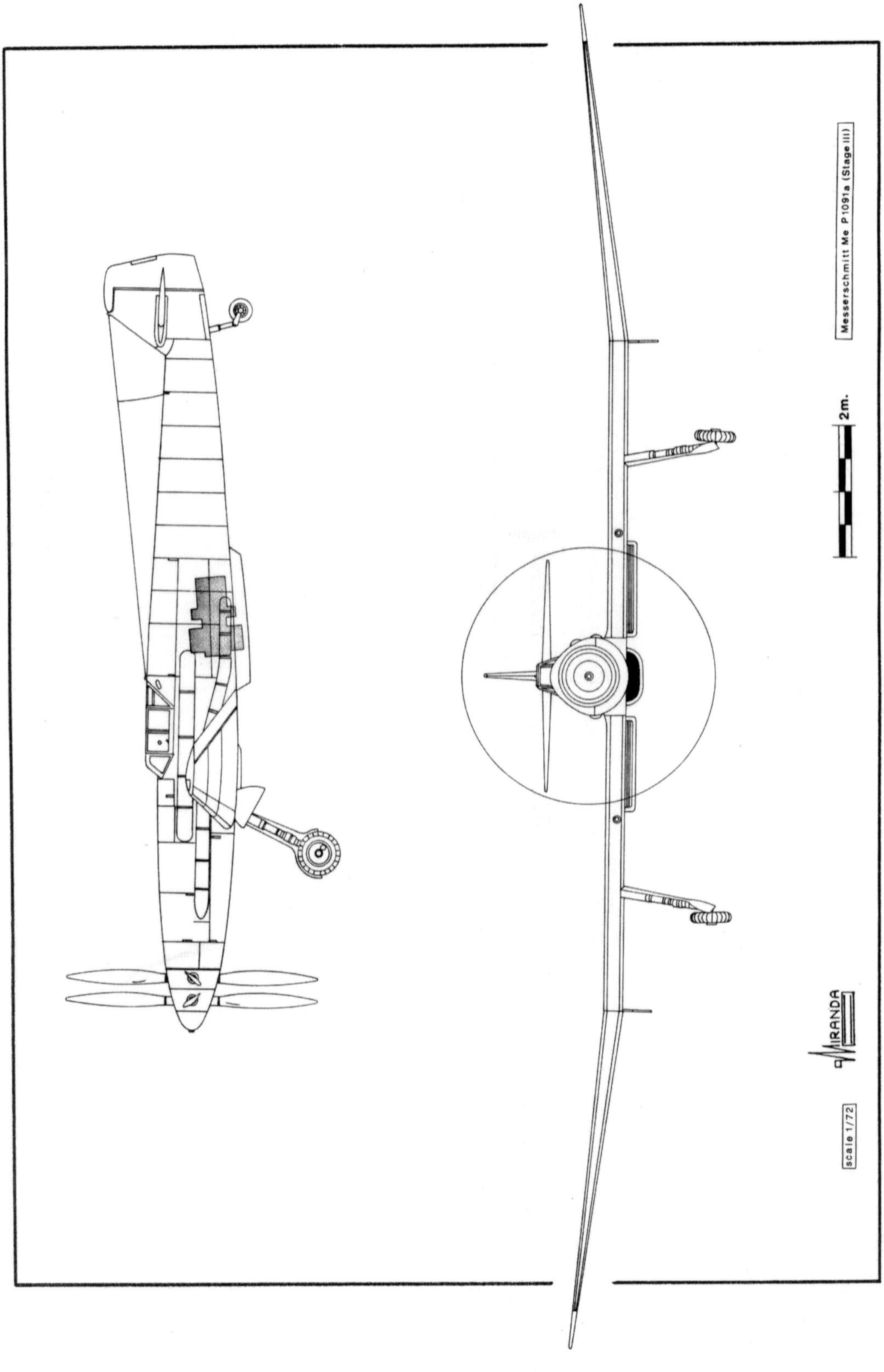
Messerschmitt Me P1091a (Stage III)
2m.
MIRANDA
scale 1/72

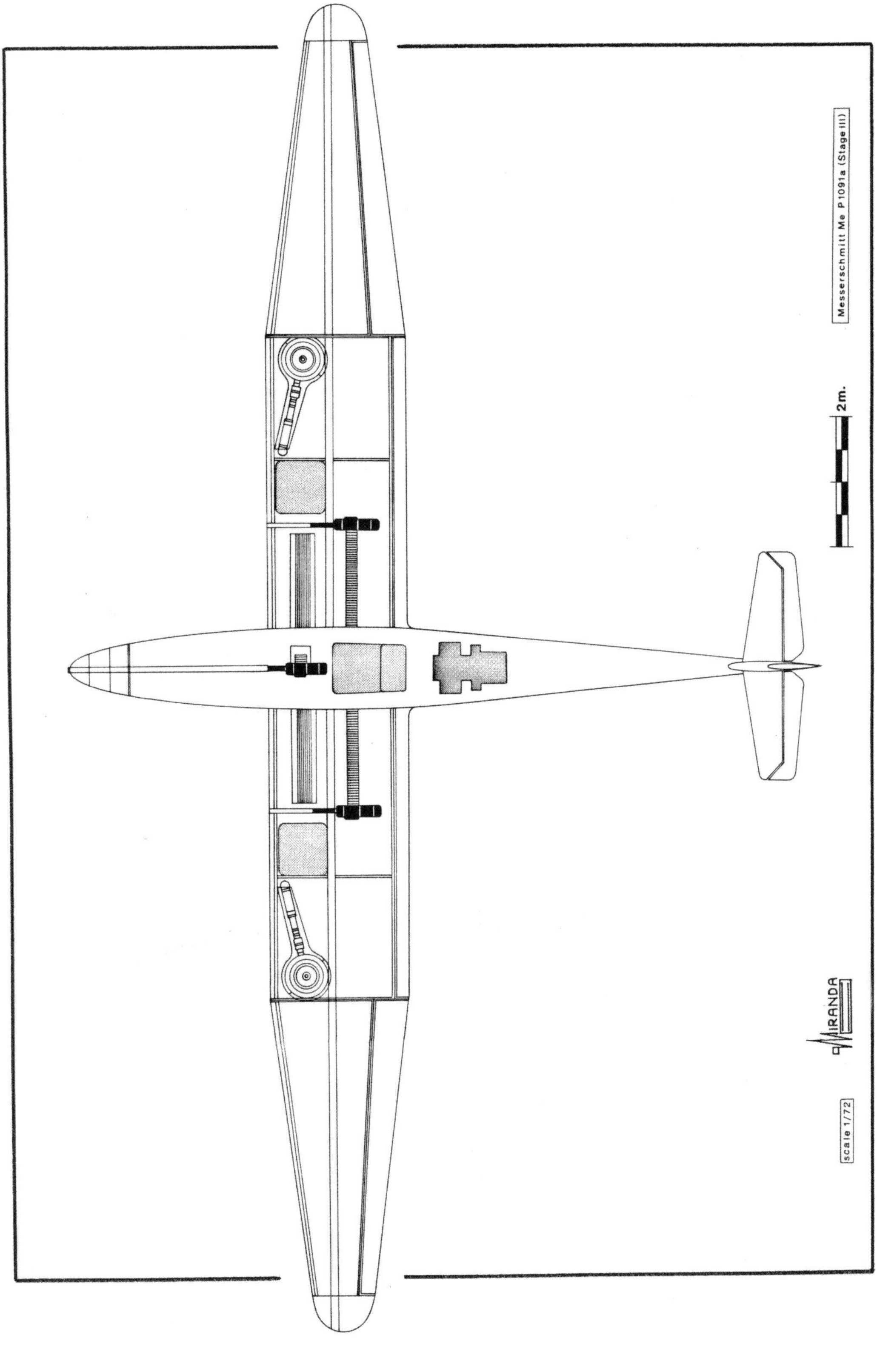
Messerschmitt Me P 1091a (Stage III)
2m.
MIRANDA
scale 1/72

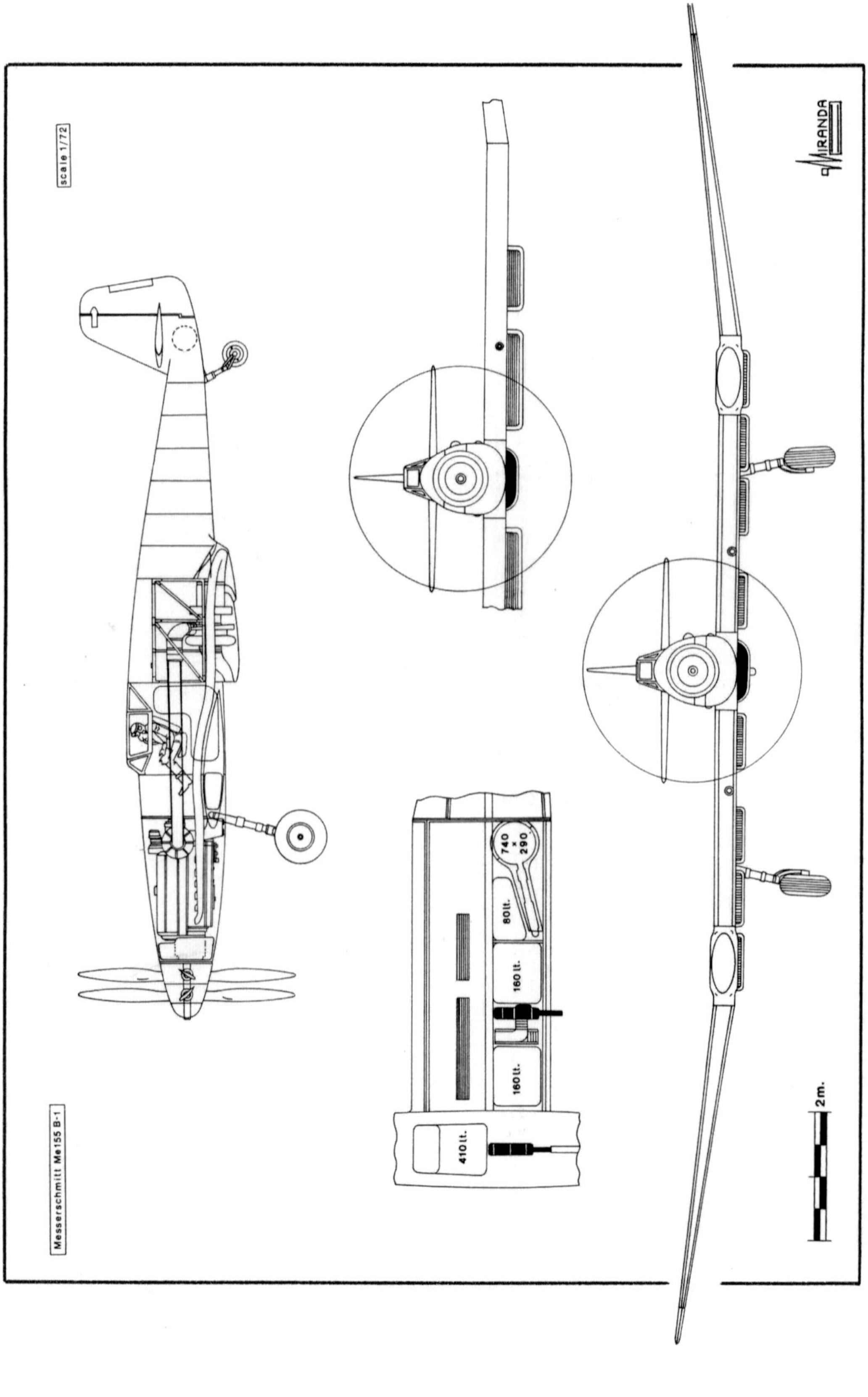
scale 1/72
Messerschmitt Me155 B-1
410 lt.
160 lt.
160 lt.
80 lt.
740
x
290
2m.

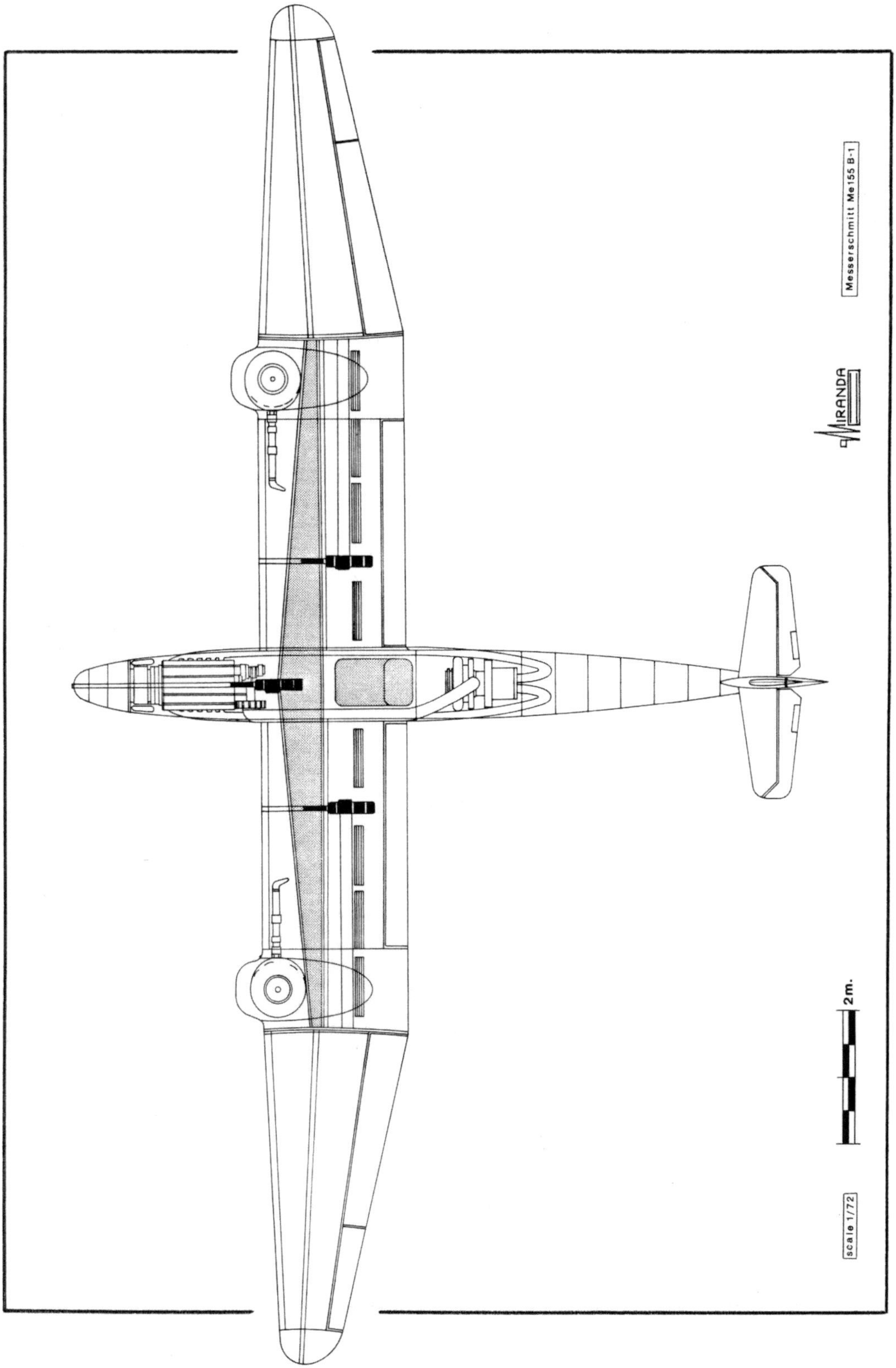
Messerschmitt Me155 B-1
MIRANDA
2m.
scale 1/72

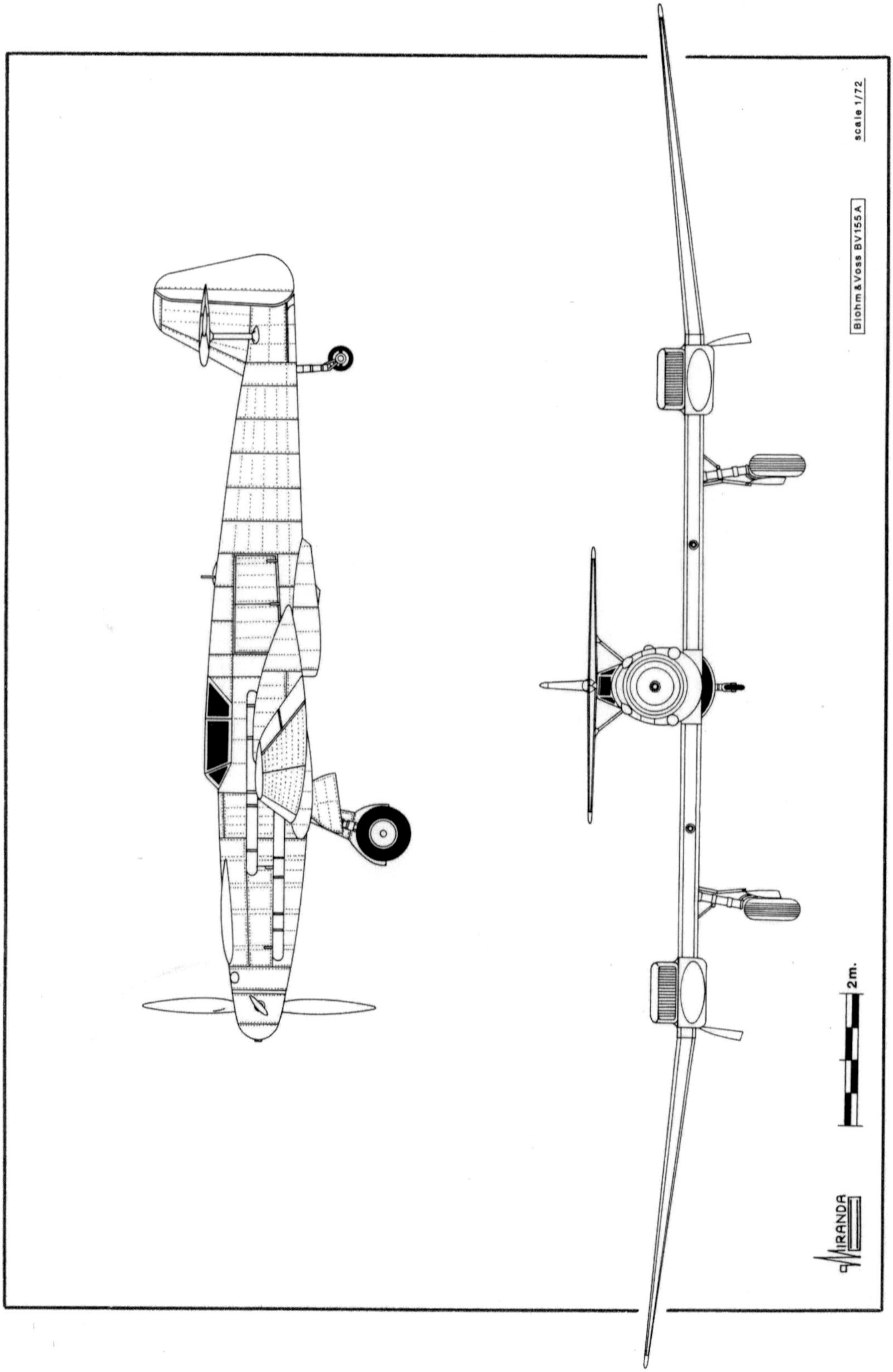
Blohm&Voss BV155A
scale 1/72
2m.
MIRANDA

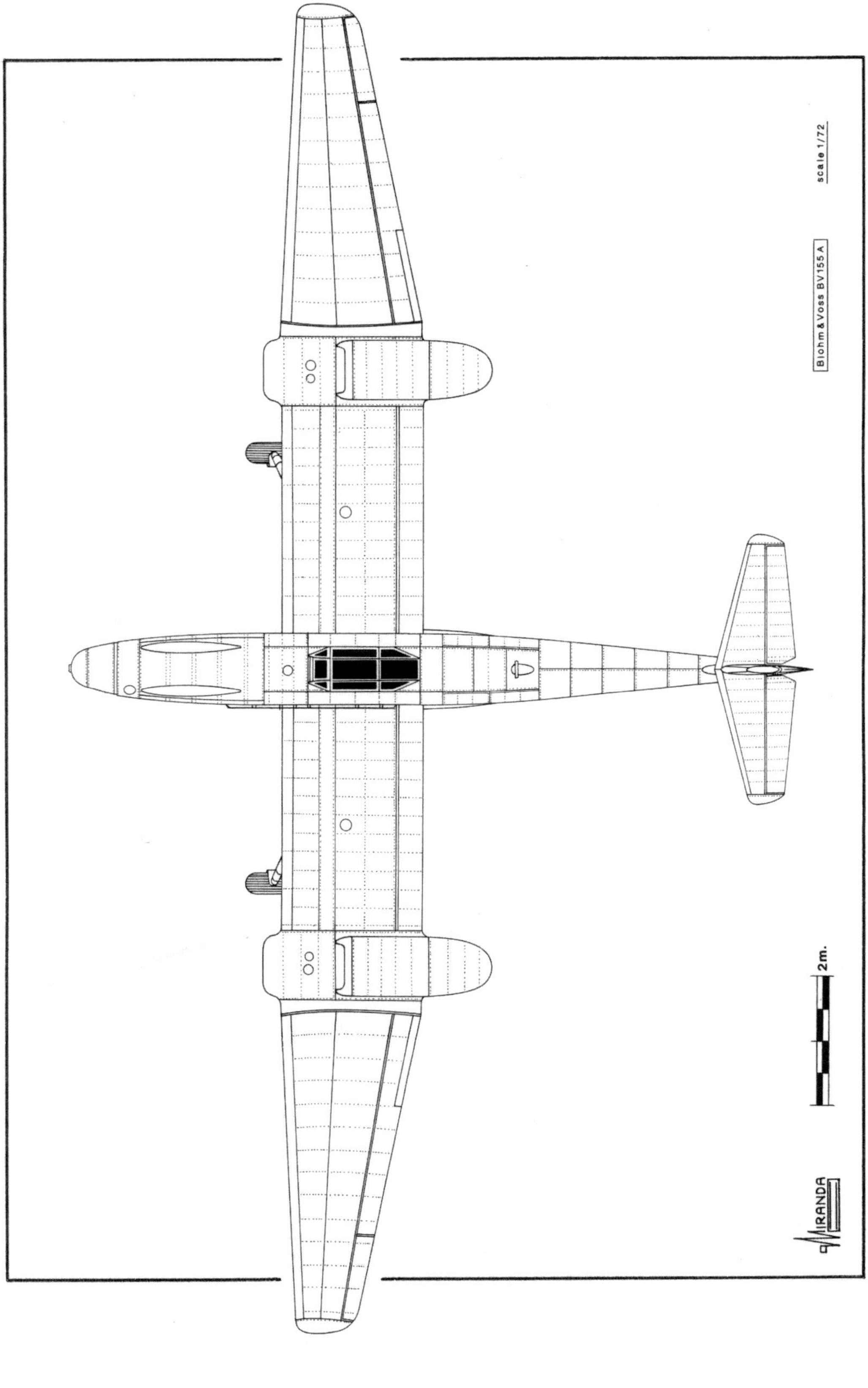
scale 1/72
Blohm & Voss BV155 A
2m.
MIRANDA

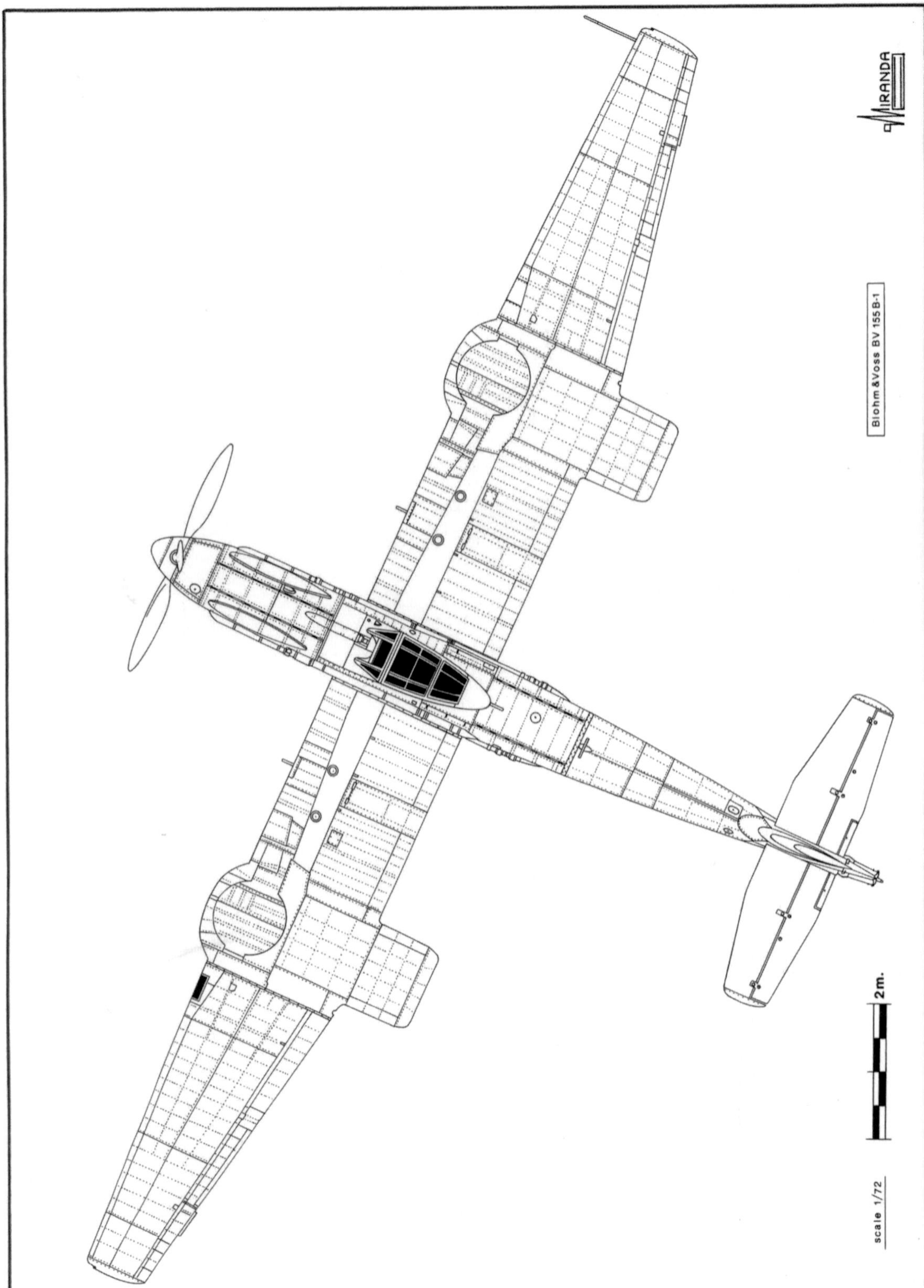
MIRANDA
Blohm&Voss BV 155 B-1
2m.
scale 1/72

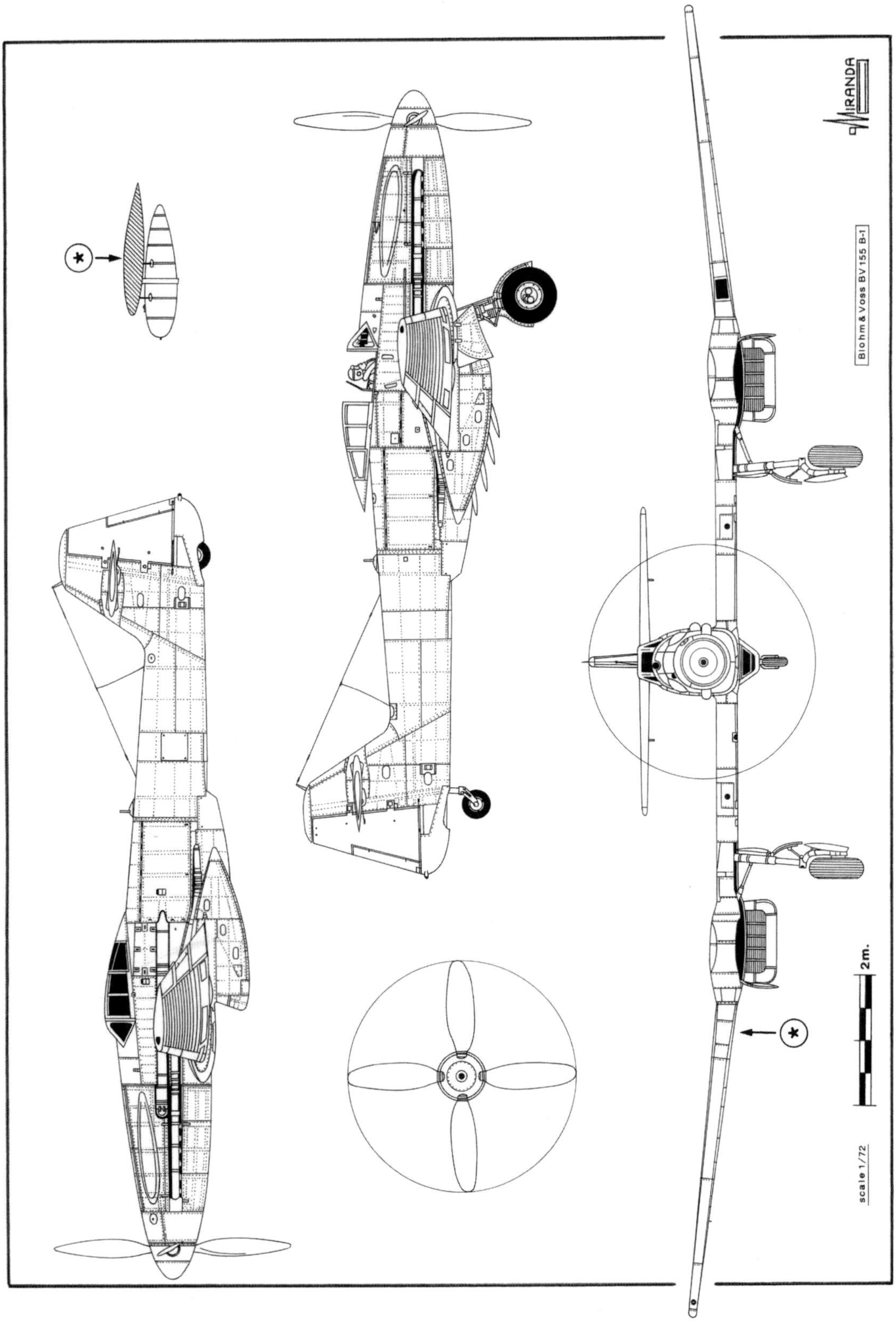
MIRANDA
Blohm & Voss BV 155 B-1
2m.
scale 1/72

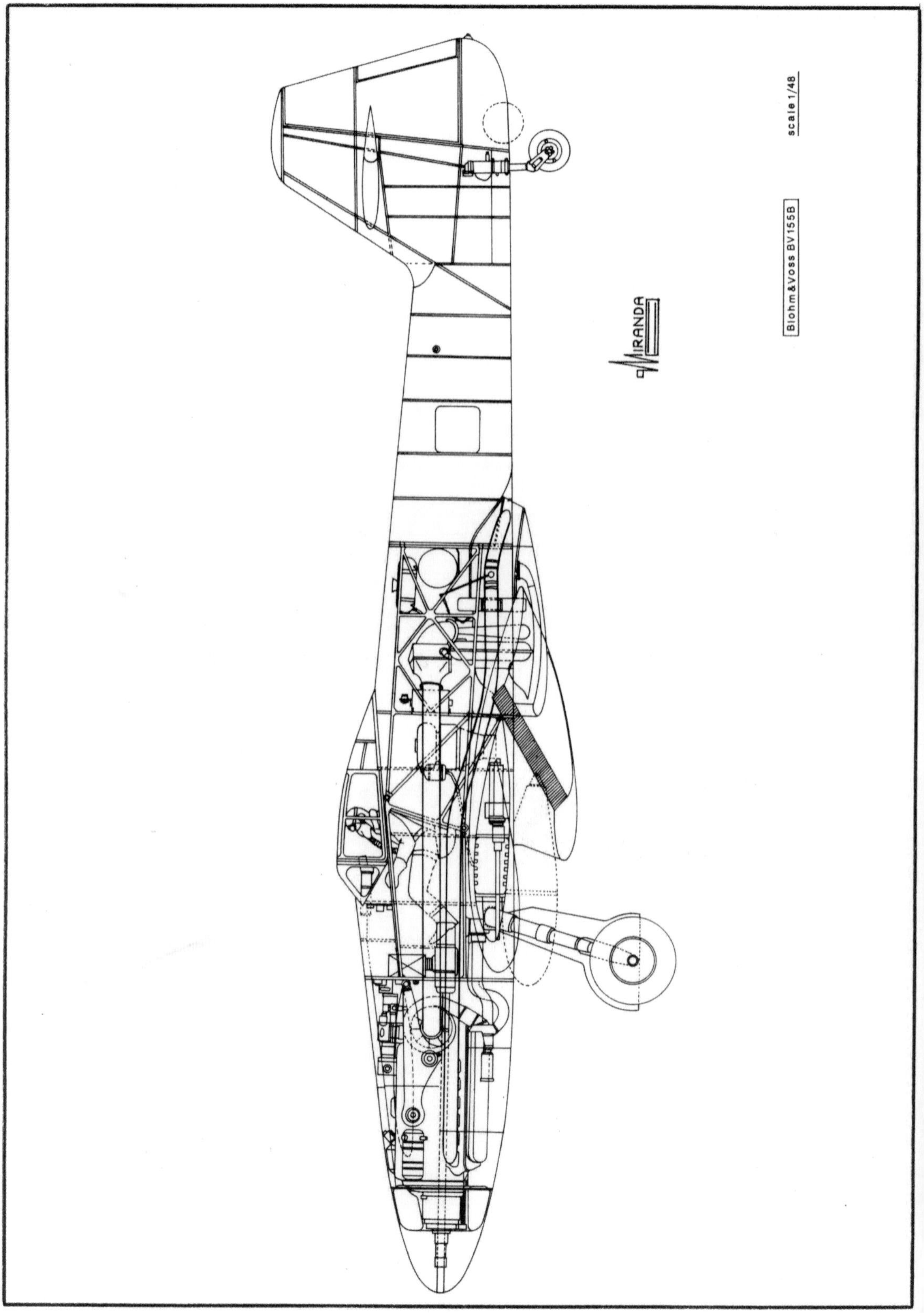
Blohm&Voss BV155B
scale 1/48
MIRANDA

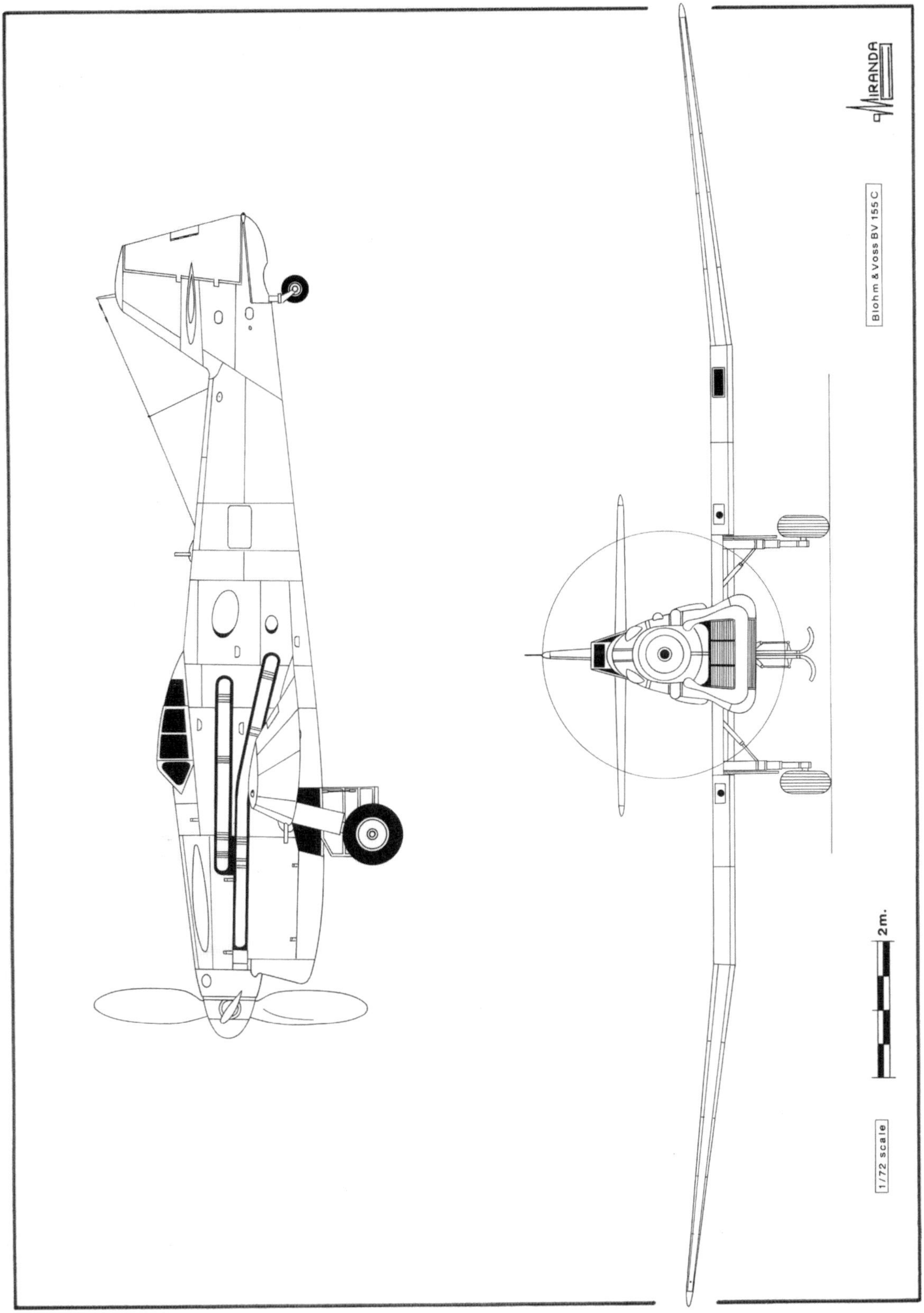
MIRANDA
Blohm & Voss BV 155 C
2m.
1/72 scale

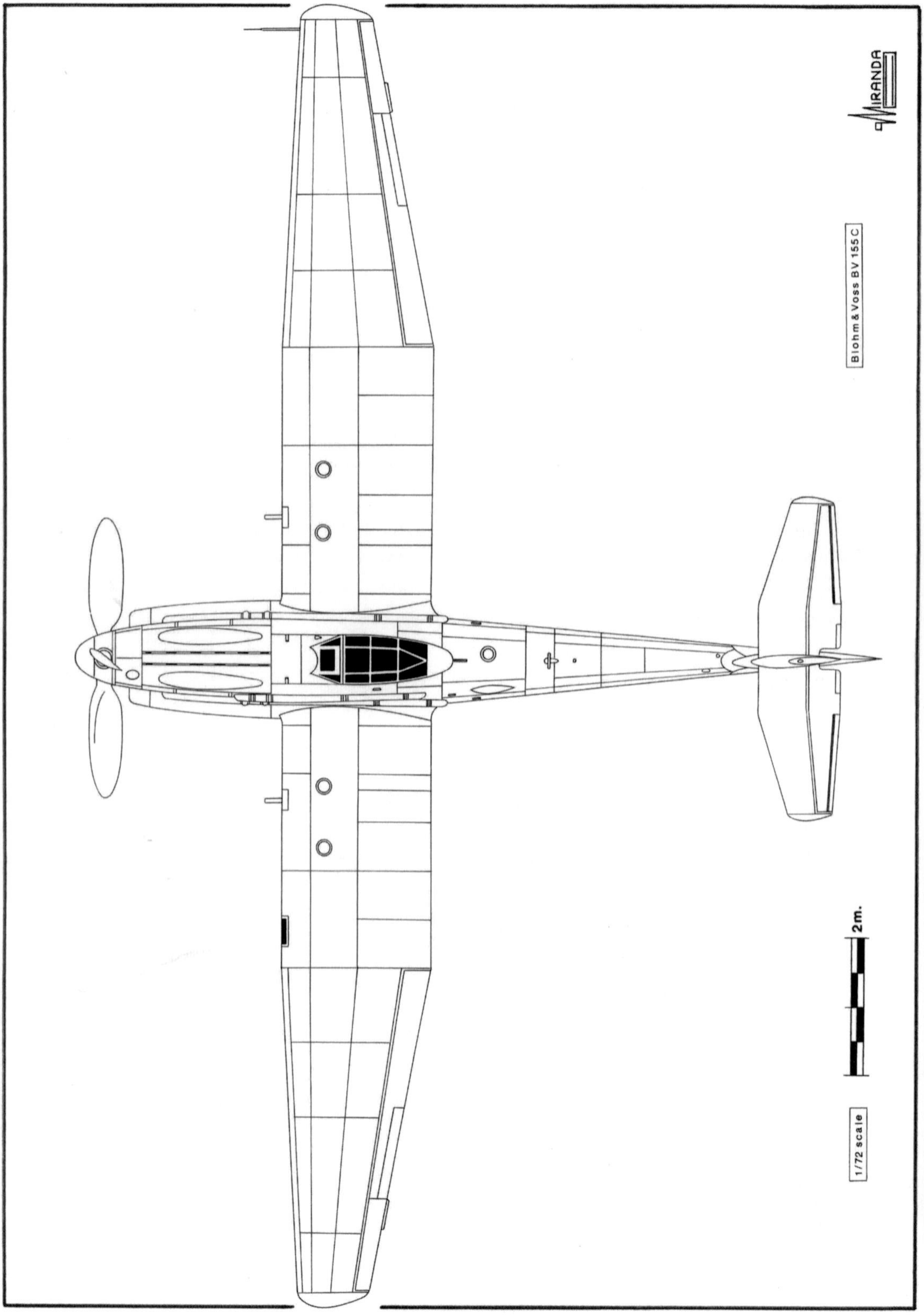
Blohm&Voss BV 155 C
2m.
1/72 scale

Chapter 2

Blohm und Voss P.205

Intended, in June 1944, to replace the BV 155 B, the BV P205 would not be more than a transitional design between the latest and the BV 155 C. The main difference with the B version was the position of the big coolers, which were moved from the wings to the fuselage.

There were good reasons to support that change. The original disposition lessened the aerodynamics of the machine and interfered with the usual working of the landing gear – a too broad landing gear track was inadequate for combat operations. It also forced the use of long and vulnerable cooling lines and reduced pilot visibility.

The plan was to use an Argus As 413 engine (4,000 hp, twenty-four cylinders in H) driving a system of contra-rotating propellers. But due to a considerable delay on its delivery, new plans were made around the DB 603 U, equipped with a TKL 15 turbosupercharger.

One of the new coolers was installed in the nose, following the same pattern as the Ta 152 H. Another two, installed in the rear fuselage, had lateral air scoops. A third intake duct, the TKL, was installed in the ventral region, as in the P-51 Mustang.

The aircraft were to carry an armament of three guns of 20 and 30 mm, four-bladed propeller, and armoured pressurised cockpit.

The project was replaced by the BV 155 C, considered to be superior from an aerodynamic point of view, in May 1945.

Technical Data	
Stage	Design (May 1944).
Type	High-altitude interceptor.
Wings	Metallic structure and cladding housing seven fuel tanks – one of 114 litres in the centre, two of 193 litres and four of 250 litres. They were also used as support for the landing gear and two guns of 20 mm
Fuselage	Metallic structure and cladding, armoured and pressurised cockpit.
Empennages	Cantilever type, built from wood.
Landing gear	Retractable inboard, fully lodged in the wings.
Engine	A Daimler Benz DB 603 U of 12 cylinders in inverted-V, liquid cooled, equipped with a Heinkel-Hirth TKL 15 turbosupercharger in addition to the normalised

	two-stage turbosupercharger, mechanically driven. It had an MW50 power boosting injection system, using methanol-water. Its estimated power was of 1,810 hp at take-off and of 1,225 hp at 13,533 m
Propeller	Four-bladed VDM built from wood and a diameter of 4,400 mm
Fuel tanks	The seven already described in the wings and another of 410 litres in the fuselage.
Armament	One Mk 108 gun of 30 mm, shooting through the propeller axis. Two MG 151/20 shooting outside the circle swept by the propeller, in the wings.
Wingspan	18.72 m
Length	12.27 m
Height	5.11 m

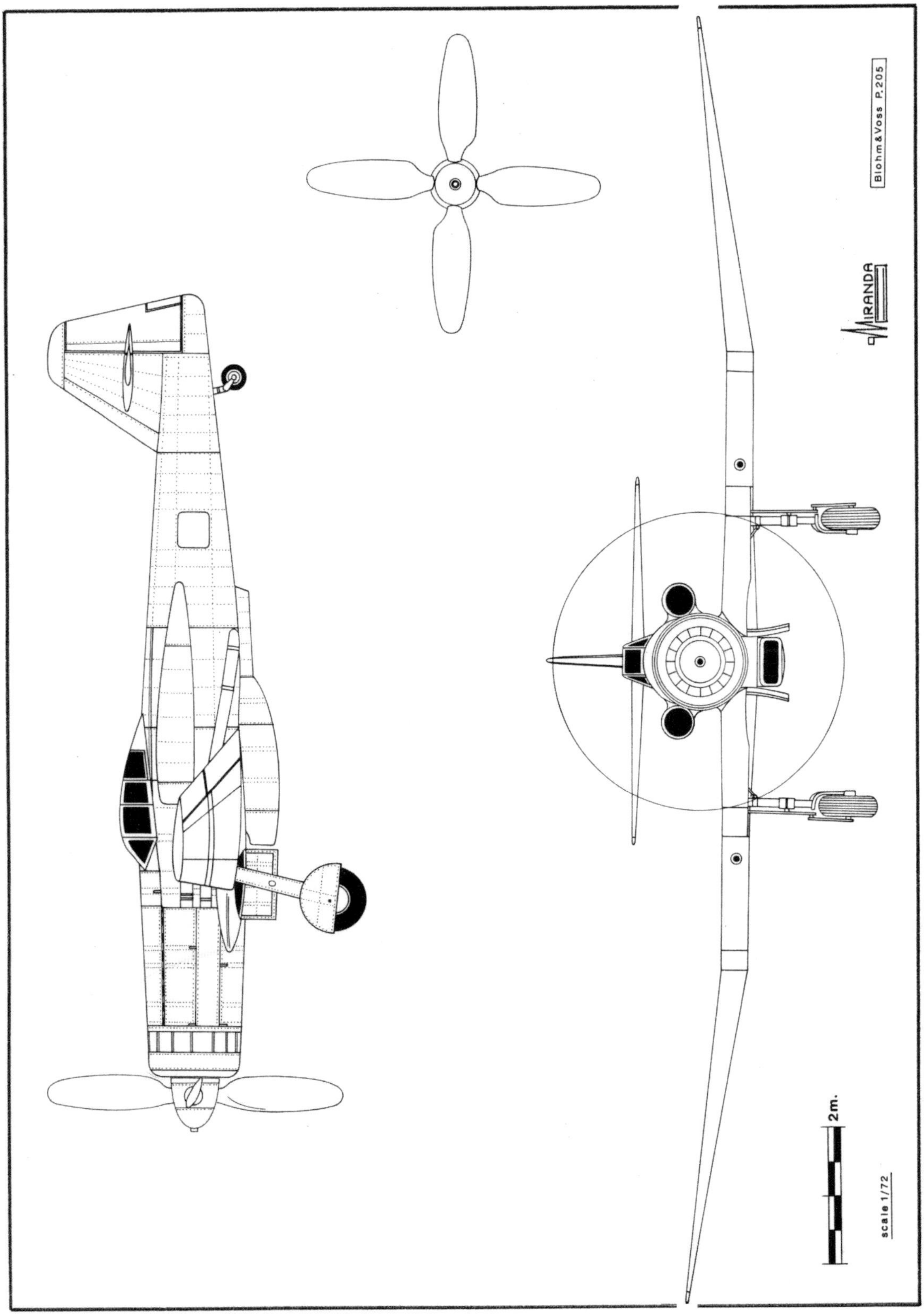
Blohm&Voss P.205
MIRANDA
2m.
scale 1/72

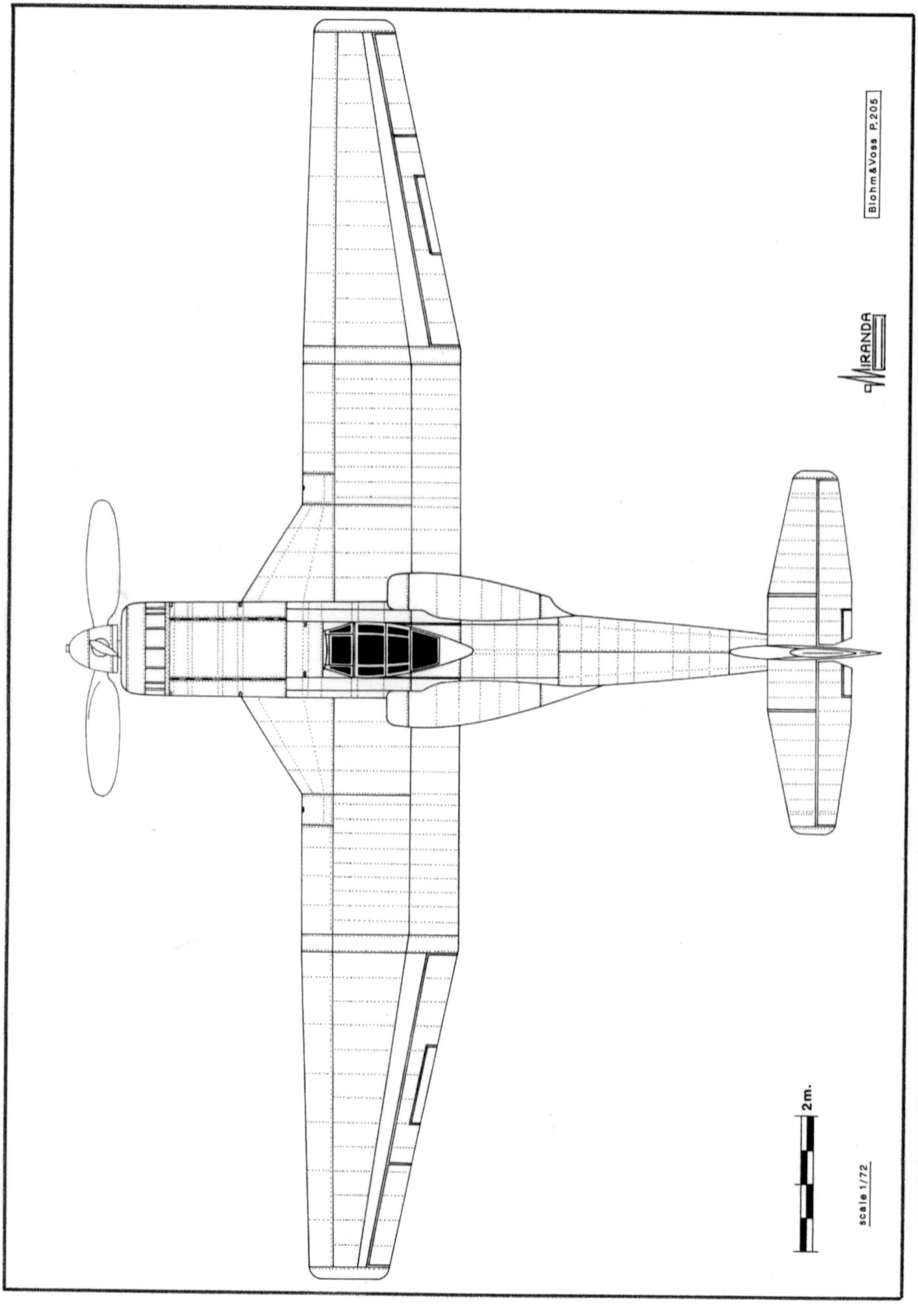
Blohm&Voss P.205
2m.
scale 1/72

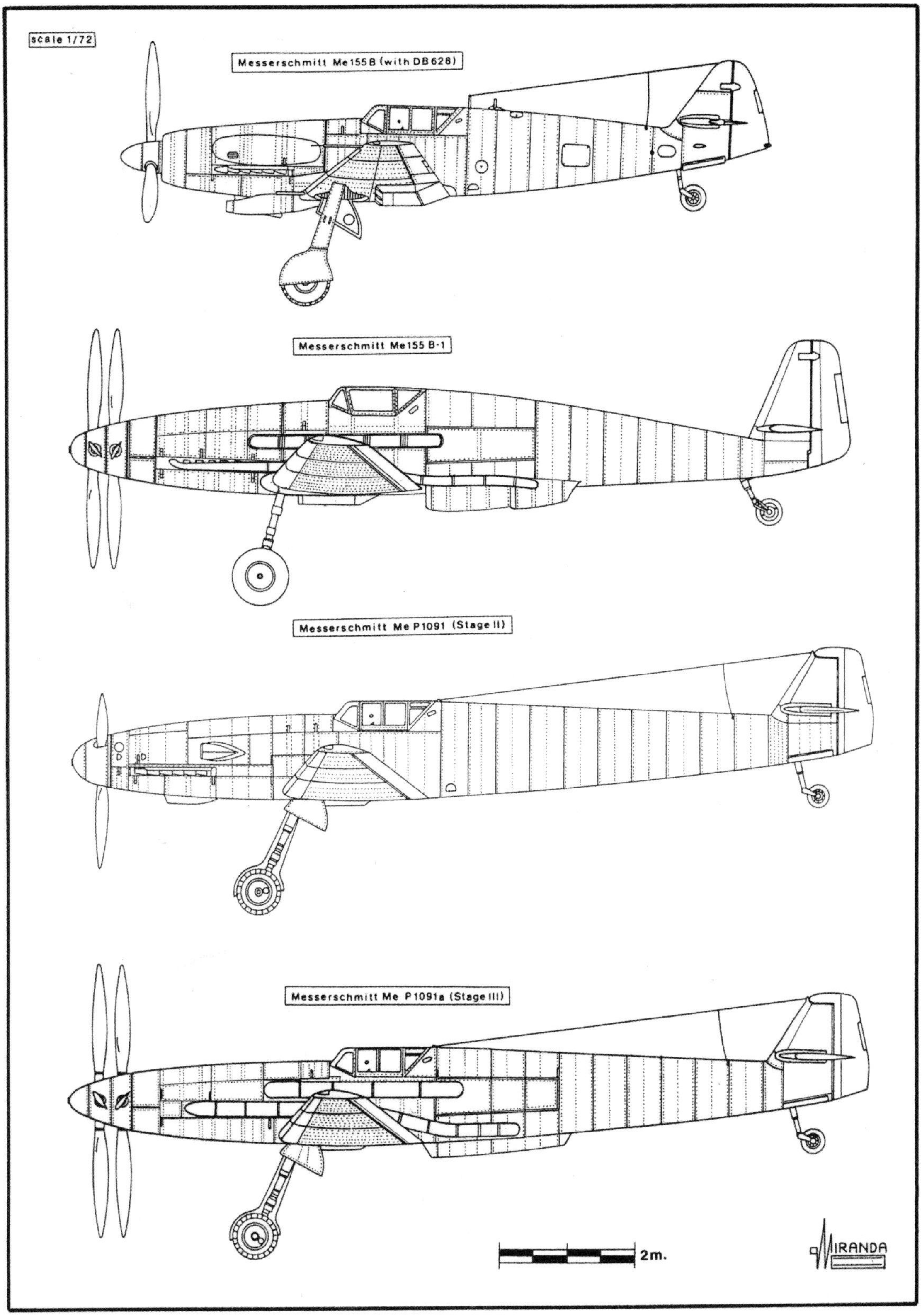
scale 1/72
Messerschmitt Me155B (with DB628)
Messerschmitt Me155 B-1
Messerschmitt Me P1091 (Stage II)
Messerschmitt Me P1091a (Stage III)
2m.
MIRANDA

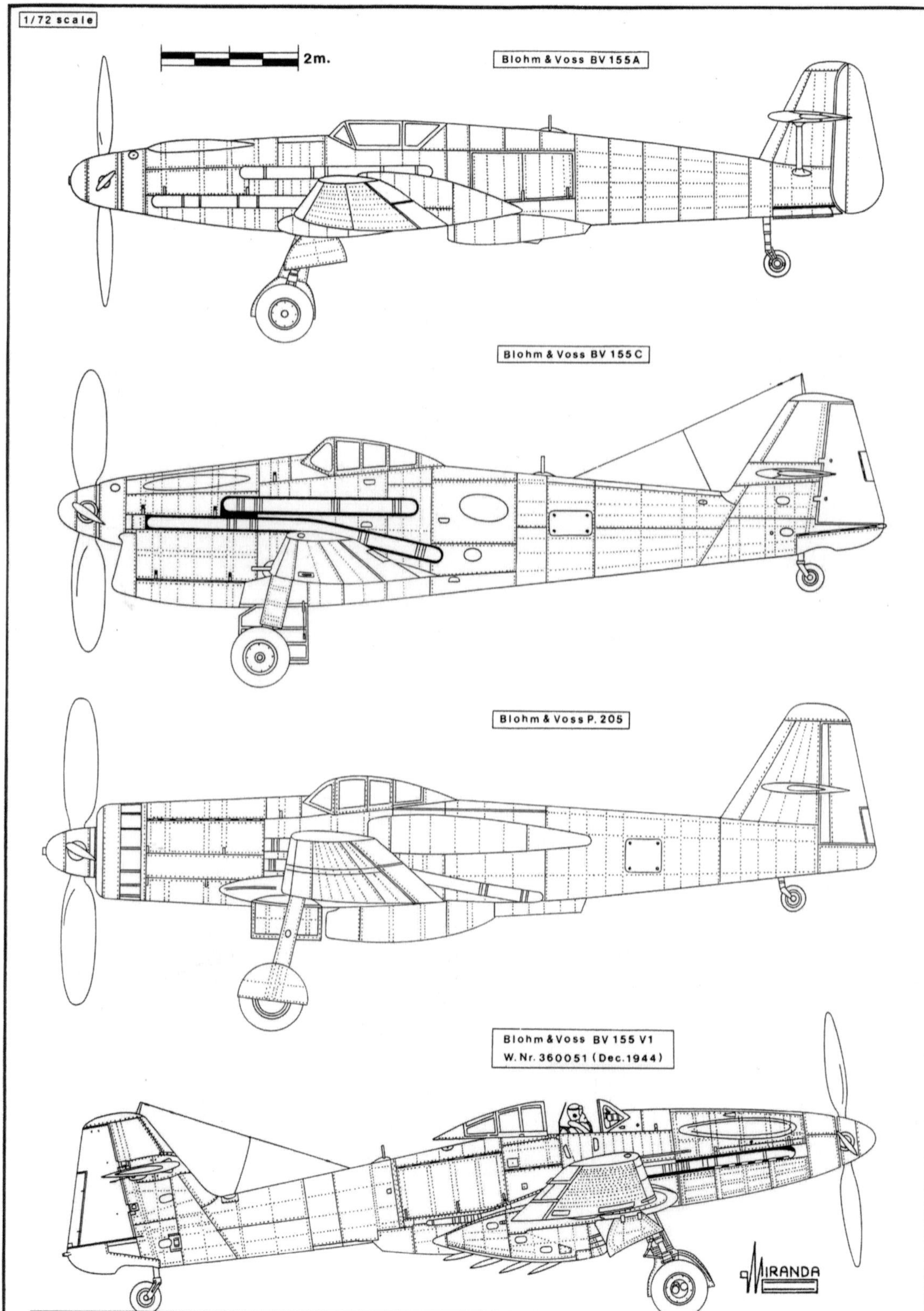
1/72 scale
2m.
Blohm & Voss BV 155A
Blohm & Voss BV 155C
Blohm & Voss P. 205
Blohm & Voss BV 155 V1
W. Nr. 360051 (Dec. 1944)
MIRANDA

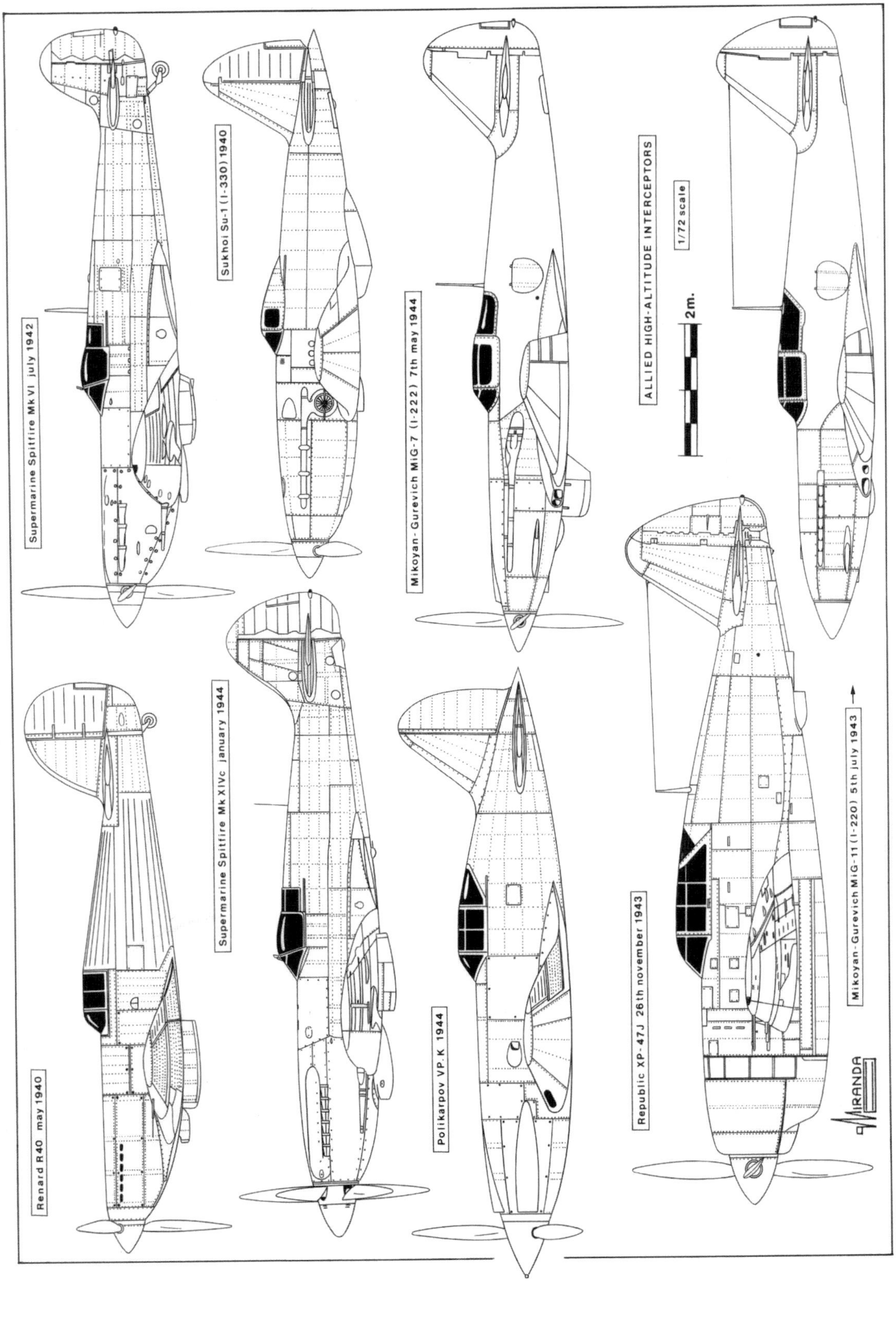
ALLIED HIGH-ALTITUDE INTERCEPTORS
1/72 scale
2m.
Supermarine Spitfire Mk VI july 1942
Sukhoi Su-1 (I-330) 1940
Mikoyan-Gurevich MiG-7 (I-222) 7th may 1944
Renard R40 may 1940
Supermarine Spitfire Mk XIVc january 1944
Polikarpov VP.K 1944
Republic XP-47J 26th november 1943
Mikoyan-Gurevich MiG-11 (I-220) 5th july 1943
MIRANDA

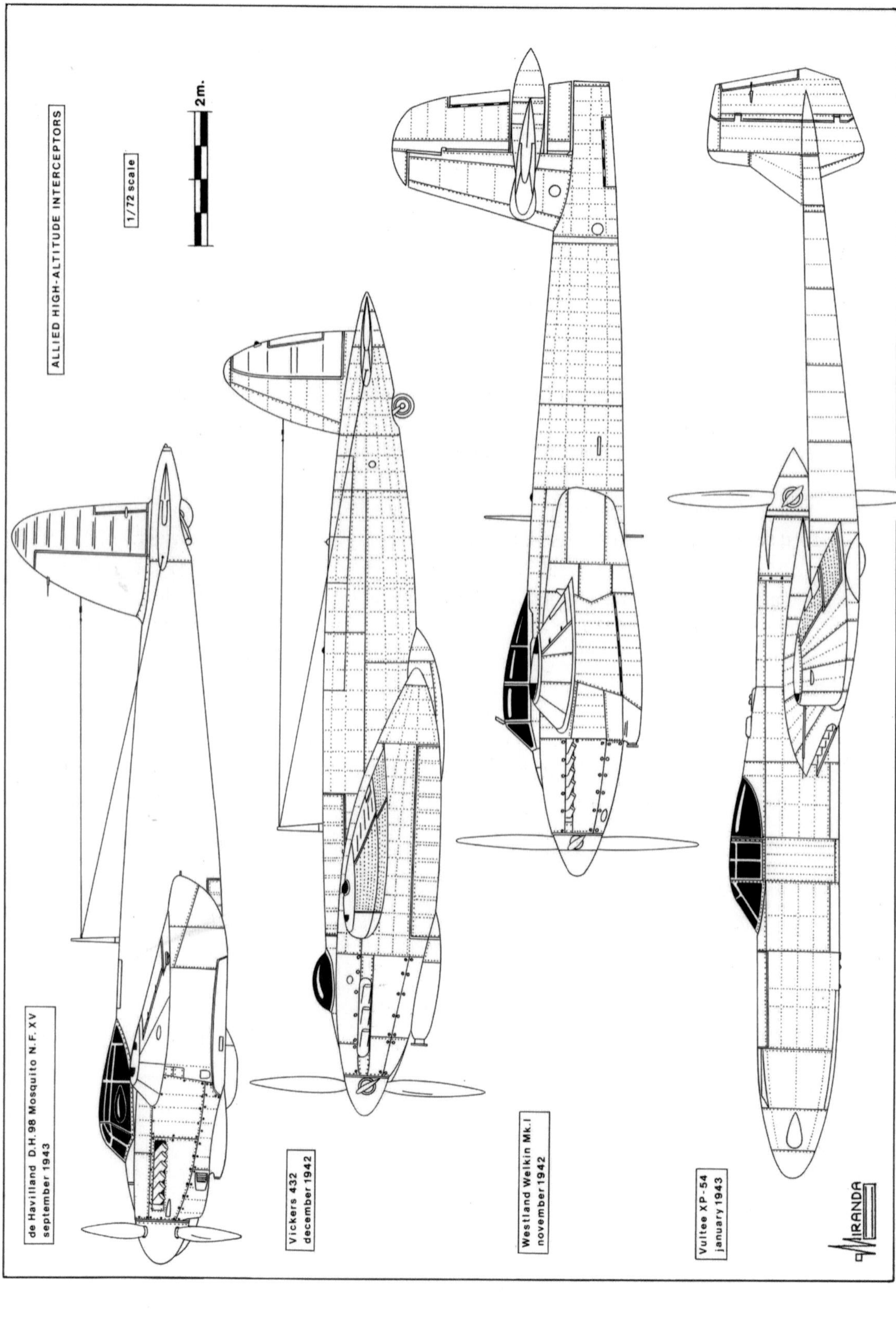
ALLIED HIGH-ALTITUDE INTERCEPTORS
1/72 scale
2m.
de Havilland D.H.98 Mosquito N.F. XV
september 1943
Vickers 432
december 1942
Westland Welkin Mk.I
november 1942
Vultee XP-54
january 1943
MIRANDA

Chapter 3

Blohm und Voss P.177

The BV P.177 was a ground attack project, or Schlachtflugzeug aircraft, based on the BV 141 aerodynamics.

The asymmetric airframe offered some advantages for the aircraft at low altitude over the battle front.

The pilot had higher visibility and more survival opportunities in case of fire or forced landing, thanks to its armoured cockpit. Also, the rear gunner had a wider vision area, without the interference of the tail surfaces. In addition, this design allowed the installation of heavy guns without interfering the movement of the propeller.

The RLM approved of the traditional construction robustness, characteristic of the firm, which used a mixture of wood and steel with just 35 per cent of light alloy, together with the use of the hollow wing spar as an armoured fuel tank, as they allowed the development of several version of Stukas and Schlacht based on the same formula.

At the beginning of 1943, the design team of Dr Ing. Richard Vogt decided to unify the P.177 with the Stuka project P.179. The result was the BV 237, which was suggested as the successor of the Ju 87 when the manufacturing of the Ju 87F was cancelled in May 1943.

Technical Data	
Type	Ground attack airplane.
Airframe	Wood, steel and aluminium, armoured crew nacelle and frontal ring of the engine.
Engines	One Jumo 213 of 12 cylinders in inverted-V, liquid cooled and 1,750 hp
Armament	Four forward fixed MG 151/20 guns and two more in a flexible montage, driven by the rear gunner. 500 kg of bombs.
Wingspan	11,95 m
Length	20.22 m
Height	3.40 m
Max. weight	6,000 kg
Max. speed	More than 600 km/h.
Electronics	FuG 16 ZY transmitter/receiver device.

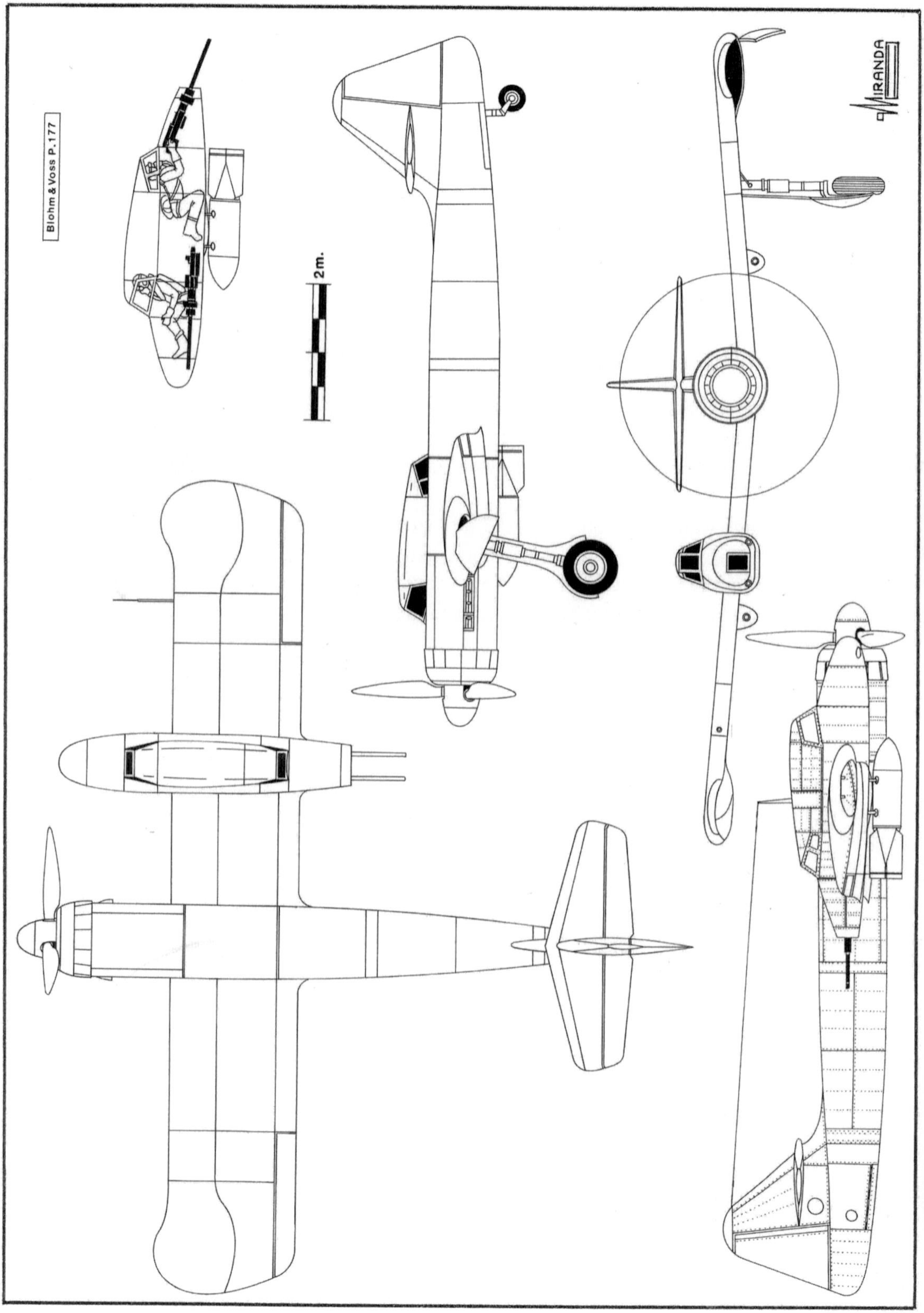
Blohm & Voss P.177
2m.
MIRANDA

Chapter 4

Blohm und Voss P.179

The P.179 was a fighter-bomber developed from the P.177, with a shorter wingspan, single seat and a BMW 801 radial engine so that it could compete against the Jabo versions of the Fw 190. It was a compact and sturdy design, but its smaller size highly reduced the advantages of the asymmetric structure that was so useful for bombers and reconnaissance aircraft.

Technical Data	
Type	Dive bomber.
Structure	Metallic.
Engine	BMW 801 D radial engine of 14 cylinders, air cooled and 1,700 hp driving a three bladed VDM propeller.
Fixed armament	Two fixed MG 151/20 guns of 20 mm under the pilot seat.
Launch armament	Up to 500 kg of bombs.
Wingspan	10,39 m
Length	8,43 m
Height	3,16 m
Max. speed	More than 600 km/h.
Electronics	FuG 16ZY transmitter/receiver device.

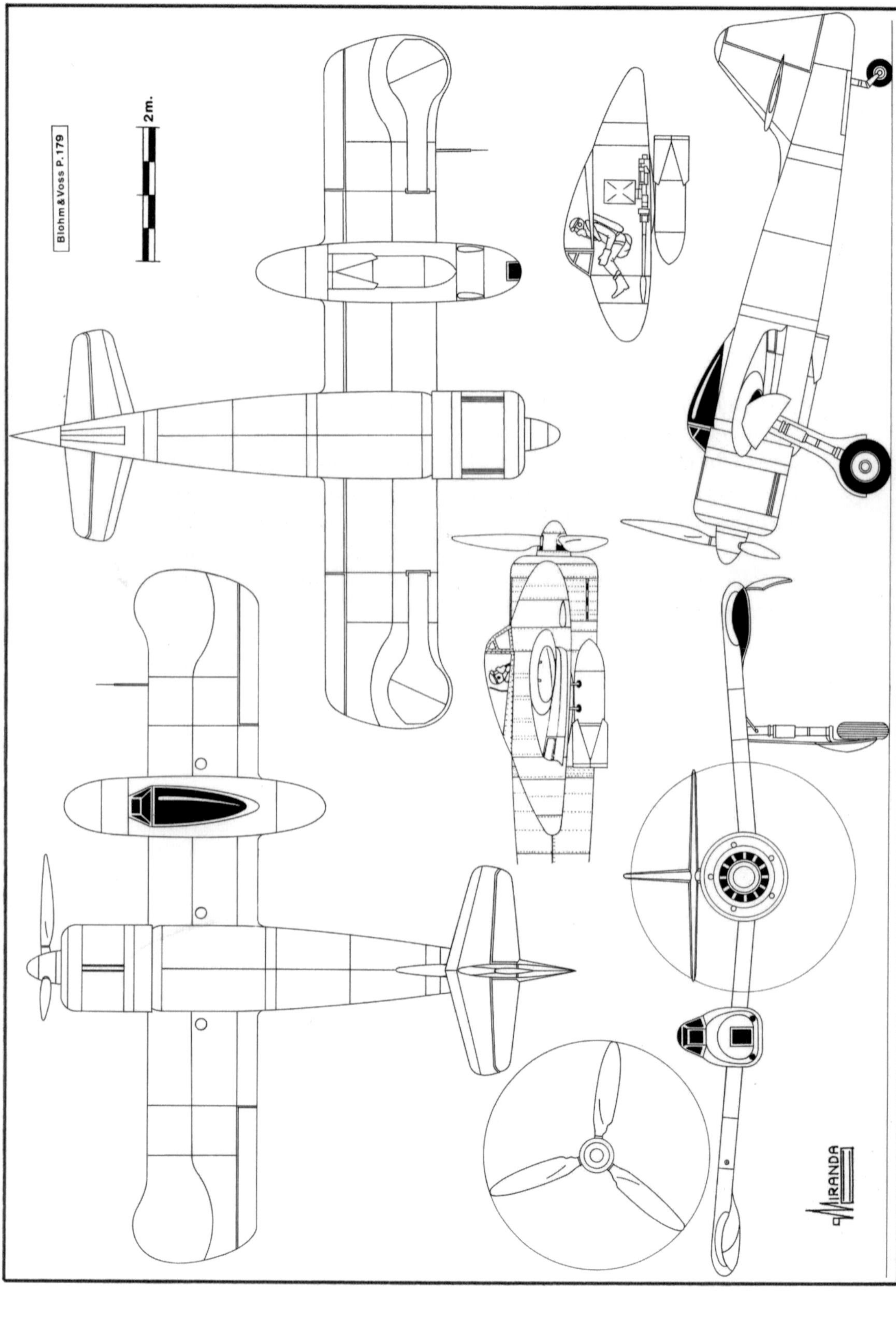
Blohm & Voss P.179
2m.
MIRANDA

Chapter 5

Blohm und Voss P.192

When manufacture of the Ju 87F was cancelled in May 1943, the Blohm und Voss firm proposed three designs of asymmetric aircraft: P.177, P.179 and BV 237, which were considered too radical by the RLM compared to the Ju 187 proposed by Junkers.

The team of Dr Vogt then designed a more conventional aircraft, the only peculiarity of which was the positioning of the armoured pilot cockpit, in front of the airscrew to protect the engine, without increasing the weight, as happened with the Soviet Shturmovik. The idea was not new. It had already been adopted, with certain success, by the French SPAD S.A. in 1915.

Unfortunately, that configuration did not allow the installation in the nose of guns of more than 30 mm for structural reasons and the fork system for dive bombing did not allow the launch of bombs heavier than 500 kg.

It was proposed to manufacture the two versions, equipped with DB 603 G (P.192.01) and Jumo 213 E (P.192.02) engines.

Technical Data	
Type	Dive bomber.
Airframe	Wood, steel and dural.
Engine	One DB 603 G of 1,900 hp or one Jumo 213 E of 2,150 hp.
Armament	Four MG 151/20 cannon and one 500 kg bomb.
Wingspan	13.20 m
Length	11.70 m
Height	4.30 m
Wing area	26.20 sq m
Max. weight	5,868 kg

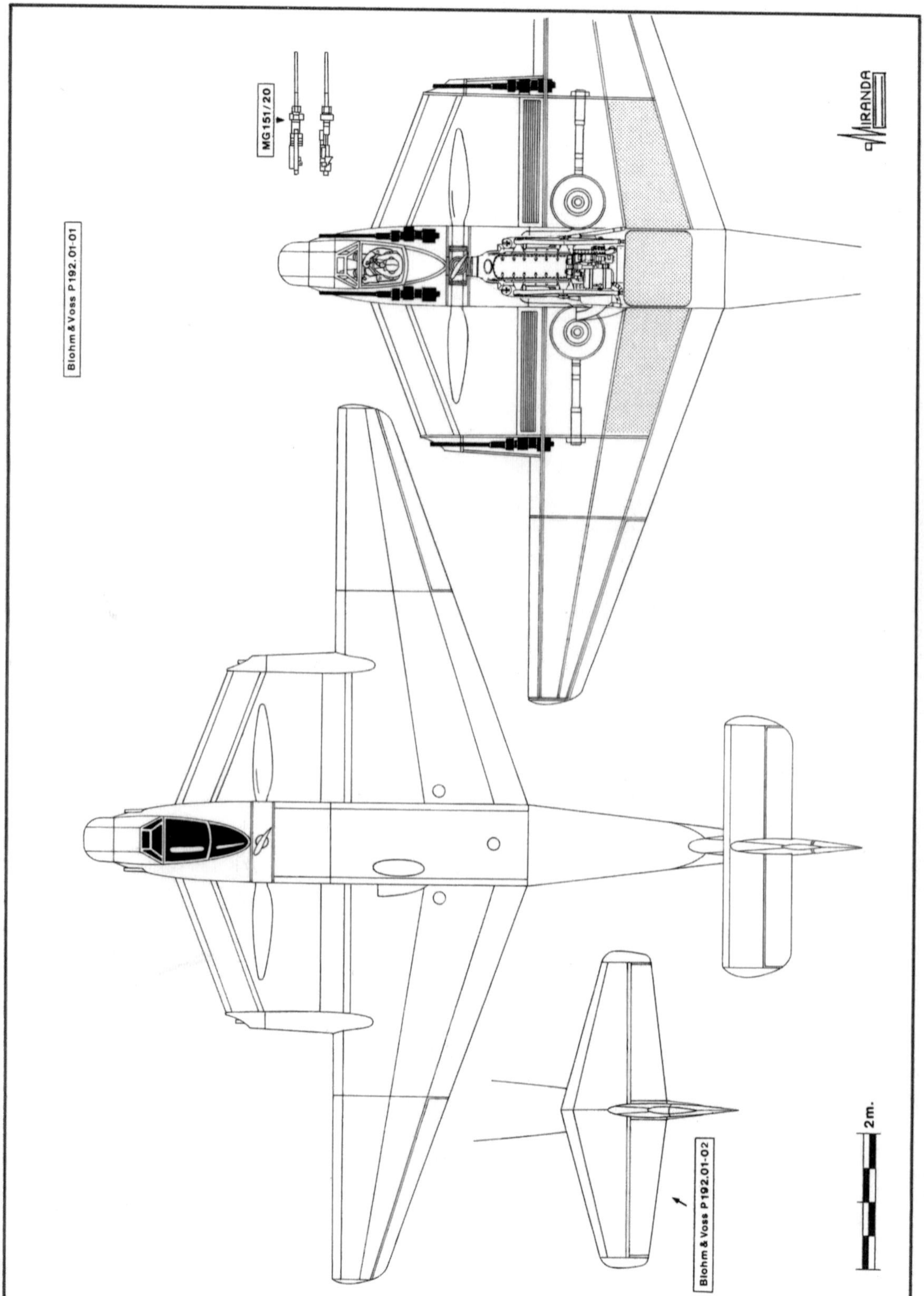
Blohm & Voss P192.01-01
MG 151/20
Blohm & Voss P192.01-02
2m.
MIRANDA

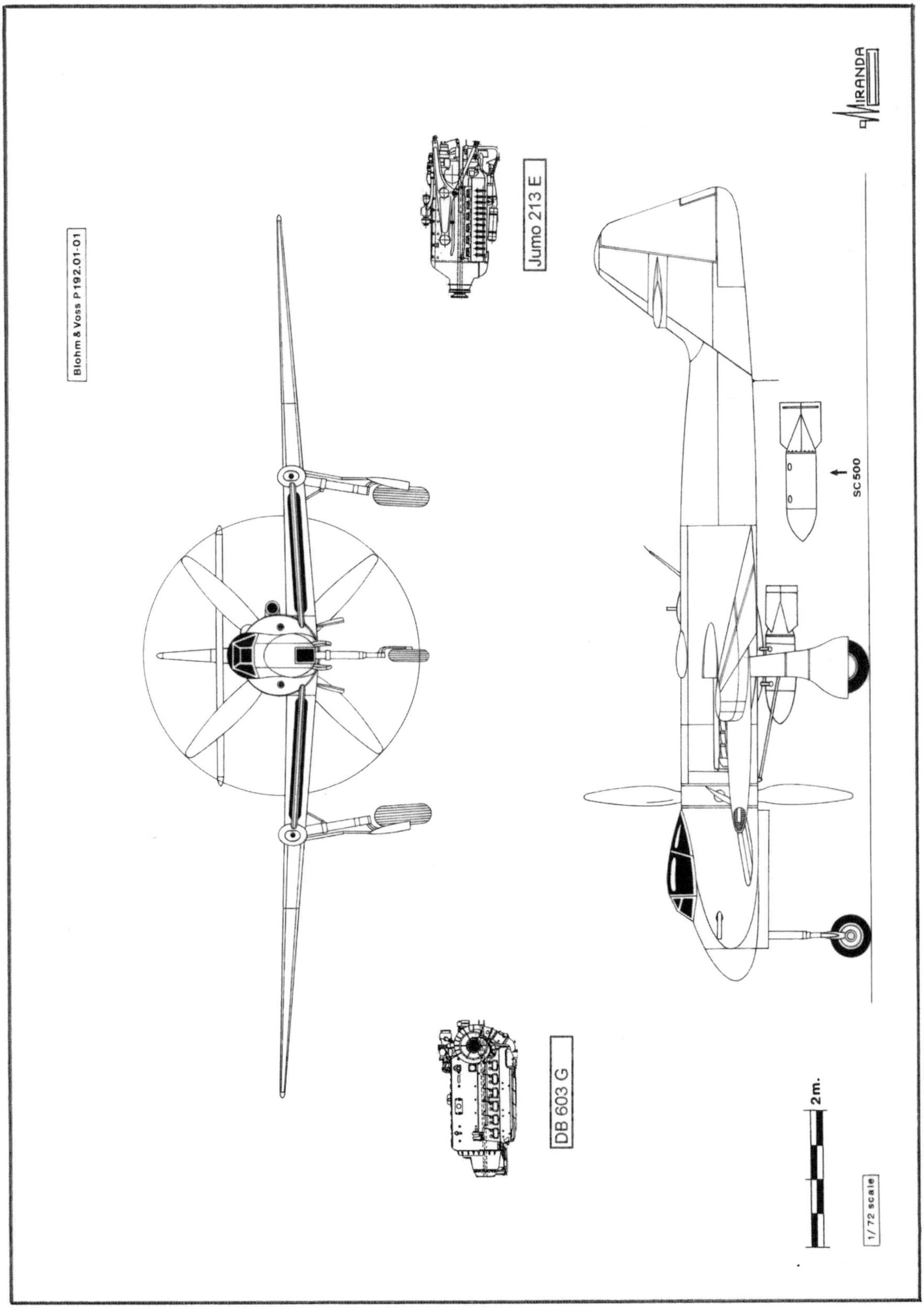
Blohm & Voss P 192.01-01
Jumo 213 E
SC 500
DB 603 G
2m.
1/72 scale

Chapter 6

Blohm und Voss P.193

The P.193 was a development of the P.192, intended to lessen its structural deficiencies by installing the airscrew, driven by a power shaft of 4.97 m, at the rear end of the fuselage. It was not the ideal solution, as it increased the weight and reduced the power in the transmission. However, the armoured cockpit was still protecting the engine and allowed the installation of anti-tank guns and dive bombing with bombs of 1,000 kg.

This proved irrelevant, however, as the OKL concluded that the dive bomber's time was past and, in February 1944, it was decided to proceed with manufacturing the Schlacht versions of the Fw 190.

Technical Data	
Type	Dive bomber.
Airframe	Wood, steel and dural.
Engine	Jumo 213 A-1 of 1,750 hp.
Armament	Two Mk 103/30 and two MG 151/20 cannon and one 1,000 kg. bomb.
Wingspan	11.40 m
Length	10.30 m
Height	3.90 m
Wing area	20 sq m
Max. weight	5,724 kg
Max. speed	520 km/h
Ceiling	7,000 m

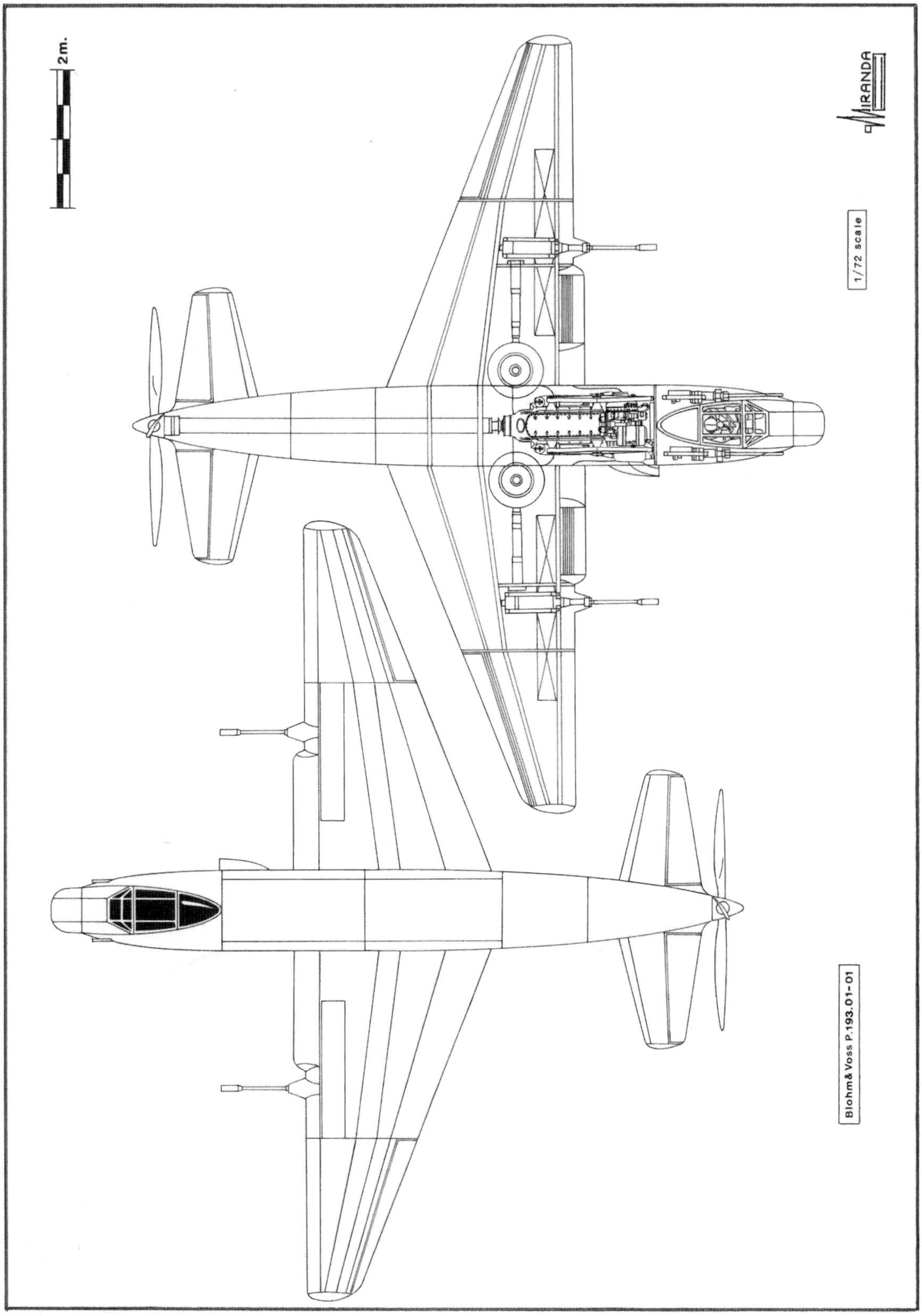
2m.
1/72 scale
Blohm& Voss P.193.01-01

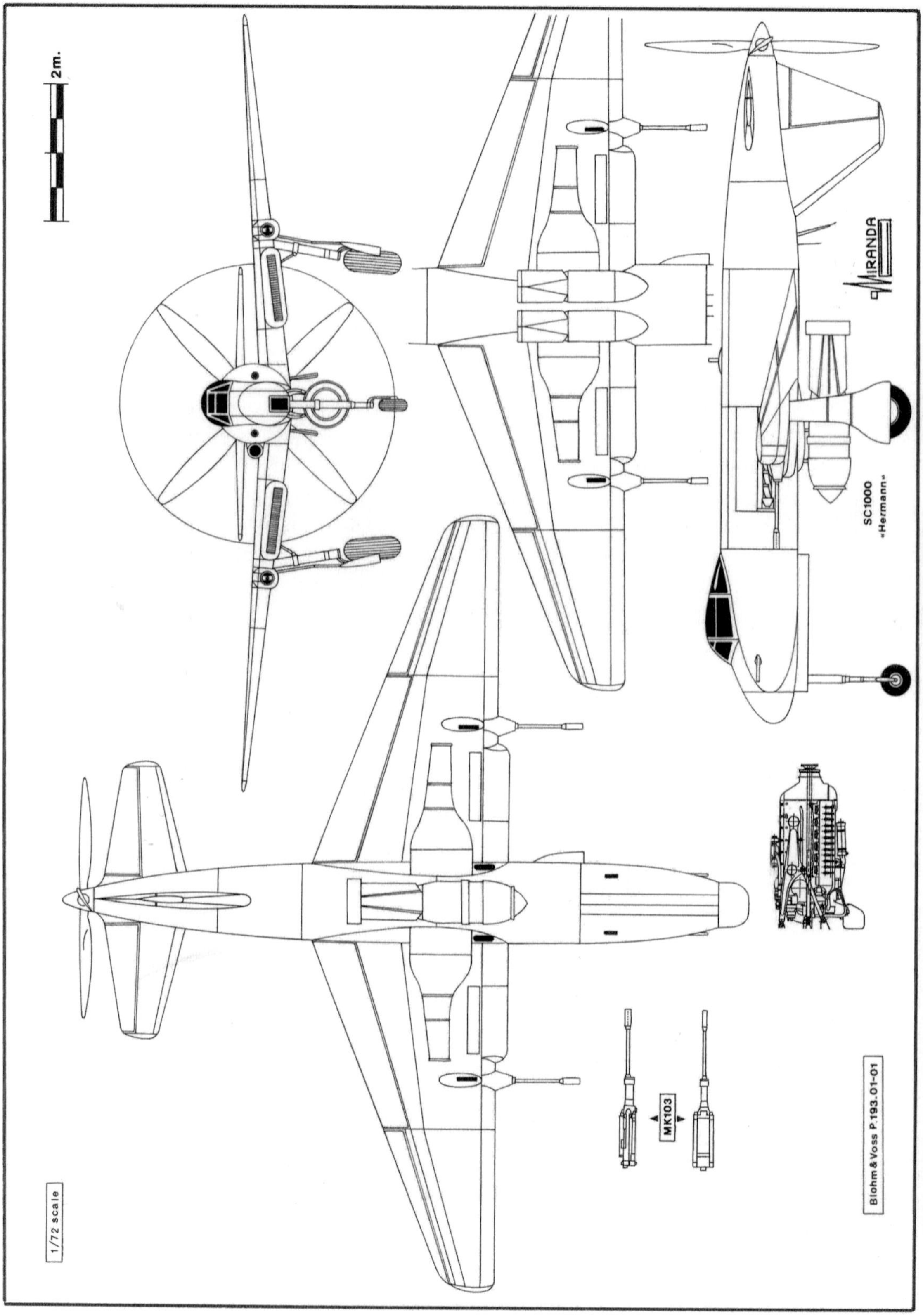
2m.
1/72 scale
MIRANDA
SC1000
«Hermann»
MK103
Blohm & Voss P.193.01-01

Chapter 7

Blohm und Voss P.194

Originally conceived as a mixed-power fast bomber, the P.194 was based on the BV 237 B-1. The project evolved, giving way to different specialised versions with anti-tank, anti-ship and night fighter roles.

Economy of fuel and turbojet speed combined to achieve a long range machine, able to operate for long periods over the sea or over the huge Russian front, thanks to its great fuel capacity and radial engine. The additional speed provided by the turbojet was used as an advantage to attack and get away from the DCA area as fast as possible.

The asymmetric position of the powerful frontal armament was not hindered by the propeller, eliminating the synchronisation problem.

The P.194.00.101 was planned as a night fighter with FuG 220 Lichtenstein SN-1 and Matratzen antenna. The P.194.00.110 was a light variant, with a single seat and reduced armament. The P.194.01.02 was designed as dive bomber. The bombs were to be housed in the fuselage engine with a launch fork to save the propeller – similar to the one in the Ju 87 – and a powerful Mk 412 gun of 55 mm, ideal for attacking ships and armoured vehicles. The P.194.02.01 was a variant of the 01.02 with the fixed armament of the 00.101. The P.194.03.01 added a forked air intake of new design, which decreased the risk of odd particles entering the turbojet and left the ventral part of the crew nacelle free to install bomb racks or fuel tanks.

P.194.00.101 Technical Data	
Type	Night fighter.
Structure	Metallic, 62 per cent steel and 38 per cent aluminium.
Engines	One BMW 801 D radial of 14 cylinders, air cooled and 1,700 hp and a Jumo 004 turbojet of 890 kp.
Fuel tanks	Three, in wings and fuselage, with a total capacity of 2,100 litres.
Fixed armament	two MG 151/20 guns of 20 mm and two Mk 103 guns of 30 mm in the forward section of the crew nacelle.
Wingspan	16 m
Length	12.35 m
Height	4.39 m
Wing area	36.40 sq m

Empty weight	6,500 kg
Loaded weight	9,350 kg
Max. speed	775 km/h
Landing speed	150 km/h
Range	1,070 km
Ceiling	11,100 m
Electronics	FuG 10P Communications system with MF and HF operating frequencies Fu Bl 2F Funklandgerät blind landing device FuG 15 Y direction finder device FuG 25a Erstling IFF discriminator FuG 136 Nachtfee command transmission device FuG 101 radioaltimeter FuG 220 Lichtenstein SN-1 active search radar FuG 217 Neptun R-1 tail radar FuG 227 Flensburg radar passive receiver (for Monica emissions) FuG 350 Z Naxos radar passive receiver (for H2S emissions)

P.194.00.110 Technical Data

Type	Fast bomber.
Structure	Metallic, 62 per cent steel and 38 per cent aluminium.
Engines	One BMW 801 D radial of 14 cylinders, air cooled and 1,700 hp and a Jumo 004 turbojet of 890 kp.
Fuel tanks	Three, in wings and fuselage, with a total capacity of 2,100 litres.
Fixed armament	Two MG 151/20 guns of 20 mm in the forward section of the crew nacelle.
Launch armament	Up to 1,000 kg
Wingspan	16 m
Length	12.17 m
Height	4.39 m
Wing area	36.40 sq m
Empty weight	6,100 kg
Loaded weight	9,000 kg
Max. speed	780 km/h
Landing speed	150 km/h
Range	1,100 km
Ceiling	11,500 m

P.194.01.02 Technical Data

Type	Anti-tank.
Structure	Metallic. 62 per cent steel and 38 per cent aluminium.
Engines	One BMW 801 D radial of 14 cylinders, air cooled and 1,700 hp and a Jumo 004 turbojet of 890 kp.
Fuel tanks	Three, in wings and fuselage, with a total capacity of 2,100 litres.
Fixed armament	One Mk 412 gun of 55 mm (or an Mk 103 of 30 mm) and two MG 151 machine guns of 15 mm in the forward section of the crew nacelle.

Launch armament	Nine SC 70 bombs, or two SC 250 or one SC 500 within the fuselage-engine. Alternatively, one SC 1,000 externally positioned.
Wingspan	15.30 m
Length	12.45 m
Height	3.70 m
Wing area	36.40 sq m
Empty weight	6,500 kg
Loaded weight	9,450 kg
Max. speed	770 km/h
Landing speed	150 km/h
Range	1,045 km
Ceiling	11,100 m

P.194.02.01 Technical Data

Type	Anti-ship
Structure	Metallic, 62 per cent steel and 38 per cent aluminium.
Engines	One BMW 801 D radial of 14 cylinders, air cooled and 1,700 hp and a Jumo 004 turbojet of 890 kp.
Fuel tanks	Three, in wings and fuselage, with a total capacity of 2,100 litres.
Fixed armament	two MG 151/20 guns of 20 mm and two Mk 103 of 30 mm in the forward section of the crew nacelle.
Launch armament	Up to 1,500 kg
Wingspan	15.30 m
Length	12.75 m
Height	3.70 m
Wing area	36.40 sq m
Empty weight	6,100 kg
Loaded weight	9,450 kg
Max. speed	780 km/h
Landing speed	150 km/h
Range	1,045 km
Ceiling	11,000 m

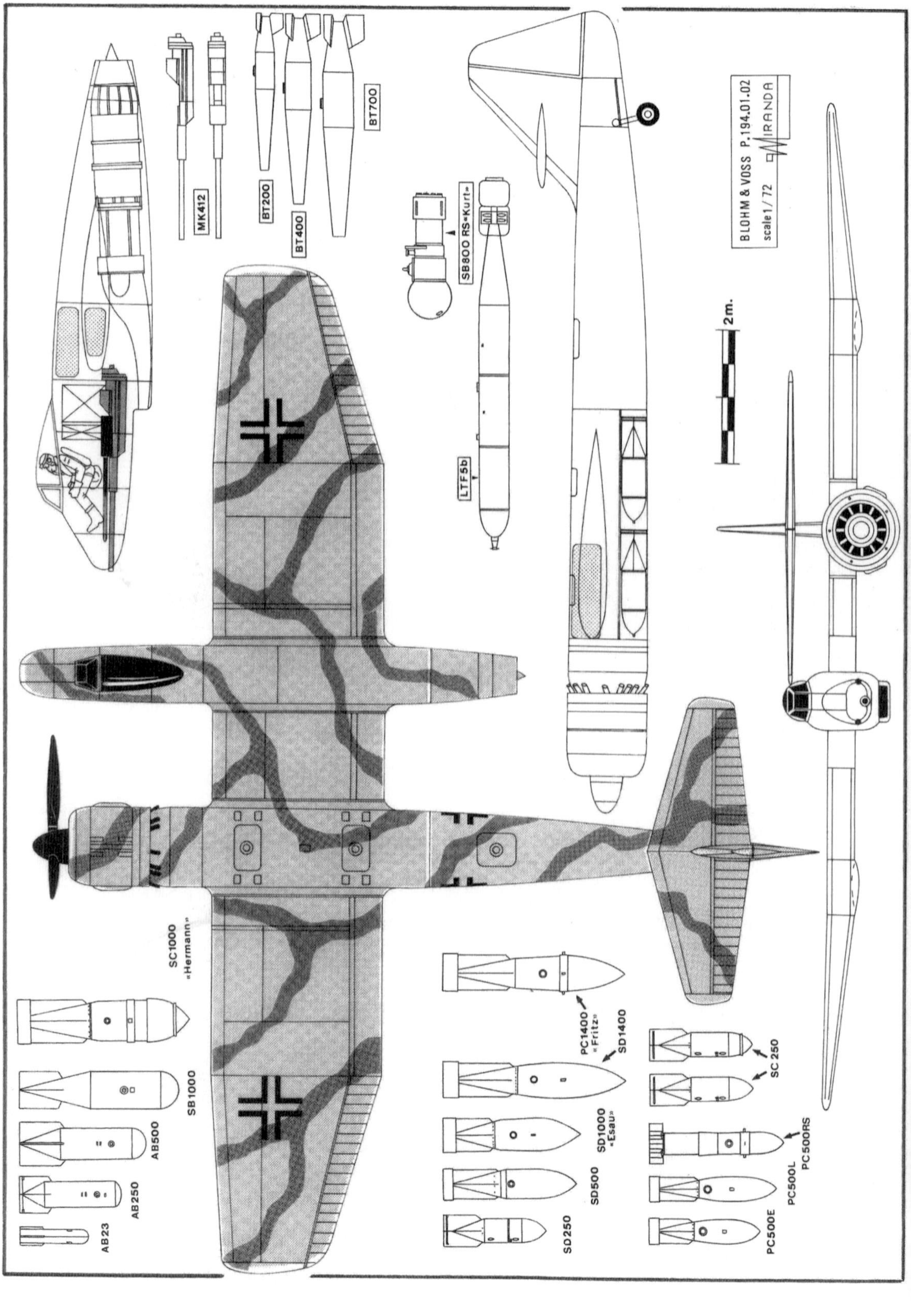
BLOHM & VOSS P.194.01.02
scale 1/72
MIRANDA
2 m.
MK412
BT200
BT400
BT700
SB800 RS «Kurt»
LTF5b
SC1000 «Hermann»
SB1000
AB500
AB250
AB23
SD250
SD500
SD1000 «Esau»
PC1400 «Fritz»
SD1400
SC 250
PC500RS
PC500L
PC500E

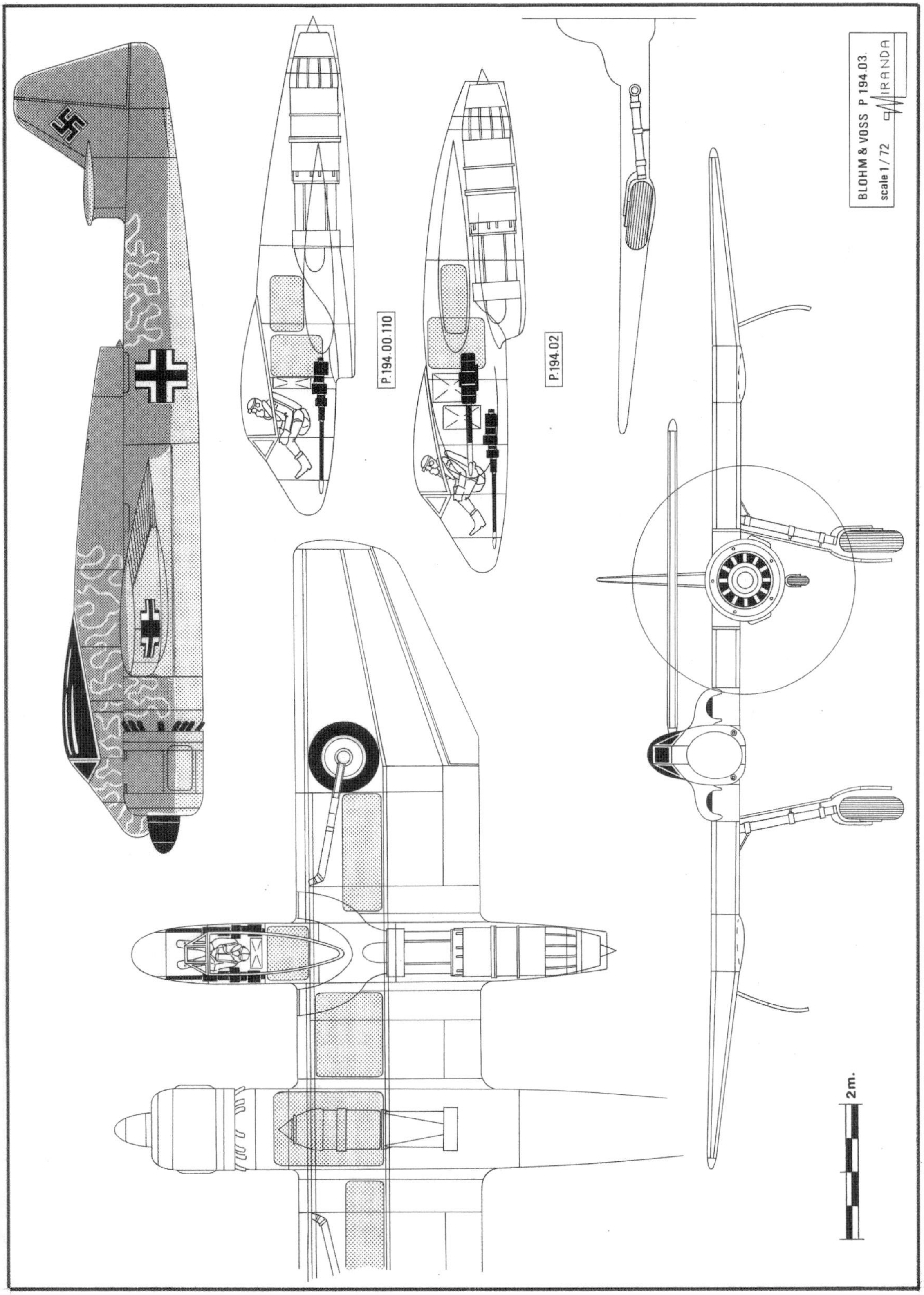
P.194.00.110
P.194.02
BLOHM & VOSS P 194.03.
scale 1/72
MIRANDA
2m.

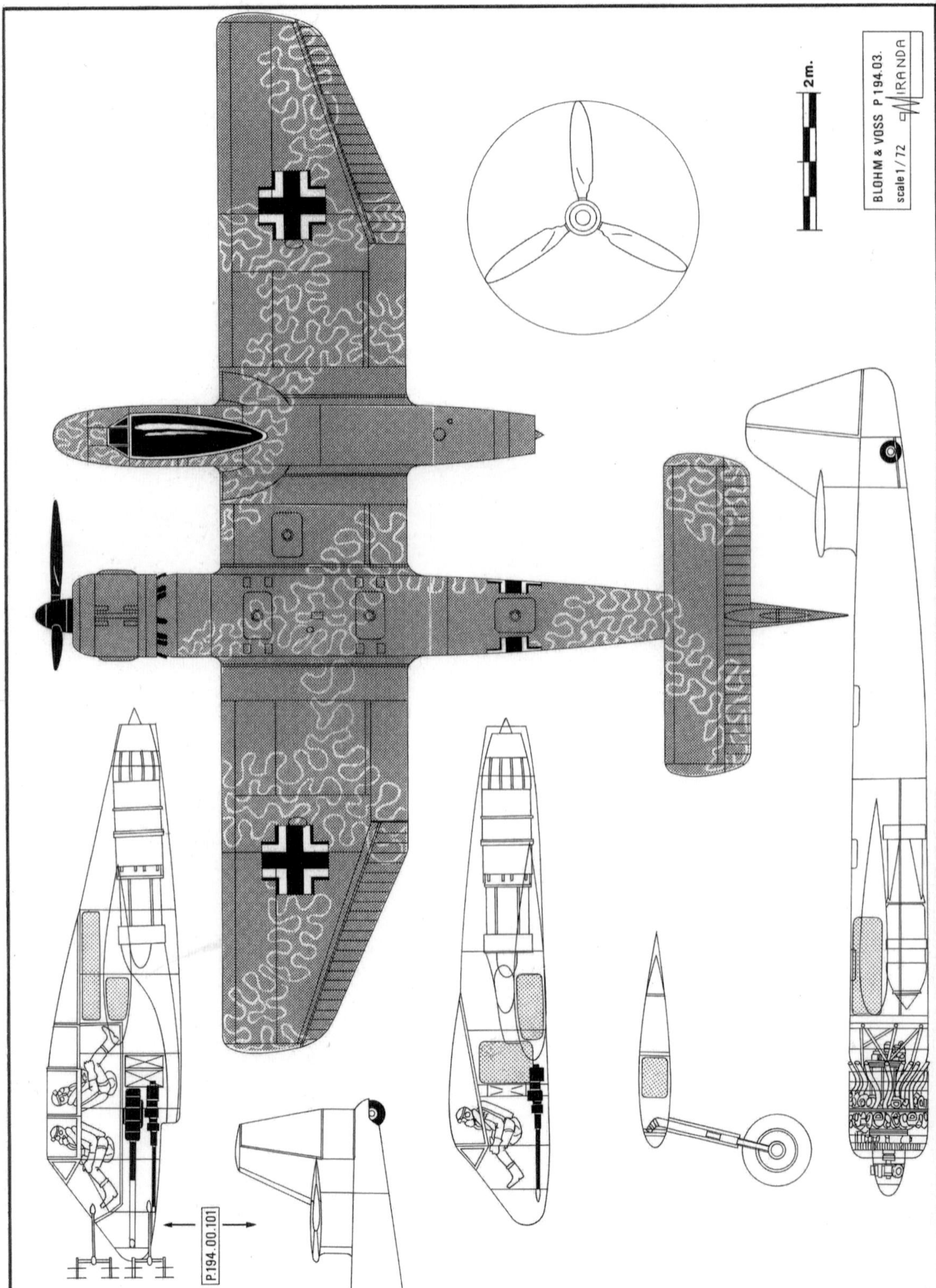
2m.
BLOHM & VOSS P 194.03.
scale 1/72
MIRANDA
P.194.00.101

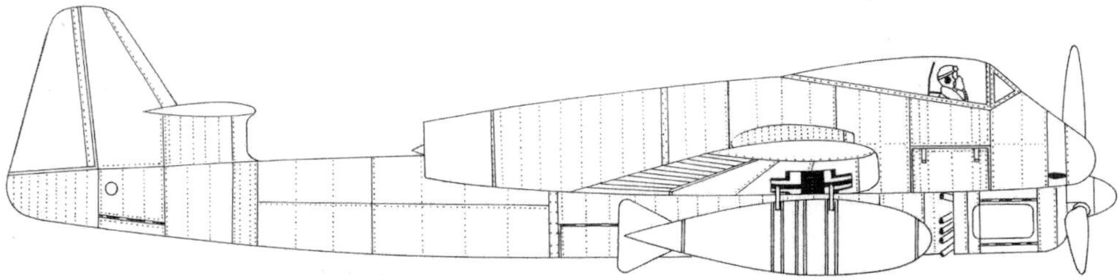

Blohm & Voss P.194.03 + 2×900 lt. fuel tank

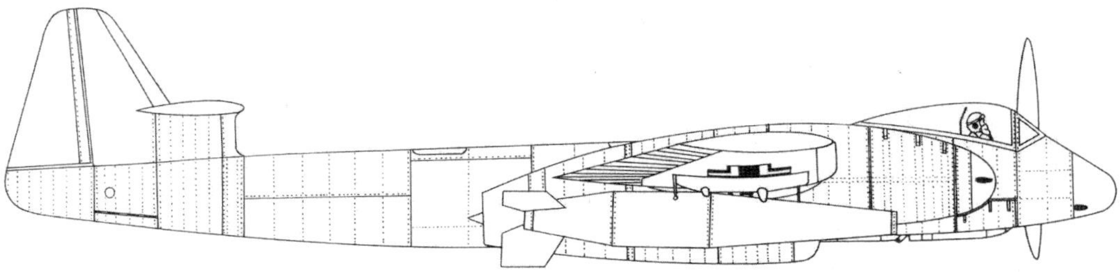

Blohm & Voss P.194.02+1×BT1400

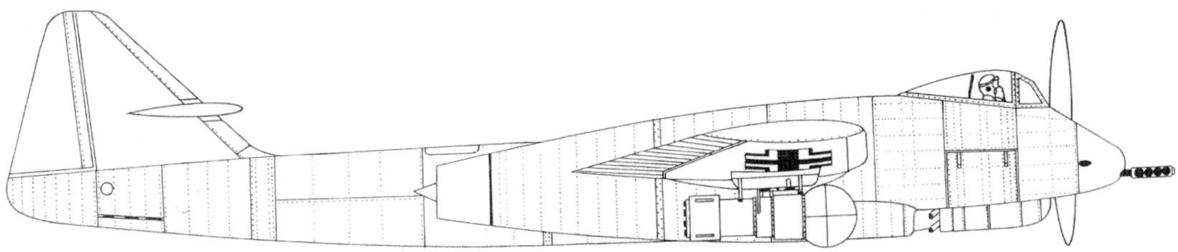

Blohm & Voss P.194.01.02+2×SB800 RS «Kurt»

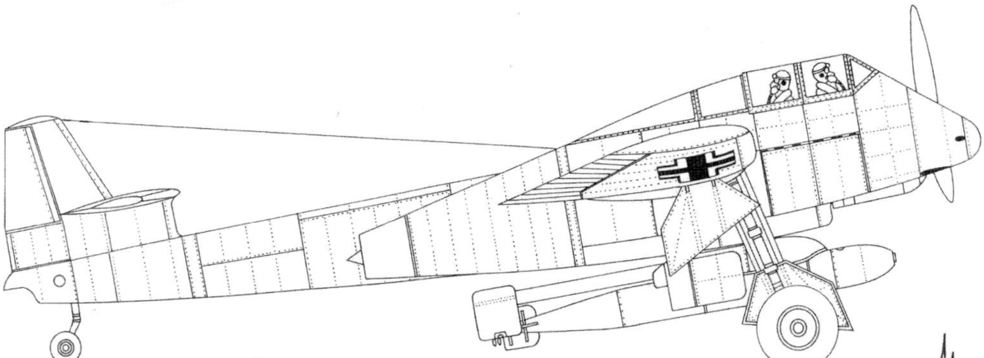

Blohm & Voss P. 194.00.101+1×L.10/LT.1

Chapter 8

Blohm und Voss P.204

The P.204 was intended as a Schnellbomber with mixed propulsion, in the same line as the P.194. It looked more conventional, except for the BMW 003 A turbojet installed in an asymmetric position, under the port side wing, to counteract the pair generated by the propeller. This configuration was successfully used in the Lockheed XH-51 A helicopter in 1964.

Its sturdy construction allowed the dive bomber role and the auxiliary engine helped to survive from the enemy DCA. The landing gear was very long so that a great number of conventional and guided weapons could be installed under its belly. It could also carry a Hermann bomb of 1,000 kg inside.

The basic design also allowed the transport and launch of the gliding bomb Bv 246 Hagelkorn.

Technical Data	
Type	Fast bomber.
Structure	Metallic (steel and duralumin).
Engine	A radial BMW 801 D, air cooled, with 1,700 hp of thrust, driving a three-bladed VDM propeller on the nose and a BMW 003 A turbojet of 800 kp in the port wing.
Fuel tanks	Three, in wings and on the back of the fuselage.
Fixed armament	Two MG 131/13 machine guns over the engine cowling and two MG 151/20 in the wing roots, synchronised with the propeller.
Launch armament	Up to 1,000 kg of bombs in the fuselage or a Bv246 gliding bomb of 730 kg suspended between the legs of the landing gear.
Wingspan	14 m
Length	12,60 m
Height	4,30 m
Wing area	33,70 sq m
Loaded weight	8,695 kg
Max. speed	760 km/h at 8,000 m
Landing speed	145 km/h
Range	530 km
Ceiling	9,540 m

Technical Data (Bv246 Hagelkorn)

Stage	Flight test over Fw 190 A-8/V 26.
Structure	Fuselage and empennages of steel and duralumin, wings of flexible concrete which drew under the carrier airplane, acting as springs during the launch sequence.
Guidance system	Directional receiver of the enemy radar.
Wingspan	6.40 m
Length	3.52 m (4.03 m in the Radieschen version)
Height	0.85 m
Launch weight	730 kg
Gliding rage	209 km
Launch height	10,500 m

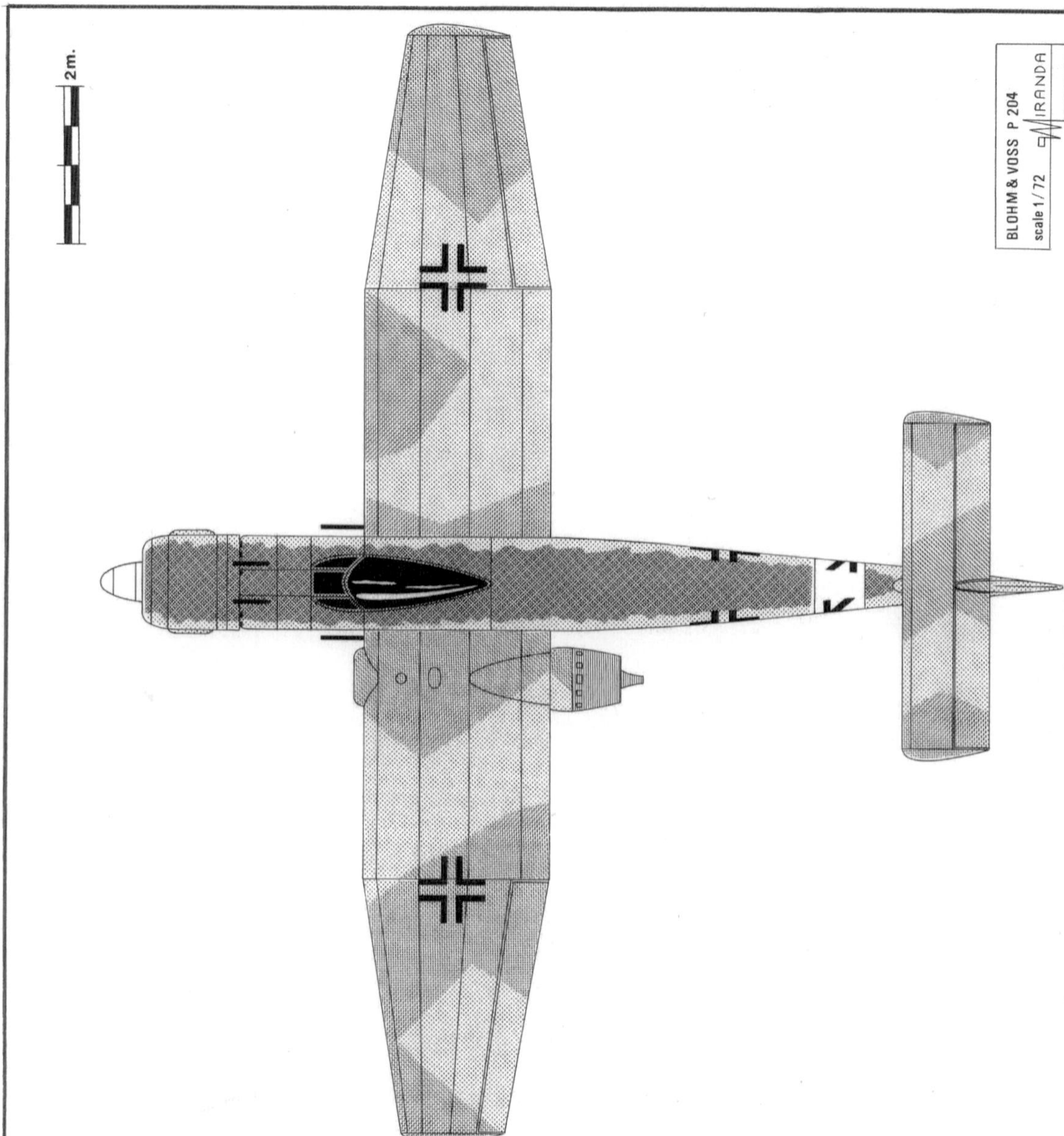
BLOHM & VOSS P 204
scale 1/72
MIRANDA
2m.

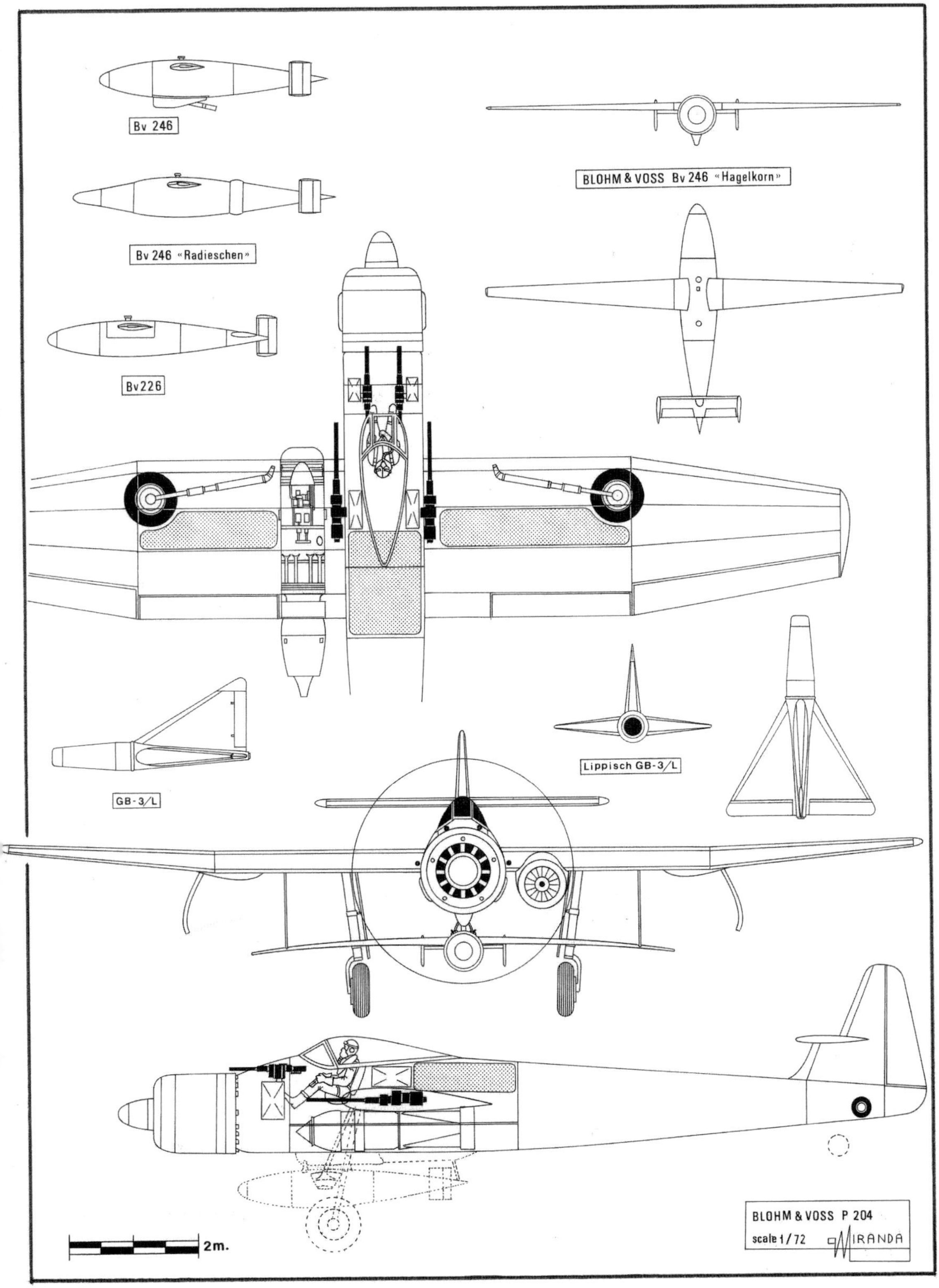
Bv 246
BLOHM & VOSS Bv 246 «Hagelkorn»
Bv 246 «Radieschen»
Bv226
GB-3/L
Lippisch GB-3/L
2m.
BLOHM & VOSS P 204
scale 1/72
MIRANDA

Chapter 9

Blohm und Voss P.207

Foreseeing that the OKL could consider that the aerodynamic solutions proposed by the P.208 –for the Otto Jäger specification of 21 July 1944 – were too radical, the design team of Dr Vogt offered three more classical versions, driven by the same engines, but with fully rectangular wings and tail planes, specially designed to be built of wood. The fuselage structure was made of steel, using just a small amount of duralumin in the outer cladding.

Technical Data P.207.02 (P.207.03)	
Type	Single-seat interceptor fighter.
Airframe	Wood, steel and dural.
Engine	One Argus As 413 of 24 cylinders in H, liquid cooled and 4,000 hp (one Daimler-Benz DB 603 L with 12 cylinders inverted-V, liquid cooled, with 2,100 hp).
Fuel tanks	Three, in wings and fuselage (idem).
Armament	four MK 108/30 cannons in the nose (two MK 108/30 mm and two MG 151/20 cannons in the nose).
Wingspan	12 m (10 m)
Length	11.37 m (9,73 m)
Height	4,46 m (3,78 m)
Wing area	(16,35 sq m)
Aspect ratio	(6.0:1)
Max. weight	(4,000 kg)
Max. speed	(more than 8,000 km/h)
Service ceiling	(10,000 m)
Endurance	3 hours

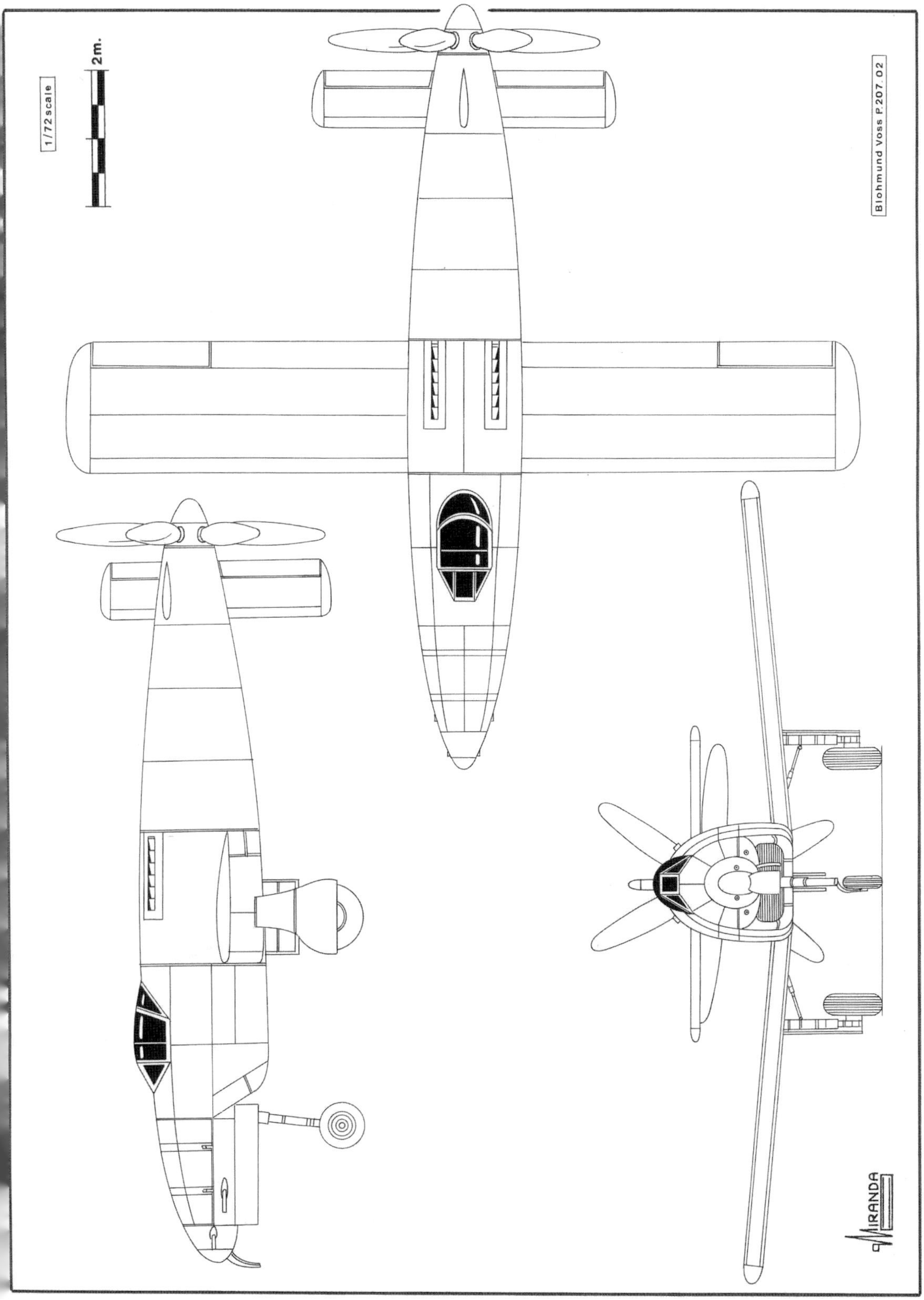
1/72 scale
2m.
Blohmund Voss P.207.02
MIRANDA

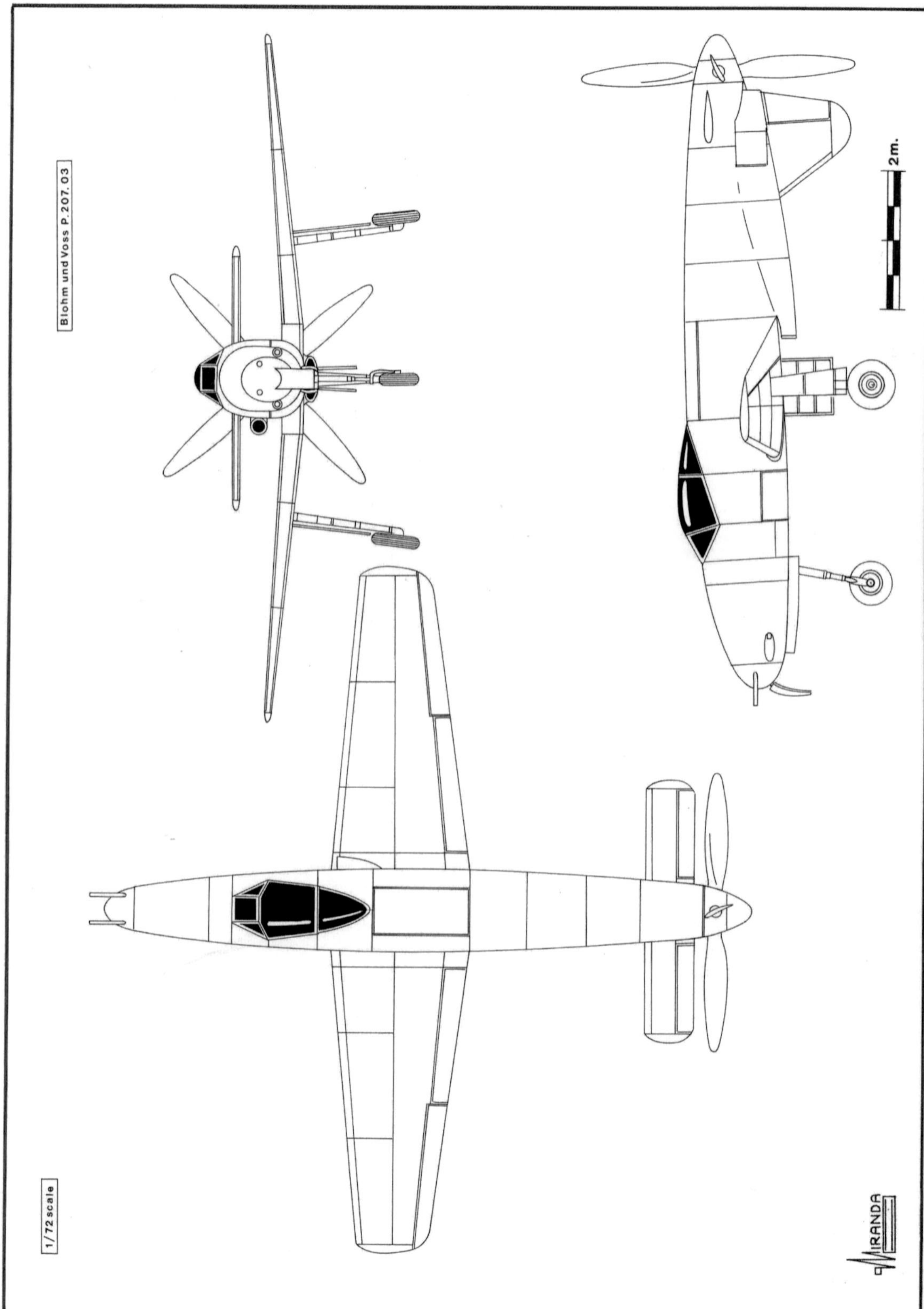
Blohm und Voss P.207.03
2m.
1/72 scale
MIRANDA

Chapter 10

Blohm und Voss P.208

The limited production of the German turbojets was reserved by the OKL for three models of aircraft: the Me 262, the Ar 234, and the He 162. The rest of manufacturers were forced to use piston engines.

To obtain faster aircraft, the engine power was increased by raising the number of cylinders, using power boost injection GM-1 (nitrous-oxide) and MW 50 (methanol-water) turbochargers, exotic fuels and multi-bladed, contra-rotating airscrews.

Tests of the first models in wind tunnels proved that pusher airscrews, combined with sweep laminar profile wings, decreased the drag, allowing the fighters with conventional engines an increase of speed of up to 900 km/h.

The installation of pusher airscrews could follow different configurations:

- Long shaft (Dornier 335)
- Twin boom (Focke Wulf Jäger mit DB 803)
- Canard (Henschel P.75)
- Tailless swept wing (Me 334)
- Bat wing (B&V P.208)

The first of these methods produced a loss of power in the transmission and an increase of weight in the shaft, bearings, double tail surfaces, tail bumper and long undercarriage legs. The second configuration was good for a jet engine, but aircraft equipped with conventional engines suffered constant troubles in control surfaces and engine cooling. The third solution was too advanced for its time and all the airplanes that got to fly using it (Curtiss XP-55, Kyushu J7W1 and S.S.I. S.S.4) suffered great problems of longitudinal stability. The fourth one flew and fought effectively, but generated violent vertical oscillations in the nose caused by the compressibility buffeting effect.

The solution suggested by Blohm und Voss had a 30-degree arrowed wing with pods on the wingtips where, on a very rear position, control surfaces acted as vertical and horizontal tailfins at the same time. This rear positioned engine-pusher propeller configuration solved the issue of the propeller air flux, acting over the empennages and allowing the concentration of armament in the nose, as well as the increase of speed and visibility up to its maximum. However, it forced the use of a high and heavy landing gear, created big problems of engine cooling and made parachuting impossible while the airscrew was working. The replacement of the conventional engine by a turbojet would solve all these problems, albeit with the penalty of higher rate of fuel consumption.

There were three variants of the BV P.208 design. The 01 had a Jumo 222 E with 24 cylinders in Star, was liquid cooled and had a thrust of 3,000 hp. The 02 used an Argus As 413, with 4,000 hp. The 03 had a Daimler Benz DB 603 L with 2,100 hp.

There existed a project to use a big internal cooler, based on the BV 155B technology, through which the air – taken in by a powerful fan on a ventral position – would flow. The installation of an ejectable seat was considered not a simple thing in an aircraft with pressure cabin and it was decided to use an explosive system to blow up the airscrew blades.

None of these were ever manufactured and, as far as I am aware, a plane with this shape has never flown. Perhaps the design was not very stable at high speed and the artificial stability could not even be tried at that time.

Technical Data P.208.02 (P.208.03)	
Type	Single-seat high-altitude interceptor. (Single-seat interceptor fighter.)
Structure	Steel, with aluminium cladding. (Idem.)
Engine	An Argus As 413 of 24 cylinders in H, liquid cooled and 4,000 hp driving a six-bladed contra-prop. (Daimler-Benz DB 603 L with 12 cylinders in V, liquid cooled, with 2,100 hp driving a four-bladed pusher airscrew with an explosive blowing up mechanism.)
Fuel tanks	Three, in wings and fuselage. (Idem.)
Fixed armament	Two MK 103 of 30 mm and two MG 151/20 in the nose. (Three MK 108 of 30 mm in the nose.)
Wingspan	16,30 m (12,20 m)
Length	10.80 m (8,64 m)
Height	3,90 m (3,60 m)
Wing area	25,30 sq m (18,90 sq m)
Empty weight	(4,185 kg)
Loaded weight	5,010 kg
Max. speed	(794 km/h at 10,000 m)
Range	(1,060 km)
Ceiling	(12,000 m)

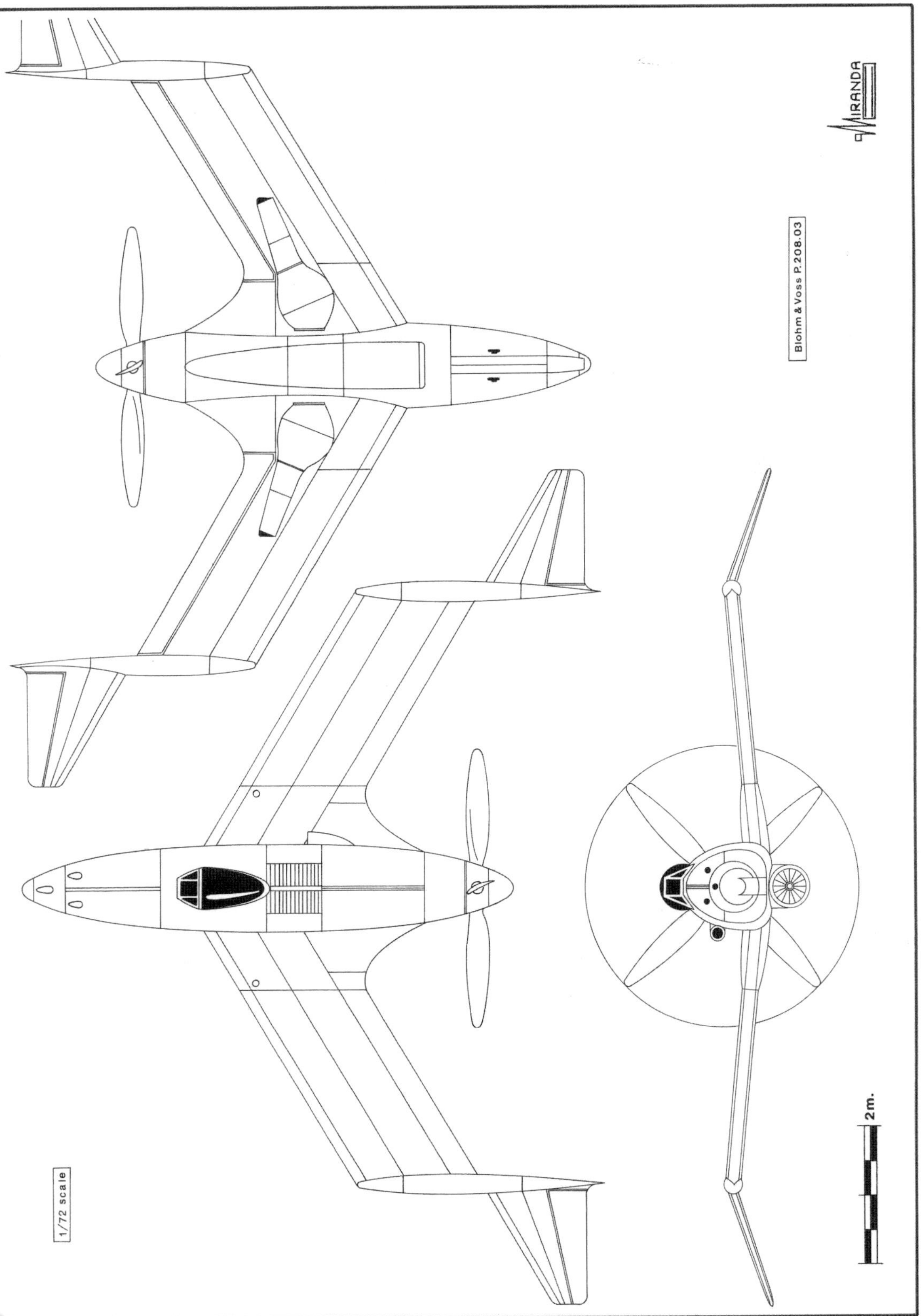
Blohm & Voss P.208.03
1/72 scale
2m.

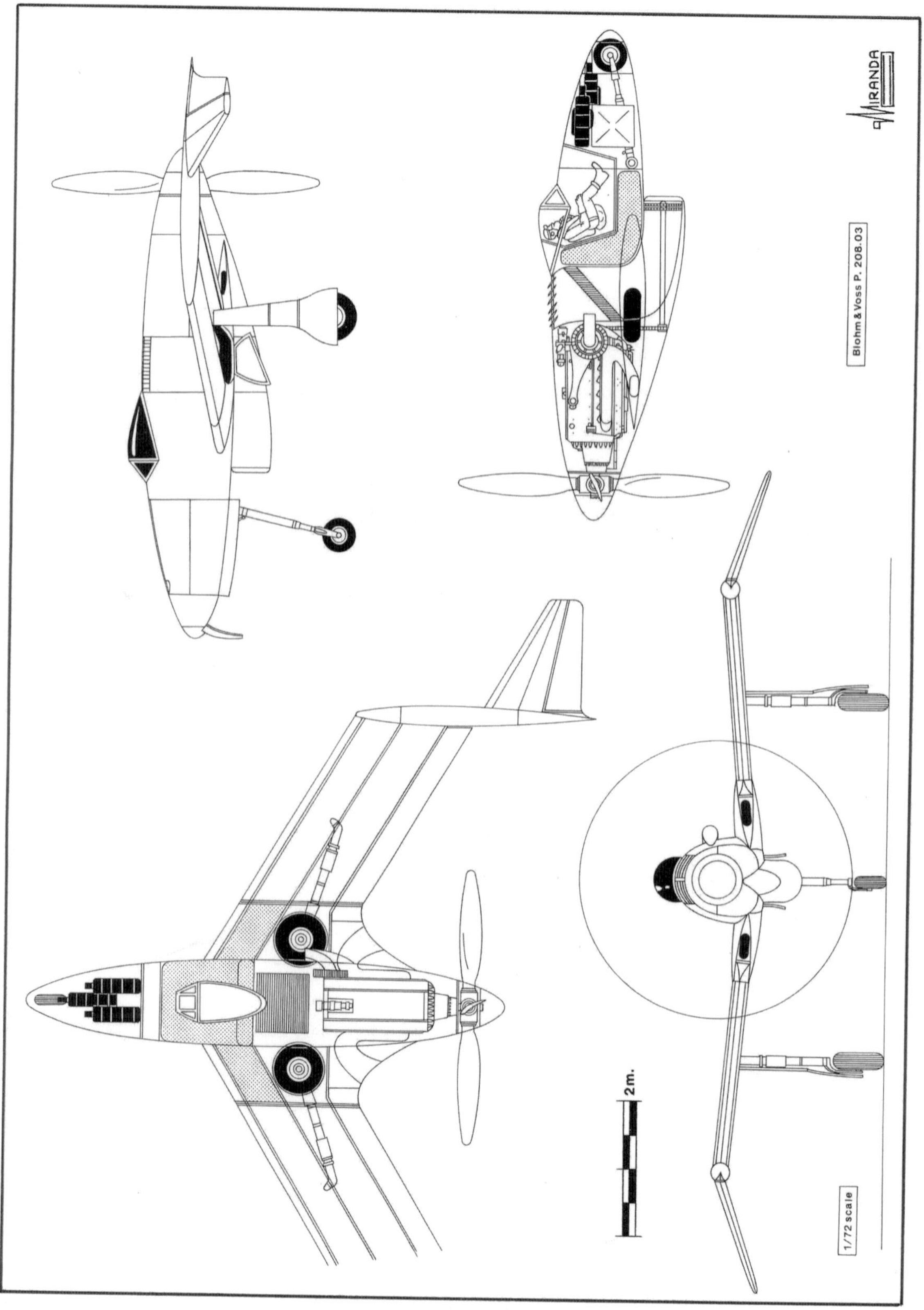
Blohm & Voss P. 208.03
MIRANDA
2m.
1/72 scale

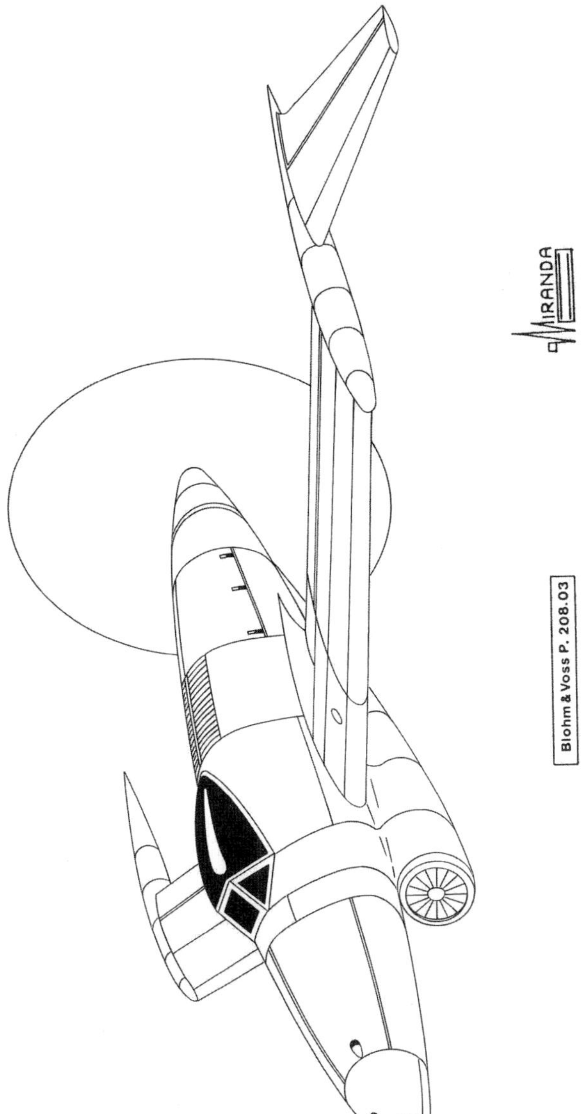
Blohm & Voss P. 208.03

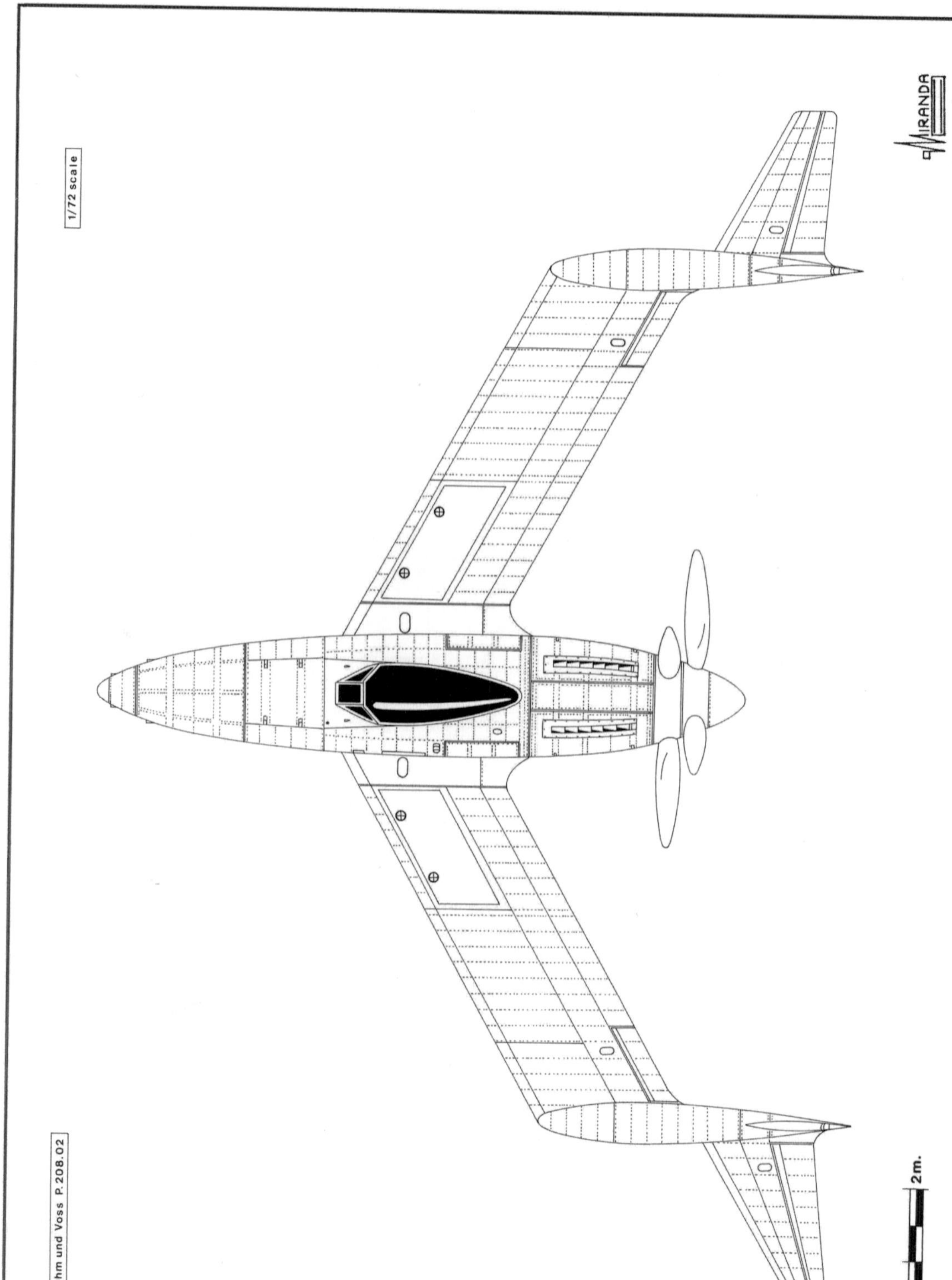
1/72 scale
Blohm und Voss P. 208.02
2m.

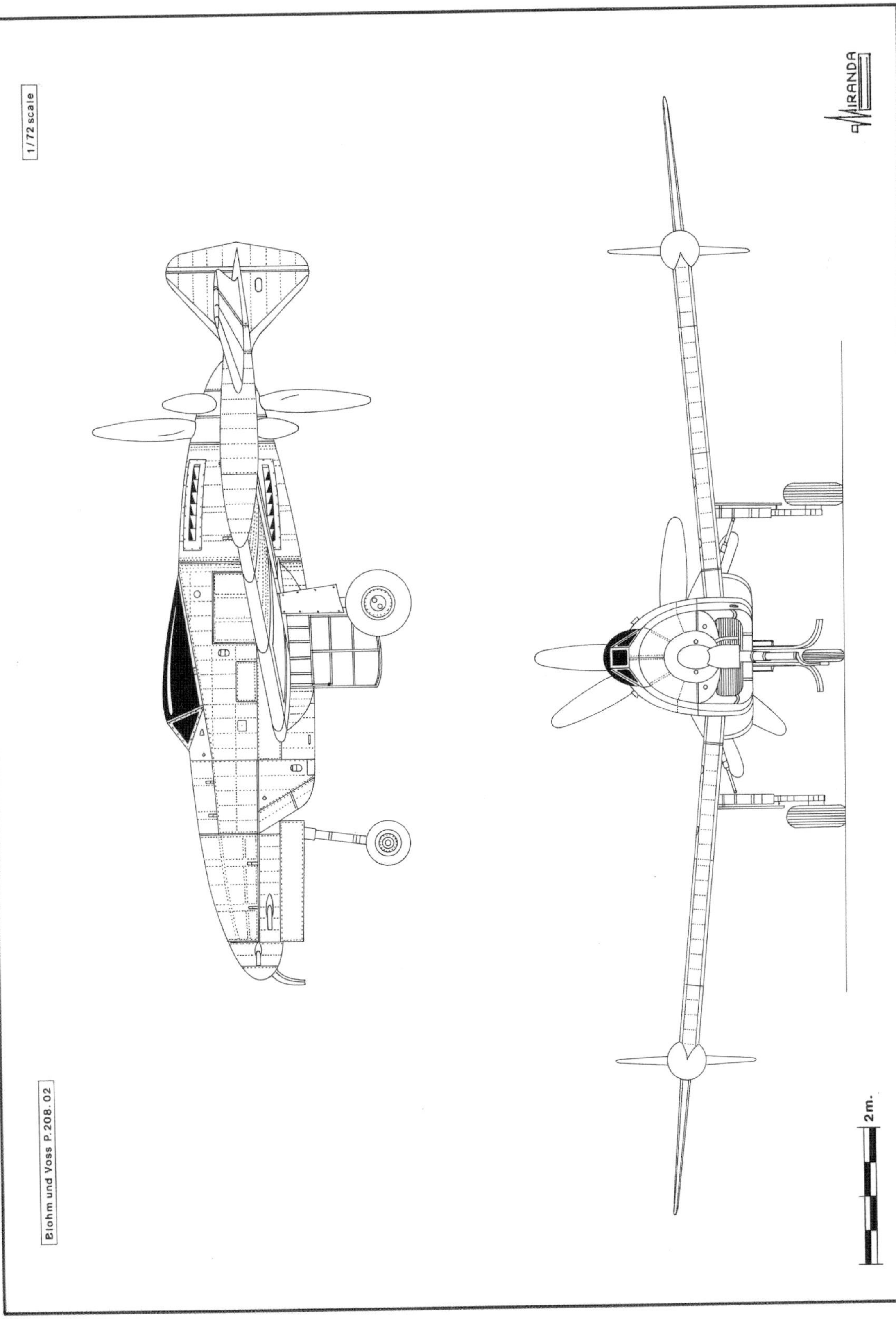
1/72 scale
Blohm und Voss P.208.02
2m.

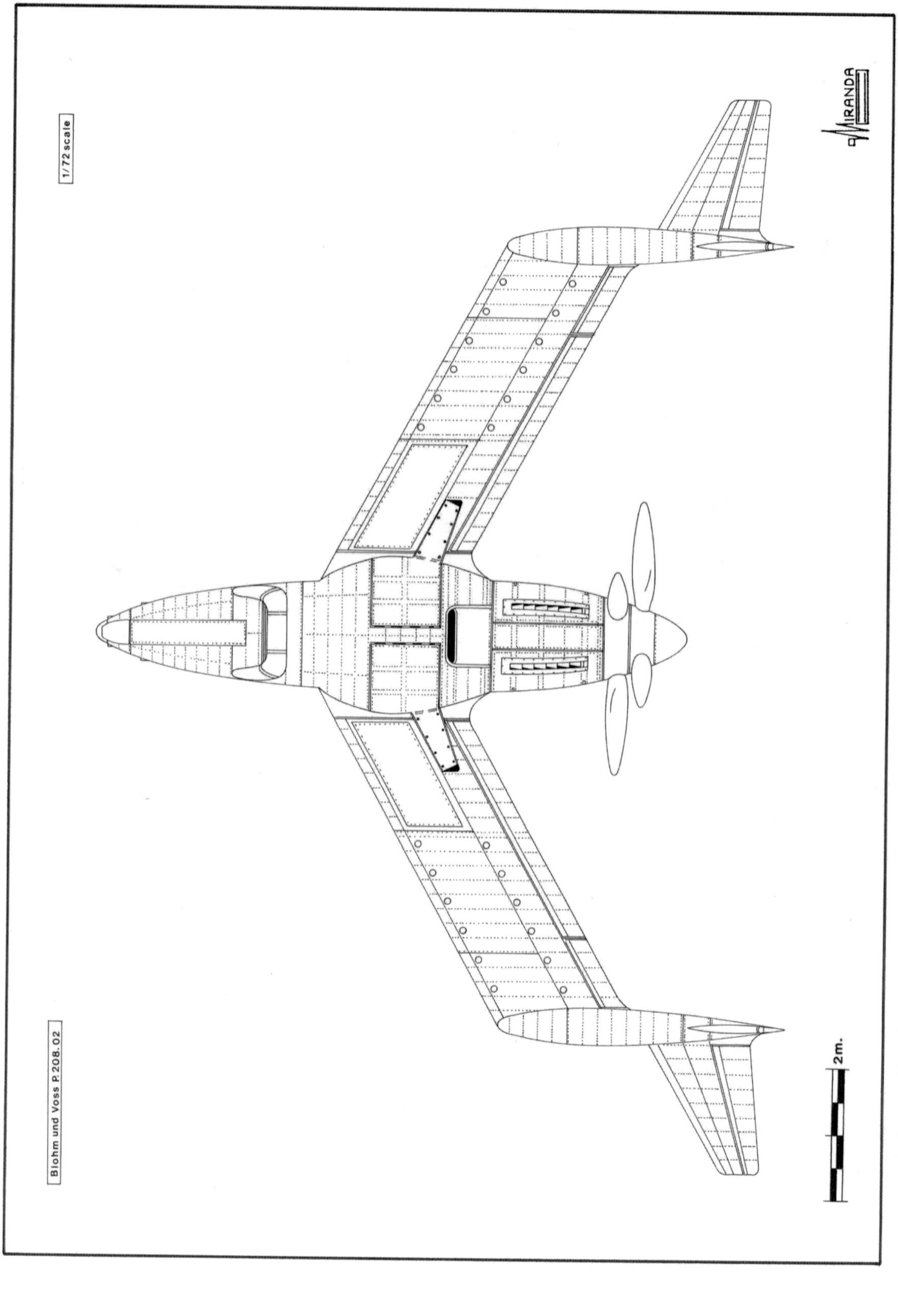
1/72 scale
Blohm und Voss P.208.02
MIRANDA
2m.

Chapter 11

Blohm und Voss BV 237

Designed at the beginning of 1943 to replace the Ju 87, manufacture of the BV 237 was proposed in three versions:

- Stuka, single seat, 2 MG 151/20, 2 MG 131/13, 1,000 kg of bombs
- Anti-tank, two seats, 3 MK 103/30 or 1 MK 101/30, 2 MG 131/13
- Schnellbomber, two seats, 2 MG 131/13, 1,000 kg bombs

The landing gear, of great width, was a considerable improvement for operations from provisional aerodromes.

The design was not successful. The Luftwaffe concept of ground attack differed from the diving bomber, which was considered poorly fitted to the fight against a constantly adapting enemy. The final decision was to use the Focke-Wulf 190 for this task. It used the same engine, was faster and lighter and could also be used as a fighter.

Technical Data	
Type	Stuka, Schlachtflugzeug, Schnellbomber.
Airframe	Wood, steel and aluminium.
Engine	A BMW 801 D, of 14 cylinders, air cooled and 1,750 hp. The BV 237 B-1 also had a Jumo 004B turbojet, with 900 kg thrust, suspended between the fuselage and the crew nacelle.
Fuel tanks	One of 900 litres in the fuselage and another of 1,000 litres within the wing spar.
Span	14,46 m
Length	10,75 m
Height	3,30 m
Wing area	42 sq m
Max. weight	6,700 kg (Stuka)
Max. speed	580 km/h (Anti-tank)
Range	2,000 km (Anti-tank)
Electronics	FuG 16ZY transmitter/receiver device

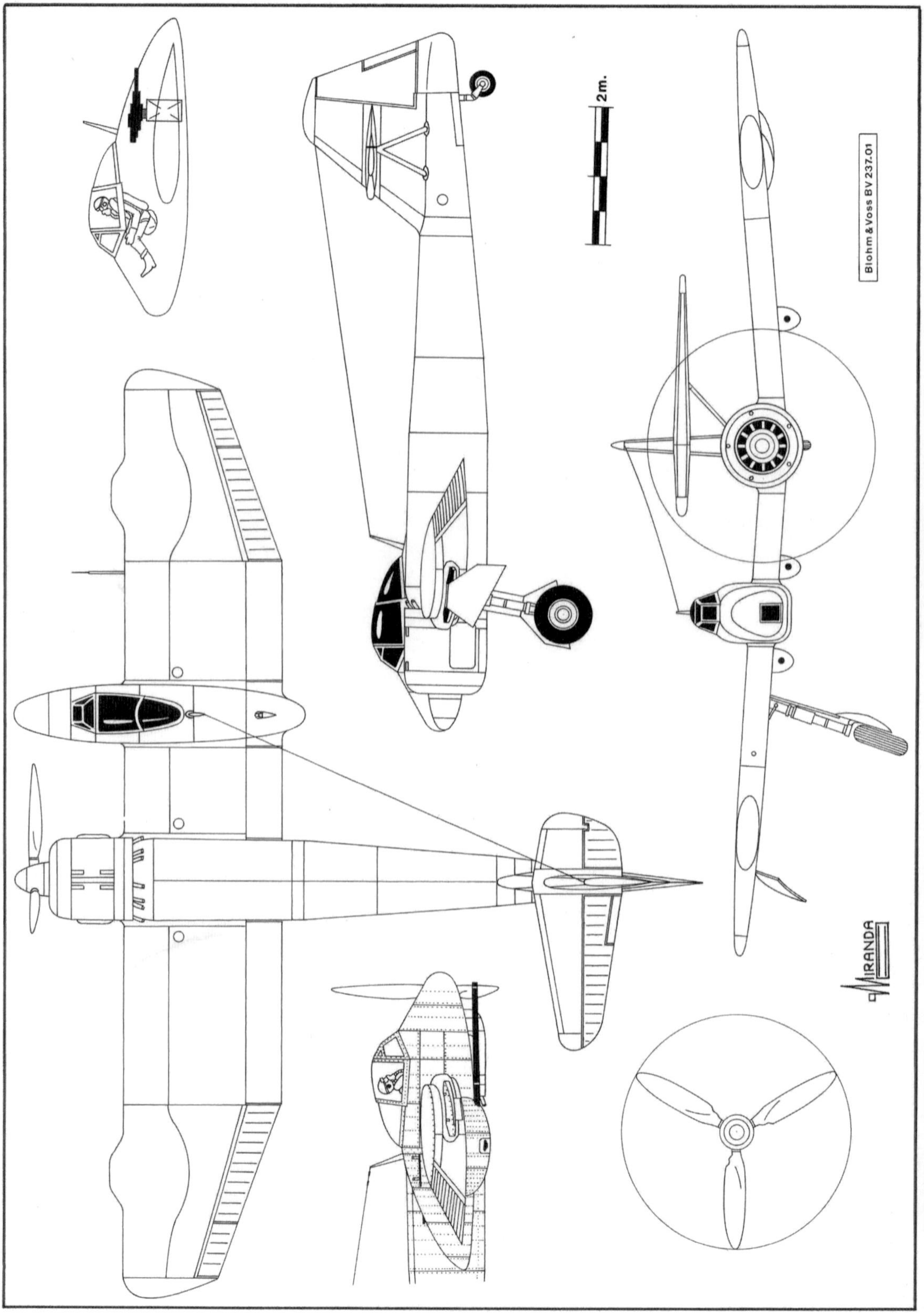
2m.
Blohm & Voss BV 237.01
MIRANDA

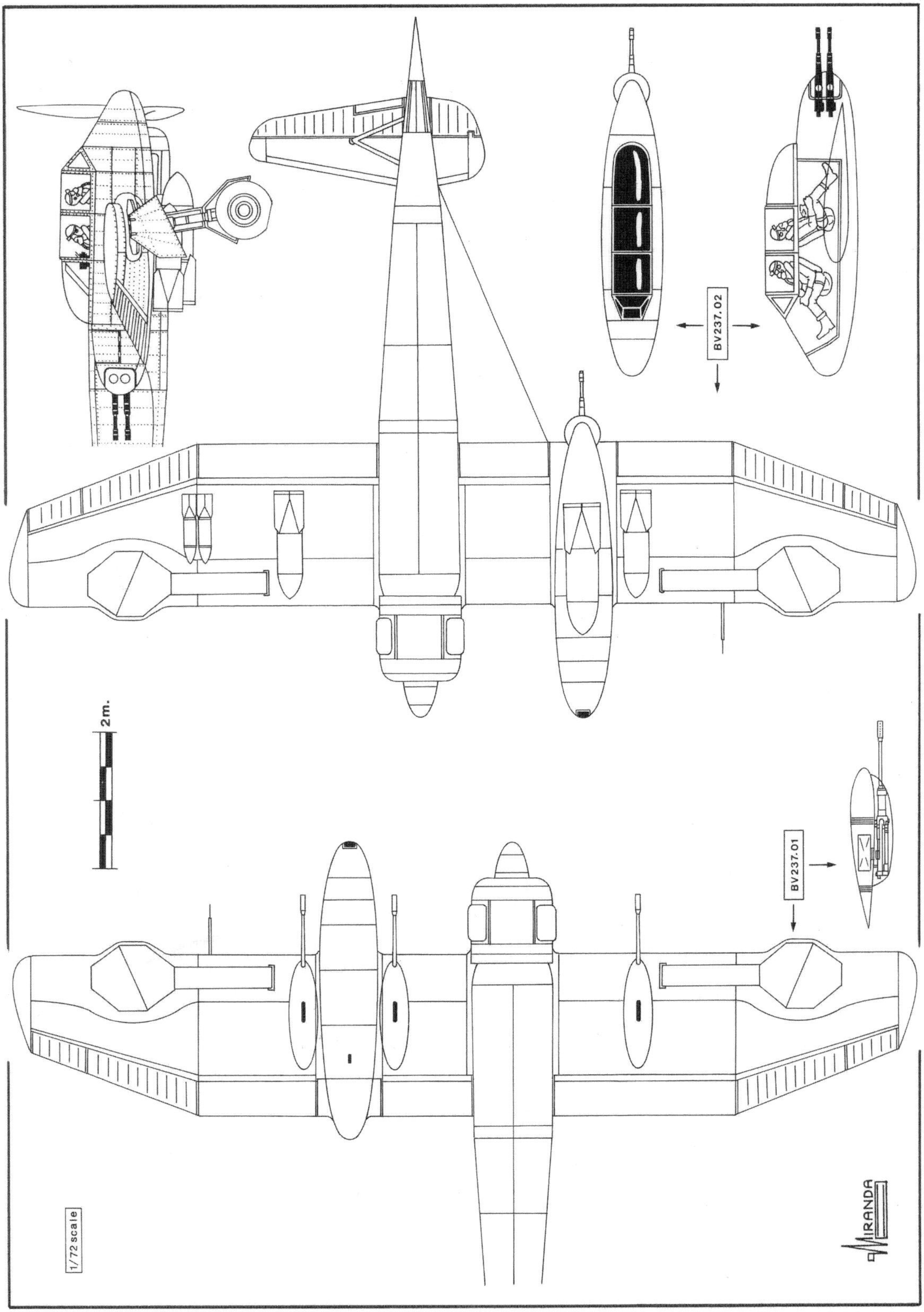
BV237.02
2m.
BV237.01
1/72 scale
MIRANDA

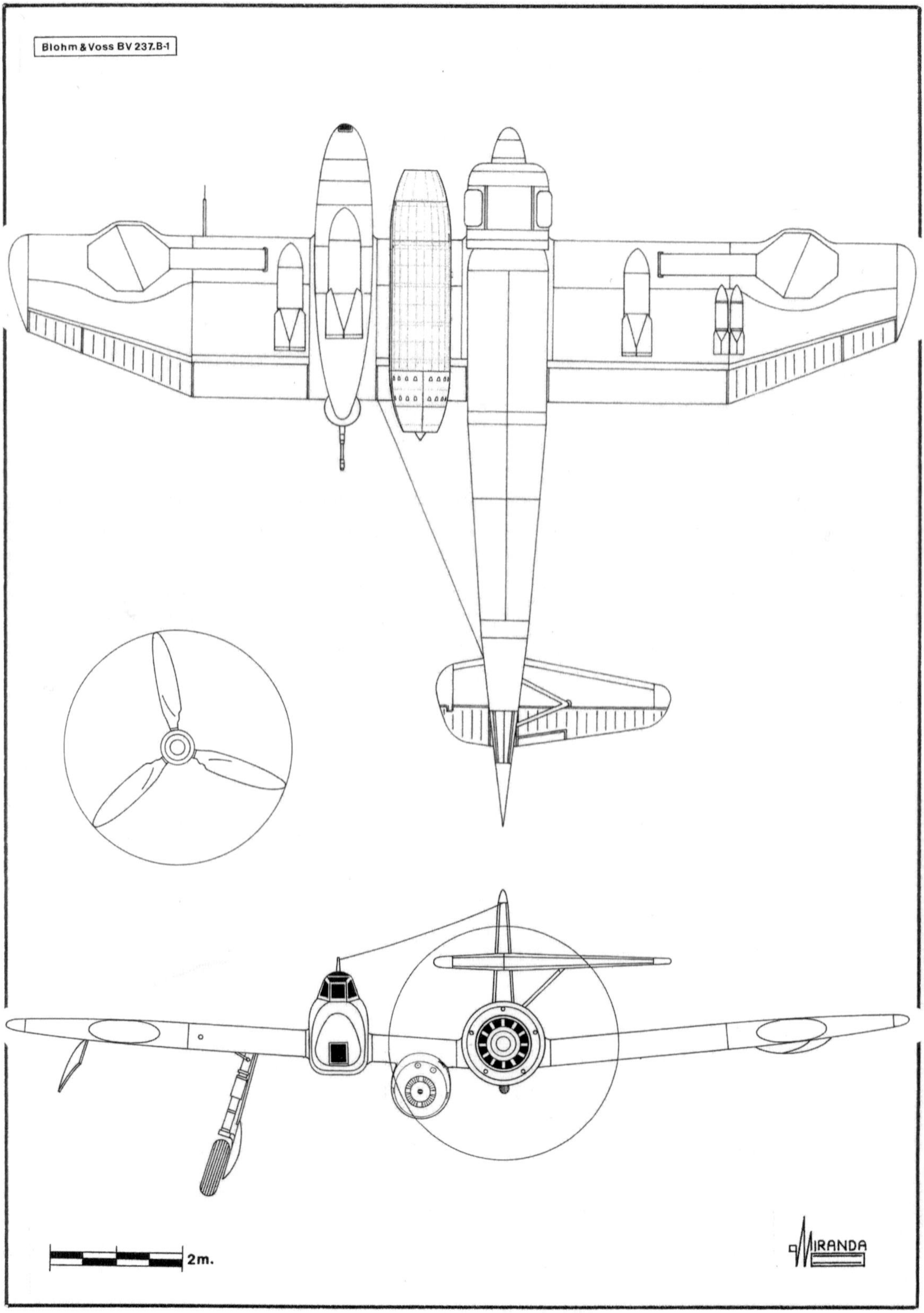
Blohm & Voss BV 237.B-1
2m.
MIRANDA

Chapter 12

Daimler Benz Hochleistungsflugzeug mit DB-609

The DB-609 looked a very promising design when its development started in mid-1942. It was powerful, it could be installed in V or inverted-V configuration and would have been ideal for a large calibre cannon installation.

Originally conceived as power plant for bombers, it consisted of a DB 603 V12, to which four additional cylinders were added, with an elongated crankshaft to achieve 2,700 hp.

It was expected to improve the design until reaching the 3,400 hp in further versions, but the development was expensive and the Luftwaffe was giving priority to the manufacturing of fighters at this stage of the war. The DB 609 was considered too long and heavy for its installation in a Single-seat fighter.

On 5 March 1942, the firm published a preliminary design to show how it could be done. The engine in the nose activated a double ring of four-blade contra-rotating airscrews – positioned in the fuselage, behind the pilot – by means of an extension shaft.

With the exception of the propellers position and the odd undercarriage, it was a very conventional and not much elaborate design. Just a simple technological demonstration of the propulsion system, on which not even the position of the armament or the fuel tanks were indicated.

In 1942, there was not yet a functional ejector seat and it may be assumed that the escape mechanism consisted of detaching the rear section of the fuselage, using explosive bolts.

The DB 609 was cancelled in May 1943 in favour of the DB 603.

Technical Data	
Type	Single-seat heavy fighter.
Airframe	Light alloy structure and cladding.
Undercarriage	Tricycle type, nosewheel would have retracted to the rear, rotating 90 degrees to lie flat in the wheel bay. The main wheels retracted inwards.
Engine	A Daimler Benz DB 609 of 2,700 hp, sixteen-cylinder, inverted-V, liquid cooled engine, driving a 3 m diameter four-blade contra-rotating propeller through an extension shaft. Frontal radiator and fan.

Armament	Some sources mention 6 x 20 mm cannons.
Electronics	FuG 16 VHF transmitter/receiver.
Measurements	(based on the engine size)
Span	11.3 m
Length	11.4 m
Height	3.8 m

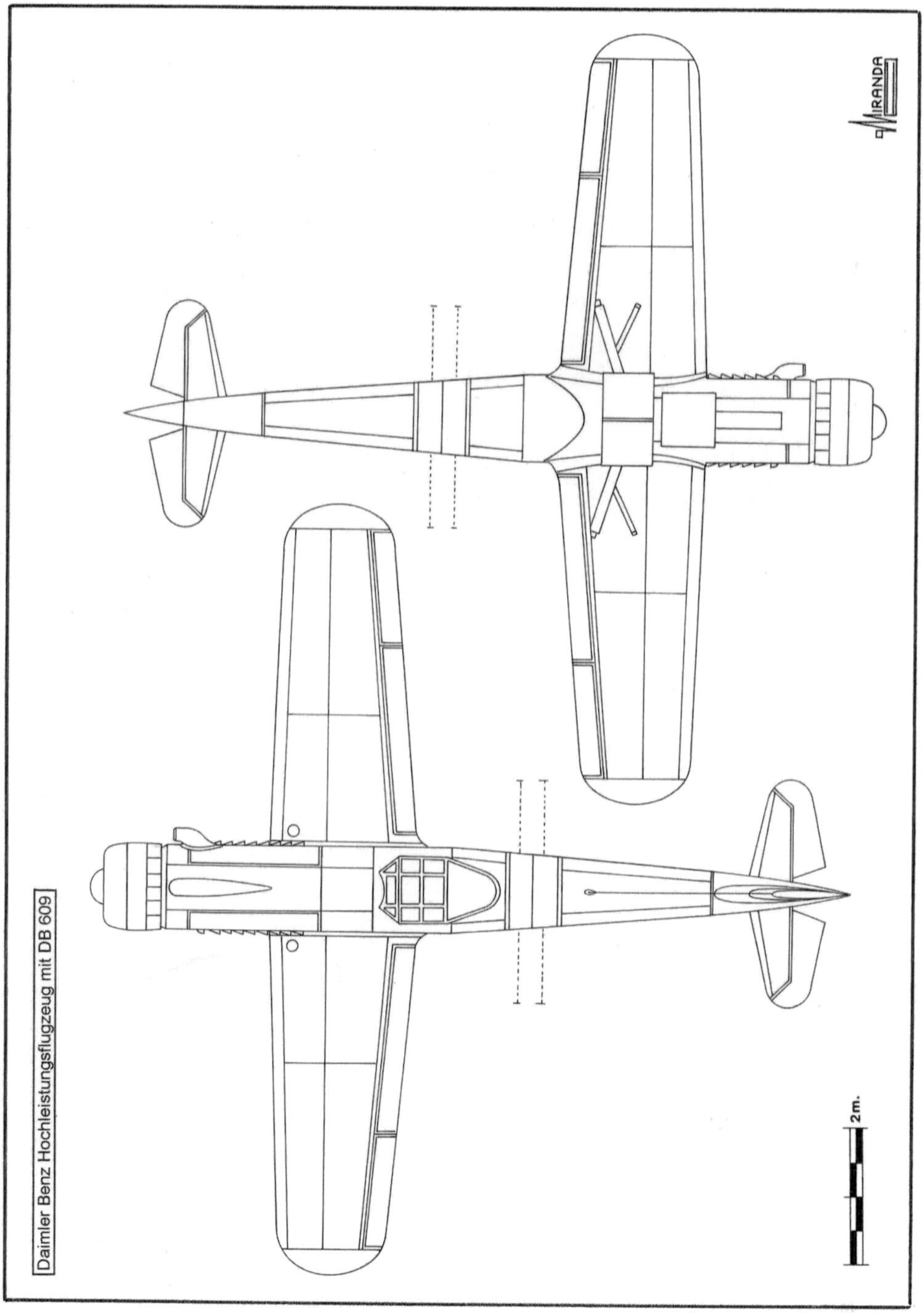

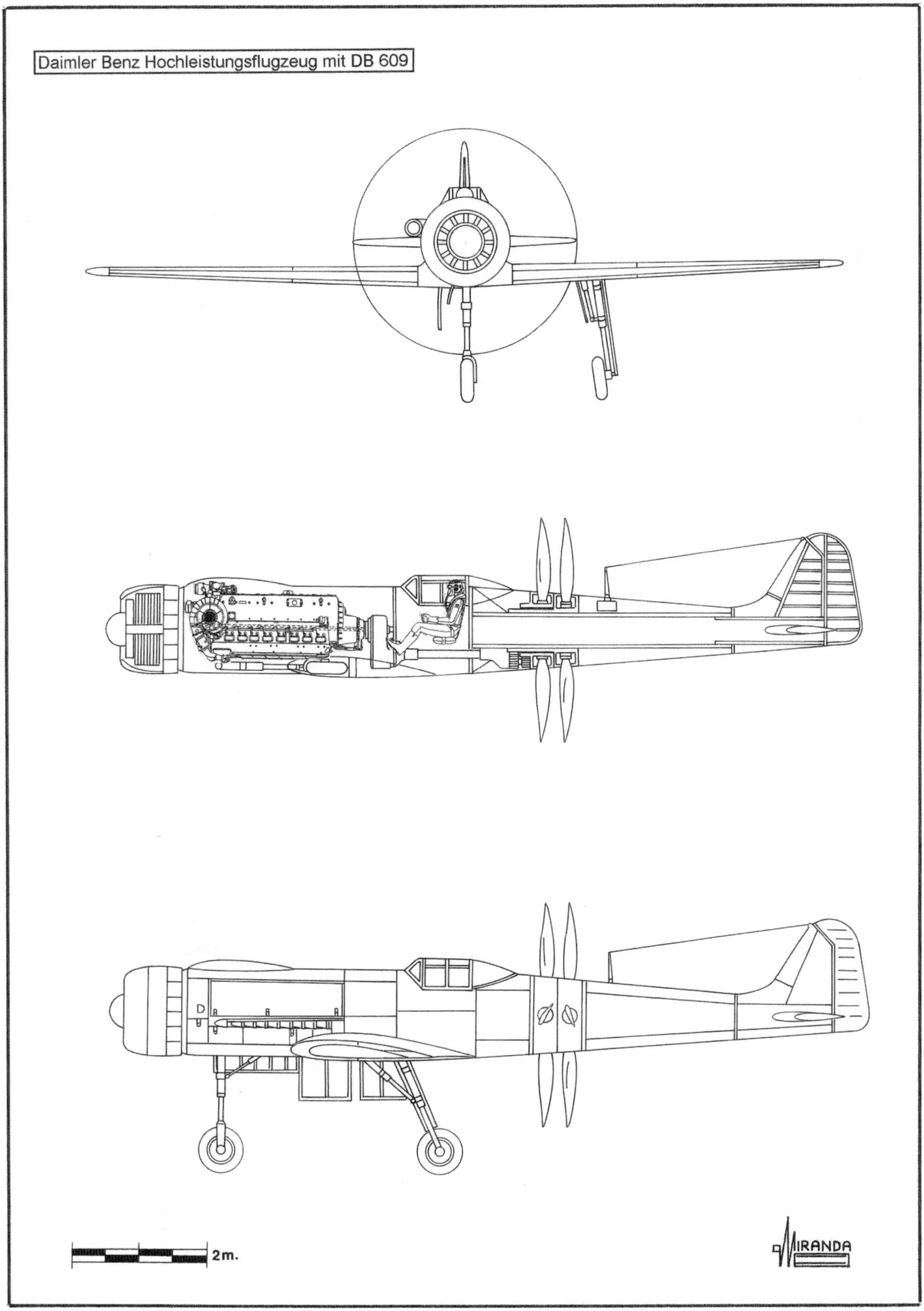
Daimler Benz Hochleistungsflugzeug mit DB 609
2m.
MIRANDA

Chapter 13

Daimler Benz Jäger mit DB 613

When the big formations of the Allied bombers began to be escorted by fighters, in their incursions over the German Reich, the Luftwaffe interceptors, equipped with heavy guns to destroy bombers, were not agile enough to elude the Allied fighters.

Additionally, the standard Mk 108 cannon did not have enough range to shoot from outside the defensive firing barrier of the B-17 and B-24 boxes and its 30 mm ammunition did not posses the required destructive power to dismantle a bomber with a single impact. The Luftwaffe's estimates suggested that this effect could only be achieved with 55 mm projectiles shot from a Mauser/Krupp Mk 214B or Mk 412 cannons.

The issue with these monsters of 630 kg was in their powerful recoil, able to cause important structural damages to the carrying airplane. They could be safely installed on the Ju-88 C-6 and Me-410 A-1, but these twin-engined Zerstörer lacked the necessary speed to escape the American P.47 and P.51.

On the contrary, the Me 262 was too fast for the low rate of fire of these weapons and did not render good results during the tests made with the 50 mm Mauser Mk 214 A in March 1945.

The solution would be a single-engined heavy fighter equipped with an engine within the 4,000 hp range, able to house a 55 mm cannon, shooting through the propeller hub.

On 21 January 1944, Daimler Benz published the report *Daimler Benz Werk 60, Konstruktionsbericht K.21* that included a study of the different possibilities for combining an Mk 412 cannon with the DB 613 engine, another monster of twenty-four cylinders and 3,800 hp, integrated by two DB 603 G engines coupled together to drive a single power shaft with contra-rotating airscrews. These were:

- Conventional configuration with the DB 613 in the aircraft nose
- A long shaft and the pilot placed forward. Annular cooler
- A long shaft and gear, in front of the pilot, the gun firing through the shaft of the gear. Cooler under the nose
- A long twin shaft and ventral cooler.

The K1 report presented several possible layouts for this engine/gun/pilot configuration, not a specific aircraft. Any aircraft able to use this engine would have been a very heavy machine, in the range of the Blackburn Firecrest, Westland Wyvern or Douglas Skyraider.

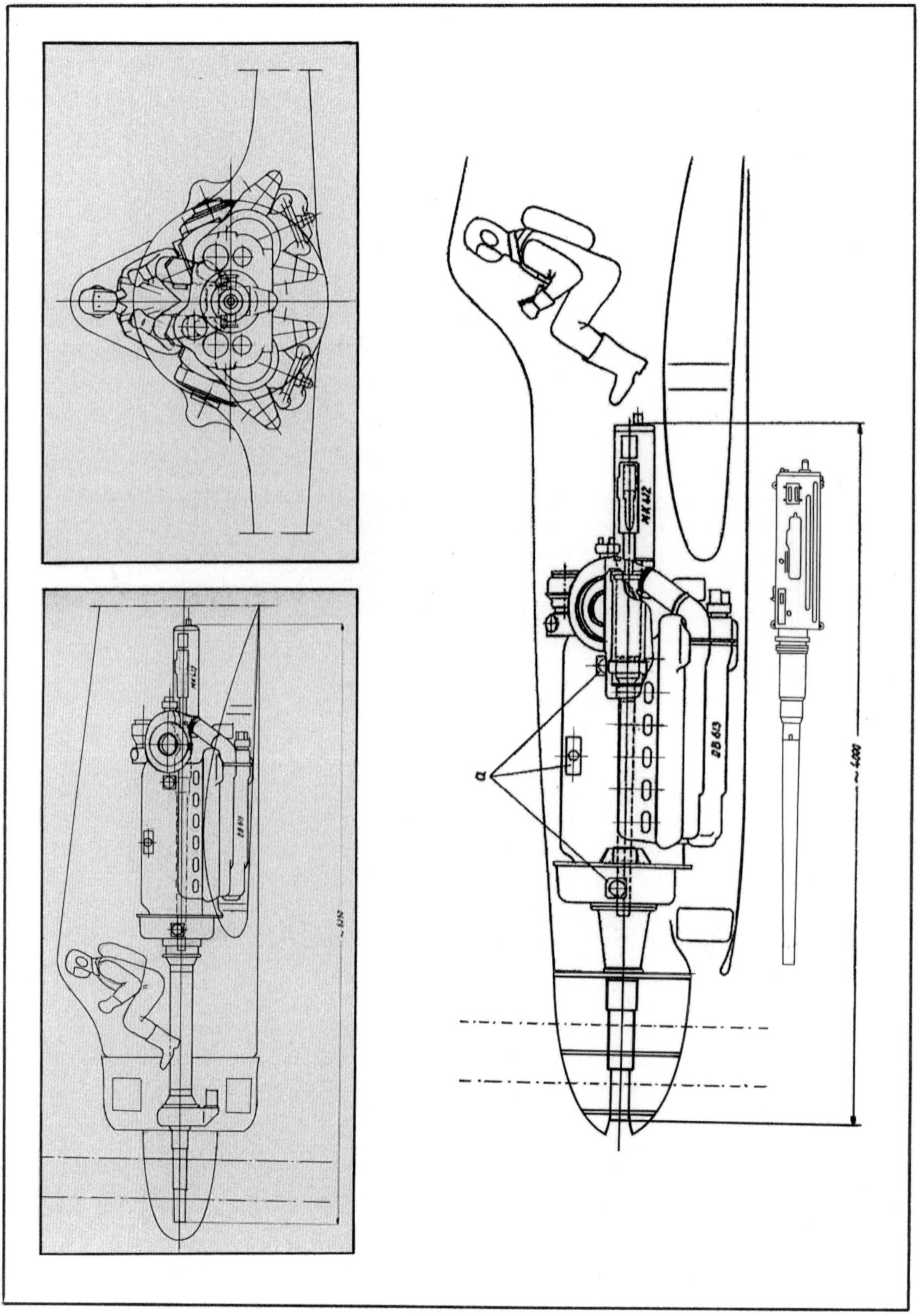
MK 412
DB 613
a

Chapter 14

Dornier P.238

The Dornier Do 335 was a formidable combat machine, with great development potential, interrupted by the end of the Second World War.

The push-pull formula, combined with the use of different types of engines, proved that it could satisfy the main needs of the Luftwaffe by the end of 1943, including:

- Conventional night fighter (Do 435 C-1, C-2, D-1 & D-2)
- Mixed power night fighter (Do 335 A&B)
- Anti-tank, Zerstörer and fighter bomber (Do 335 B-2, B-1 & A-1)
- Light bomber (Do 335 A-2)
- Trainer (Do 335 B-5)
- Recce (Do 435 B-4)
- High-altitude Recce (Do 335 B-4)
- Long range Recce (Do 335 Z)

This twin fuselage design served as the base for the four-engined, 8,000 km-range Junkers Ju 635.

The last push-pull Dornier was the P.238, derived from the Do 435 with elongated fuselage of up to 17.10 m and Jumo 222 E/F engines.

The P.238/1 had the wing and tail surfaces of a standard Do 335 and it was presented in two versions: Zerstörer (A-1) and fighter bomber (B-1).

The P.238/2 had the new wing with a 18.33 m span designed by Heinkel for the Do 335 B-4 and it was presented in the escort fighter version (A-2) and high-altitude interceptor (B-2) capable to face the Boeing B-29 of the Allies.

There were some night fighter versions. At the time when the project was presented, the old Hirschgeweigh antennae of the Lichtenstein radar had been replaced by parabolic ones, designed to be installed on the nose cone of the aircraft, but this was not possible in the P.238.

For this reason, and because of the excessive drag produced by the frontal cooler, the manufacturing of the Do 435 has already been discontinued on 28 August 1944. By the end of that year, the Dornier Project Office decided to interrupt the push-pull developments in favour of the P.247 and P.252 projects, which possessed more advanced aerodynamics and allowed higher speed and the installation of last generation radars.

Technical Data	
Type	Single-seat Zerstörer, escort fighter and high-altitude interceptor.
Airframe	Light alloy structure and cladding with wooden outer wings panels in the P.238/2.
Cockpit	Pressurised, control heating, frontal armour against 12.7 mm shelling and from the rear against 20 mm Heinkel kartusche ejector seat.
Undercarriage	Tricycle type. The main legs retracted inwards and the front gear retractable to the rear after switching 90 degrees to lie flat in the wheel bay.
Engine	Two (tractor and pusher) Jumo 222 E/F, 24-cylinder supercharged, liquid cooled, in Star with six banks of four cylinder each and 2,465 hp (3,000 with MW-50 injection) at take-off, driving two Junkers VS-19 four-blade airscrews with a 3.60 m diameter and fed by two-stage, three-speed superchargers with three intercoolers each.
Armament	Two MG 151/20 (synchro) cannons in the fuselage and two MK 103/30 cannons in the wings.
Wingspan	13.80 m (P.238/1) 18.33 m (P.238/2)
Length	17.10 m
Height	5.30 m
Wing area	38.50 sq m (P.238/1) 51 sq m (P.238/2)
Maximum speed	800 km/h (P.238/1) 770 km/h (P.238/2)
Service ceiling	14,000 m (P.238/2)
Electronics	One EZ42 gyrogunsight, FuG 16 ZY VHF transmitter/receiver, FuG 25a IFF radio set, FuG 125, K23 automatic pilot.

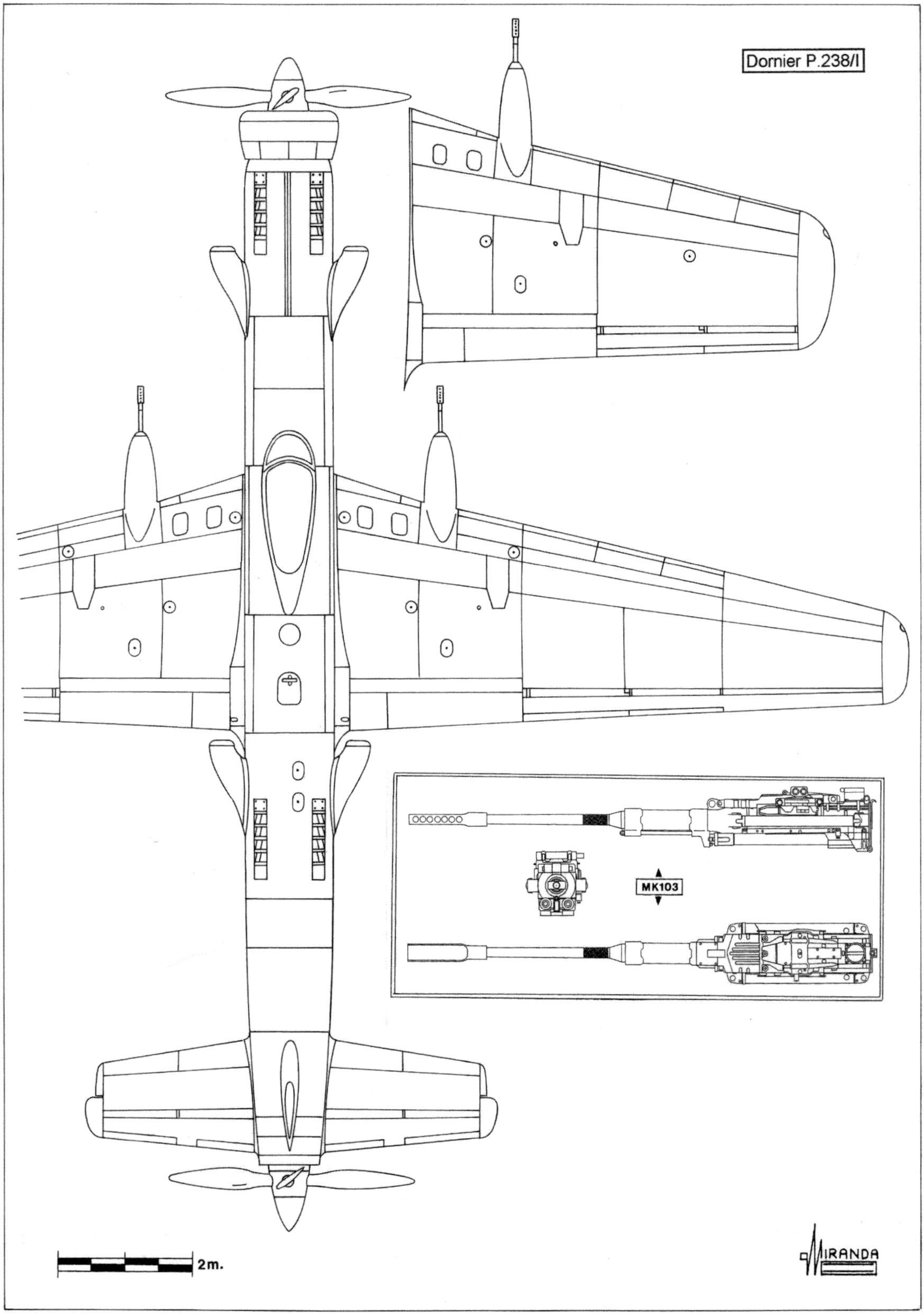
Dornier P.238/I
MK103
2m.
MIRANDA

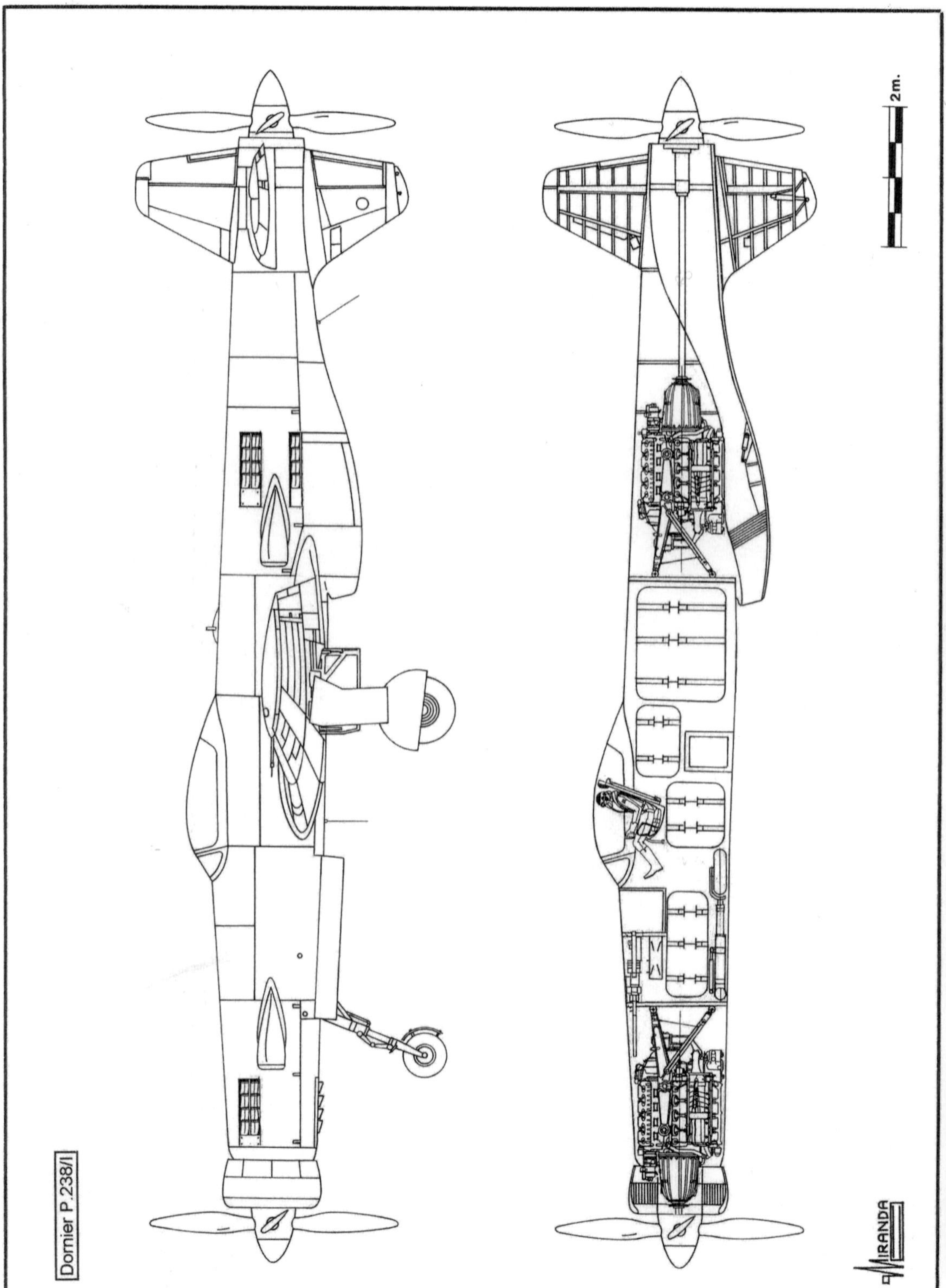
Dornier P.238/I
2m.

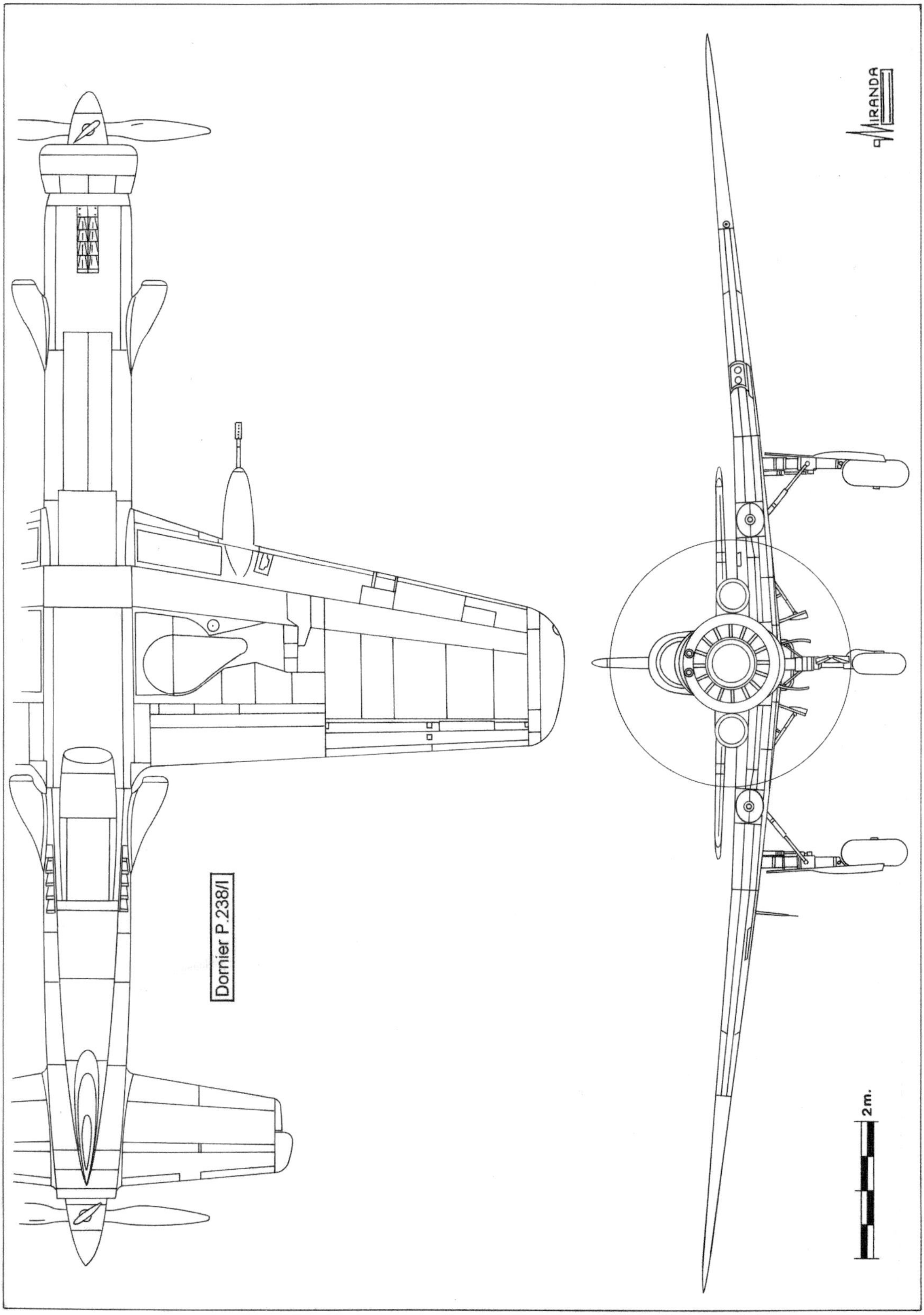
MIRANDA
Dornier P.238/I
2m.

Chapter 15

Dornier P.247

Started in 1944, the P.247 was part of an aerodynamic research program that aimed to avoid the drag produced by the frontal engine of the Do 335. Up to six configurations of wings and engines were tested using the Jumo 213 J, Jumo 213 T, DB 603 A, DB 603 G and DB 603 LA, based on previous studies made with the Göppingen Gö 9.

The first design had an unswept wing with a 12.5 mm span, based on the wing of the Do P.213/1. The last one had evolved to a swept wing of 30 degrees and a cooler integrated in the fuselage.

The drag reduction achieved enabled it to reach estimated speeds of between 835 and 875 km/h, armed with three 30 mm guns, a fact that made it superior to any Allied fighter with the possible exception of the Lockheed P.80A.

At the beginning of 1945, the OKL ordered the cancellation of the program, but the data obtained were used as the base to design the P.252 Moskitojäger.

Technical Data (P.247/6)	
Type	Single-seat interceptor fighter.
Wings	Light alloy structure and cladding, 30 degrees swept back (28 degrees at 0.25 chord), aspect ratio 6.0:1.
Fuselage	Light alloy structure and cladding.
Cockpit	Pressurised, control heating, frontal armour against 12.7 mm shelling and from the rear against 20 mm Heinkel kartusche ejector seat.
Tailfin	Light alloy structure and cladding with tail bumper/
Undercarriage	Tricycle type. The main legs retracted inwards and the front gear retractable to the rear. Tyres of 630 x 220 and 840 x 300.
Engine	One Jumo 213 J, 12-cylinder, 60-degree inverted-V, pressure cooled, with direct fuel injection, three-speed supercharger and 2,600 hp, with MW 50 power boost, driving a 3.2 m pusher propeller via an extension shaft.
Fuel tanks	Two of 120 litres each in the wing roots and another two of 260 and 400 litres in the fuselage.
Oil tank	One of 110 litres in the fuselage.
MW 50 tank	One of 75 litres in the fuselage.
Armament	Three MK 108/30 cannons in the fuselage nose.

Electronics	EZ 42 gyrogunsight, FuG 16 ZY VHF transmitter/receiver, FuG 25a IFF radioset.
Wingspan	12 m
Length	12.06 m
Height	4.30 m
Wing area	25 sq m
Maximum weight	6,200 kg
Maximum speed	875 km/h
Service ceiling	11,300 m

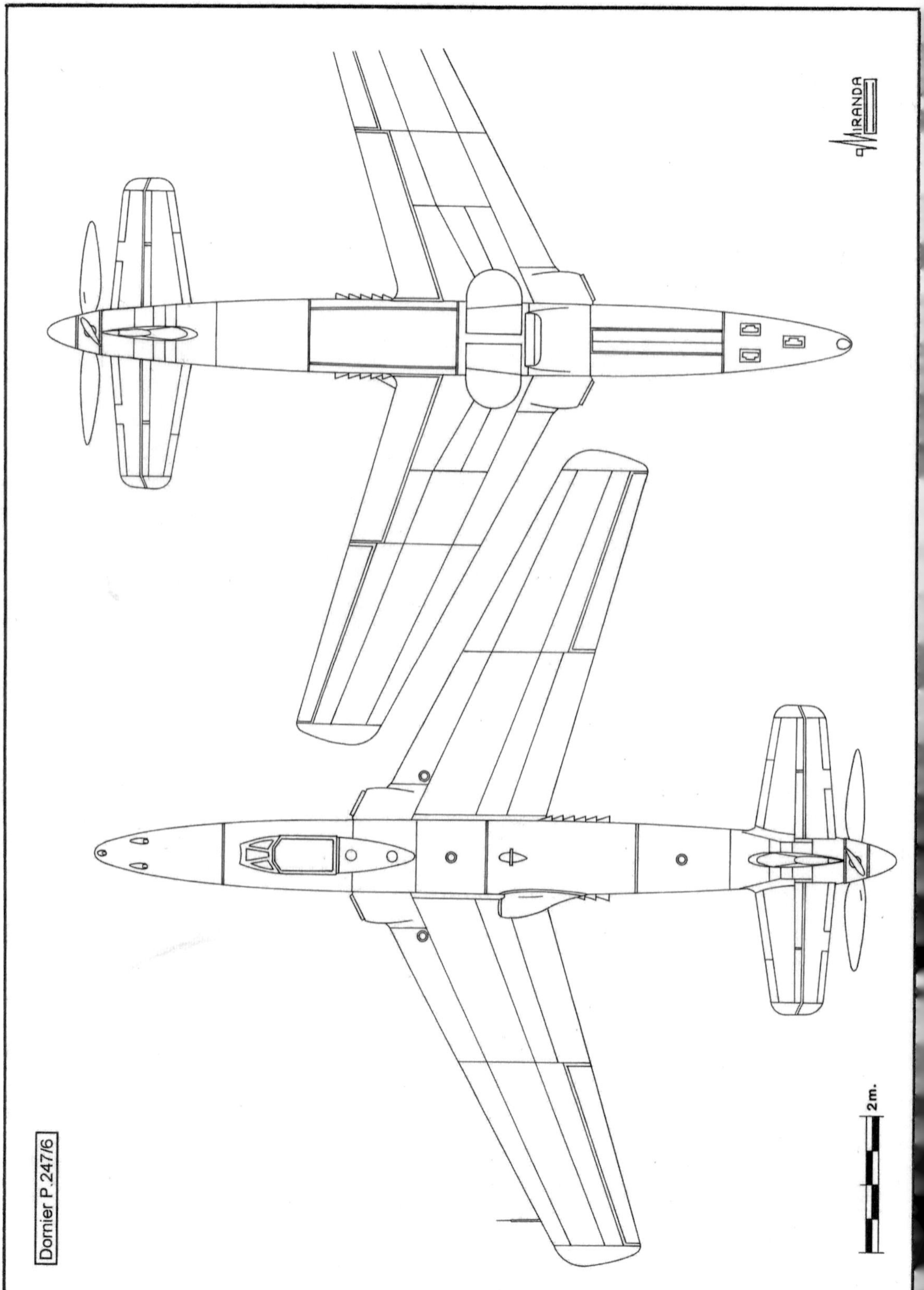
Dornier P.247/6
2m.

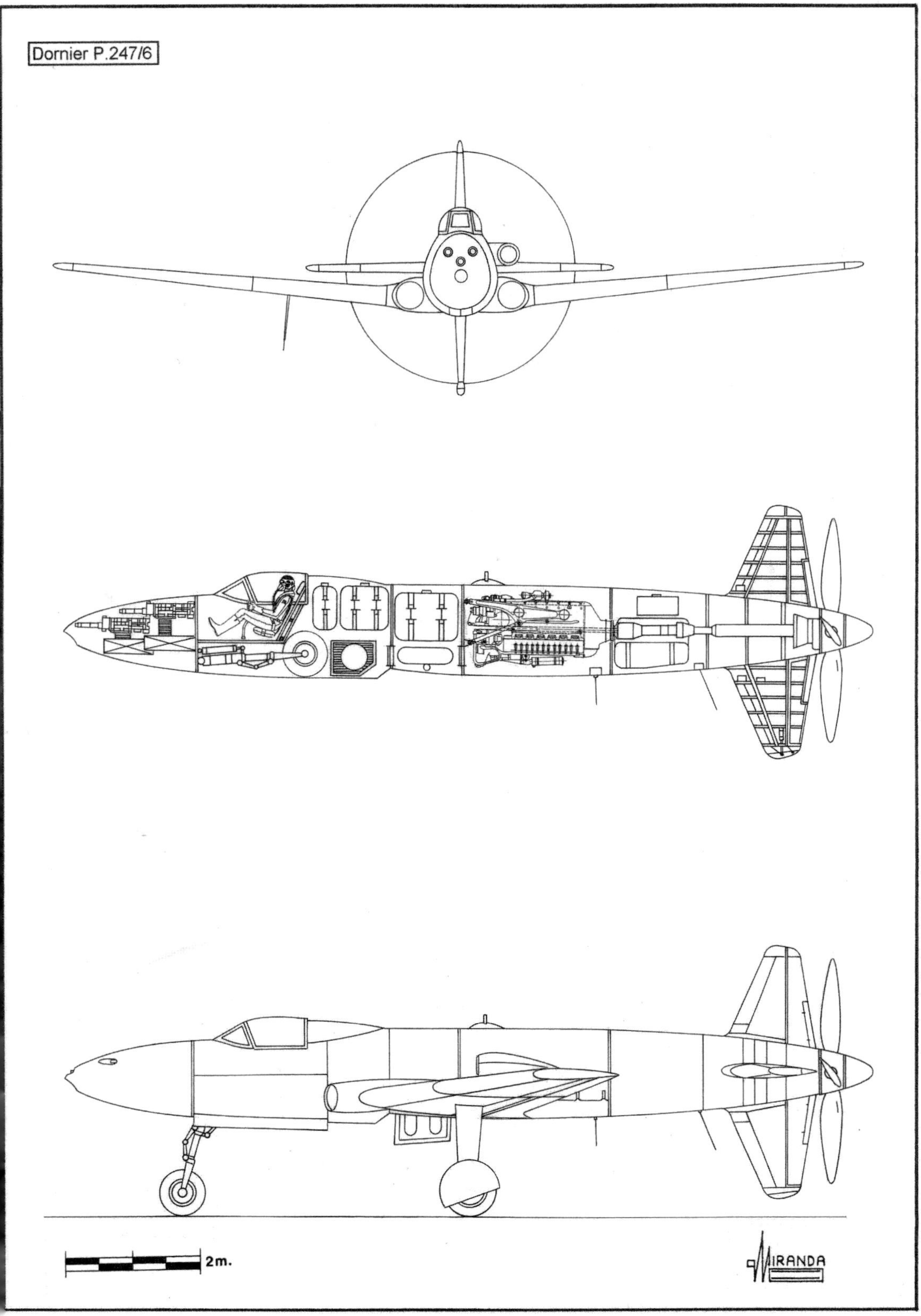
Dornier P.247/6
2m.
MIRANDA

Chapter 16

Dornier P.252/1

By mid-1942, Germany had to face the unpleasant fact of not having any night fighters capable of dealing with the RAF Mosquito. The Heinkel He 219 had potential, but the aerodynamic drag produced by the external antennae Hirschgeweih and the weight of the first generation ejector seats (activated by compressed air) reduced its speed and ceiling.

The Focke Wulf Ta 154, designed to hunt Mosquitoes, was never mass produced. Its manufacture was cancelled in July 1944 when the factory of the Tego-film glue – required for assembling subcomponents – was destroyed during the raid of Wuppertal.

In August 1944 the OKL proposed the transformation of available jet airplanes into night fighters as an immediate solution:

- Messerschmitt modified its trainer Me 262 B-1a obtaining the emergency night fighter Me 262 B-1a/U1
- Arado transformed an Ar 234 B into the Ar 234 B-2/N
- Horten proposed the Ho 229 V6, two-seat radar-equipped variant

In spite of the powerful jet engines and the advanced aerodynamics, these airplanes still had outer antennae that considerably hindered their performances.

The appearance of the new centimetric radars of Telefunken FuG 240/3 Berlin N-3 and FuG 244/245 Bremen – the parabolic antennae of which could be installed within the airplane – and the near availability of the HeS 011 turbojets, favoured the specification of 27 January 1945 – a specification by which the Technical Department of the Luftwaffe ordered the construction of a night fighter able to fly at 900 km/h and reaching a ceiling of 9,000 m, armed with four cannons, and capable of an overall endurance of four hours.

By the end of February a new requirement was added to the aircraft. It should use an oblique, upward-firing Schräge Musik armament.

Several options were presented: a variant of the Me 262 HG III (12 February 1945), a Focke Wulf with three turbojets, and a jet version (P.256/1) of the Dornier Do 335. There were also six flying wings: Arado E-583 (two-seat version of the E-581 heavy fighter), Blohm und Voss P.215 (scaled-up variant of the P.212), Gotha P.60 C-1a (a modified P.60 B *Zerstörer*), Heinkel P.1079B (without tailfin), Horten He 229 V6 (two seat variant), and a two seat version of the Junkers EF-128.

Except the Ho229, all these projects were to use the HeS 011 turbojet and, except the Go P.60 C-1a, all of them used the Bremen O radar.

The design of the Do P.256, based on the Do 435, was aerodynamically inefficient, due to the large drag induced by tail surfaces and engine nacelles, with an endurance of 1 hour 45 minutes, which was also considered insufficient. Given the scarcity of jet engines – top priority being given to Messerschmitt and Arado in terms of delivery time – both Dornier and Focke Wulf dedicated their efforts to twin-engined piston fighters with pusher propellers and advanced aerodynamics.

The Dornier Project Office of Friedrichshafen designed an all-weather interceptor driven by two DB 603LA, Bremen O radar, Schräge Musik and a crew of two, based on the P.247/1 aerodynamics.

It had an unswept laminar flow wing originally designed by Heinkel for the Do.335 B-4, modified to reach 16.44 m of span. The vertical tail surfaces were the same as in the standard Do 435 and for the horizontal surfaces they used the ones originally designed for the Do 535.

The project was presented to the RLM on 27 January 1945 as Do P.252/1 Moskitojäger but its manufacture was set aside in March 1945, in favour of the faster Messerschmitt Me 262 B-2.

Technical Data	
Type	Two-seat all-weather interceptor.
Airframe	Light alloy structure and cladding.
Cockpit	Based on the cockpit of the Do 435 A-1, pressurised, with control heating. The pilot and radar operator sat side by side, although only the pilot had an ejector seat, which meant the existence of some kind of mechanism to detach the propeller blades in an emergency. The crew was protected, in the forward part, by armoured glass against 12.7 mm rounds from the bombers and in the rear part, by metal plates, against 20 mm rounds from the fighters.
Undercarriage	Of a standard Do 435.
Engine	Two DB 603 LA, 12-cylinder, inverted-V, liquid cooled, 1,900 hp emergency power boost, with MW 50 and two-stage supercharger. The forward engine drove the rear propeller by means of an 8.9 m extension shaft that went through the rear engine and its corresponding extension shaft of bigger diameter. Both engines were installed in different directions so that their respective propellers (2 x 3 blades, 3.2 m diameter) rotated also in opposite directions.
Fuel tanks	Two of 300 litres in the wing roots and two in the central section of the fuselage with 1,900 litres in total.
MW 50 tank	One of 220 litres in the fuselage.
Armament	Four MK 108/30 cannons in the fuselage nose. Two of them were firing 80 degrees upwards in Schräge Musik and two MG 213C/20 cannons to both sides of the cockpit.

Wingspan	16.44 m
Length	15.20 m
Height	4,95 m
Wing area	43.20 sq m
Max. speed	755 km/h
Service ceiling	12,500 m
Max. weight	10,730 kg
Electronics	Telefunken FuG 244 Bremen O preproduction series radar, which could aim its 70 cm diameter Parabolspiegel antenna up to 100 degrees in each direction. Lorenz FuG SE, a VHF transmitter/receiver with whip antenna in the lower section of the fuselage. GEMA FuG 25a IFF device with 300 mm rod antenna (10 degrees rear swept) in the lower section of the fuselage. Lorenz radio-beacon receiver FuG 125A that operated in combination with the FuG 16ZY direction finder device using the Morane mast and D/F loop of the FuG 16 R/T standard equipment. FuG 139 Barbarossa command relay device, operating in combination with the FuG 25a and using its antenna. FuG 101a radioaltimeter with two inverted T antennae under the port wing (Morane mast under the starboard wing). FFO EiV125 crew intercom. EZ 42 Adler gyroscopic gunsight and auxiliary Revi C16 A-N gunsight for aiming the Schräge Musik cannons.

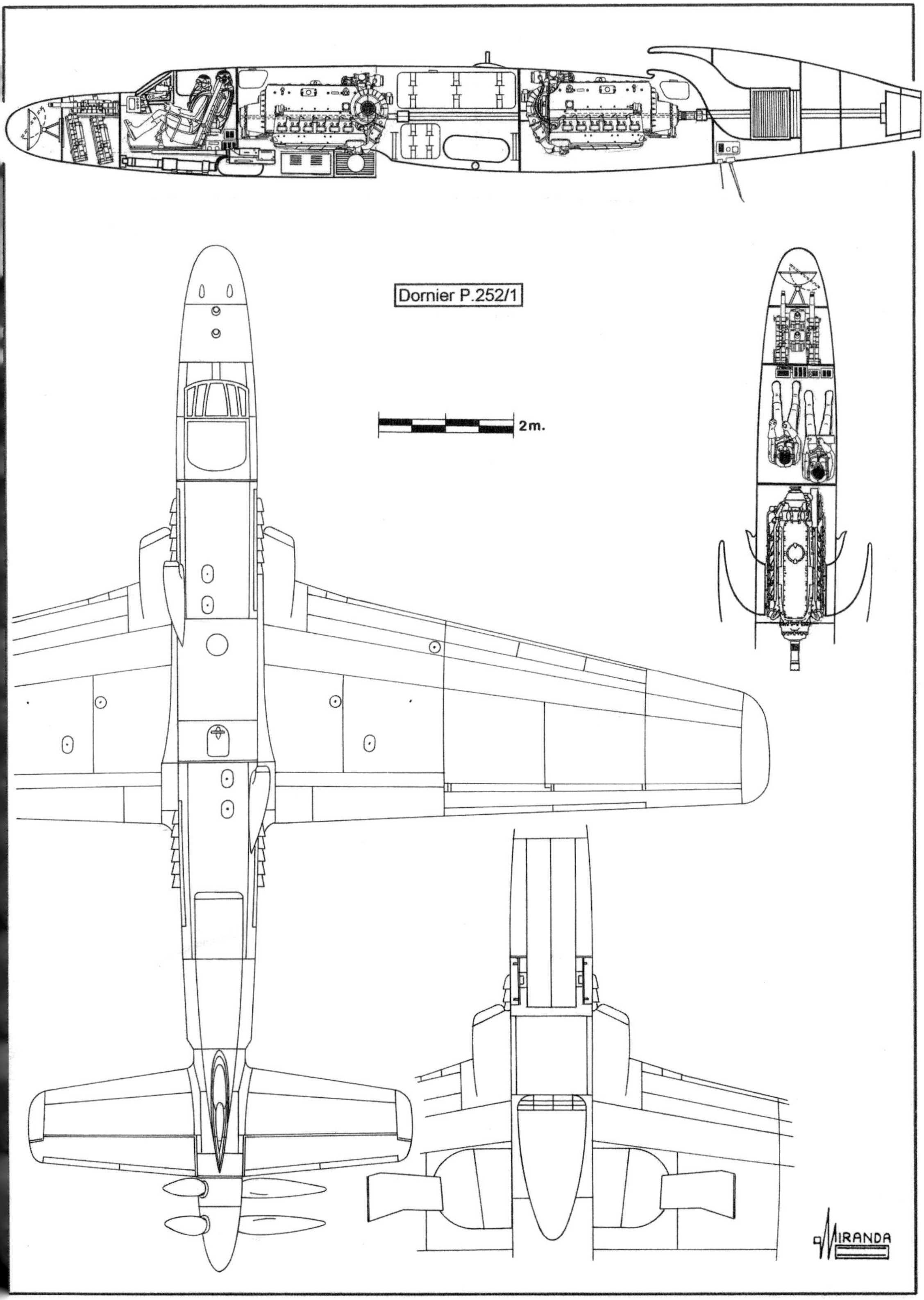
Dornier P.252/1
2m.
MIRANDA

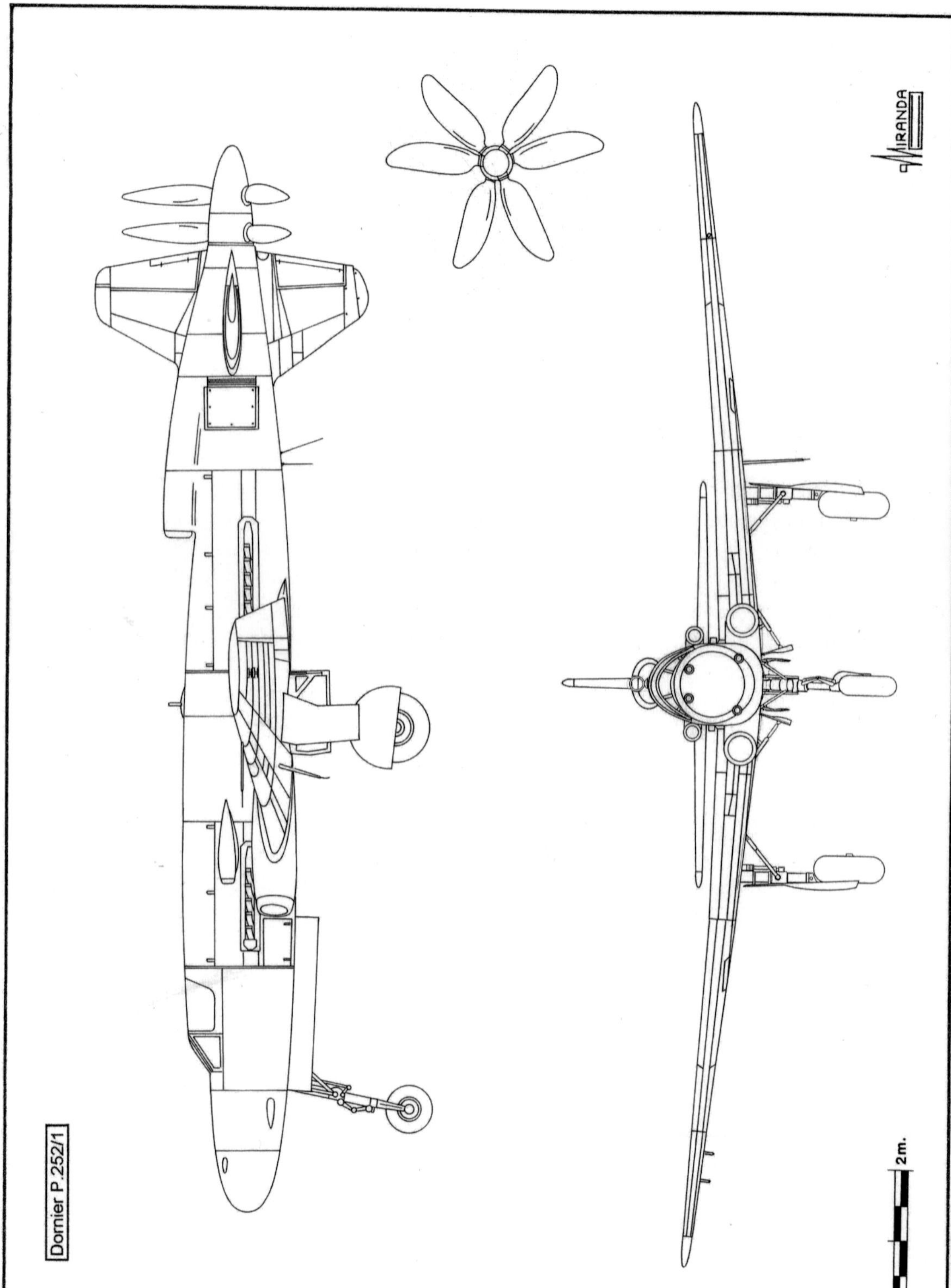
Dornier P.252/1
MIRANDA
2m.

Chapter 17

Dornier P.252

By the beginning of March 1945, the Luftwaffe no longer need an all-weather interceptor Moskitojäger but a heavy night fighter with a great amount of electronic equipment, this in turn requiring the inclusion of a third crew member.

This left the Junkers EF-128, Heinkel P.1079B and Horten Ho229V6 designs out of the contest, as they could not increase the crew room for structural reasons.

Messerschmitt was forced to enlarge the fuselage and redesign the wings of its Me 262 B-2 (17 March 1945) being finally left out for three reasons: it used light alloys for its construction, it could not transport enough fuel and the Siemens Antler antenna of its radar was fixed.

The designs dependent on the HeS 011 turbojet – Arado Ar234P, Ar.I and E-583, Blohm und Voss P.215, Focke Wulf P.011.045, P.0310251-51, P.011-046 and P.011-047 and Gotha P.60C – consumed too much fuel, lacking the endurance required in the 27 January 1945 specification. Only the Dornier P.252 and the Focke Wulf P.0310251-22 with mixed propulsion could make it.

Based on the aerodynamic solutions of the P.247/6, the Dornier Project Office produced two swept-wing, very fast designs, with two Jumo 213J piston engines in tandem driving contra-rotating 50-degree sweep, multi-bladed Scimitar propellers, especially designed to counteract an effect known as wave drag which occurs just below supersonic speeds.

The first design, denominated P.252/2, was a high-altitude all-weather interceptor, with 35-degree swept wings and 50 mm cannons, to fight against the American B-29s when they appeared over Europe.

To the standard night equipment, some day combat features were added: armoured windshield against 20 mm shelling, ceiling and rear of the cockpit protected by metal plates against 20 mm ammo, GM-1 power boost and several Vertikalbordwaffen SG116 or SG117, capable of shooting vertically against the belly of a bomber when passing underneath it, activated by a photoelectric cell. These devices allowed the P.252 to fly at full speed under the boxes, without the need of aiming the armament.

The second design, known as P.252/3, was faster and with a smaller wingspan. Equipped as a night fighter, it could stay up to seven hours in the air, harassing the stream of enemy bombers the whole way back to England.

Although the general opinion was that the piston fighter had reached the limit of its potential development (Göring, 22 February 1945), the Dornier engineers continued working on the P.252 until the end of the war in Europe.

P.252.2 Technical Data	
Type	Three seat high-altitude all-weather interceptor.
Airframe	Light alloy structure and cladding.
Cockpit	Pressurised, control heating. The pilot and navigator-radio operator sat side by side under the clear canopy, the radar operator sat with his back to the pilot, under the armoured plates of the ceiling. Only the pilot had an ejector seat, which meant the existence of some kind of mechanism to detach the propeller blades in an emergency.
Undercarriage	Of a standard Do 435.
Engine	Two Junkers Jumo 213J, 12-cylinder, 60-degree inverted-V, pressure cooled, with direct fuel injection, three-speed supercharger and special emergency 2600 hp, 2000 hp at 8000 m with GM-1 power boost. The forward engine drove the rear propeller by means of an 8.3 m extension shaft that went through the rear engine and its corresponding extension shaft of bigger diameter. Both engines were installed in different directions so that their respective propellers (3.2 m diameter, 50-degree sweep) rotated also in opposite directions. Both engines shared the same configuration of coolers.
Fuel tanks	One of 2100 litres in the fuselage and two of 650 litres each in the wings.
GM-1 tank	One of 350 litres in the fuselage.
Armament	Two Rheinmetall MK 108/30 cannons in the nose with 80 rounds each. Two MK 108/30 cannons with 100 rounds each, firing 70 degrees upwards in Schräge Musik configuration behind the cockpit. Two Rheinmetall-Borsig SG 116/30 Zellendusche recoilless cannons vertically installed in the fuselage, with photoelectric trigger Opta Radio Fotozellenfühler. Alternatively, four Rheinmetall-Borsig SG 117/30 Rohrblock recoilless cannons, vertically installed in the wings, with photoelectric trigger AEG Zossen.
Wingspan	18.4 m (swept 35 degrees at the leading edge, 32.5 degrees at 0.25 chord)
Length	17.80 m
Height	5.05 m
Wing area	55 sq m
Max. speed	900 km/h
Service ceiling	13,000 m to 16,000 m
Electronics	Telefunken FuG 244 Bremen O radar preproduction series with 70 cm diameter Parabolspiegel antenna, searching range of 100 degrees to the sides and 20 degrees downwards. Range of 200 to 5,00 m Siemens/LGW FuG 101a radioaltimeter Lorenz Hermine FuG 125a radio-beacon receiver Lorenz FuG 16 R/T transmitter/receiver Lorenz FuG 16 ZY Zypresse direction finder device GEMA FuG 25a IFF device Erstling

FuG 139 Barbarossa command relay device
Lorenz FuG 350 Zc Naxos passive radar receiver
EiV125 crew intercom
AEG Zossen photoelectric trigger
Opta radio Fotozellenfühler photoelectric trigger
Askania EZ42 Adler gyroscopic gunsight
Zeiss Revi C16 A-N auxiliary gunsight for aiming the Schräge Musik cannons

P.252.3 Technical Data

Type	Three-seat heavy night fighter.
Airframe	Light alloy structure and cladding.
Cockpit	Pressurised, control heating. The pilot and navigator-radio operator sat side by side, the radar operator sat with his back to the pilot. The crew was protected in the forward part by armoured glass windscreen against 12.7 mm shelling and in the rear part by metal plates against 20 mm rounds from the fighters. Only the pilot had an ejector seat, which meant the existence of some kind of mechanism to detach the propeller blades in an emergency.
Undercarriage	Of a standard Do 435.
Engine	Two Junkers Jumo 213J, 12-cylinder, 60-degree inverted-V, pressure cooled, with direct fuel injection, three-speed supercharger and special emergency 2600 hp with MW-50 power boost. The forward engine drove the rear propeller by means of a 9.3 m extension shaft that went through the rear engine and its corresponding extension shaft, of bigger diameter. Both engines were installed in different directions so that their respective propellers (3.2 m diameter, 50-degree sweep) rotated also in opposite directions. Each engine had its own cooler and air intakes in the wings roots and at the upper end of the fuselage.
Fuel tanks	One of 1500 litres and another of 1,000 litres in the fuselage and two of 450 litres each in the wings.
Oil tanks	Two of 110 litres each in the fuselage.
MW-50 tanks	One of 100 litres in the fuselage.
Armament	Two Rheinmetall MK 108/30 cannons in the nose with 80 rounds each. Two Rheinmetall MK 108/30 cannons with 100 rounds each, firing 70 degrees upwards in *Schräge Musik* configuration behind the cockpit. Two Mauser MK 213/20 cannons with 240 rounds each under the fuselage.
Wingspan	15.80 m (22.5-degree sweep at the leading edge, 20 degrees at 0.25 chord)
Length	17.20 m
Height	5.05 m
Wing area	50 sq m
Aspect ratio	5,0:1
Max. speed	930 km/h
Max. weight	12,300 kg.
Ceiling	12,500 m

Electronics

One Telefunken FuG 244 Bremen O radar preproduction series with 70 cm diameter Parabolspiegel antenna, searching a range of 100 degrees to the sides and 20 degrees downwards.
One FFO FuG 218 Neptun R-3 rear warning radar, with a Stachel antenna of two asymmetric horizontal dipoles, located in the upper end of the tailfin, defending against the Mosquito Serrate system.
Lorenz FuG 10P communications system with MF and HF operating frequencies and two types of antennae: the rod-shaped FuG 24 system under the fuselage and an MF electrically powered trailing wire of 75 m of length located under the port wing.
Lorenz FuG 226 Neuling discriminator that combined the identification and range finder functions, had two flat Breitbanddipolen antennae located over the starboard engine.
The autopilot was an FuG 130 associated to a blind landing device FuBl3E with AWG1. Both systems shared a comb shaped antenna covered by fairing, located under the fuselage.
The navigation systems included a Lorenz FuG 125a Hermine radio-beacon receiver and a Siemens FuG 120A Bernhardine teleprinter. Both of them used the Morane antenna of the Lorenz FuG 16Y located under the fuselage.
The Askania EZ42 Adler gyroscopic gunsight could combine with the FuG 244 radar and with the automatic FFO EG3 Elfe 3 trigger to launch the air to air unguided R100 rockets.
The Naxos was replaced by a Telefunken Peil G6 radiogoniometer with automatic search system APZ6 and flat antenna with radial ribs, located over the fuselage.
One Siemens/LGW radioaltimeter FuG 101a with two different dipolar antennae in inverted T, located under the starboard wing.
One crew intercom EiV125.
Some passive antiradar defences included painting with Schornsteinfeger.

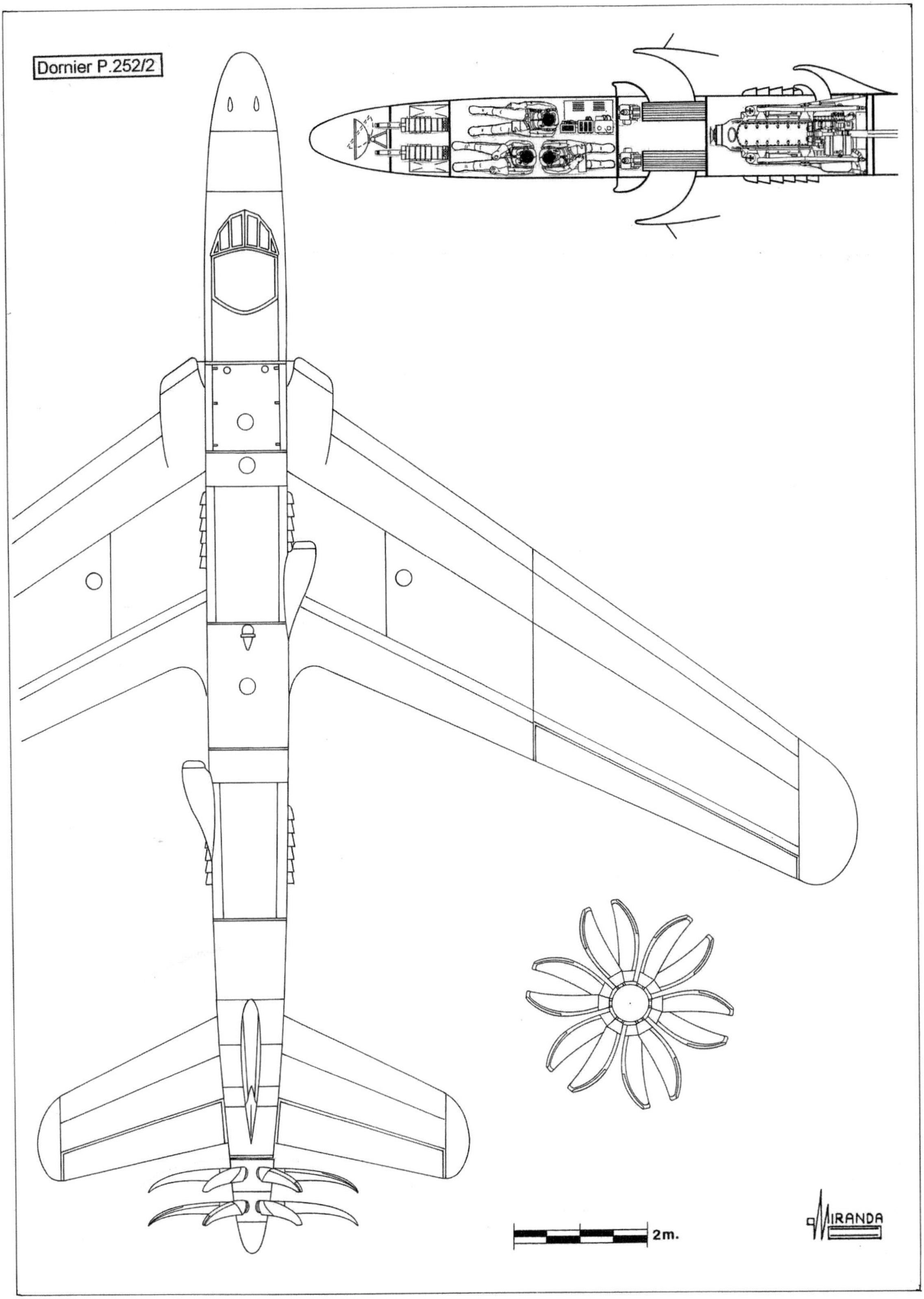
Dornier P.252/2
2m.
MIRANDA

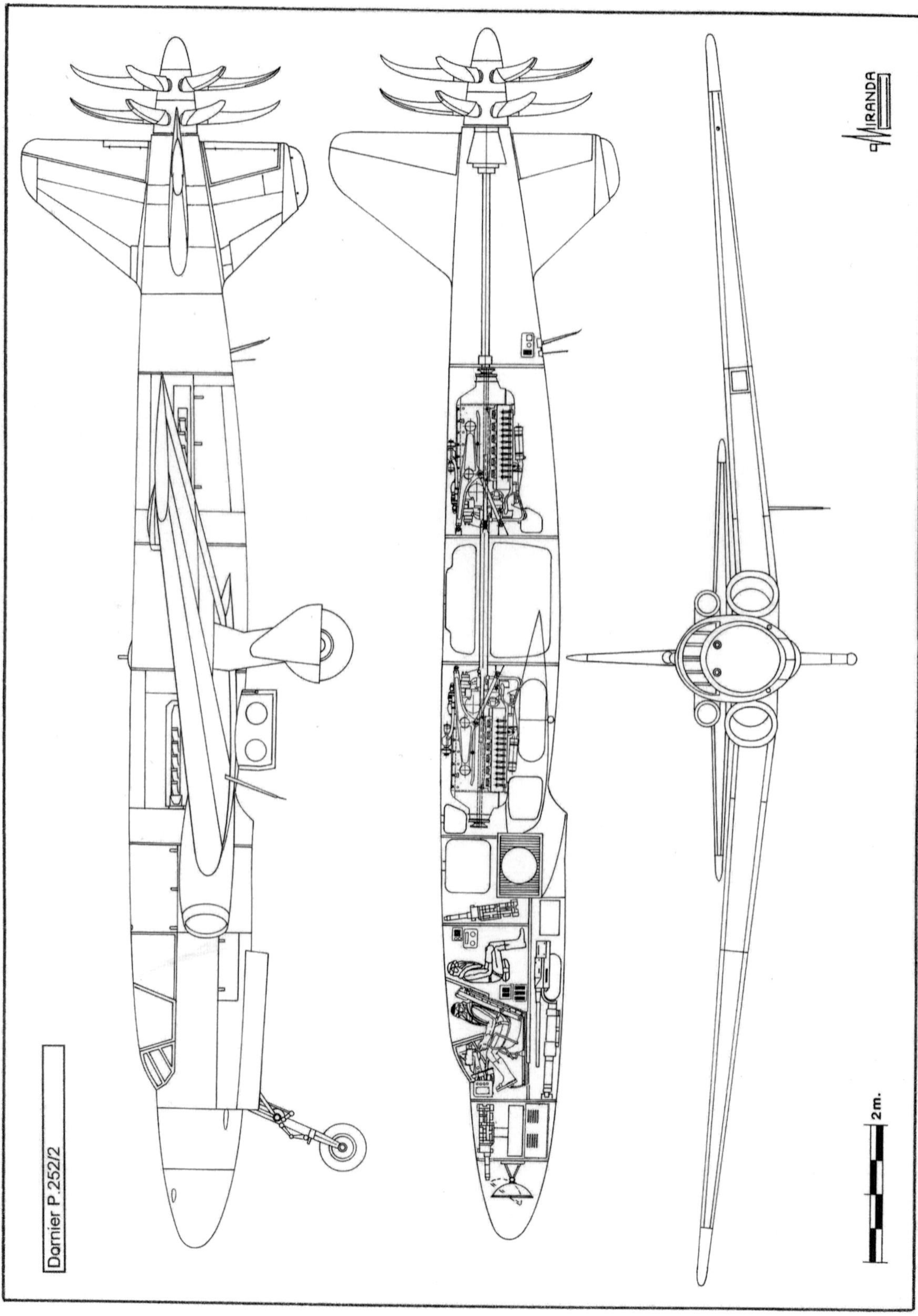
Dornier P.252/2
2m.
MIRANDA

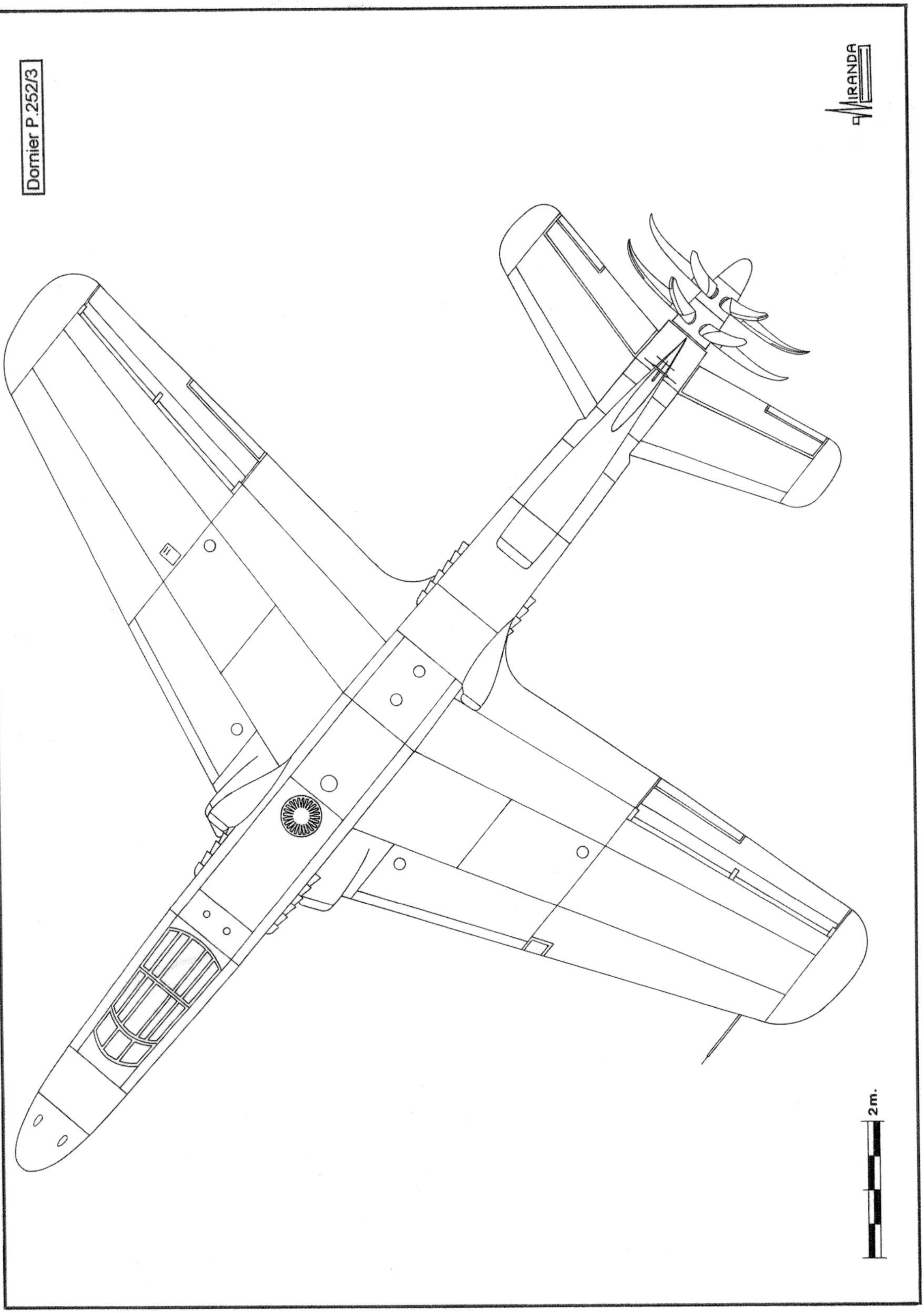
Dornier P.252/3
MIRANDA
2m.

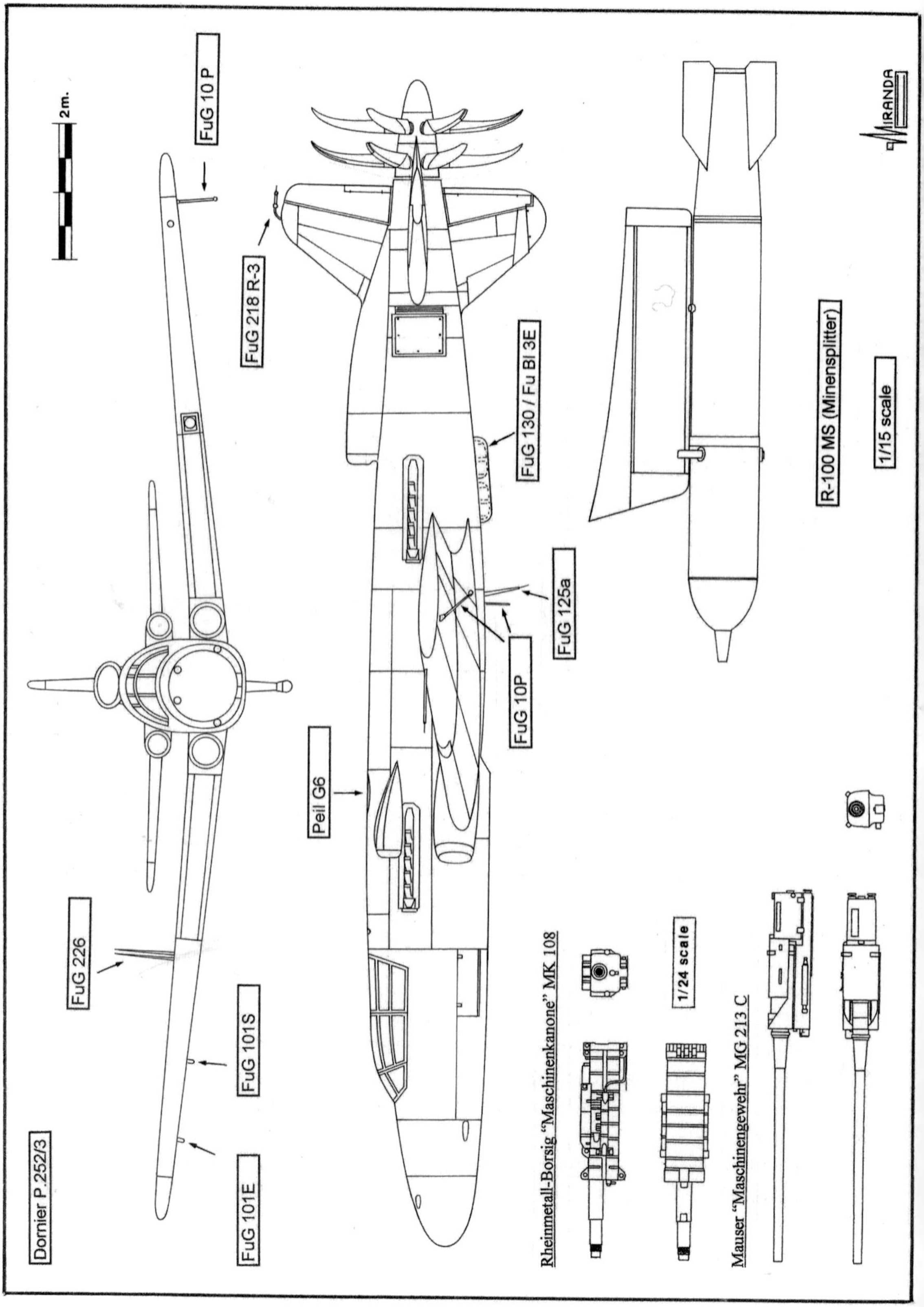
Dornier P.252/3
FuG 101E
FuG 101S
FuG 226
FuG 10 P
2 m.
FuG 218 R-3
Peil G6
FuG 10P
FuG 125a
FuG 130 / Fu Bl 3E
R-100 MS (Minensplitter)
1/15 scale
Rheinmetall-Borsig "Maschinenkanone" MK 108
1/24 scale
Mauser "Maschinengewehr" MG 213 C

Chapter 18

Focke Wulf Höhenjäger

The Fw 190's inadequate performance at altitude was a constant source of concern for the Technisches Amt. Officially, the BMW 801 was supposed to produce its full power at 22,600 ft. but in fact it had difficulties above 19,700 ft.

Three Fw 190A-3/U7 (works no. 137528, 530 and 531) were built in September 1942. They were intended as light high-altitude fighters with BMW 801 D-2, two superchargers and a ceiling of 11,900 m fitted with a new 12.5 m span wing, two MG 151, two air intakes and external Kiemenklappen cooling flaps.

The operational tests performed by the Stab of II. Jagdkorps between July 1943 and May 1944 were unsatisfactory and no additional units were built. The V45 (works no. 7347) and V47 (works no. 530115) prototypes, fitted with a 12.3 m span wing, were also built to test manoeuvrability at high altitude.

On 20 May 1942, some RLM officials met with Messerschmitt and Focke Wulf representatives in Augsburg, to set forth their requirement for a special high-altitude fighter, capable of intercepting high flying bombers above the Me 262 combat ceiling.

The answer from Messerschmitt was the Me 155B project, powered by the DB 628 engine, sharing a high degree of component commonality with the standard Bf 109G. On 3 January 1944, the project was transferred to Blohm und Voss as BV 155A. This firm built up to four prototypes by the beginning of 1945. On its side, Focke Wulf initiated three projects known as Höhenjäger 1, 2 and 3 (Ta 152H).

Höhenjäger-1

In 1943, four airplanes of the FW 190 A-1 type (works no. 0046, 0047, 0048 and 0049) were modified to be transformed into the B series prototypes.

This conversion consisted on the installation of a pressure cabin and BMW 801 D-2 engine with GM-1 power boost injection system. The 0046 had a new wing with a span of 10.24 m.

Flying tests were performed between January and August 1943 in Hannover-Langenhagen and Rechlin.

The problems encountered with the canopy pressurisation system had not been overcome and the B-0 series were then abandoned in favour of the planned C series at the end of 1943.

Höhenjäger-2

The Fw 190C were never mass produced, with only twelve prototypes ever built.

The initial tests made with the V13, equipped with a DB 603 A and a 10.5 m span wing, showed excellent performance over 33,000 ft, although the turbo-supercharger intended for the C series was not yet fitted at this stage.

The V18/U2, fitted with a new 12.30 m span wing, four-bladed propeller and powered by one of the first Hirth TK 11 turbochargers, was flight tested on November 19, 1944.

The shortage of raw materials in Germany meant it was not possible to produce a suitably heat-resistant alloy before the war ended. The turbo-superchargers themselves worked well but the pipes for the engine exhausts were unable to withstand the high temperatures.

In October 1944 it was impossible to increase the life of turbo-superchargers to more than twenty hours. It was only when the Jumo 213 was available that it was made feasible to build fighters with ceilings of 36,000 ft.

Projects

The Fw 190 A-10, developed from the A-3/U7 with a BMW 801 F engine and a 12.3 m span wing, was to begin arriving in pilots hands by March 1945.

Two versions of the A-10 are known. One of them, dated 23 April 1944 has 10.8 m wing span and two Lorin ramjets of 10,850 hp each in the wingtips. The other tried to solve the problem of the turbo-superchargers using a Heinkel HeS 8 turbojet, suspended under the fuselage, that provided pressurised air to the BMW 801D-2 through a vertical duct installed within the pod. This version is known in the specialised literature as Fw 190 H and was possibly derived from the A-3 with 12.3 m wingspan, 20.3 sq m wing surface and 4,000 kg maximum weight.

The Fw 190 C, derived from the V18/U2 – with 12.3 m wing span, a length of 9,5 m, 20.3 sq m wing area and an HMZ turbosupercharger – should have reached mass production stage should the Focke Wulf engineers have solved the issue of the heat resistant alloy of the engine exhaust pipes on time. Instead, the Höhenjager-3 program gained priority, culminating with the construction of the excellent Ta 152 H in 1945.

An advanced version, fitted with laminar profile wing with 13.68 m span and Jumo 222 E engine, was ready for construction at the end of the war. The new airplane, with a length of 10.77 m and a weight of 5.815 kg, would have a four-bladed VS-19 propeller and armament of two MG 151 plus two Mk 103.

Finally, to compete against the Me 155 B, the Extreme-Höhenjäger was designed. It was fitted with a TKL 15 turbo-supercharger at the fuselage rear and a DB 603 G engine able to generate 1,810 hp at 2,700 rpm in altitude. The planned armament was four MG 151/20 installed on one elliptical wing of 34 sq m and 14.4 m wingspan. Two very similar designs were created, one with a length of 11.4 m and another 11.32 m long.

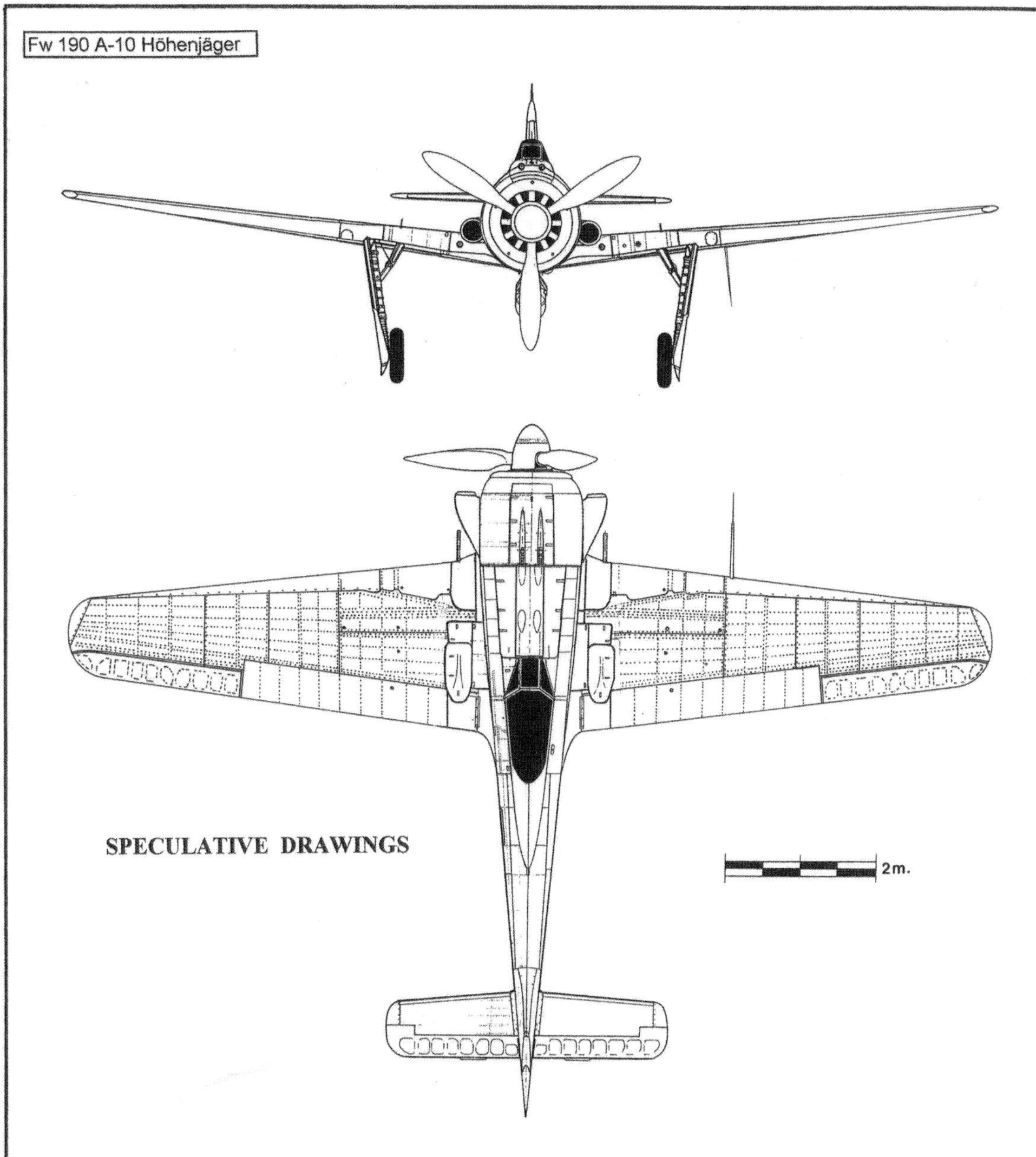
Fw 190 A-10 Höhenjäger
SPECULATIVE DRAWINGS
2m.
MIRANDA

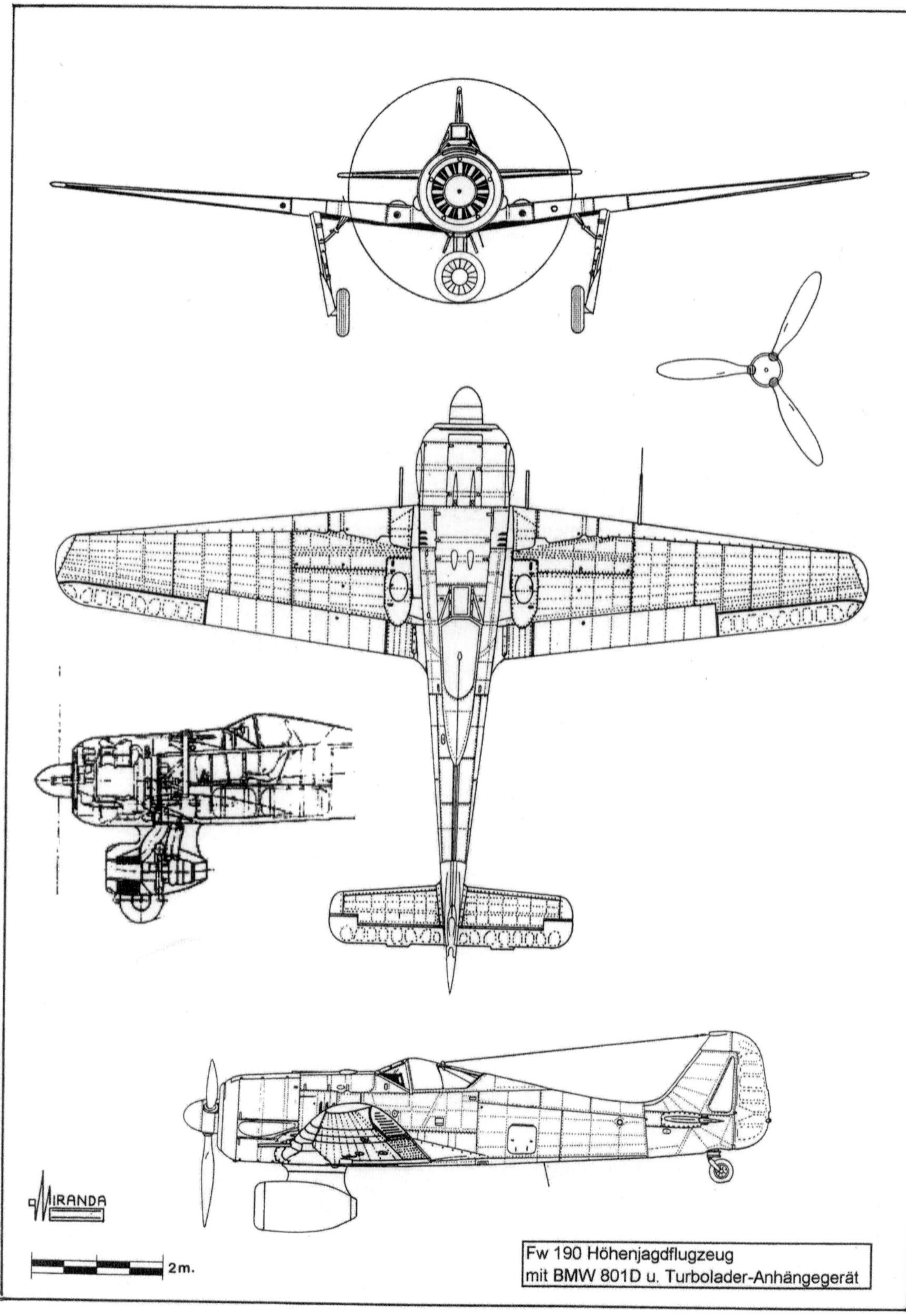
IRANDA
2 m.
Fw 190 Höhenjagdflugzeug
mit BMW 801D u. Turbolader-Anhängegerät

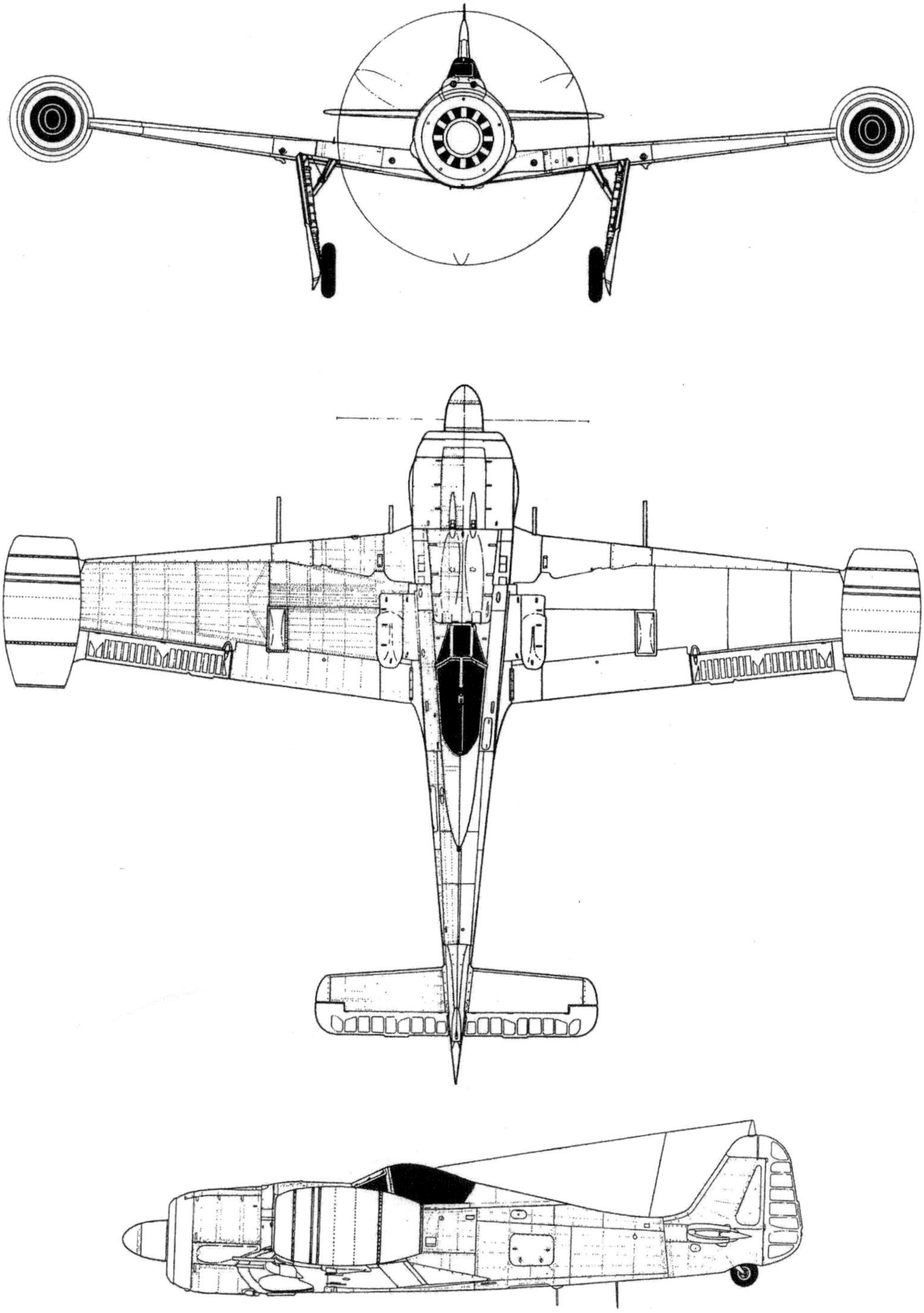

Fw 190 A-10 mit Strahlrohr

1/72 scale

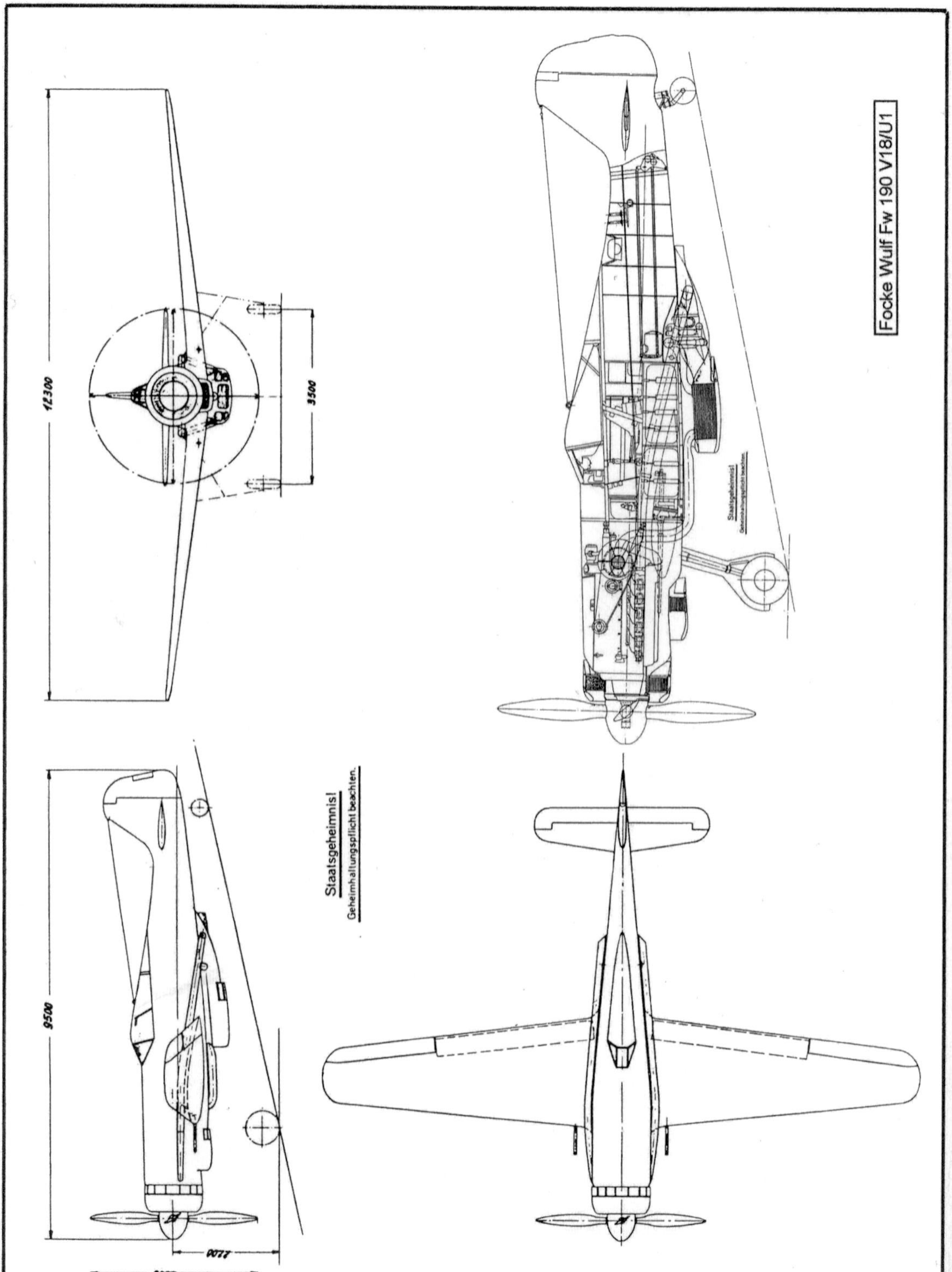
Focke Wulf Fw 190 V18/U1
Staatsgeheimnis!
Geheimhaltungspflicht beachten.
12300
3500
9500
2200
3500

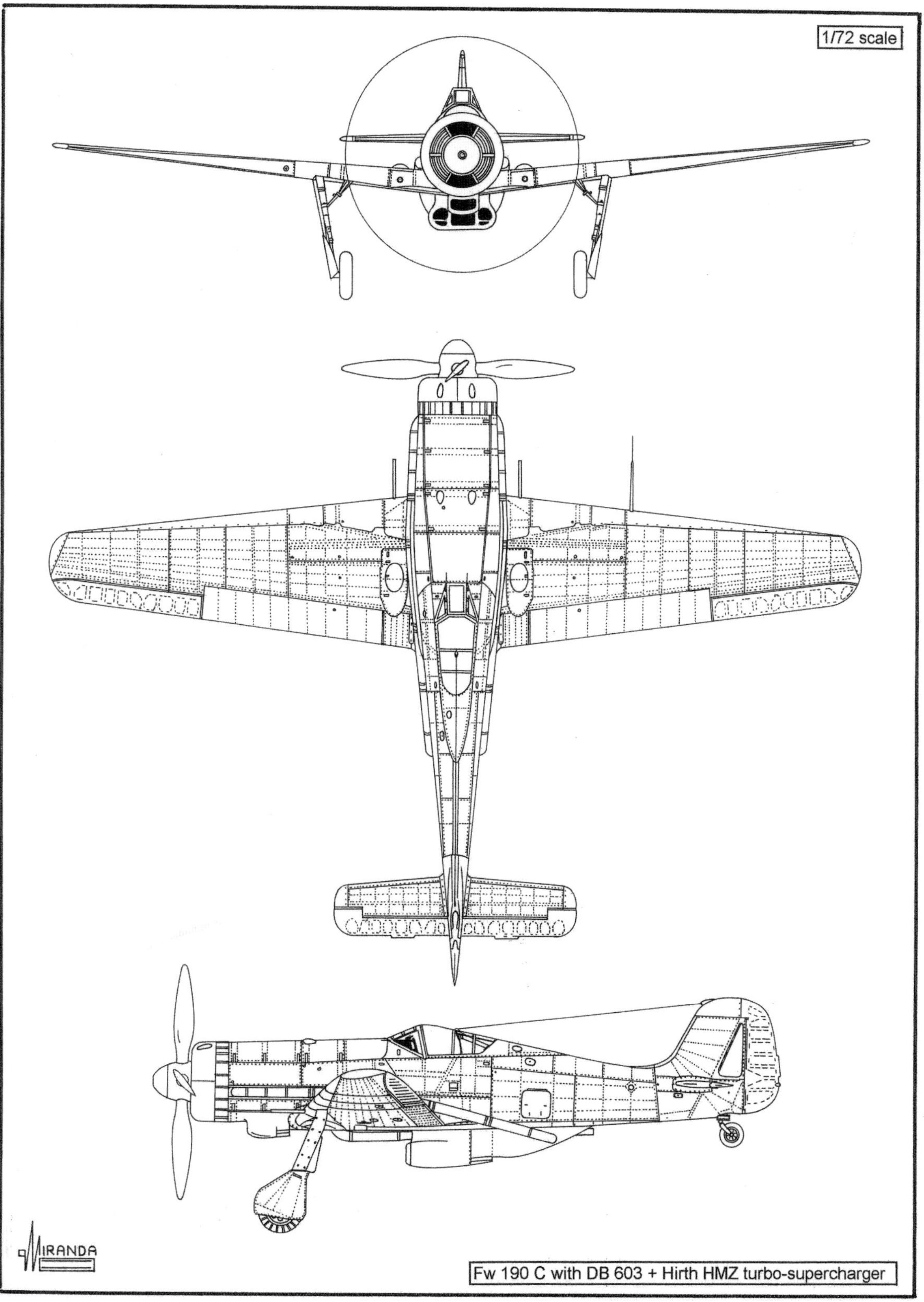
1/72 scale
MIRANDA
Fw 190 C with DB 603 + Hirth HMZ turbo-supercharger

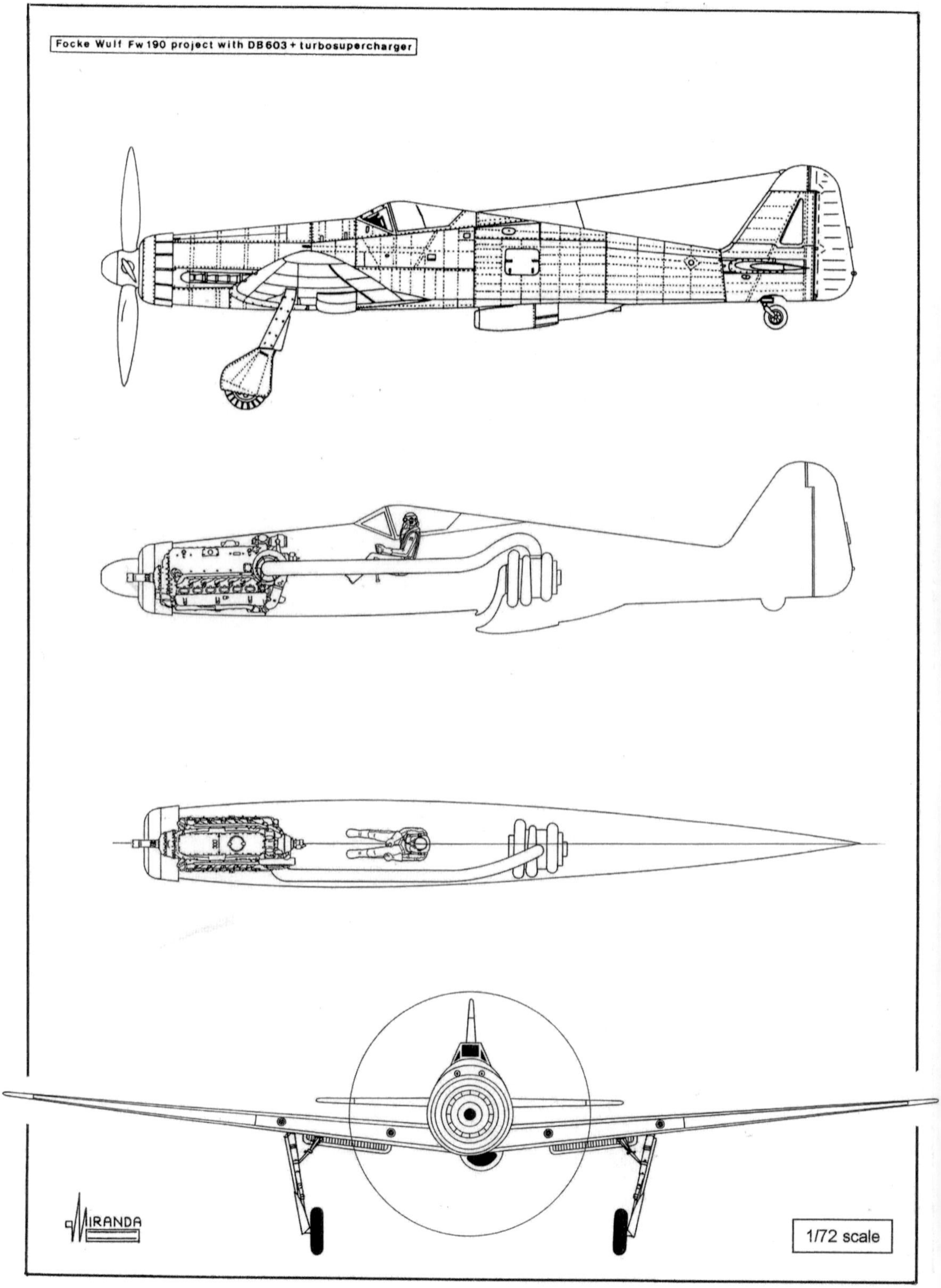
Focke Wulf Fw 190 project with DB603 + turbosupercharger
MIRANDA
1/72 scale

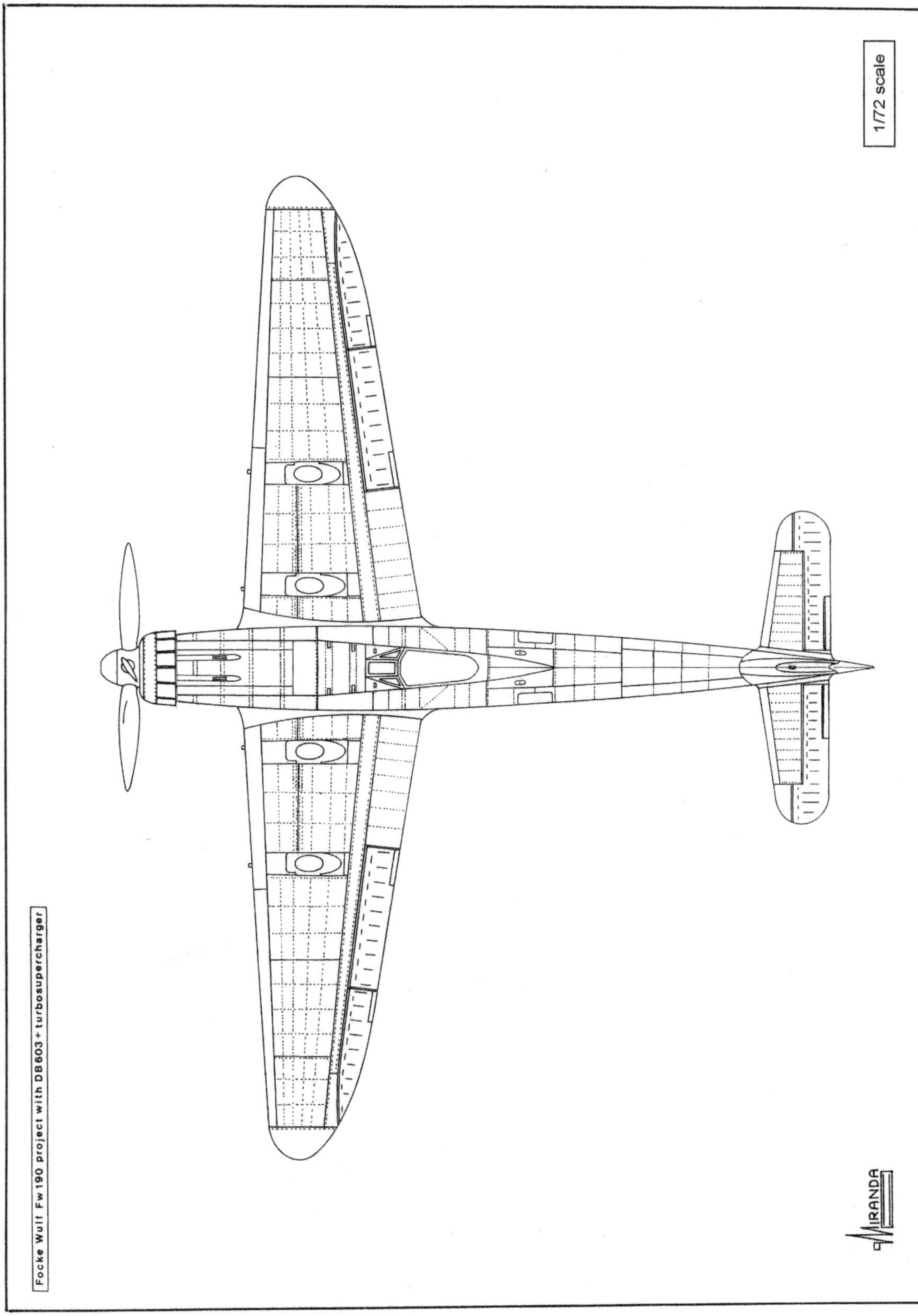
Focke Wulf Fw 190 project with DB603 + turbosupercharger
1/72 scale
MIRANDA

Chapter 19

Focke Wulf Ta 152 mit Jumo 222

By mid-1944 it looked as if the production issues of the Jumo 222 were finally fixed and the Focke Wulf designers started working on potential use of the engine for the Ta 152.

In a first phase (December 1944) a Jumo 222A would be installed in a Ta 152C, a low-altitude-optimised version with MW50 power boost and four synchronised MG 151/20 cannons:

Wingspan: 11.0 m

Length: 10.62 m

Wing area: 19.6 sq m

Afterwards, the combination Jumo 222E/Ta 152C would be tested with same characteristics and a length of 10.67 m.

Finally, the production version (early December 1944) would be a Jumo 222E/Ta 152H with GM-1 injection for altitudes above 10,000 m a new wing with laminar profile of d/ti=15.85 per cent and d/ta=10 per cent and monocoque structure with two spars and 23.8 sq m.

Technical Data (Ta 152H)	
Type	Single-seat high-altitude interceptor.
Wingspan	13.68 m
Length	10.77 m
Height	3.75 m
Wing area	23.8 sq m
Maximum weight	5,800 kg
Maximum speed	740 km/h
Service ceiling	15,000 m
Range	1,290 km
Engine	One Jumo 222E, 24-cylinder supercharged, liquid cooled, in Star with six banks of four cylinders each and 2,465 hp (3,000 with MW.50 injection) at take-off, driving a Junkers VS-19 four-blade airscrew with 3.6 m of diameter. Two-stage, three-speed supercharger with three intercoolers.
Armament	Two MG 151/20 cannons in the fuselage, two MK 103 cannons in wing roots, possibility to install vertical recoilless weapons SG 500 or Rohrblock 108 in the wings.
Electronics	FuG 16 ZY, FuG 25a, FuG 125, K23 automatic pilot, Revi 16b or EZ42 gyrogunsight.

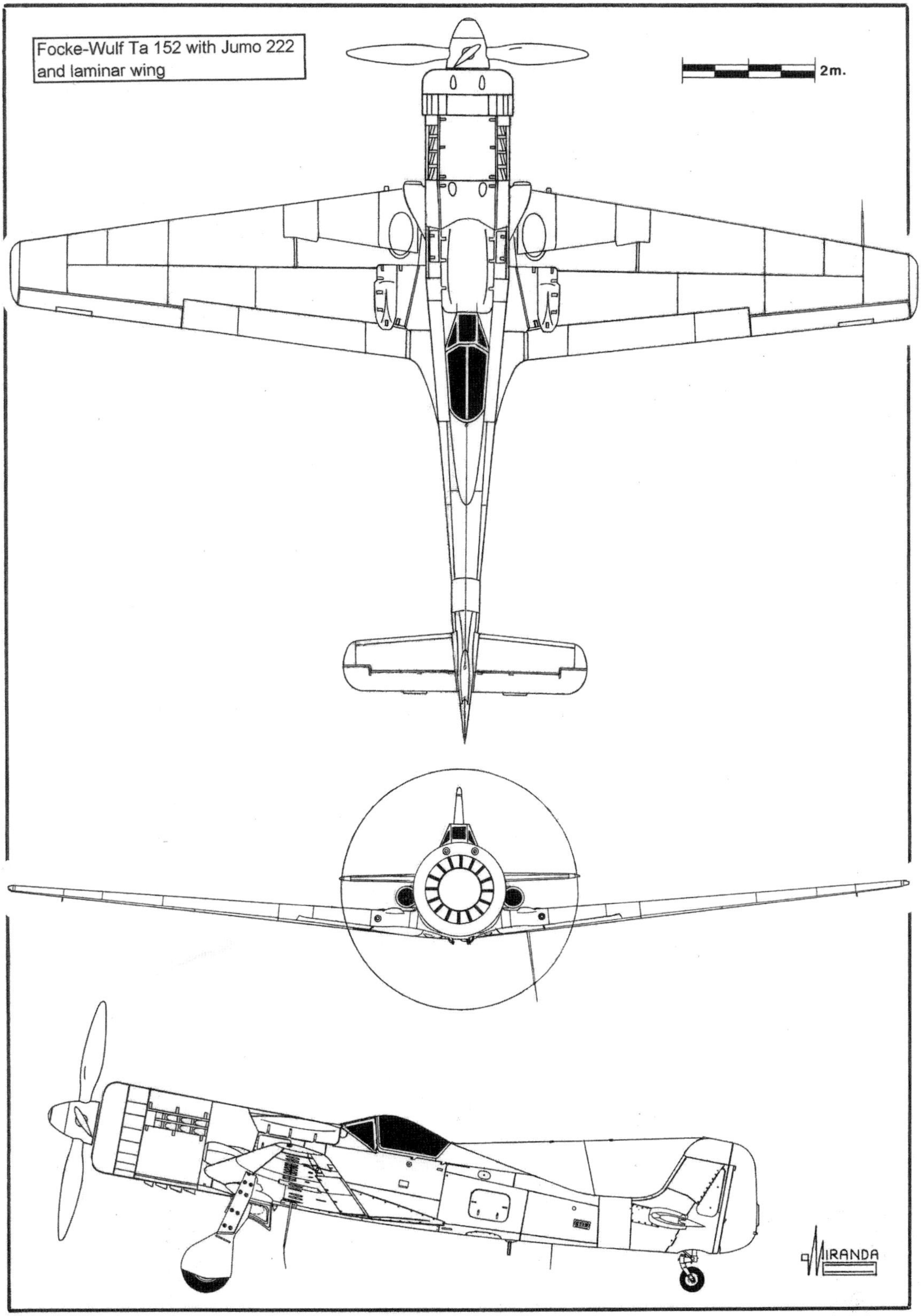
Focke-Wulf Ta 152 with Jumo 222
and laminar wing
2m.
MIRANDA

Chapter 20

Focke Wulf FW 190 mit Jumo 222

At the end of 1941, the development of the Jumo 222 engine had reached the preproduction level, generating high expectations amongst German aircraft manufacturers for its great potential.

Messerschmitt having priority over the best Daimler Benz models, the firm Focke Wulf always tried to match the airframe of the Fw 190 to any available engine, in an effort to improve its performances. The V19 prototype was used as test bed for the BMW 801J and P.8028, the Daimler Benz 603, 609 and 614 and the Jumo 213 A-1 and A-2.

The possibility of installing a pre-series Jumo 222A in the V19 was also considered. The aircraft equipped with this engine would have a length of 9.54 m and it was estimated that the production version would reach 435 mph with a standard armament of two MG 131 and two MK 151/20.

However, it soon became evident that the weight and power of the 222 surpassed the structural resistance of the V19 airframe. Additional issues appeared with the heavy torque and longitudinal stability, besides the high fuel consumption that required a bigger aircraft. The experiment was therefore cancelled.

Technical Data	
Wingspan	10.5 m
Length	9.54 m
Height	3.15 m
Wing area	18.3 sq m
Estimated maximum speed	435 km/h

Fw 190 with Jumo 222

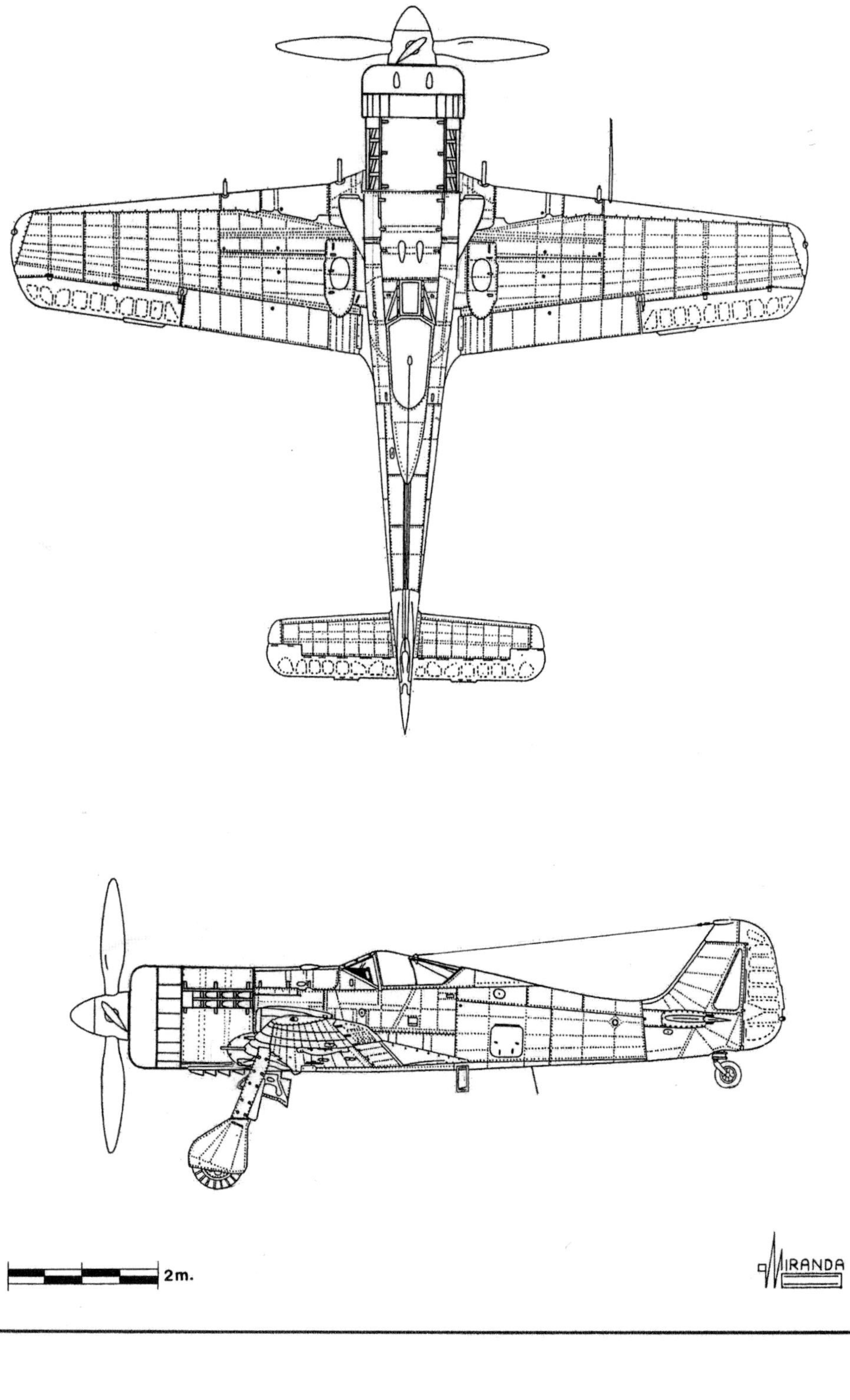

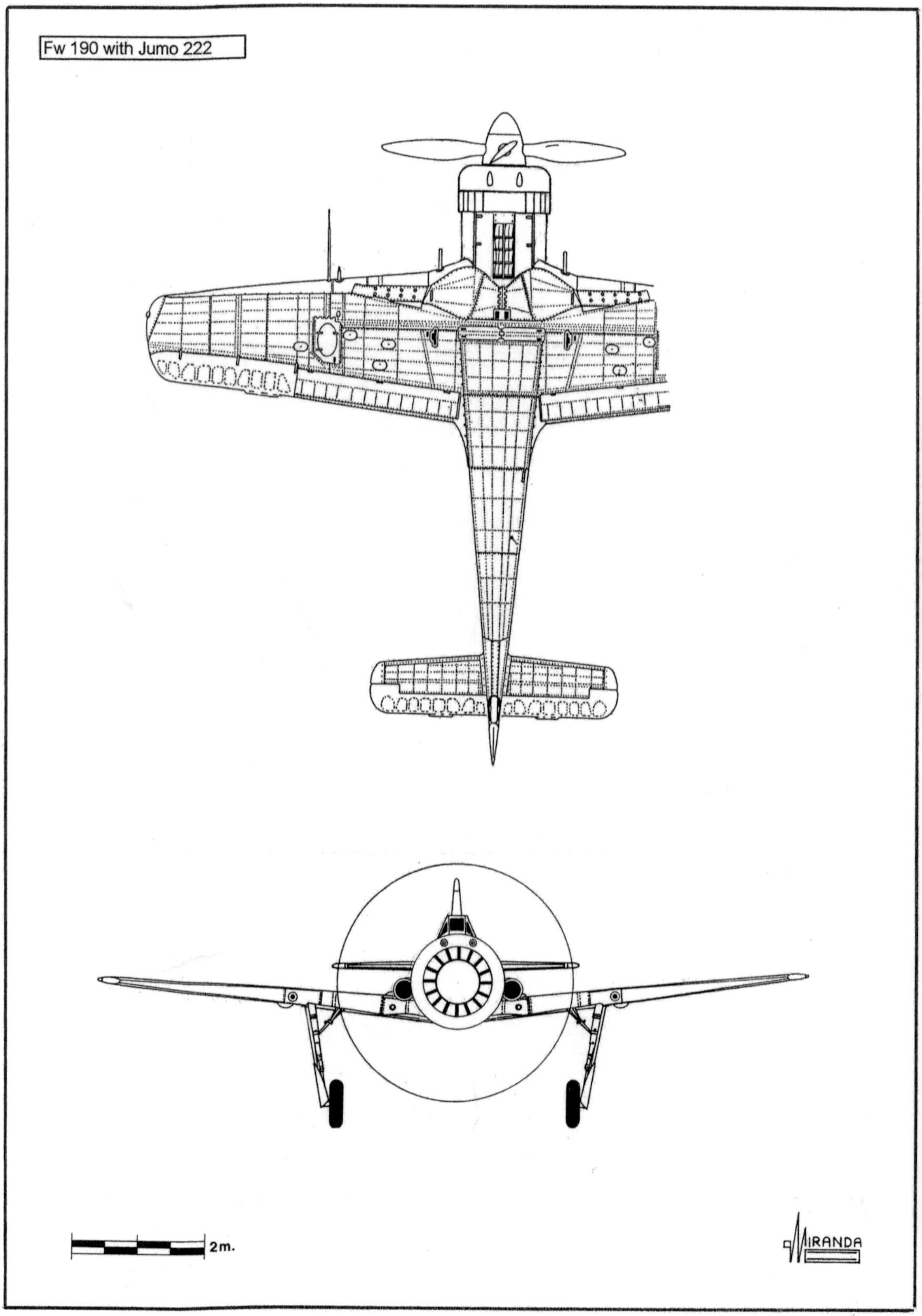
Fw 190 with Jumo 222
2m.
MIRANDA

Focke Wulf Jäger mit DB 609

The biggest success of the Focke Wulf Company was the choice of a radial engine for the Fw 190 in 1938, thus avoiding competing against Messerschmitt for the in-line engines.

During the rest of the war, the Kurt Tank team systematically researched the possibility of utilising all available – or in the design stage – engines for their fighters.

The V19 prototype of the Fw 190 (c/n 0042, GH+KP) was used to test the BMW 801 J and P.8028, The DB 603, 609, 614 and 623 and the Jumo 213 A-1, 213 A-2 and 213 S engines.

Although the rule of the firm was to install an annular radiator in the aft area of the in-line engines, an exception was made with the DB 609. The radiator was installed in the rear area of the fuselage, following the style of the American P-38, in a try to obtain a faster design.

Technical Data

Type	Experimental.
Airframe	Light alloy structure and cladding.
Undercarriage	Fw 190 standard.
Engine	A Daimler Benz DB 609 of 2,700 hp, sixteen-cylinder, inverted-V, liquid cooled engine.
Armament	None.
Electronics	FuG 16 VHF transmitter/receiver.
Measurements	
Span	10,58 m
Length	10,15 m
Height	3.52 m

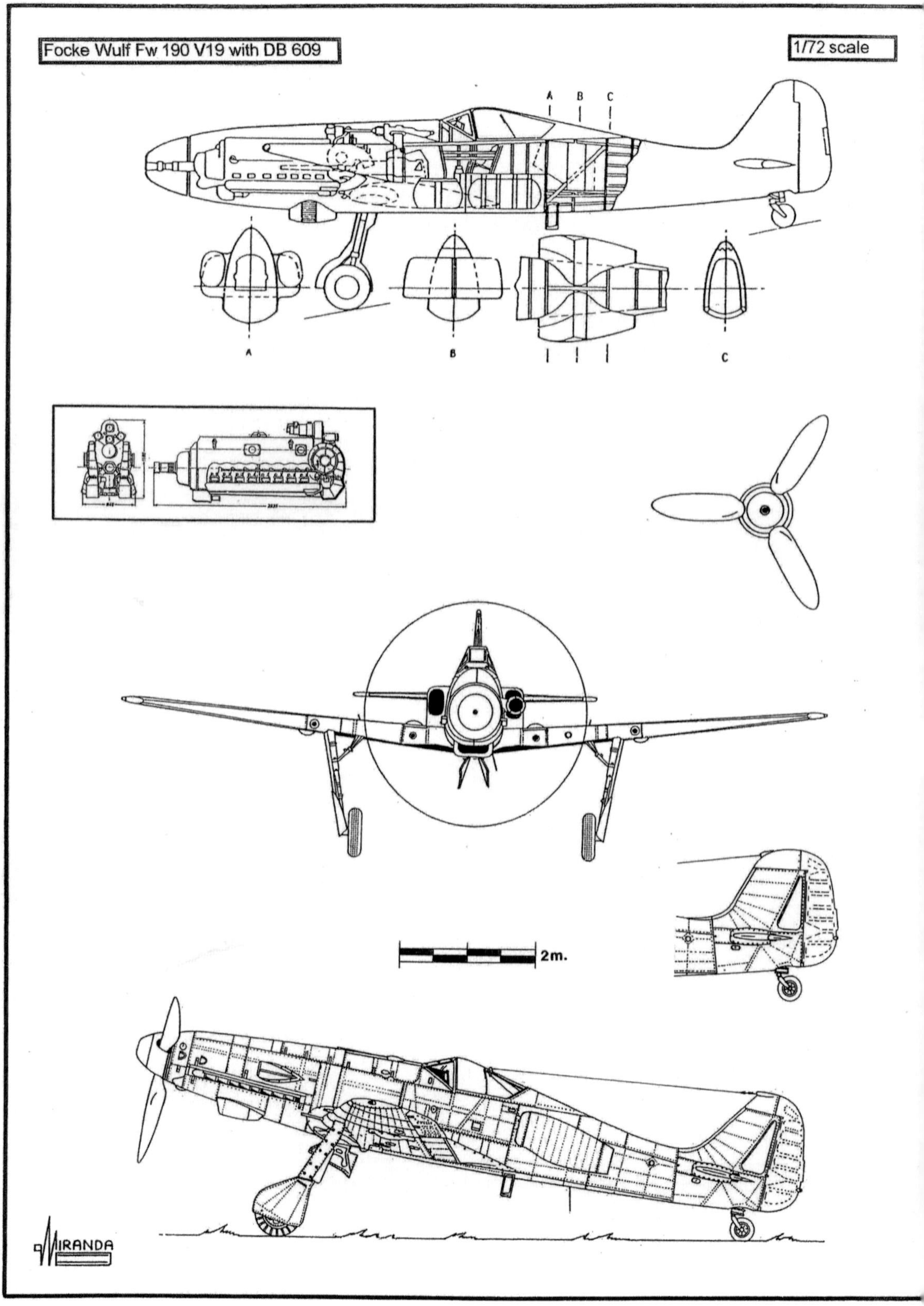
Focke Wulf Fw 190 V19 with DB 609
1/72 scale
A
B
C
2m.

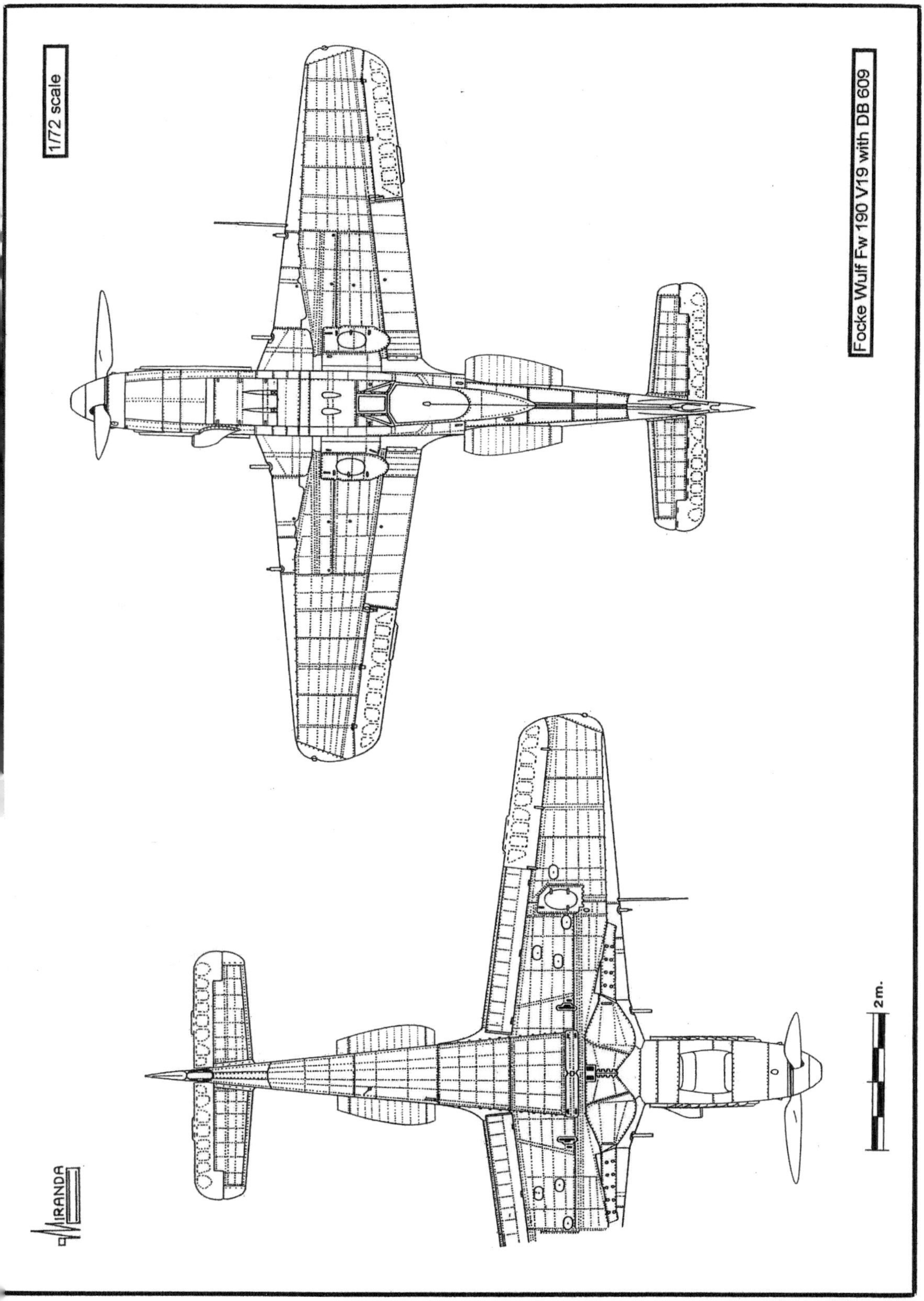
1/72 scale
Focke Wulf Fw 190 V19 with DB 609
2 m.

Chapter 21

Fw 190 Wb-1

The swept wing was not easy to adapt to the conventional piston-engined fighters. The aerodynamicist found great difficulties of longitudinal stability caused by the backwards displacement of the wing pressure centre at high speed and dangerous stall at low speed. The forward swept solution could not be adopted because materials resistance did not allow the construction of a wing rigid enough to avoid vibration on the wingtips.

On 14 November 1941 Focke Wulf published a study based on observations of the shape taken by the wings of prey birds during diving. The result was an inverted W shaped wing, 25-degree double-swept, known as 25 degree gepfeilter Flügel mit grosse Fläche. To test its behaviour in flight, a sample was built, installing it on the Fw 190 V19 prototype that had already been previously modified to change the position of the conventional wing. The static testing gave unsatisfactory results (possibly due to the appearance of vibrations at the ailerons, typical of these first swept designs).

The V19 denomination was changed by the Fw WB-1.

There are no records kept of the tests made but the V19 was built again as A-3 standard with tail section from Fw 190 C, being destroyed when crashing on 16 February 1944.

Technical Data	
Type	Experimental.
Airframe	Light alloy structure and cladding.
Undercarriage	Fw 190 standard.
Engine	One BMW 801 D/2, 14-cylinder radial, air-cooled with 1700 hp.
Armament	none
Electronics	FuG 16 VHF transmitter/receiver
Measurements	
Span	10,72 m
Length	8,78 m
Height	2.88 m

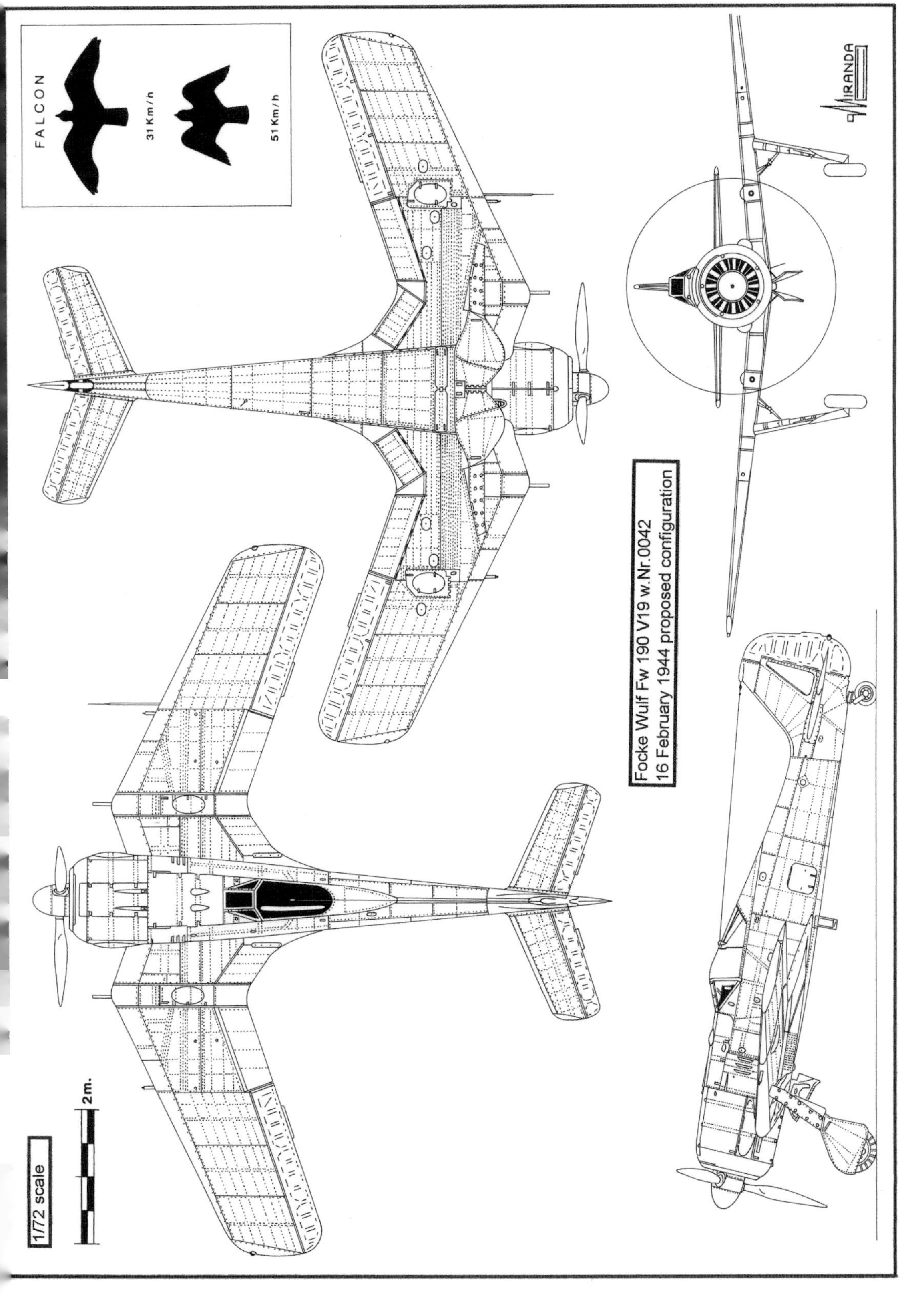
FALCON
31 Km/h
51 Km/h
MIRANDA
Focke Wulf Fw 190 V19 w.Nr.0042
16 February 1944 proposed configuration
1/72 scale
2m.

Chapter 22

Focke Wulf Jäger mit Jumo 222 C/D

The poor octane ratings of the B4 fuel and the poor quality of the lubrication oil that obliged engines to run at high revolutions (3,200 rpm and 6.5 to 1 compression ratio) to deliver the required horsepower were the cause of all the problems suffered by the A series of the Jumo 222. Rather deficient cooling, vibration fractures and disintegration of bearings were due to the shortage of tin during its manufacturing, causing corrosion and piston seizure. The poor performance, of just thirty minutes, of the one-stage supercharger and the low time between overhauls led the RLM to cancel production of the A and B series in December 1941.

To avoid these deficiencies, the engine was redesigned with bigger cylinders and an improved supercharger. The new C and D series of 55.5 litres and 2,200-3,000 hp were authorised for mass production in the summer of 1942, for the bombers of the 'Bomber B' program.

In autumn, the decision was taken to promote the production of fighters, to adapt to war needs.

Benefiting from the possibility of having a new engine and from the experience obtained with the Fw 190 V19, the Kurt Tank team designed an optimised heavy fighter for ground attack.

The 22 October 1942 project was 25 per cent bigger that the 190, so that it could have double fuel capacity. The engine was fixed to the central section of the wing, driving a four-blade of 4 m by means of an extension shaft. This allowed the installation of one heavy cannon in the nose, which fired through the propeller hub.

The fuselage, of circular section, housed the engine, the fuel tank, the pilot cockpit and the main armament. The wings contained two Bf 109 style coolers, the undercarriage and the secondary weapons.

After the bombing of the Junkers Motorenwerke's headquarters in the spring of 1943, the C and D series were cancelled. The Focke Wulf project would be modified as Fw 0310.226-32 to be powered by a Jumo 004 turbojet. It competed against the Me.P1095 on 7 June 1943 as Strahljäger Projekt II.

Technical Data (P.247/6)

Type	Single-seat heavy fighter and ground attack aircraft.
Airframe	Light alloy.
Engine	One Jumo 222 C/D, 24-cylinder, liquid cooled, in Star with six banks of four cylinders each and 2,465-3,000 hp take-off.
Fuel tank	One of 140 litres behind the pilot.
Armament	As a fighter, it carried an MK 103/30 cannon in the nose, shooting through the propeller hub, and two MK 108/30 (synchro) in the wing roots. As Zerstörer, one MK 103 in the nose and four Mk 108/30 in the wings. As ground attack, two MG 151/20 in the nose, four MG 151/20 in the wings and two 500 kg of bombs under wings racks.
Wingspan	11.5 m
Length	12.4 m
Height	4.05 m
Wing area	22.3 sq m
Maximum weight	5,290 kg (Fighter)
6,328 kg (Attack)	
Estimated maximum speed	750 km/h at 6,000 m

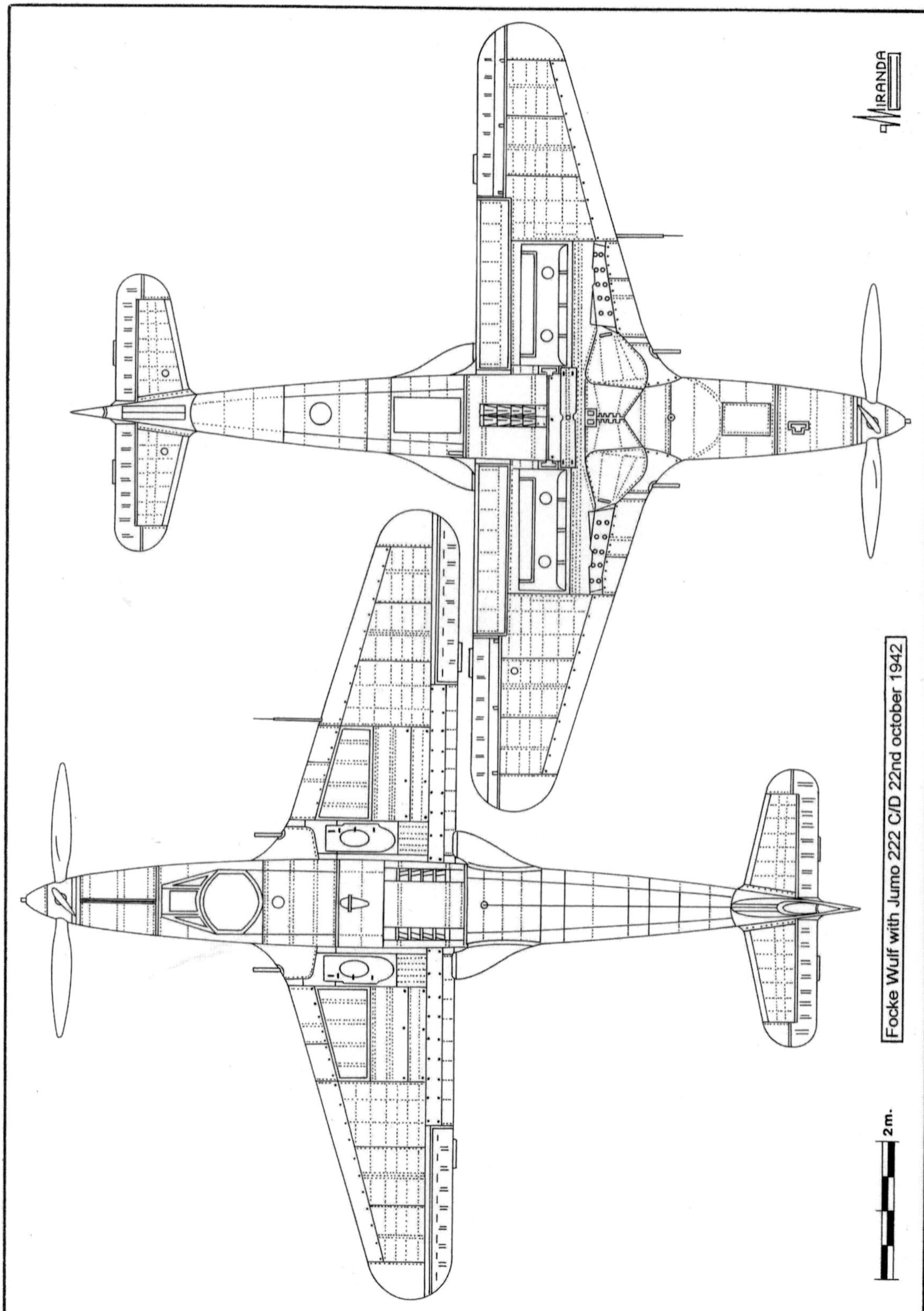
MIRANDA
Focke Wulf with Jumo 222 C/D 22nd october 1942
2 m.

Focke Wulf with Jumo 222 C/D 22nd october 1942

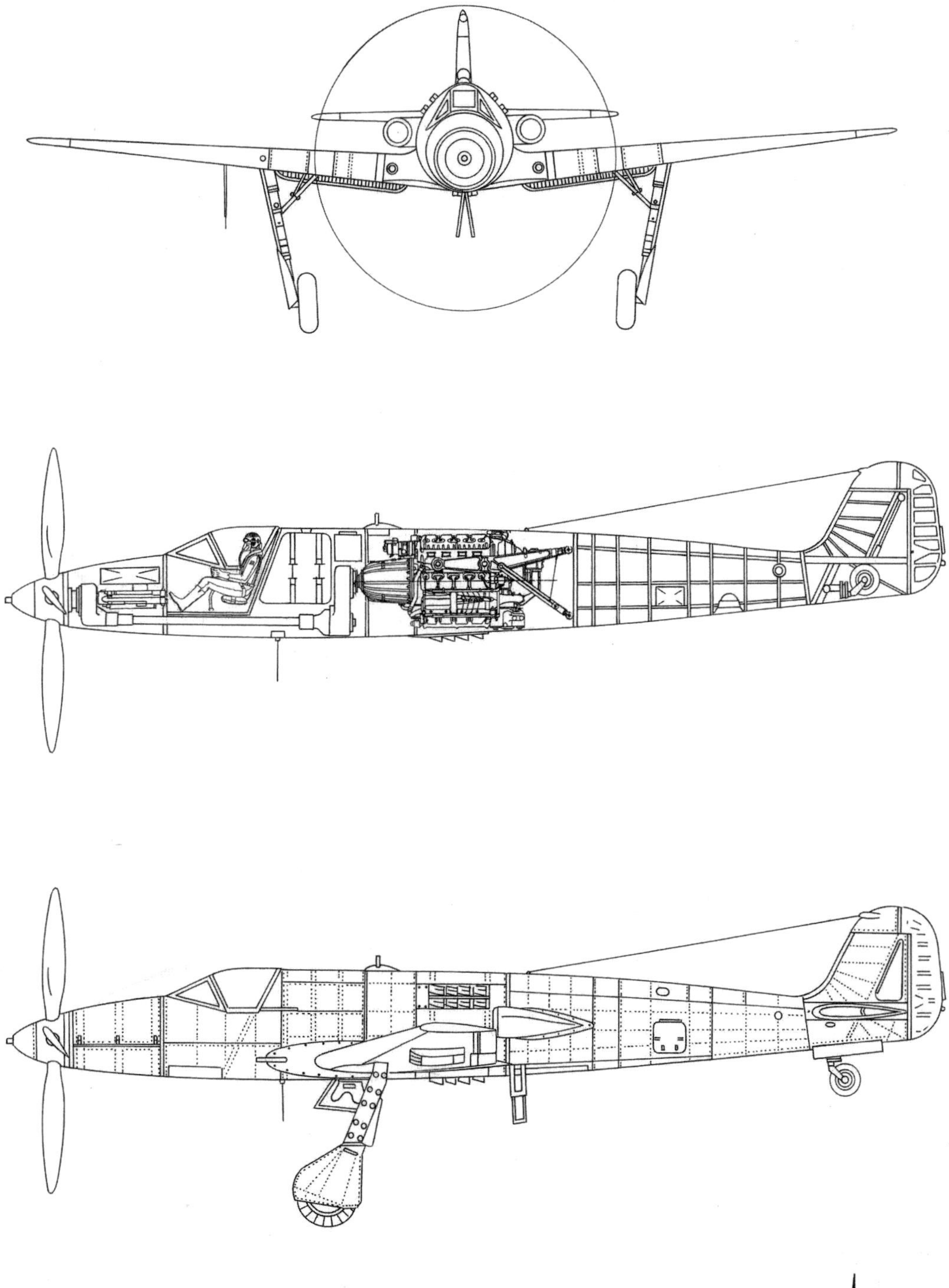

Chapter 23

Focke Wulf Jäger mit BMW 802

Projected in 1939 as a scaled up version of the BMW 801, the BMW 803 was an air-cooled 18-cylinder, twin-row radial engine, with the same cylinder type as the BMW 801.

Equipped with a two-stage, two-speed supercharger placed in front of the engine and a 3.8 m diameter, four-bladed variable pitch propeller, it was capable of delivering 2,600 hp at take-off and 1.600 hp at 12,000 m.

A prototype, named BMW 8028, equipped with a three-speed supercharger and 1,550 hp at take-off, was tested on the Fw 190 V19. To benefit from the potential of the new BMW 802 engine, a new homothetic enlarged (125 per cent) version of the Fw 190 was designed on 24 June 1941.

The BMW 802 was a 2600 hp, 18-cylinder twin-row radial engine, with exhaust gas turbocharger and bullet-shaped ducted spinner similar to the one used in the Fw 190 V-1.

Similar devices had been tested in British and American airplanes (Northrop A-1, Curtiss XP-42, Vultee Model 48 and Hawker Tempest Mk V NV 768) since 1938 without success due to overheating. To overcome this problem the new design had a very powerful system of ducted cooling fans.

BMW P.8011

The P.8011 was a project derived from the BMW 802, able to produce 2900 hp at take-off. The supercharger was replaced by two gas turbines enclosed in an aerodynamic engine cowling and driving two contra-rotating propellers. The project was cancelled in mid-1942.

These engines were too heavy and powerful for the standard Fw 190 airframe. It was necessary to design heavier airplanes for them. The quickest answer was two 125 per cent scaled up versions of the Fw 190, both with a wing of 13 m span and 34.5 sq m surface. The BMW 802 had a length of 11.15 m and 5,400 kg of maximum weight. The BMW P.8011 version was 11.8 m long. The armament in both versions consisted in 4 x MG 151/20 placed in the wing roots and above the engine.

These monster planes lacked any official designation and were known as 'Focke Wulf einsitzer mit BMW 802' (although an article by General Arnold published on 29 May 1944 in *Aviation News* refers to it as the 'Focke Wulf Fw 290') and 'Focke Wulf einsitzer mit BMW P.8011'.

This project was considered again at the end of 1944 as high-altitude interceptor with BMW P.8011 and armoured pressure cabin.

Focke Wulf Single Seater with BMW 802 **(Technical Data for BMW 8011 in brackets)**	
Type	Project of high-altitude interceptor.
Structure and cladding	Metallic.
Landing gear	Fw 190 style enlarged 120 per cent.
Engine	One BMW 802, a 2600 hp and 18-cylinder twin-row radial engine, air cooled with exhaust gas with turbocharger. (One BMW 8011, a 2900 hp and 18 cylinder twin-row radial engine, air-cooled with two centrifugal turbochargers.)
Propeller	Four-bladed, with a diameter of 3.8 m. (Two/three-bladed contra-rotating, with a diameter of 3.7 m.)
Fuel tank	Two in the fuselage and two in the wings.
Armament	Four MG 151/20 of 20 mm, two in the wings and two in the aft upper area of the fuselage.
Wingspan	13 m
Length	11.15 m (11.8 m)
Height	3.8 m
Wing area	34.5 sq m
Empty weight	4475 kg
Max. weight	5400 kg
Max. speed	725 km/h

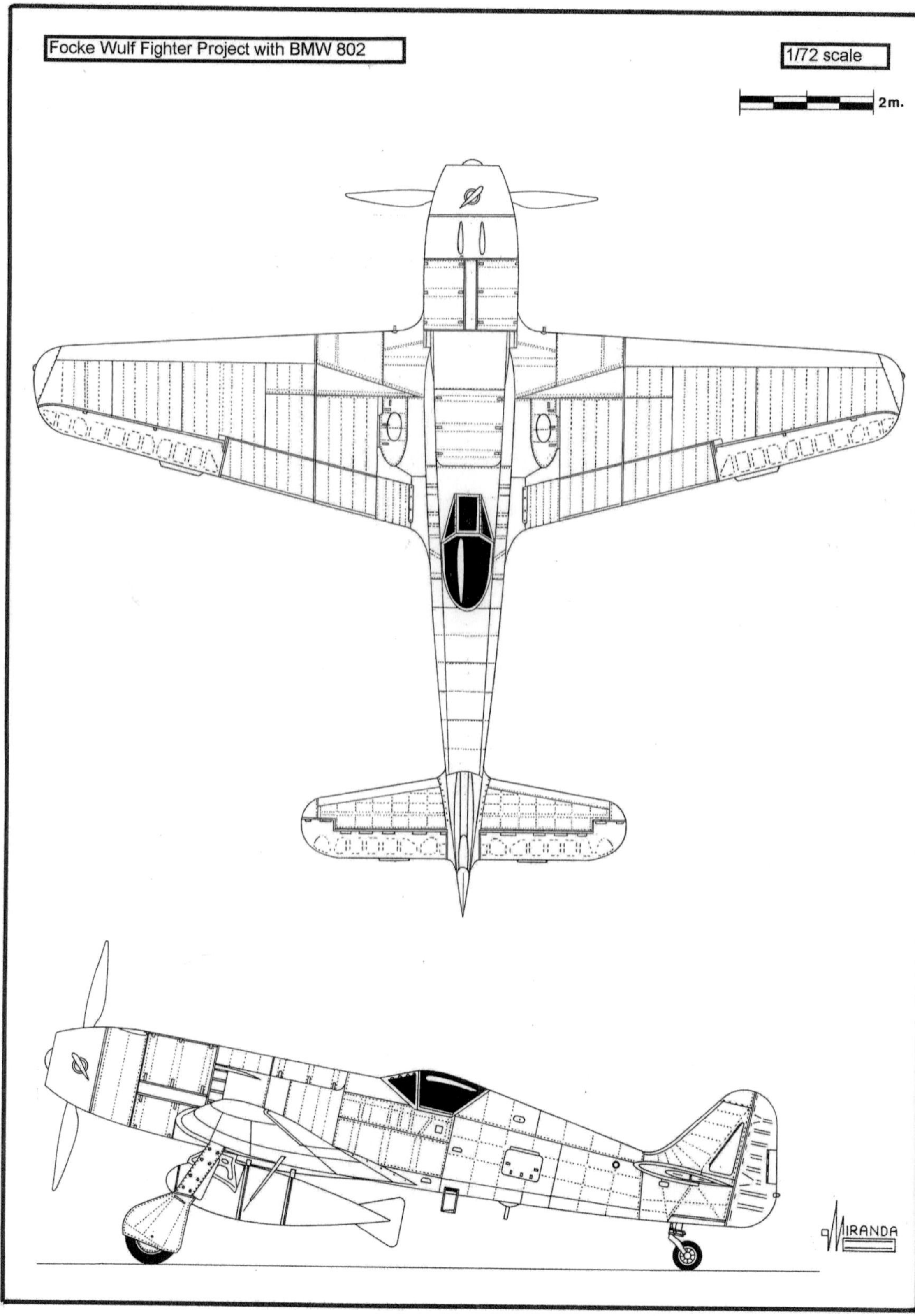
Focke Wulf Fighter Project with BMW 802
1/72 scale
2m.
MIRANDA

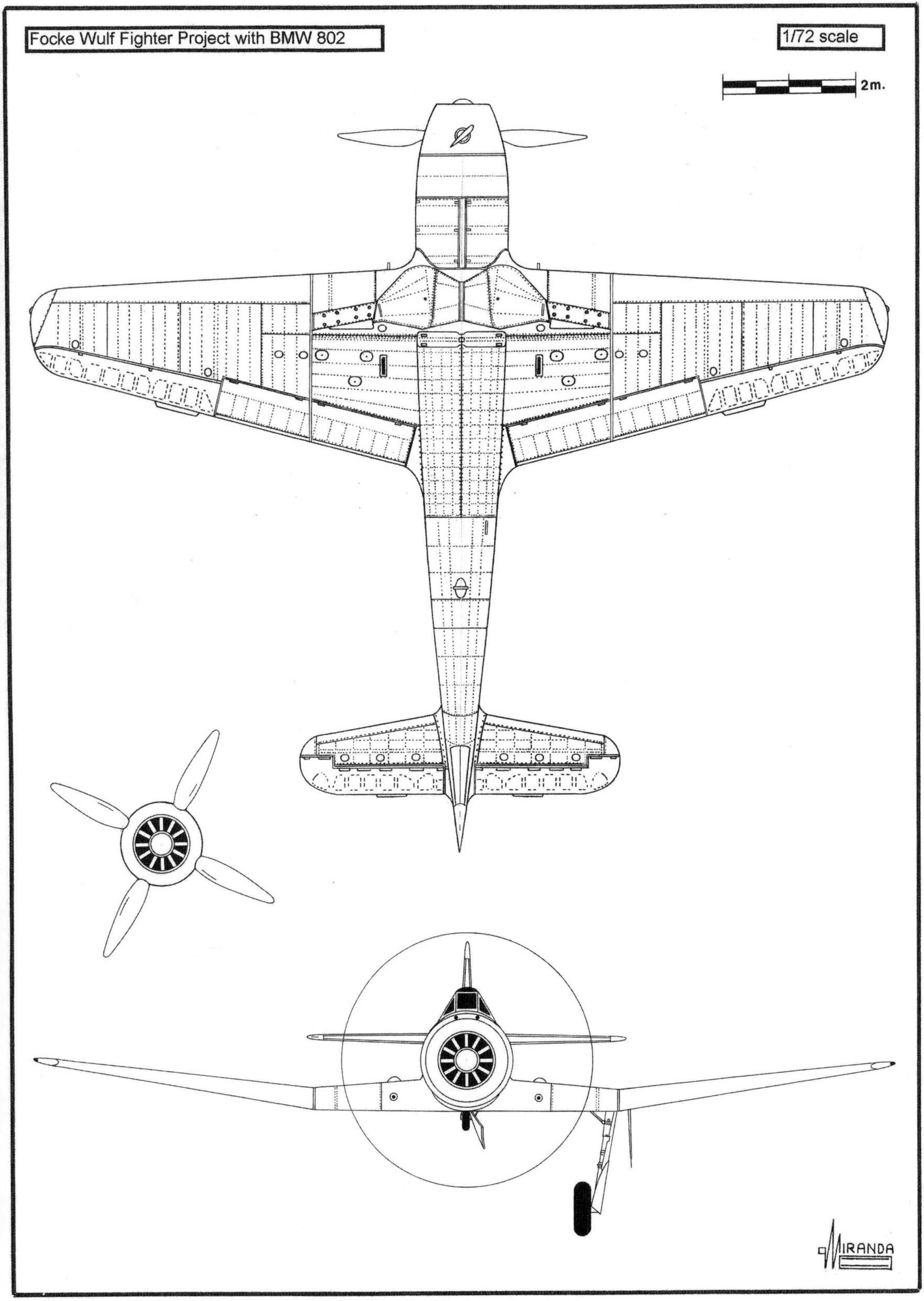
Focke Wulf Fighter Project with BMW 802
1/72 scale
2m.
MIRANDA

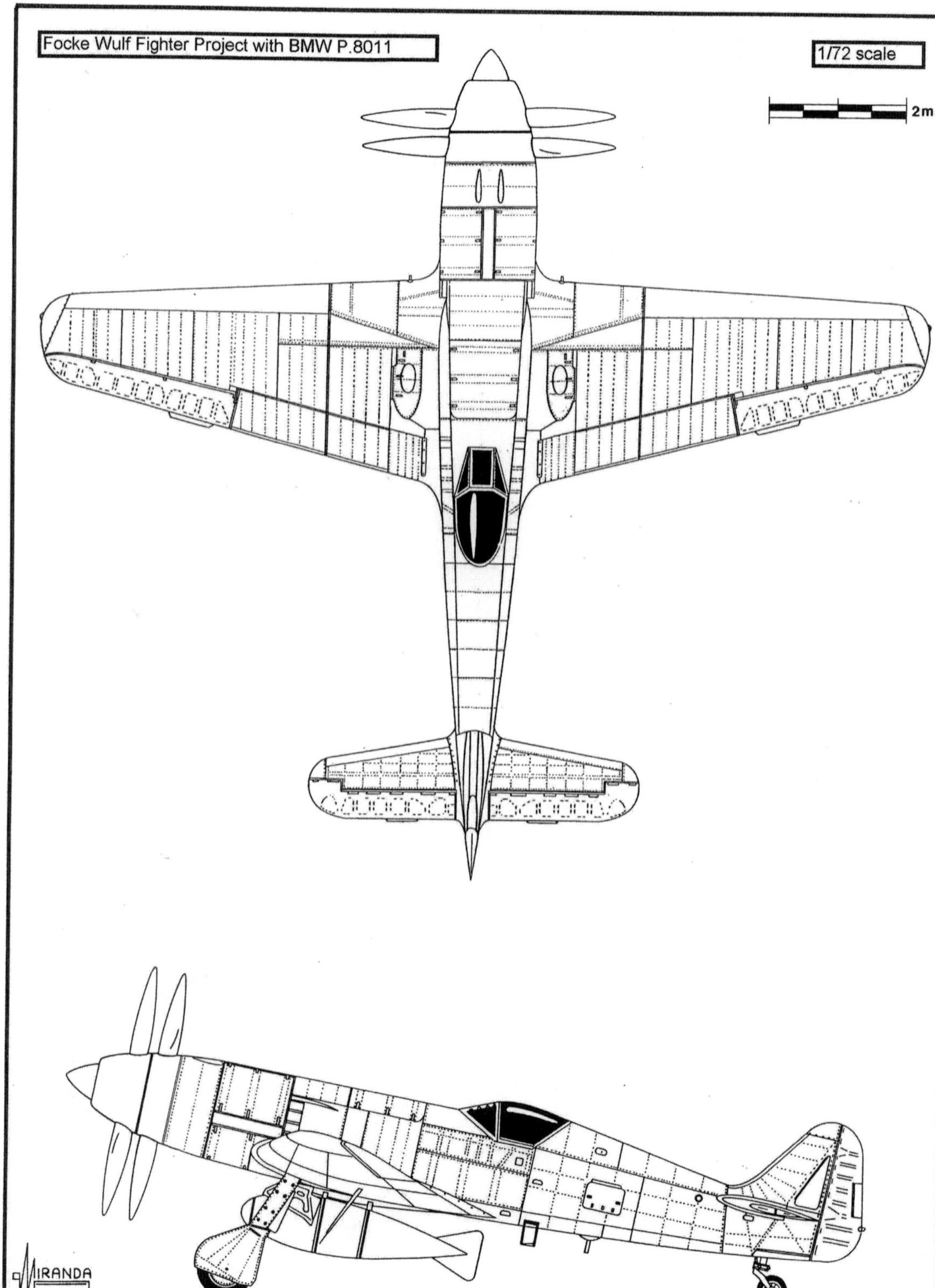
Focke Wulf Fighter Project with BMW P.8011
1/72 scale
2m.

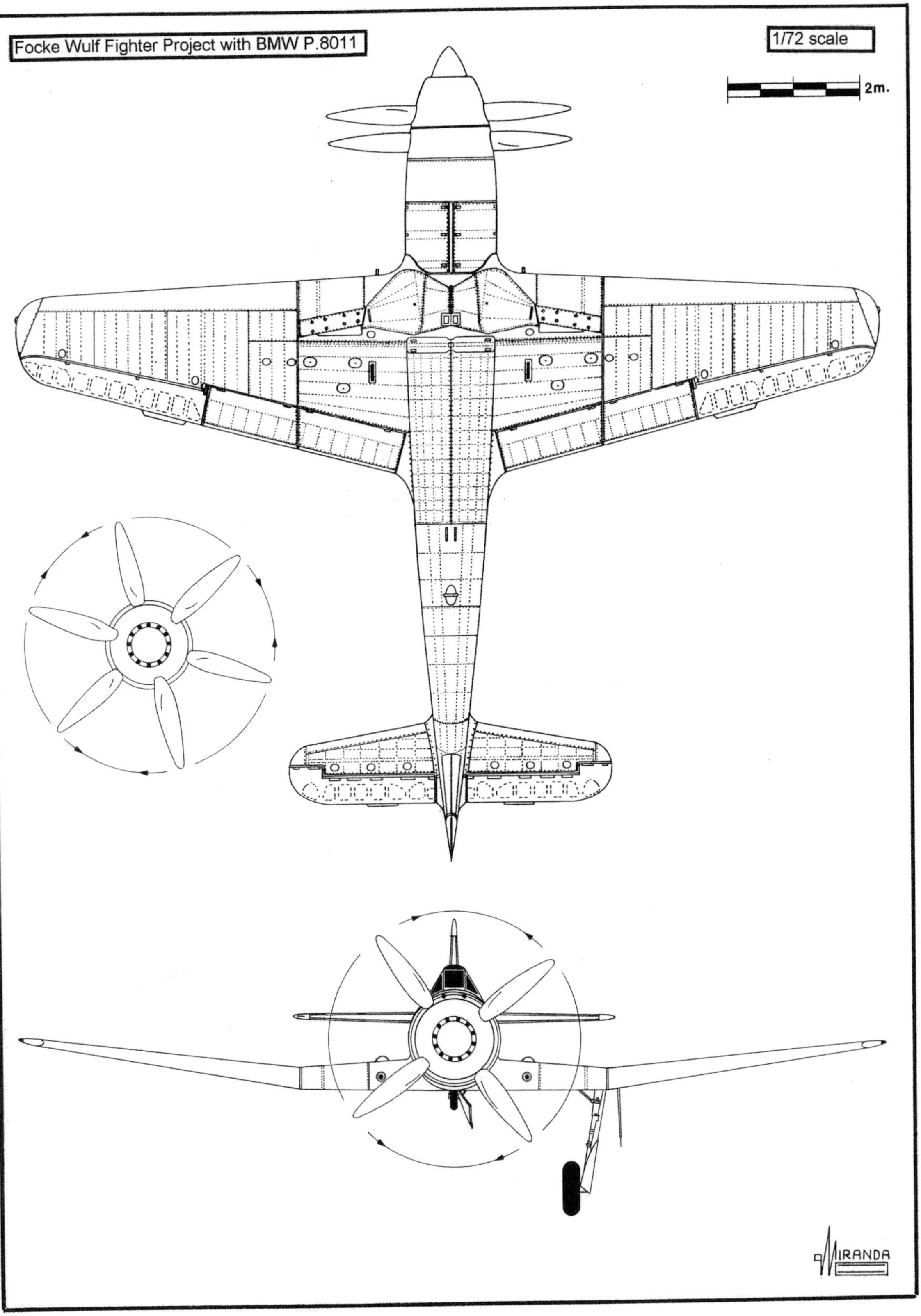
Focke Wulf Fighter Project with BMW P.8011
1/72 scale
2m.
MIRANDA

Chapter 24

Focke Wulf Jäger mit BMW 803 A

This monster engine was developed from 1941 onwards to propel the long range bomber Fw 238 and the Blohm und Voss P200 flying boat. It was a double engine composed of two BMW 801, bolted back to back and driving contra-rotating propellers.

The result was a 28-cylinder, 4-row radial engine, liquid cooled. Equipped with a two-stage, four-speed supercharger, the engine should have had an output of 4,000 hp at take-off and 4,500 hp with auxiliary injection. There was no common crankshaft and each BMW 801 drove a set of independent contra-rotating propellers.

The rear engine drove a number of smaller shafts that passed between the cylinders of the front engine, being geared together in a rather large gearbox on the front of the BMW 803. The supercharger and engine accessories were powered by the rear 801.

By the middle of 1944, a preproduction order was given with delivery expected from May 1945 onwards. The prototype built was extremely heavy (2,950 kg) and was expressly designed for the heavy fighter of 9,000 kg known as Focke Wulf Jäger Projekt mit BMW 803. Projected in three versions, between June 1941 and April 1943, it was not derived from the Fw 190 but from a twin-boom pusher propeller very similar to the S.O. 8000 Narval built by the French in 1949. In error, some authors cite this project as Fw 190 when it was actually a development from the Fw 189.

The first design, dated April 1941, had a fuselage with circular section and an annular air intake for the fan of the cooler, which was installed in front of the engine. The air circulated through the inner fuselage and was expelled, together with the engine exhaust gases, through two annular nozzles located at the rear.

The armament, insufficient for a heavy fighter, was of four 20 mm guns. The pilot had ejector seat. The wing was swept 24 degrees at leading edge and had a 4.98:1 aspect ratio.

Wind tunnel simulations proved that the cooling system was inefficient and the design was modified in April 1943, with the cooler and fan being located in the nose, within the cylindrical container.

A second Entwurf II design was presented on the same date. It had two smaller coolers, installed at the frontal end of the tail booms.

Both designs had two oil coolers in the wing roots, increased span and replaced two of the guns with others of 30 mm.

Additionally, it was proposed to install four machine guns in the wing roots.

Technical Data (June 1941)

Type	Single-seat heavy fighter.
Airframe	Light alloy.
Engine	A BMW 803 of 28 cylinders, liquid cooled and 4,000 hp
Fuel tank	One in the fuselage, behind the pilot, and two jettisonable of 300 litres below each tail boom.
Armament	Four MG 151/20 cannons in the nose.
Wingspan	13.20 m
Length	13.80 m
Height	3.20 m
Wing area	35 sq m
Max. weight	7,500 kg
Max. speed	730 km/h
Service ceiling	11,200 m
Endurance	1.5 hours

Technical Data (April 1943)

Type	High-altitude interceptor.
Airframe	Light alloy.
Engine	A BMW 803 of 28 cylinders, liquid cooled and 4,000 hp.
Armament	Two MG 151/20 and two Mk 103/30 cannons in the nose and four MG 131/13 machine guns in the wing roots.
Wingspan	15.50 m
Length	14.30 m (13.70 m Entwurf II)
Height	4.70 m
Wing area	40 sq m
Max. weight	9,000 kg

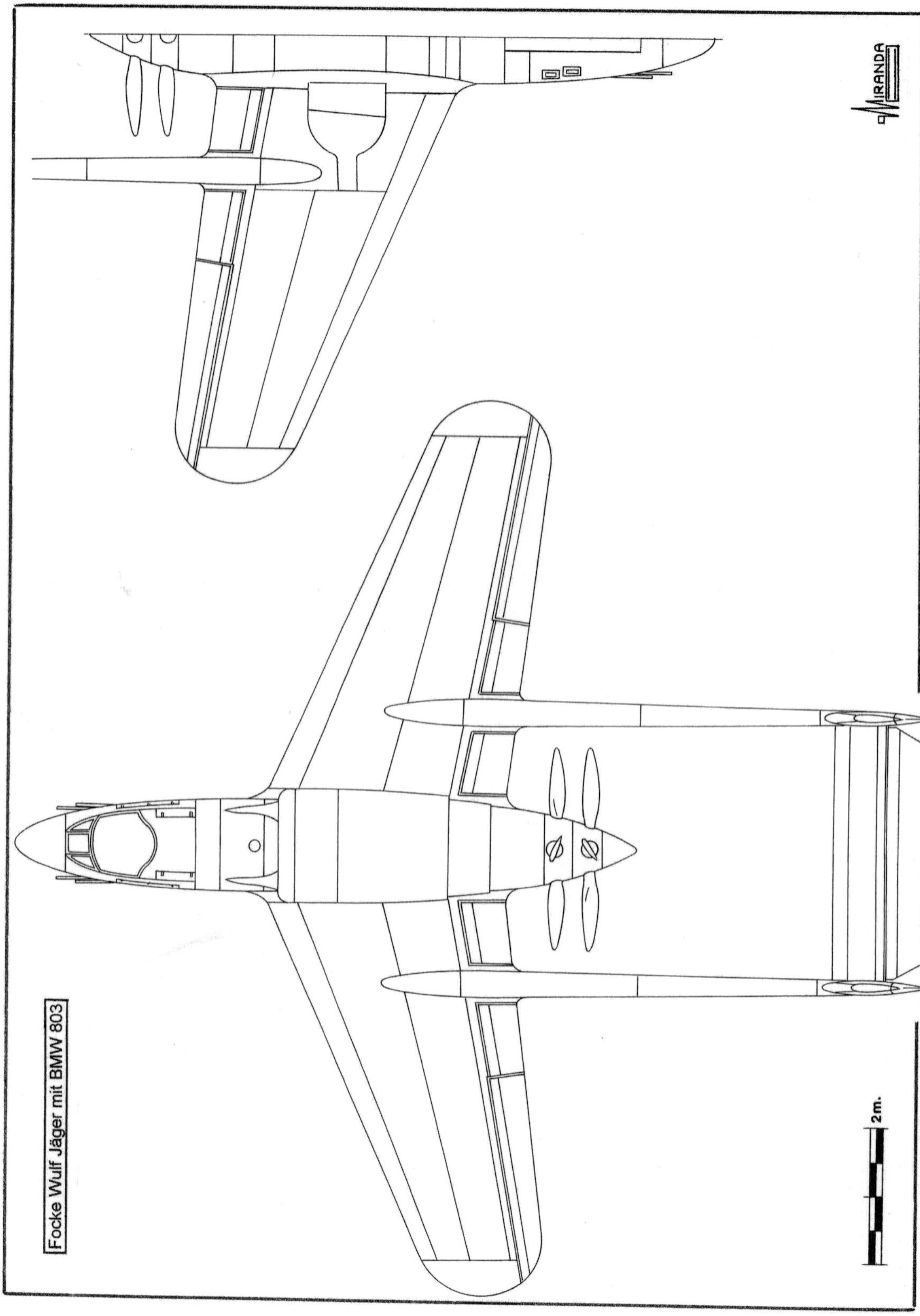
Focke Wulf Jäger mit BMW 803
2m.
MIRANDA

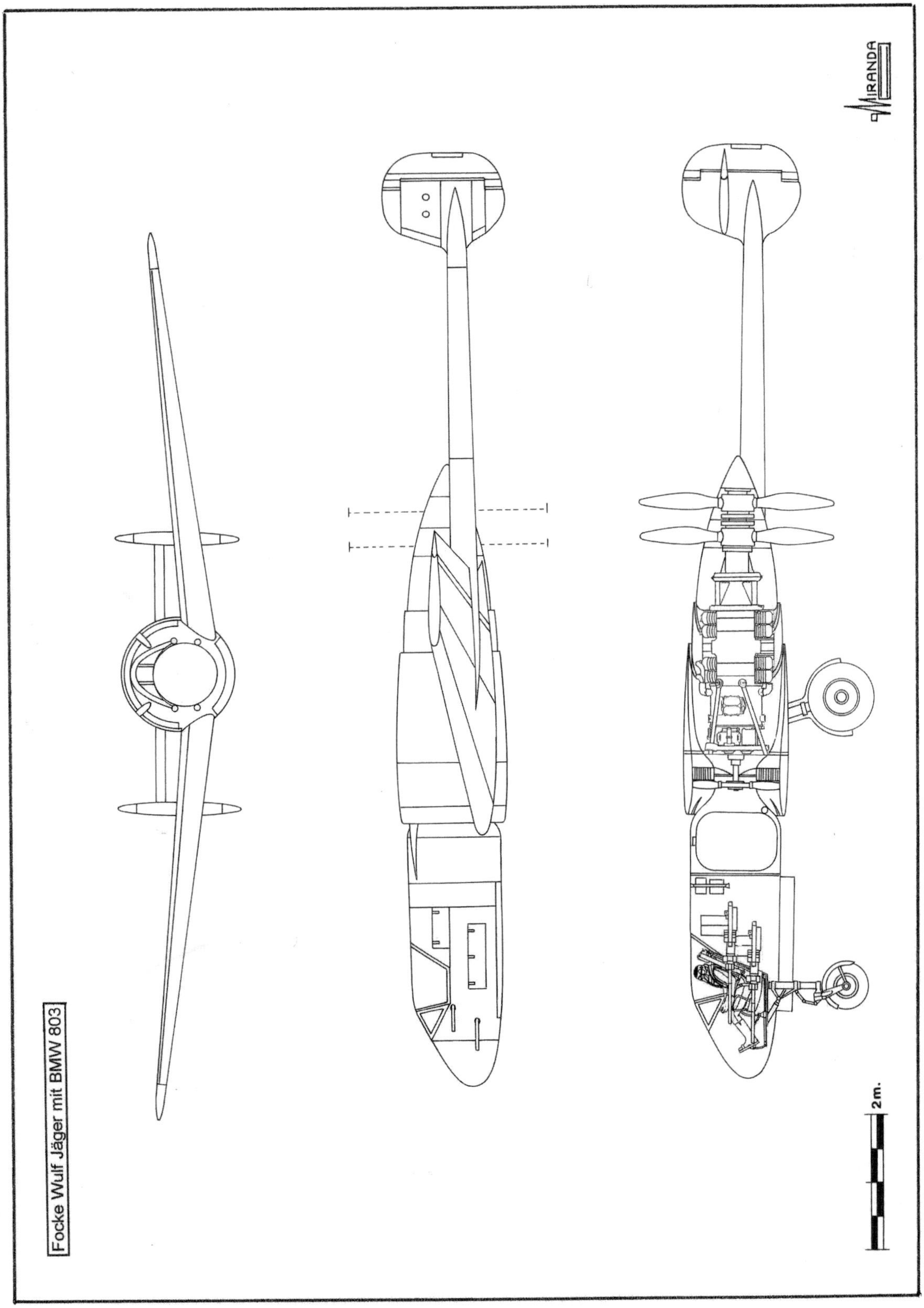
Focke Wulf Jäger mit BMW 803
2m.

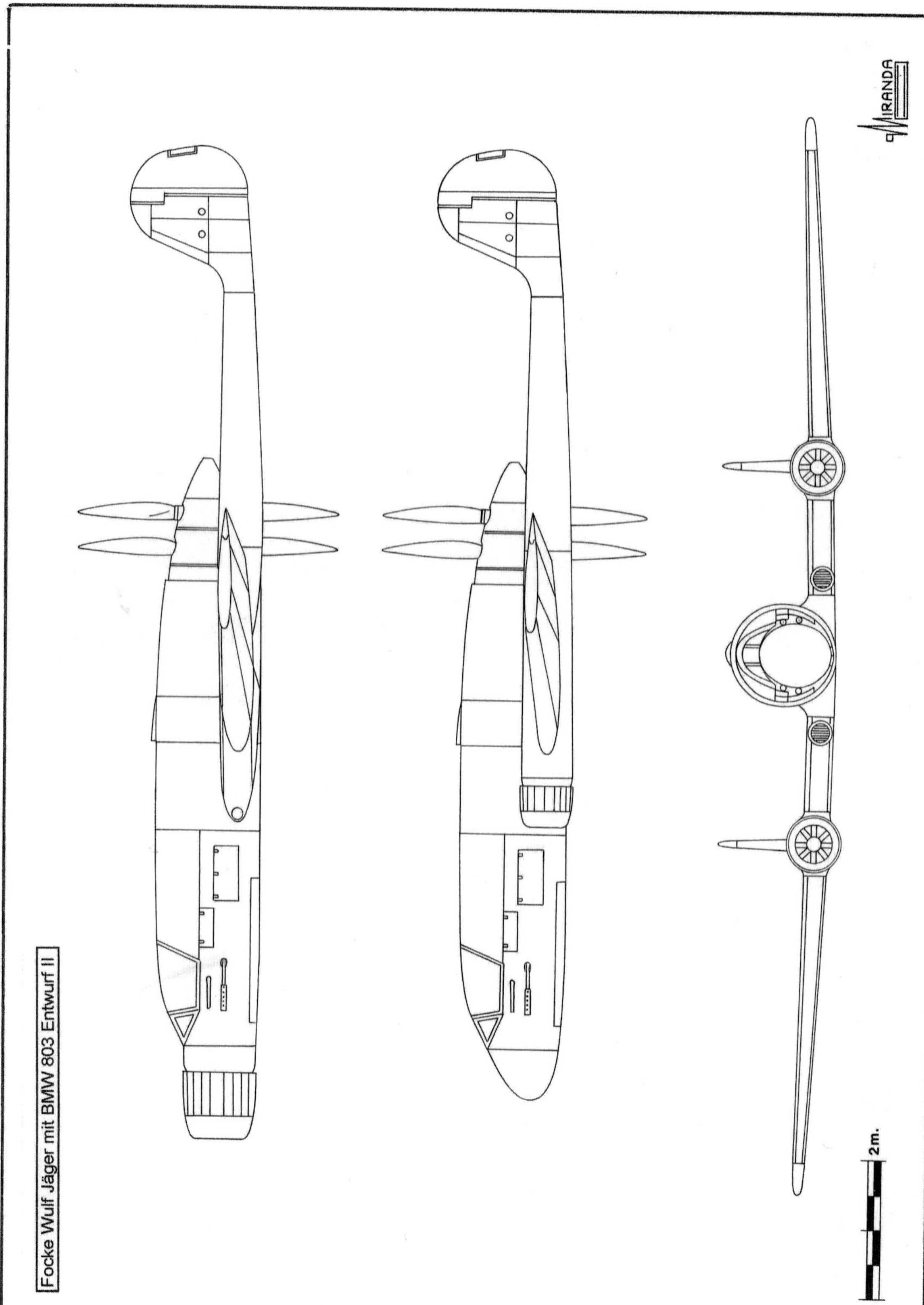
Focke Wulf Jäger mit BMW 803 Entwurf II
2m.
MIRANDA

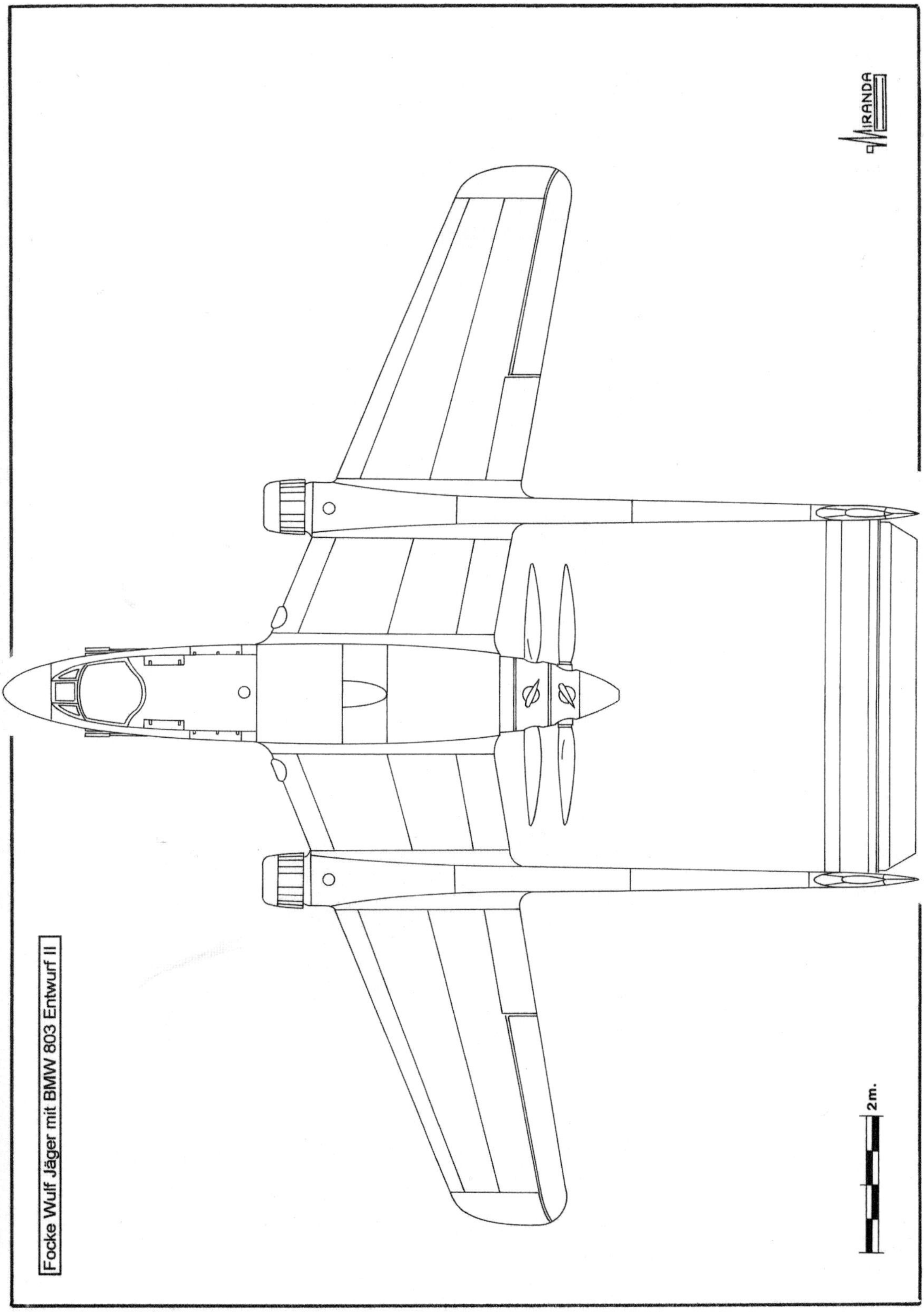
Focke Wulf Jäger mit BMW 803 Entwurf II
2m.

Chapter 25

Focke Wulf P.0310.025-1006

On 21 July 1944, the RLM published the Otto Jäger specification for a high-altitude piston fighter.

Focke Wulf answered in October with a great rhomboid wing and pusher airscrews aircraft, powered by an 4,000 hp Argus As 413 engine and armed with four guns of 30 mm. The plan included a bad-weather Moskitojäger two seat variant equipped with a FuG 218/219 radar with Siemens fixed 20 cm diameter parabolic antenna, able to fly and fight at an altitude superior to the Me 262 B-2a.

Neither the Argus As 413 nor the Jumo 222 E/F, proposed as replacement, were available when Göring ordered a stop to the development of any type of piston engine on 22 February 1945.

Technical Data	
Type	High-altitude interceptor and bad-weather fighter.
Airframe	Light alloy structure and cladding, 31-degree swept wing at 0.25 chord
Cockpit	pressurised, control heating, armoured front and rear, ejector seat.
Engine	One Argus As 413, water cooled, 24 cylinders H ,with 4,000 hp, and GM-1 power boost, driving two counter rotating propellers by means of an extension shaft.
Fuel tanks	One of 1,300 litres in the fuselage, behind the pilot, and two of 300 litres each in the wings.
Oil tank	One of 130 litres in the fuselage.
Armament	Two Mk 103/30 and two MG 213C/30 cannon in forward fuselage.
Wingspan	16.40 m
Length	14.20 m
Height	4.70 m
Wing area	55 sq m
Aspect ratio	4,9:1
Max. weight	9,800 kg
Max. speed	840 km/h
Ceiling	14,100 m
Endurance	2 hours
Electronics	FuG 16 ZY, FuG 25a, FuG 125

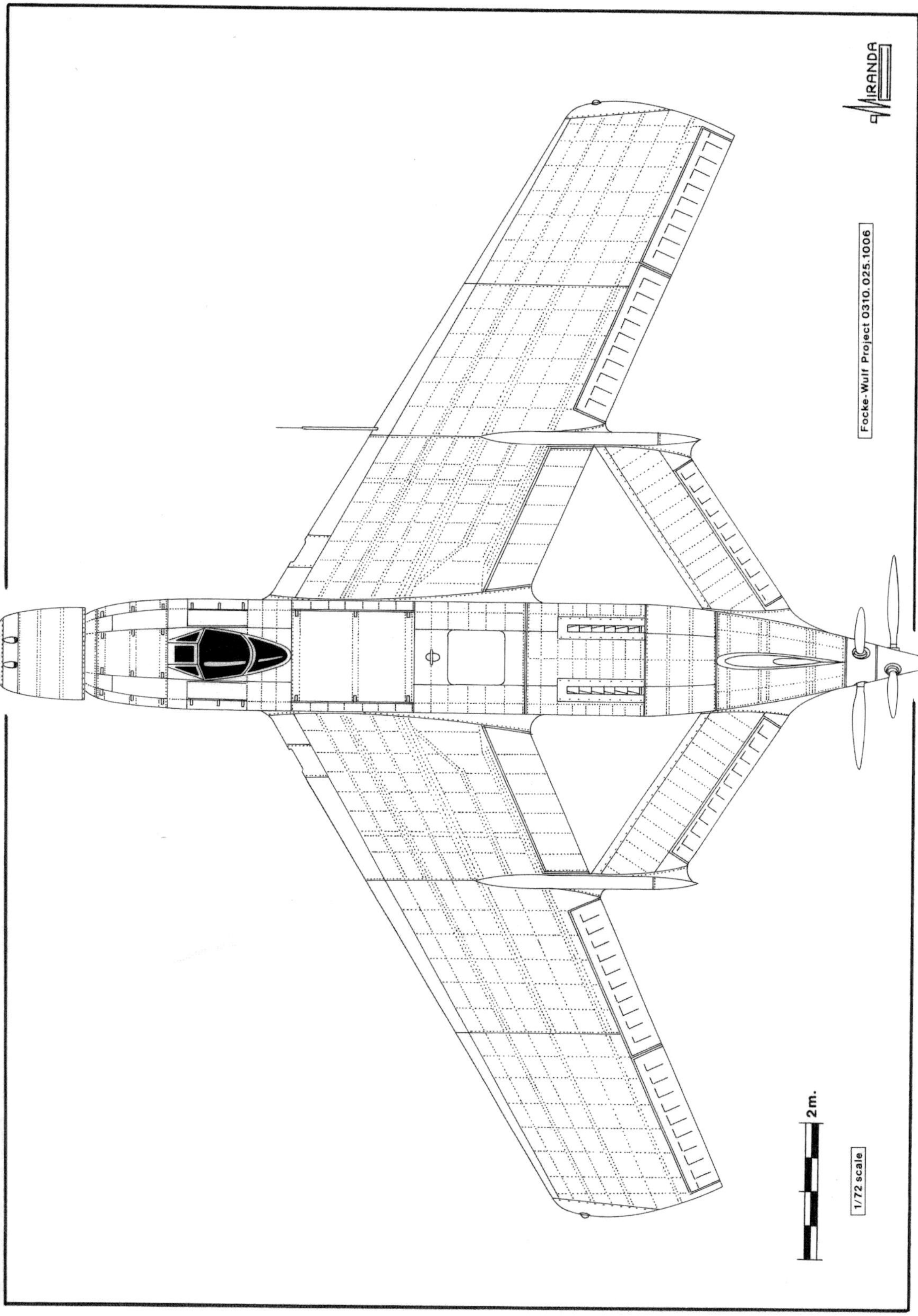
Focke-Wulf Project 0310.025.1006
1/72 scale
2m.

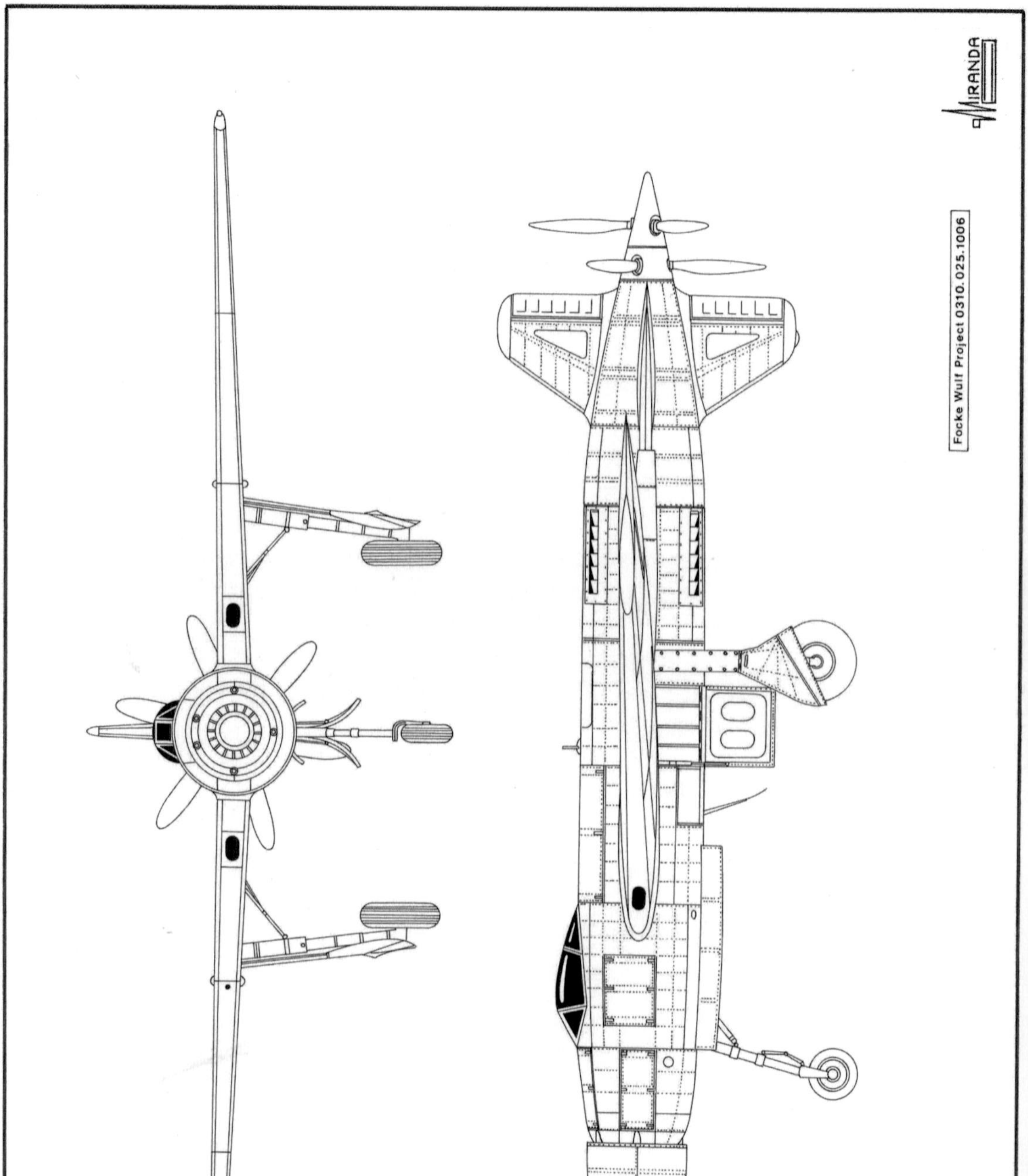
Focke Wulf Project 0310.025.1006
1/72 scale
2 m.

Chapter 26

Focke Wulf Hochleistungsjäger

The Kurt Tank design team proposed three different designs, based on the three types of available engines, in response to the Otto Jäger specification, all using the same aerodynamic solution:

The P.222.01/018, driven by a Jumo 222 E/F, was presented in three versions:

1. Fw 0310.025-501 (30 August 1944) with 35-degree swept wing at 0.25 chord, 12.6 m wingspan and MW 50 power boost for medium altitude.
2. Fw 0310.025-506 (2 October 1944) with 28-degree swept wing at 0.25 chord, 12.8 m wingspan and GM-1 power boost for high altitude, equipped with the same engine and contra-rotating propellers
3. Fw 0310.025-509 (23 November 1944) with 28-degree swept wing, 13.8 m wingspan and 13.7 m length.

P.603 No. 1 (January 1945) version reduced to 85 per cent driven by a DB 603N.

Fw 0310.035-512 (20 February 1945) version augmented to 115 per cent driven by an Argus As 413.

All projects were cancelled by Göring on 22 February 1945.

P.222.01/018 Technical Data	
Type	Single-seat interceptor fighter and high-altitude interceptor.
Engine	A Jumo 222 E/F of 24-cylinders, liquid-cooled, in 'star', with six banks of four cylinders each and 2,500 hp with two-stage supercharger, MW50 emergency power boost and GM-1 injection for altitudes above 10,000 m driving a Junkers VS 13, five-bladed pusher airscrew by means of an extension shaft in the August 1944 version and six-bladed 3.4 m diameter contraprop in the October 44 version.
Wingspan	12.60 m (August 1944)
	12.80 m (October 1944)
	12.80 m (November 1944)
Length	13.70 m (August 1944)
	14.11 m (October 1944)
	13.70 m (November 1944)
Height	4.30 m (August 1944)
	4.50m. (October 1944)

Wing area	33 sq m (October 1944)
Aspect ratio	5.0:1 (October 1944)
Max. weight	6,730 kg (October 1944)
Max. speed	805 km/h (October 1944)
Ceiling	13,900 m (October 1944)
Endurance	5.5 hours (October 1944)
Armament	One Mk 103/30 and two MG 213C/30 cannons in the nose.
Electronics	FuG 16 ZY, FuG 25, FuG 125
Cockpit	Pressurised, control heating, armoured front and rear, ejector seat.

P.603 No. 1 Technical Data

Type	Single-seat interceptor fighter.
Engine	One Daimler Benz DB 603N of 12 cylinders, inverted-V, liquid-cooled, with 2,830 hp, emergency power.
Cockpit	Pressurised, control heating, armoured front and rear, ejector seat.
Armament	One Mk 103/30 and two MG 213C/30 cannons in the nose.
Wingspan	11.00 m
Length	11.70 m
Height	3.13 m
Wing area	26 sq m
Max. weight	6,000 kg
Max. speed	703 km/h
Ceiling	12,600 m
Electronics	FuG 16 ZY, FuG 25, FuG 125

Fw 0310.035-512 Technical Data

Type	Single-seat high-altitude interceptor.
Engine	One Argus As 413, water cooled, 24 cylinders in 'H', with 4,000 hp and GM-1 power boost, driving two contra-rotating propeller by means of an extension shaft.
Cockpit	Pressurised, control heating, armoured front and rear, ejector seat.
Wingspan	15.20 m (24 degrees swept at 0.25 chord)
Length	15.35 m
Height	4.70 m
Wing area	42 sq m
Aspect ratio	5.5:1
Max. weight	10,600 kg
Endurance	3 hours
Armament	One Mk 103/30 and two MG 213C/30 cannons in the nose
Electronics	FuG 16 ZY, FuG 25, FuG 125

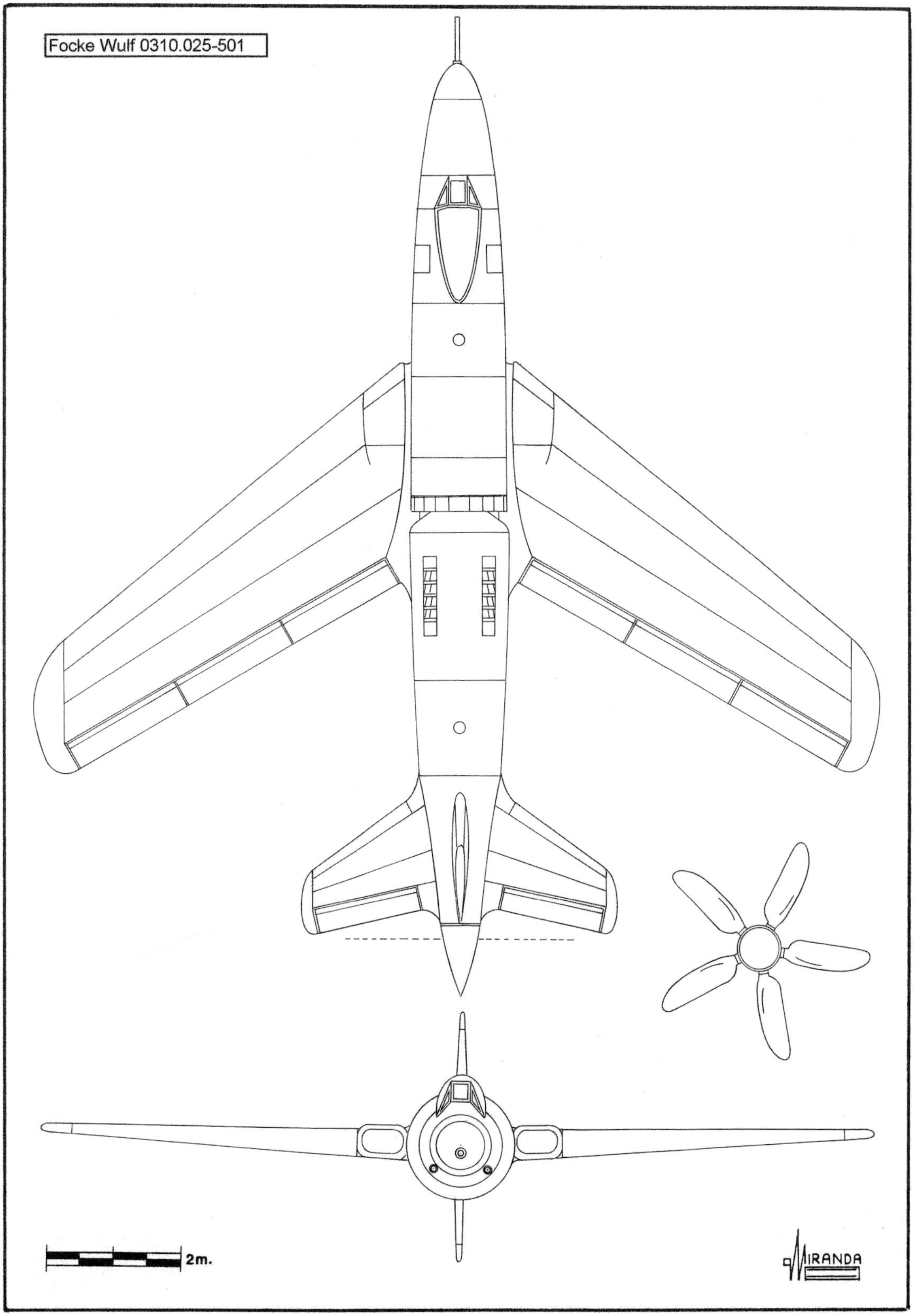
Focke Wulf 0310.025-501
2m.
MIRANDA

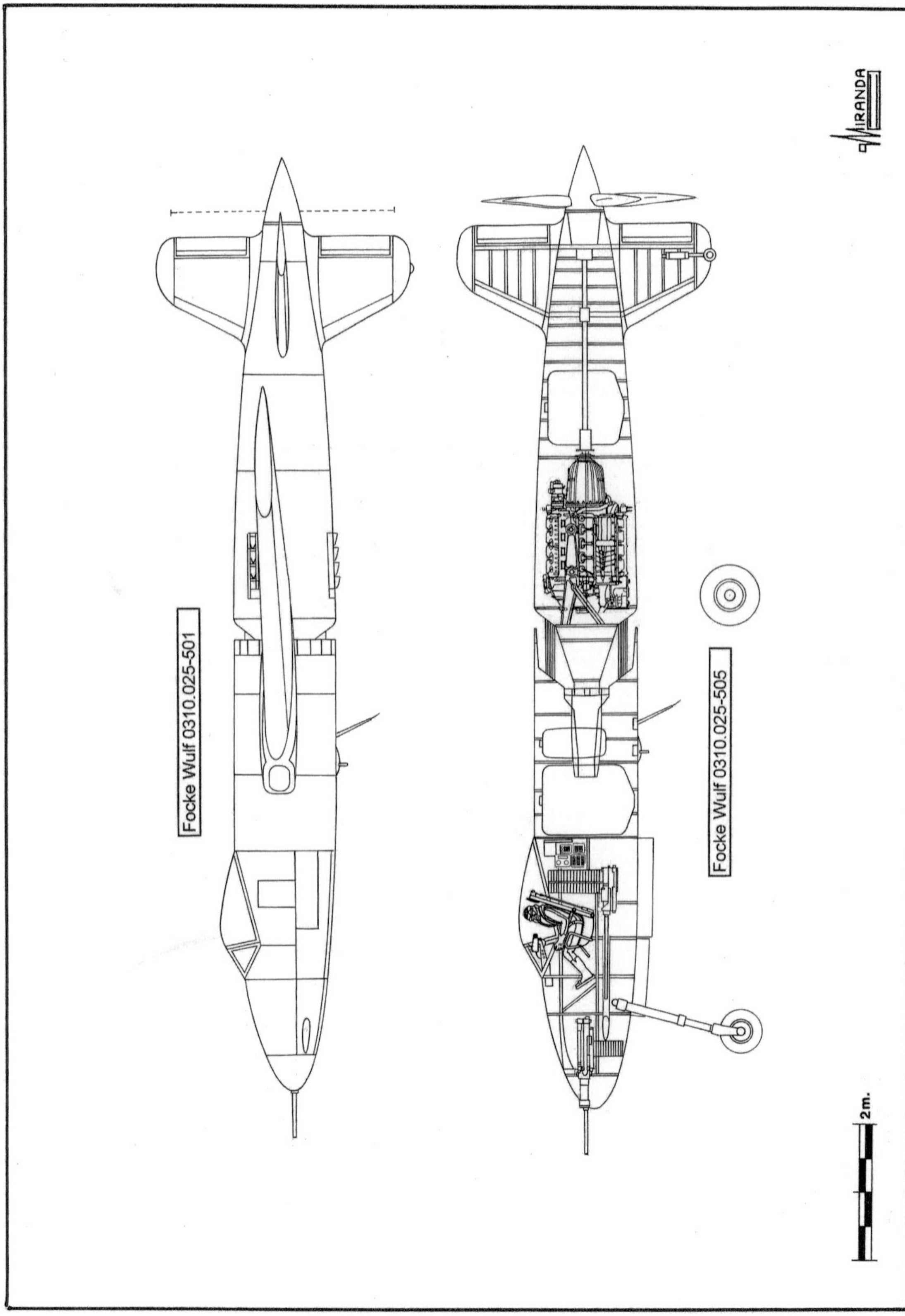
Focke Wulf 0310.025-501
Focke Wulf 0310.025-505
2 m.

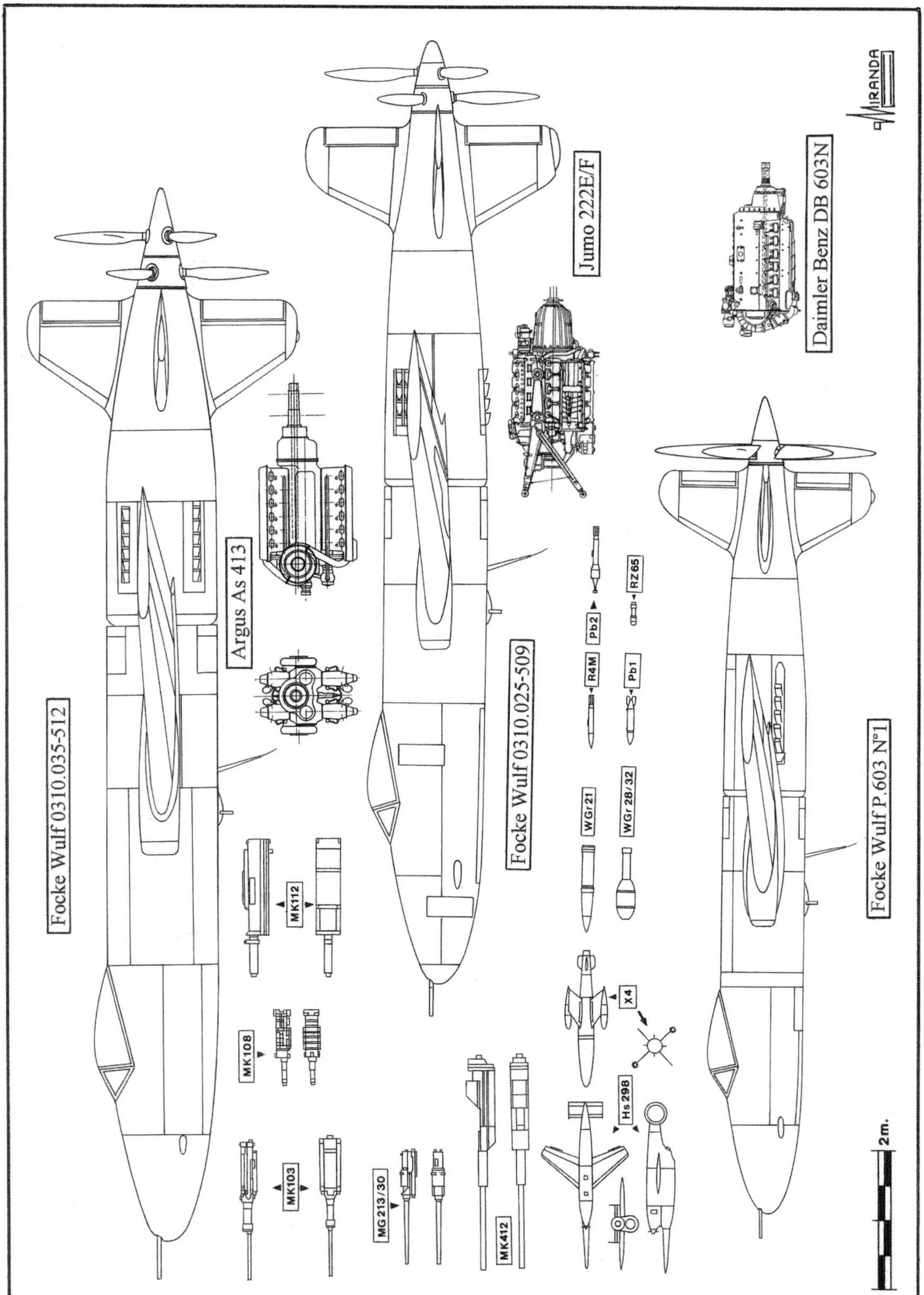
Focke Wulf 0310.035-512
Argus As 413
Focke Wulf 0310.025-509
Jumo 222E/F
Daimler Benz DB 603N
Focke Wulf P.603 N°1
MK112
MK108
MK103
MG 213/30
MK412
WGr21
WGr 28/32
R4M
Pb2
Pb1
RZ65
X4
Hs 298
2m.

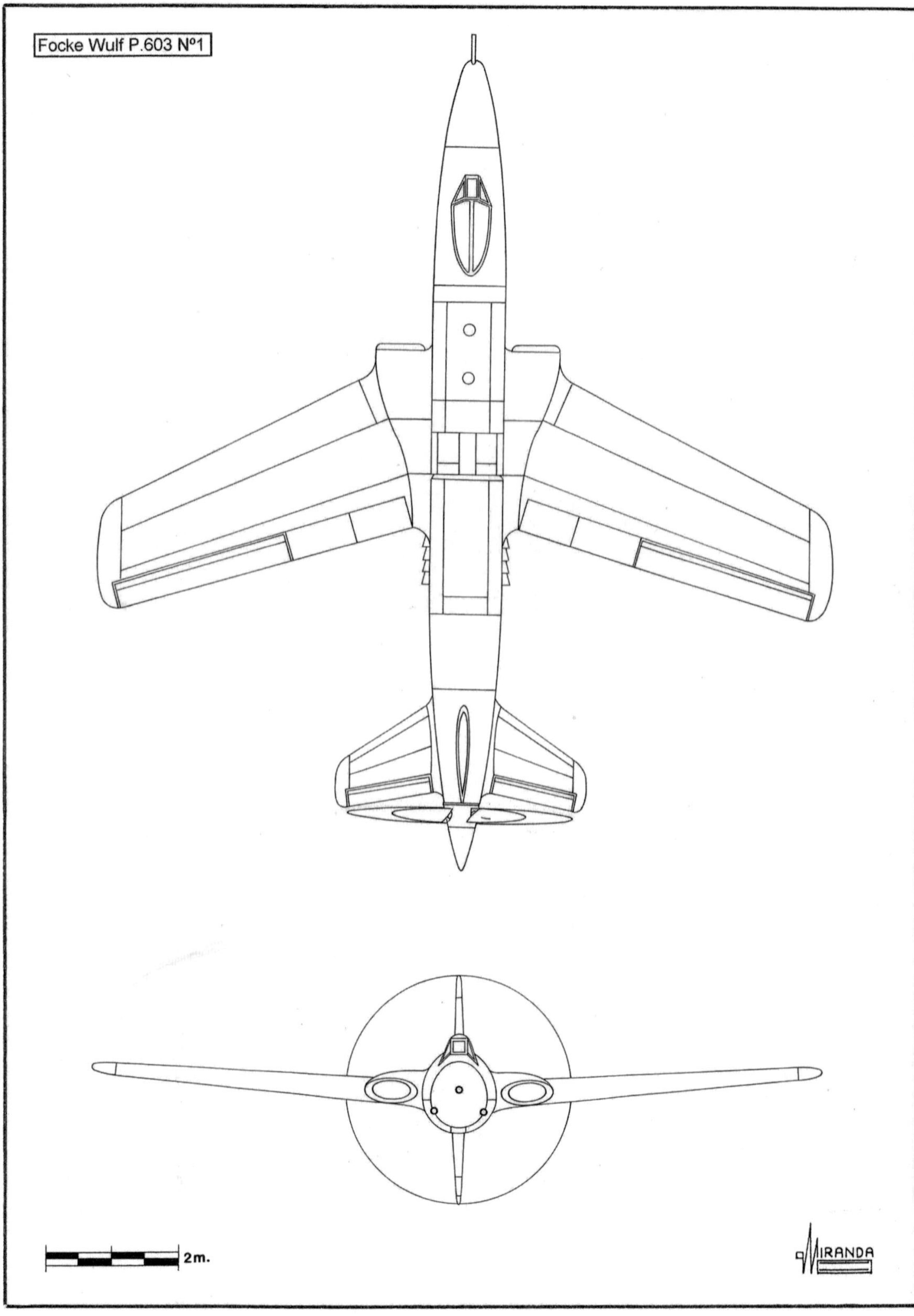
Focke Wulf P.603 Nº1
2m.
MIRANDA

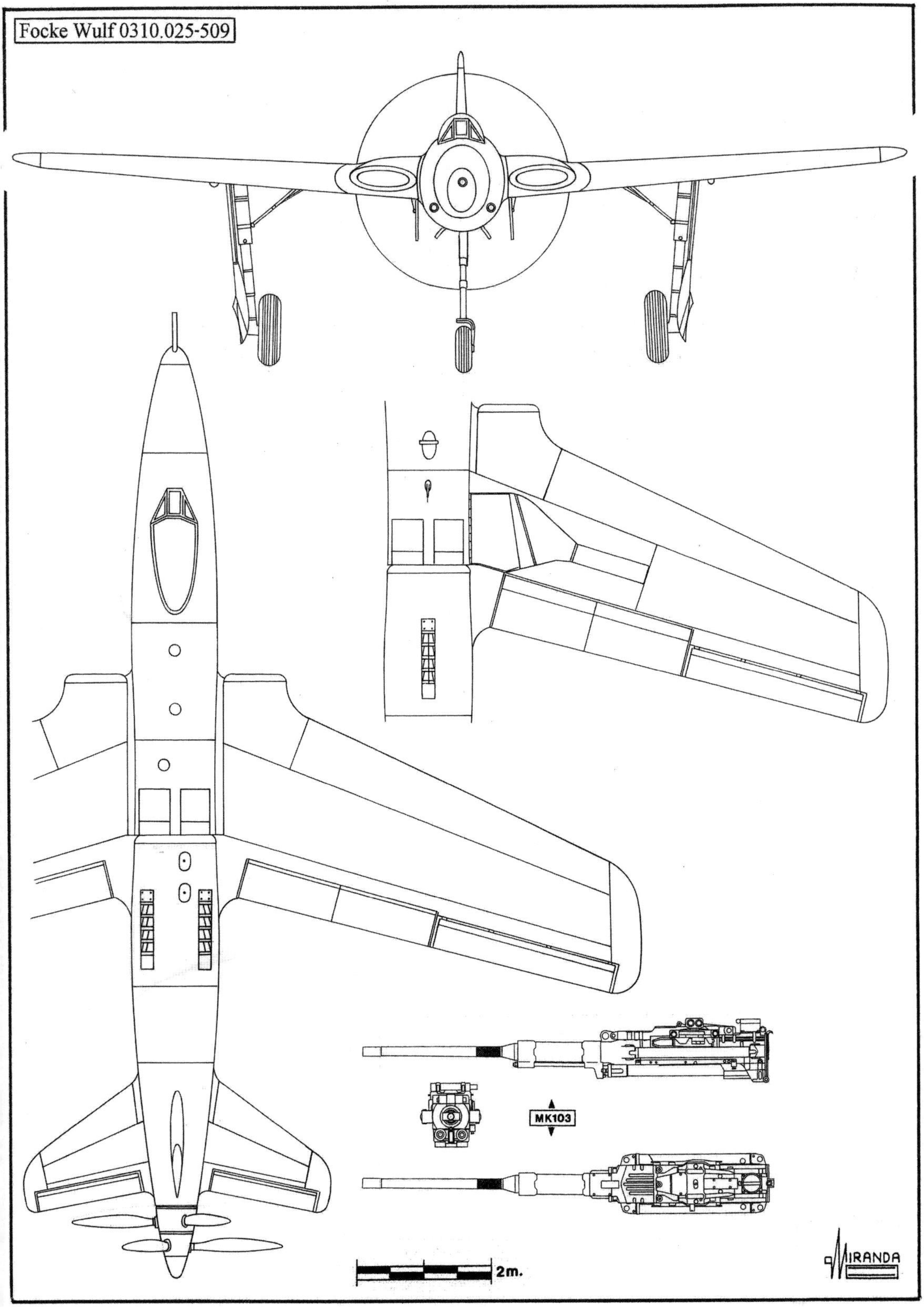
Focke Wulf 0310.025-509
MK103
2m.
MIRANDA

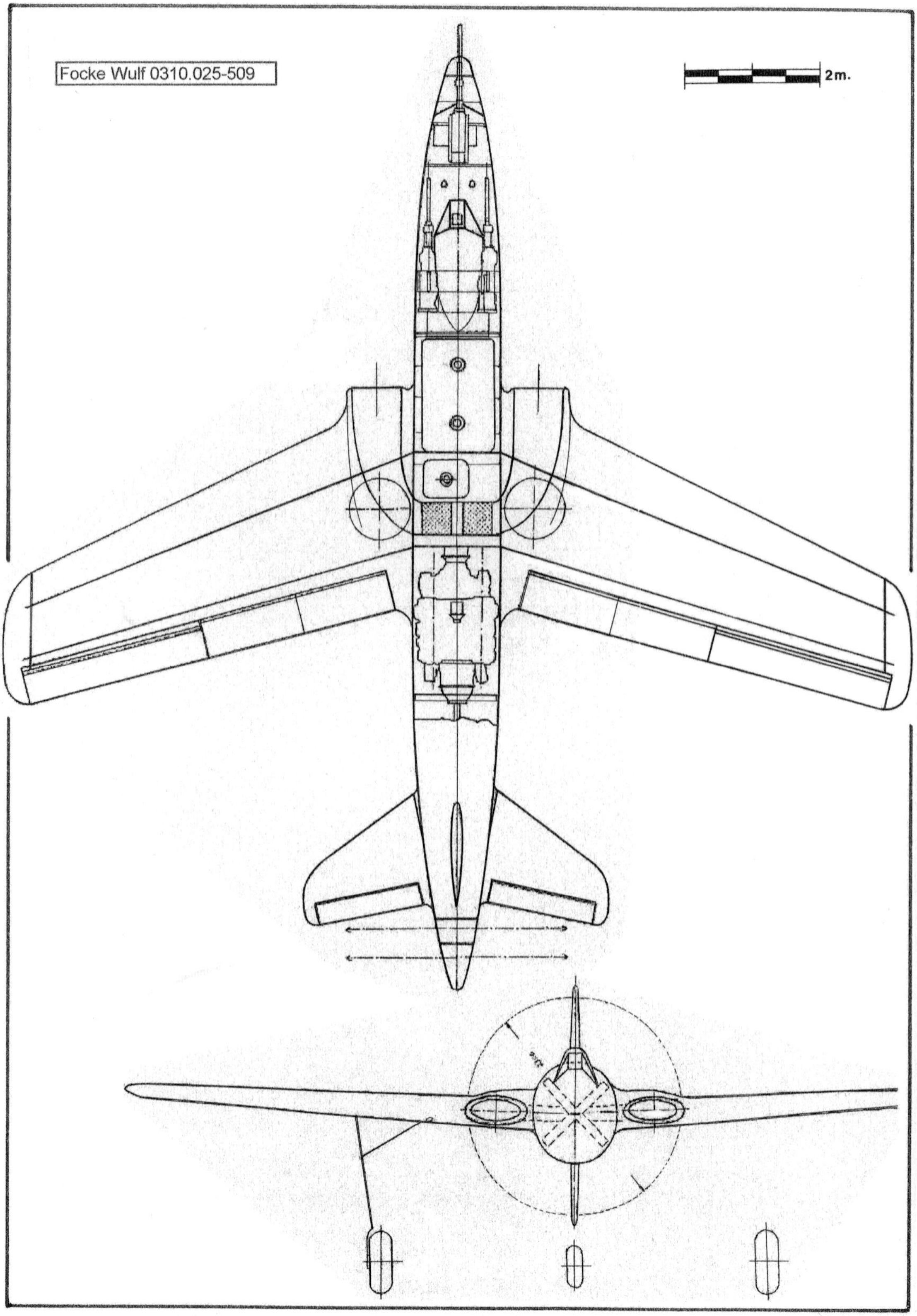
Focke Wulf 0310.025-509
2m.

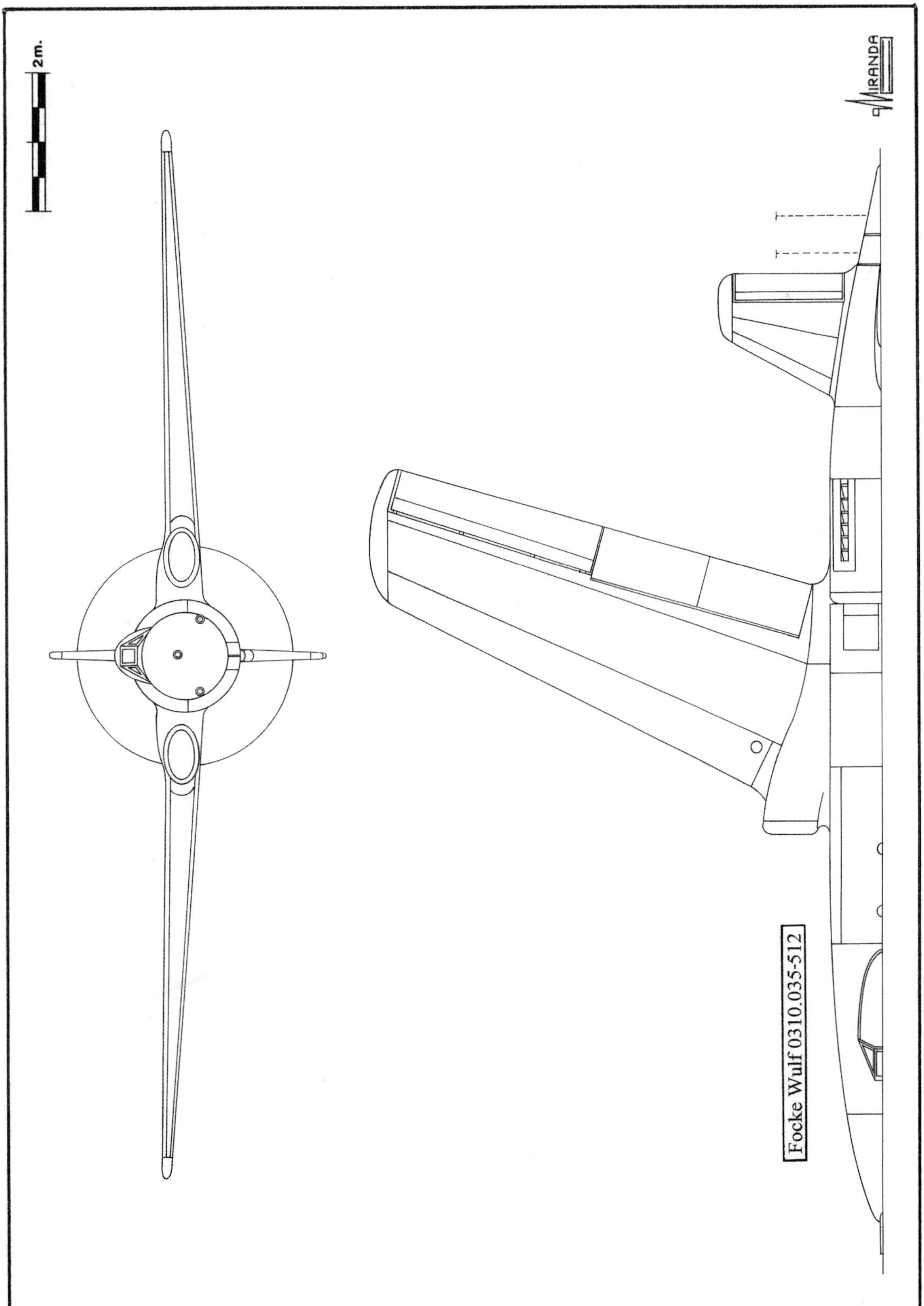
2m.
Focke Wulf 0310.035-512

Chapter 27

Focke Wulf Projekt 0310251

By the end of 1944, the design team of Kurt Tank had proposed a series of heavy night/all-weather fighters, based on the aerodynamics of the Fw P.413.002, increased to 110 per cent and 28-degree swept wing. The RLM had planned the Fw 272 designation, although, in practice, it was never applied to the project.

They were big aircraft, equipped with the FuG 244 Bremen radar and a crew of three: pilot, navigator and radar operator. The formula was similar to the one in the Dornier P.247/252, but instead of two Otto engines in tandem, it had just one for extra-long-range CAP, complemented by two turbojets in underslung wing nacelles, for take-off and combat only.

The usual uncertainty about the future availability of high-performance piston engines, gave way to three different designs, adapted to the three most promising engines in development.

- The Fw 0310251-13 (23 November 1944) would be driven by a Junkers Jumo 213 C/D (medium altitude version) with MW 50 power boost.
- The Fw 0310251-22 (2 February 1944) to be driven by a Daimler Benz DB 603N with MW 50 power boost.
- The Fw 0310251-23 (December 1944) would be driven by an Argus As 413 with GM-1 power boost.

The electronic equipment consisted of:

FuG 244 Bremen O active search radar
FuG 226 Neuling IFF discriminator
FuG 139 Barbarossa command relay equipment
FuG 130 autopilot
FuG 101a radio altimeter
FuG 24 SN R/T homing device
Fu Bl 3F radio navigation equipment
Peil G6 Ludwig direction finder device

The standard armament of 4 MK 108/30 could be complemented by another two guns in 80-degree Schräge Musik configuration, of the same type, positioned in the place usually allocated to the triangular fuel tank, between the main wheel bays. It could also fire R 100 rockets with the Oberon-Elfe system associated to the FuG 244.

The crew did not have ejector seats. Therefore, it can be assumed that there was an explosive device to detach the propeller blades in an emergency.

Fw 0310251-13 Technical Data

Type	Heavy all-weather fighter.
Cockpit	Three-seat, pressurised, control heating, armoured windscreen.
Engine	A Jumo 222 C/D of 24 cylinders, liquid cooled, star, with six banks of four cylinders each and 3,000 hp, driving a single 3.4 m diameter 2 x 3 blades contra-rotating propeller by means of an extension shaft and two BMW 003 A-1 turbojets with 800 kg thrust each.
Armament	Four Mk 103/30 guns in the nose.
Wingspan	21 m
Length	16.55 m
Wing area	55 sq m
Max. weight	14,000 kg
Max. speed	880 km/h
Service veiling	14,000 m
Endurance	8 hours

Fw 0310251-22 Technical Data

Type	Heavy night fighter.
Cockpit	Three-seat, pressurised, control heating, armoured windscreen.
Engine	One Daimler Benz DB 603N of 12 cylinders, inverted-V, liquid-cooled, with 2,830 hp emergency power driving a single 3.4 m diameter four-bladed propeller by means of a 4.40 m extension shaft and two BMW 003 A-1 turbojets with 800 kg thrust each
Armament	Four Mk 103/30 guns in the nose.
Wingspan	20.40 m
Length	16.60 m
Height	4.65 m
Wing area	52 sq m
Max. weight	13,000 kg
Max. speed	848 km/h
Service veiling	13,400 m

Fw 0310251-123 Technical Data

Type	Heavy night fighter.
Cockpit	Three-seat, pressurised, control heating, armoured windscreen.
Engine	One Argus As 413 of 24 cylinders, water cooled, with 4,000 hp driving a single 3.10 m diameter 2 x 3 blades, contra-props by means of an extension shaft and two BMW 003 A-1 turbojets with 800 kg thrust each.
Armament	Four Mk 103/30 guns in the nose.
Wingspan	22.80 m
Length	16.75 m

Height	5.10 m
Wing area	65 sq m
Max. weight	19,000 kg
Max. speed	850 km/h
Service veiling	13,000 m

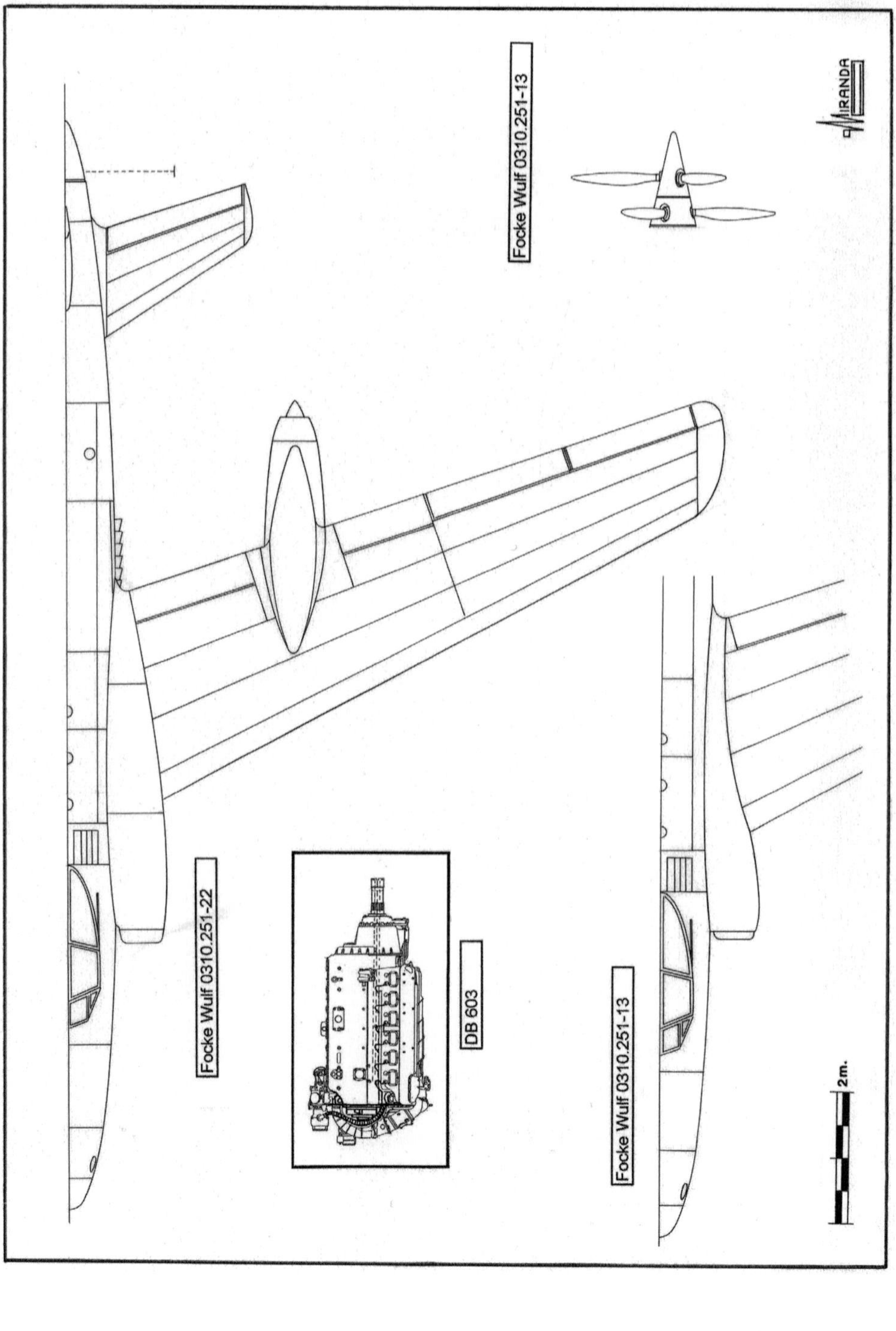

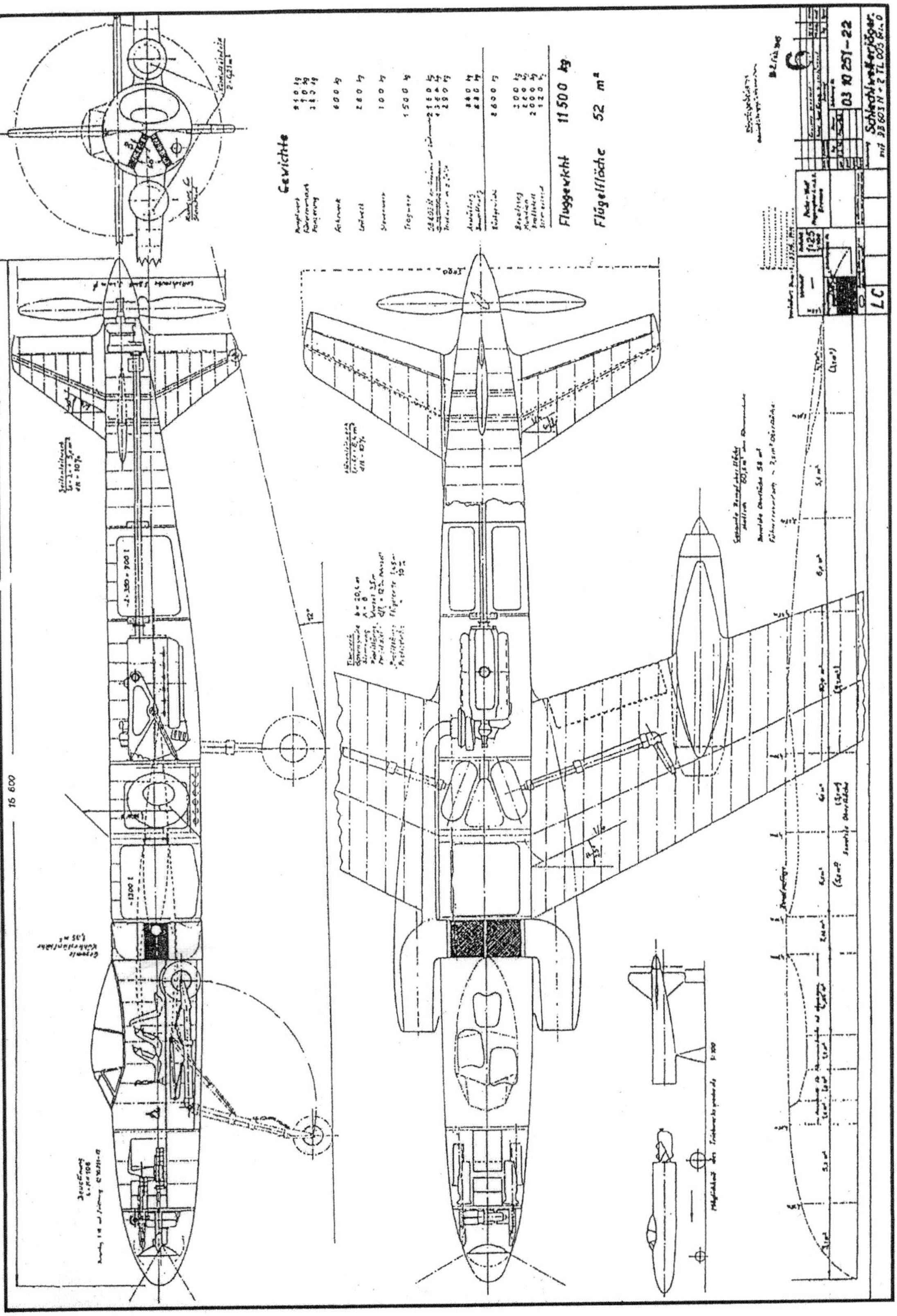
Gewichte
Fluggewicht 11 500 kg
Flügelfläche 52 m²
03 10 251-22
15 600

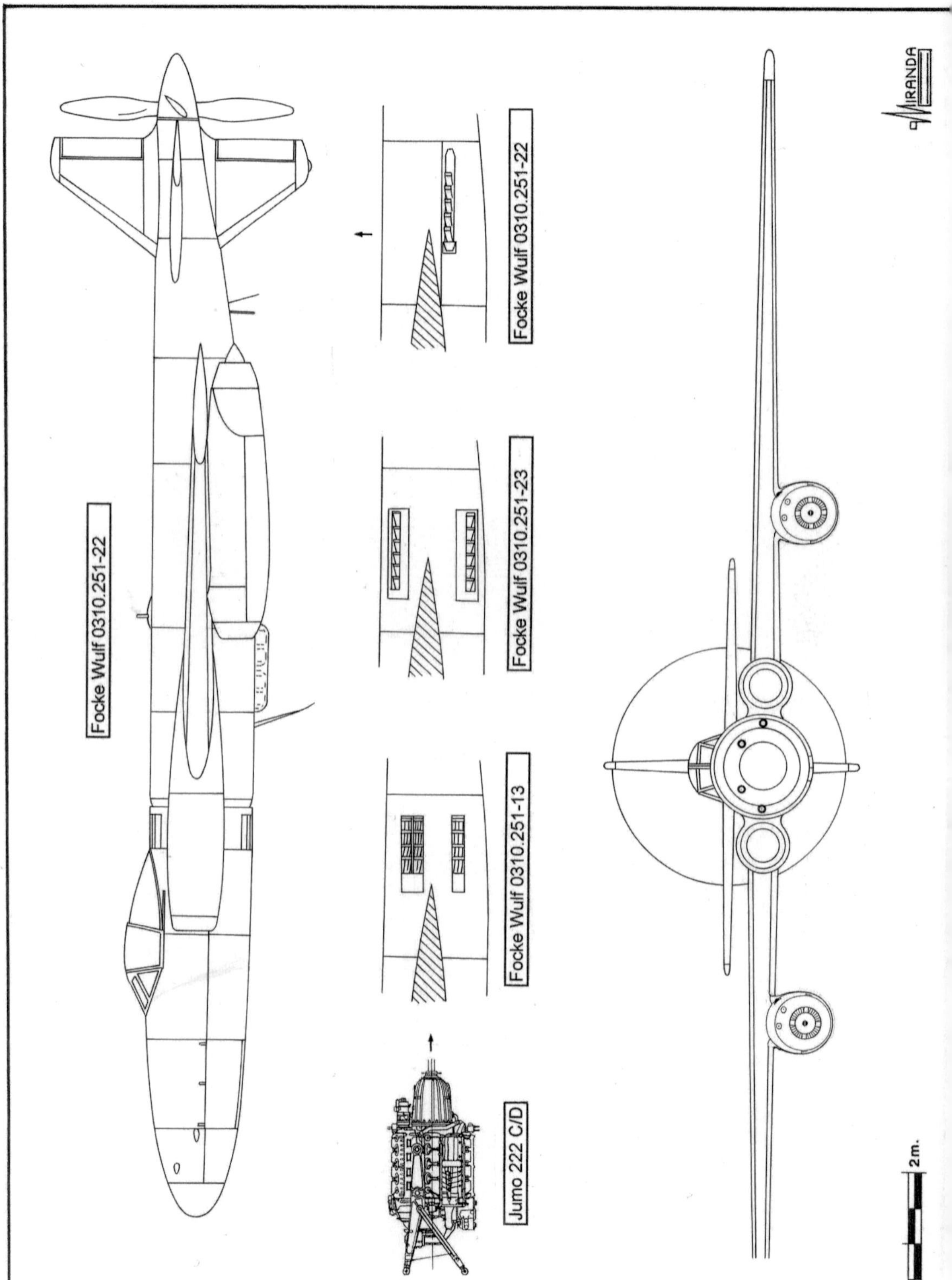
Focke Wulf 0310.251-22
Focke Wulf 0310.251-22
Focke Wulf 0310.251-23
Focke Wulf 0310.251-13
Jumo 222 C/D
MIRANDA
2m.

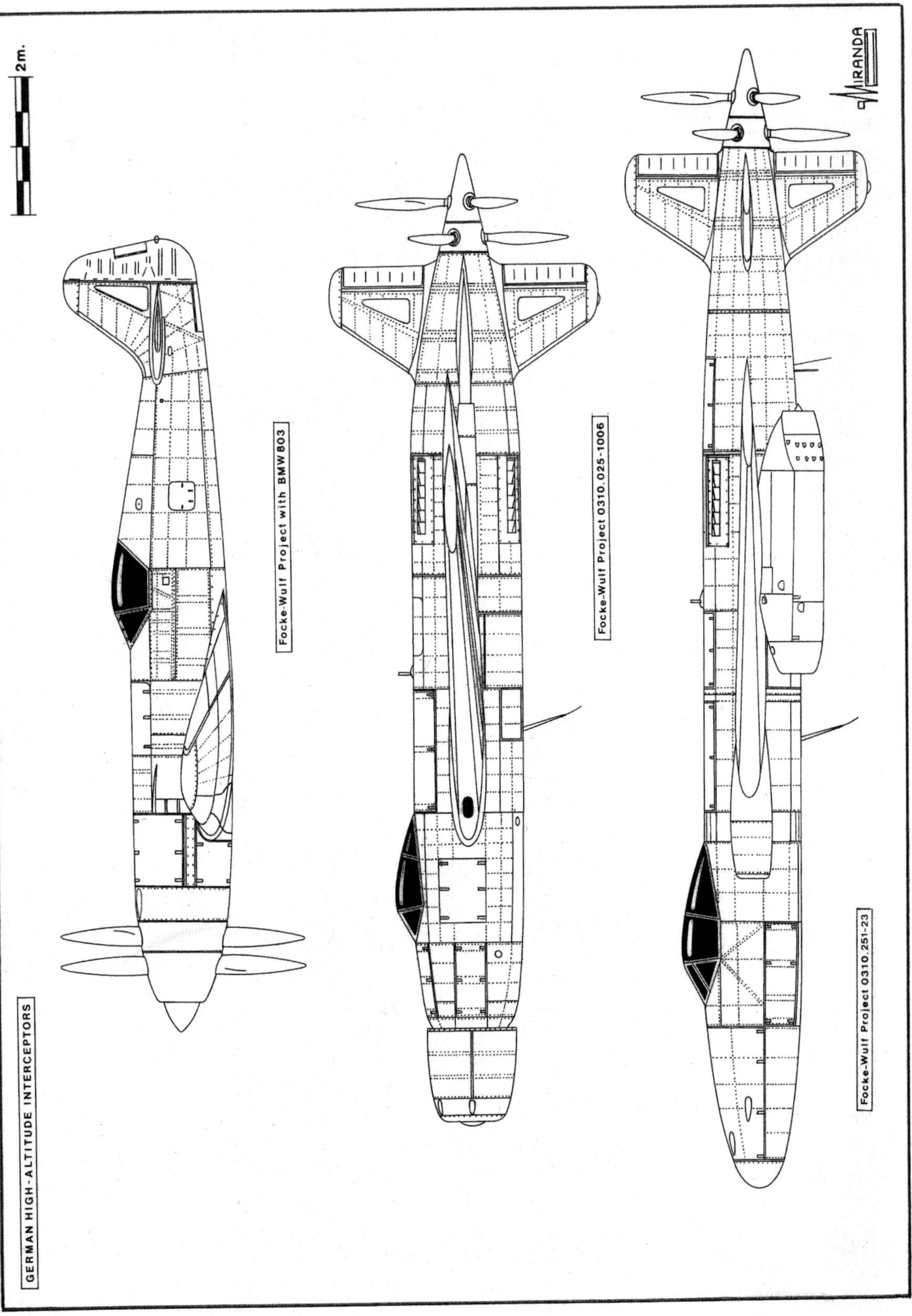
2m.
MIRANDA
Focke-Wulf Project with BMW803
Focke-Wulf Project 0310.025-1006
Focke-Wulf Project 0310.251-23
GERMAN HIGH-ALTITUDE INTERCEPTORS

Chapter 28

Heinkel He P.1076

In 1935's contest for future fighter airplanes of the Luftwaffe, the Heinkel He 112 lost against the Messerschmitt Bf 109 because of its elliptic wing, more difficult to manufacture.

In 1937, in an effort to remain in the contest, Dr Heinkel promised to General Luftzeugmeister Udet that he would be able to manufacture a fighter that, propelled by a Daimler Benz DB 601, would be capable of reaching 700 km/h.

Although Udet considered it impossible, the project – named Heinkel P1035 – began on 25 May 1937. The design team, led by Siegfried Günter, had the streamlining and drag reduction as the main guidelines. They adopted a well-faired cockpit, a fully-retractable tail wheel and a stressed-skin wing covering, reducing the number of Butter rivets.

The DB 601 engine had exhaust ejectors for a small amount of thrust and the supercharger inlet was moved from the side of the cowling to a location under the propeller hub. The frontal radiator was replaced by a surface cooling system, inspired by the Macchi seaplane racers, which was already being tested on the He 119 V1.

Steam at high temperature was separated from the cooling fluid coming from the engine, using a centrifugal compressor and an expansion chamber. The heat exchangers, located in the wings, had a total capacity of 345 litres and transferred the heat outside through the light alloy stressed covering. The steam was then condensed into liquid by cooling and returned to the engine circuit by means of twenty-two electric driven centrifugal pumps.

A similar system was designed to refrigerate the oil, by passing it through a heat exchanger where methyl alcohol was added. The resulting vapour was then ducted to the tail surfaces, where it was to be condensed back to liquid form before returning to the heat exchanger.

By the end of October the project was presented to the Technisches Amt of the Luftwaffe, receiving number type He 100.

During the flight tests of the first prototype, it turned out that the wing suffered a structural distortion, caused by the high temperatures. It was also confirmed that the oil cooling system did not work at all.

The second prototype had a reinforced wing cladding and was equipped with a retractable auxiliary cooler for the ground running and another, on the port wing root, for the oil.

More prototypes and a short preproduction series were built and the He 100 achieved several speed records. But its little reliable cooling system – which made it very vulnerable in combat – together with its maintenance problems and the lack of DB 601 engines, advised against its mass production, foreseen for 1939.

However, Ernst Heinkel tried it again, following the RLM specifications for a piston-engined fighter which was to combine speed and high-altitude performance.

By the end of 1944, the team of Siegfried Günter started to work on the P1076, possibly the fastest airplane of its class ever designed. Based on the He 100, a more sophisticated version of the surface-cooling technology was adopted, where the steam circulated within the double layer of stressed-skin covering that integrated the wings, the engine cowling, the rear fuselage and the tailfin. The centrifugal compressor and the expansion chamber were located at the rear of the fuselage.

The design of the wings was very advanced for its time, with a perfectly smooth surface, and slightly swept forward at 8 degrees, constructed as a two piece, two spar, all metal structure. The section between the spars housed the condensation deposits of the heat exchangers, the electric driven centrifugal pumps, the main undercarriage and two Mk 108/30 cannon and ammo tanks. Flaps and ailerons spanned the entire trailing edge, with the outermost as ailerons and the inside ones as landing flaps.

The armoured cockpit was pressurised for high-altitude flying and covered with a clear vision bubble canopy that was hinged to the port side. The 700 litres fuel tank was located behind the pilot seat. The tail wheel was fully retractable.

To facilitate its cooling on both sides, the tailfin was designed with a 0 degrees angle to the fuselage axis. As a consequence, all the installed engines had to be fitted with counter-rotating three-blade VDM propellers. The P.1076 was projected in four different versions, to adjust to the new 2,000 hp class engines that were expected to be available in 1945.

The P.1076/I was designed as a competitor of the Bf 109 K-14. Equipped with a DB 603 M, it would have been faster and climbed to higher altitude, carrying heavier armament.

The P.1076/II, fitted with a Jumo 213, should reach similar performances. Its production was to compete against the Fw 190 D-9, to which could have equally exceeded in armament, maximum speed and ceiling.

The P.1076/III was designed as a competitor of the Fw Ta 152 H. Equipped with a DB 603N and a wingspan expanded to 12.40 m, it would have been a formidable high-altitude interceptor, so fast and well armed as the Me 262, but with a superior ceiling.

The design of a V16 variant of the DB 603, known as DB 609, was started in September 1942. It had a 16-cylinder and 2,500 hp engine, the prototype of which showed serious problems of vibration, when tested in the Focke Wulf 190 V19, due to the excessive length of the crankshaft.

The expectation was that the DB 609, with two-stage twin supercharger, integrated heat exchanger cooler and contra-rotating three-blade VDM propellers, would reach the 3,400 hp at a ceiling of 12,000 m, but the vibration issue could not be solved and the program was cancelled in 1943. From some drawings of the time can be inferred that the purpose was to install it on the P.1076. The version III, with increased span, would possibly serve to compensate the lengthier engine. The new airplane would have had a length of 9.86m and a central armament of 55 mm Mk 112B, Mk 214 or Mk 412.

He P.1076/I Technical Data	
Engine	A Daimler Benz DB 603M, twin supercharged, with take-off power of 1,825 hp and 2,100 hp with MW50 injection boost.
Wingspan	11 m
Length	9.60 m
Sweep	-8 degrees at 0.25 chord
Wing area	18.00 sq m
Height	2.90 m
Max. weight	3,260 kg
Max. speed	860 km/h at 11,000 m
Rate of climb	17.2 m/sec at 9,000 m
Service ceiling	14,500 m
Max. range	1,340 km.
Landing speed	167 km/h
Armament	One Mk 103/30 engine mounted cannon plus two Mk 108/30 wing mounted cannon.

He P.1076/II Technical Data	
Engine	A Junkers Jumo 213 E, two-stage, three-speed supercharger with take-off power of 1,750 hp and 2,100 hp with MW50 injection boost.
Wingspan	11 m
Length	9.64 m
Sweep	-8 degrees at 0.25 chord
Wing area	18.00 sq m
Height	2.90 m
Max. weight	4,480 kg
Max. speed	860 km/h at 11,000 m
Rate of climb	17.2 m/sec at 9,000 m
Service ceiling	14,500 m
Max. range	1,340 km
Landing speed	167 km/h
Armament	One Mk 103/30 engine mounted cannon plus two Mk 108/30 wing mounted cannon.

He P.1076/III Technical Data	
Engine	A Daimler Benz DB 603N, with two-stage twin supercharger, integrated heat exchanger cooler and contra-rotating three-blade VDM propellers. Take-off power of 2,750 hp and 1,500 hp at 9,200 m.

Wingspan	12.40 m
Length	9.60 m
Sweep	-8 degrees at 0.25 chord
Height	2.90 m
Max. weight	5,230 kg
Max. speed	880 km/h at 11,000 m
Armament	One Mk 103/30 engine mounted cannon plus two Mk 108/30 wing mounted cannon.

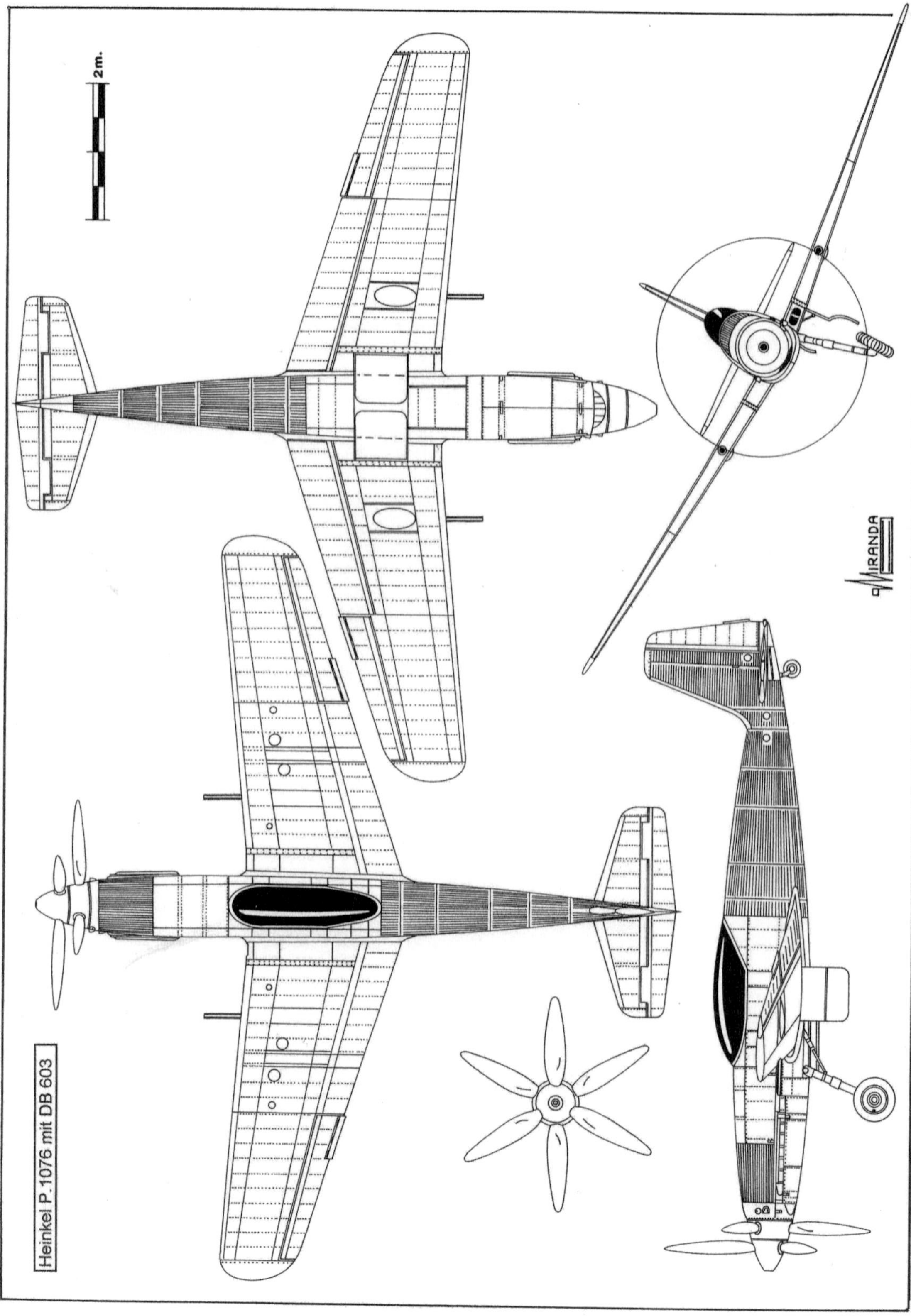
2m.
Heinkel P.1076 mit DB 603
MIRANDA

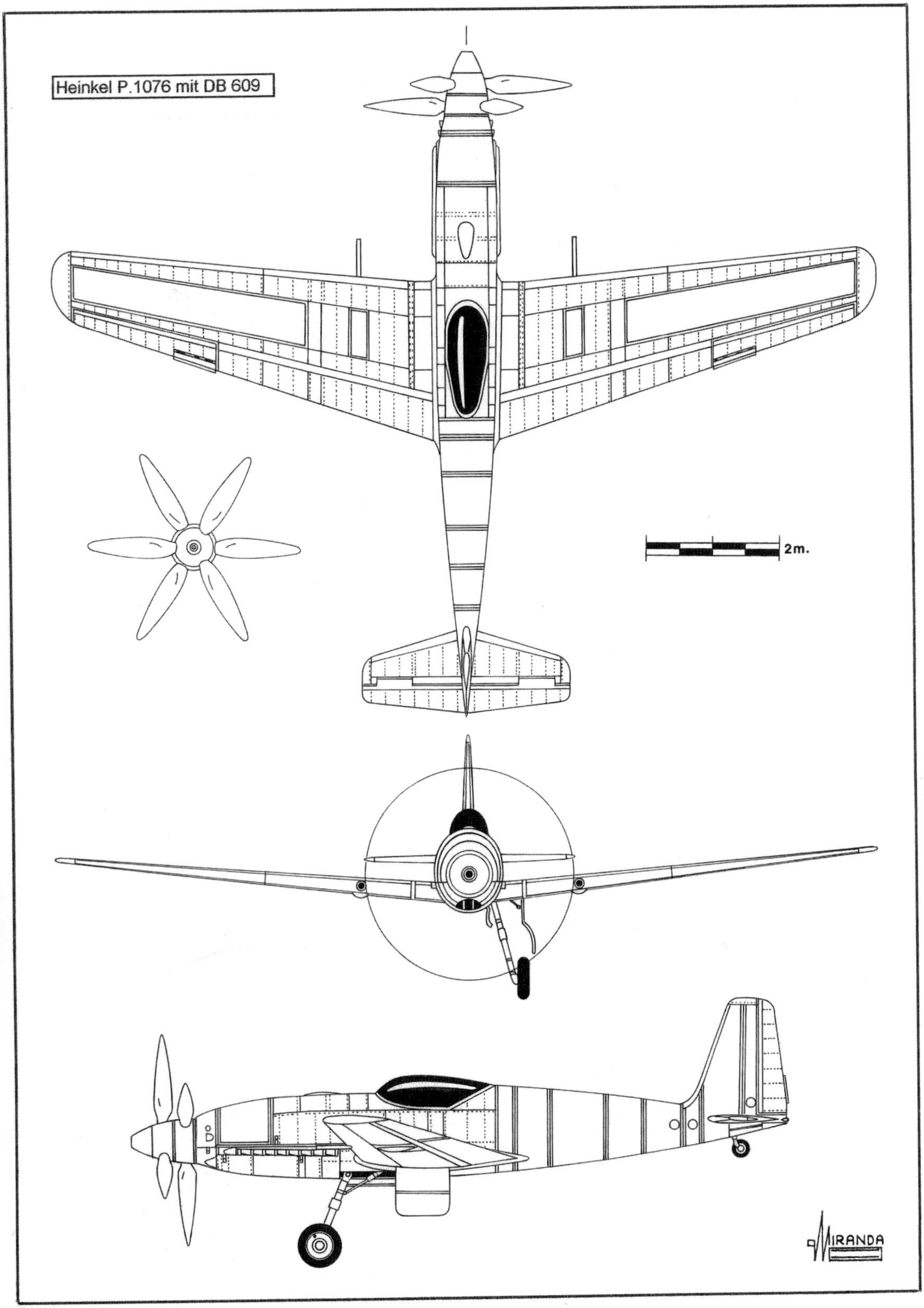
Heinkel P.1076 mit DB 609
2m.
MIRANDA

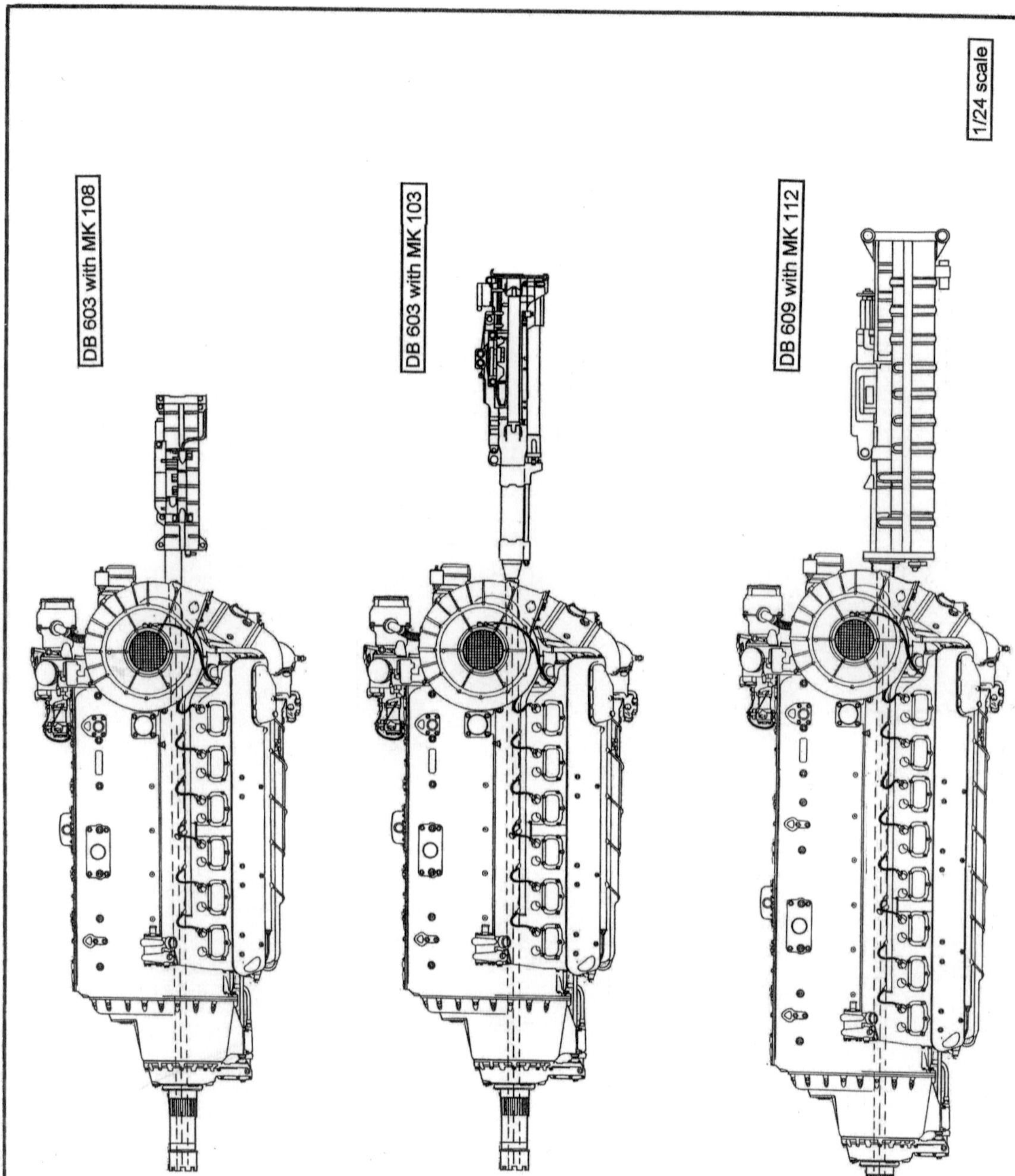
1/24 scale
DB 603 with MK 108
DB 603 with MK 103
DB 609 with MK 112
MIRANDA

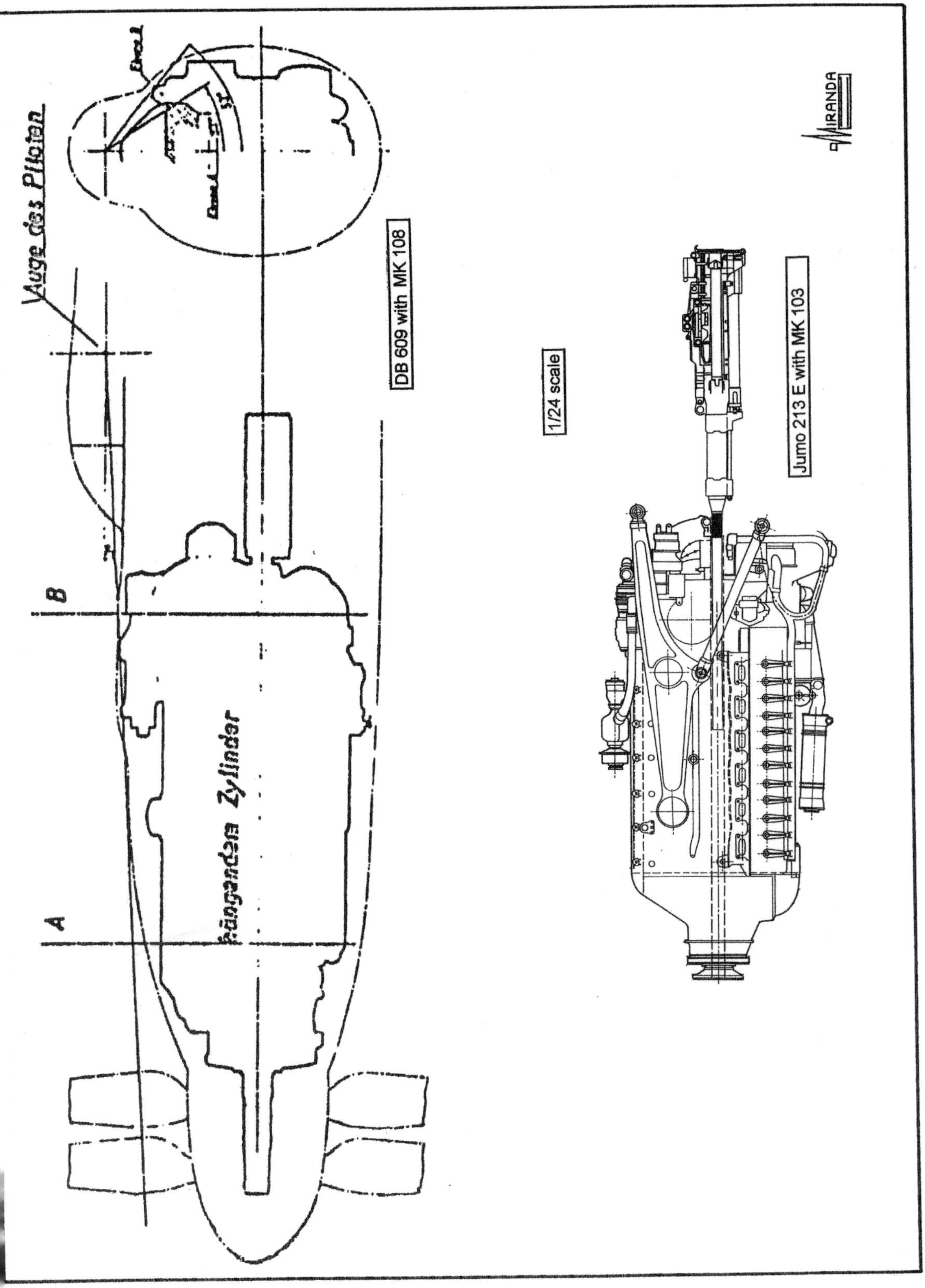
Auge des Piloten
DB 609 with MK 108
1/24 scale
Jumo 213 E with MK 103
B
A
hängenden Zylinder

Chapter 29

Henschel P.75

Designed in 1941 to replace the Messerschmitt Bf 110 applying the 'canard' formula, the most advanced at that time. The canard was also used for the S.A.I. S.S.4 fighter in Italy, for the Kyushu J7W1 Shinden in Japan, and for the Curtis XP.55 'Ascender' and Lockheed L-133 in USA.

With this new configuration the designers tried to elude the problem of compressibility buffeting by installing the wing behind the centre of gravity.

The system had the advantages of allowing the installation of the armament in the nose and improving the pilot visibility.

The downside was that the pusher configuration required the installation of an ejector seat or a detaching system for the propeller blades, to abandon the airplane during flight in an emergency.

The P. 75 was originally designed around the DB 610 power plant. However due to the bad results rendered by this engine during its service career with the He 177 bomber, it was necessary to adapt the project to the new DB 613 (of bigger size) in 1942. This engine was formed by two coupled DB 603 driving two contra-rotating propellers via an extension shaft.

Technical Data	
Type	Canard-pusher heavy fighter.
Engine	One Daimler Benz DB 613 A/B liquid-cooled, 24 cylinders coupled engine with 3500 hp and contra-rotating propellers of 3.2 m of diameter.
Fuel tanks	Two in the wings and one in the fuselage behind the pilot.
Armament	Four 30 mm Mk 108 cannon in the nose.
Equipment	Pressurised cockpit, ejector seat.
Wingspan	11.3 m
Length	12.2 m
Height	3.96 m
Wing area	28.4 sq m
Max. weight	7,500 kg
Max. speed	790 km/h at 7000 m
Service ceiling	12,000 m

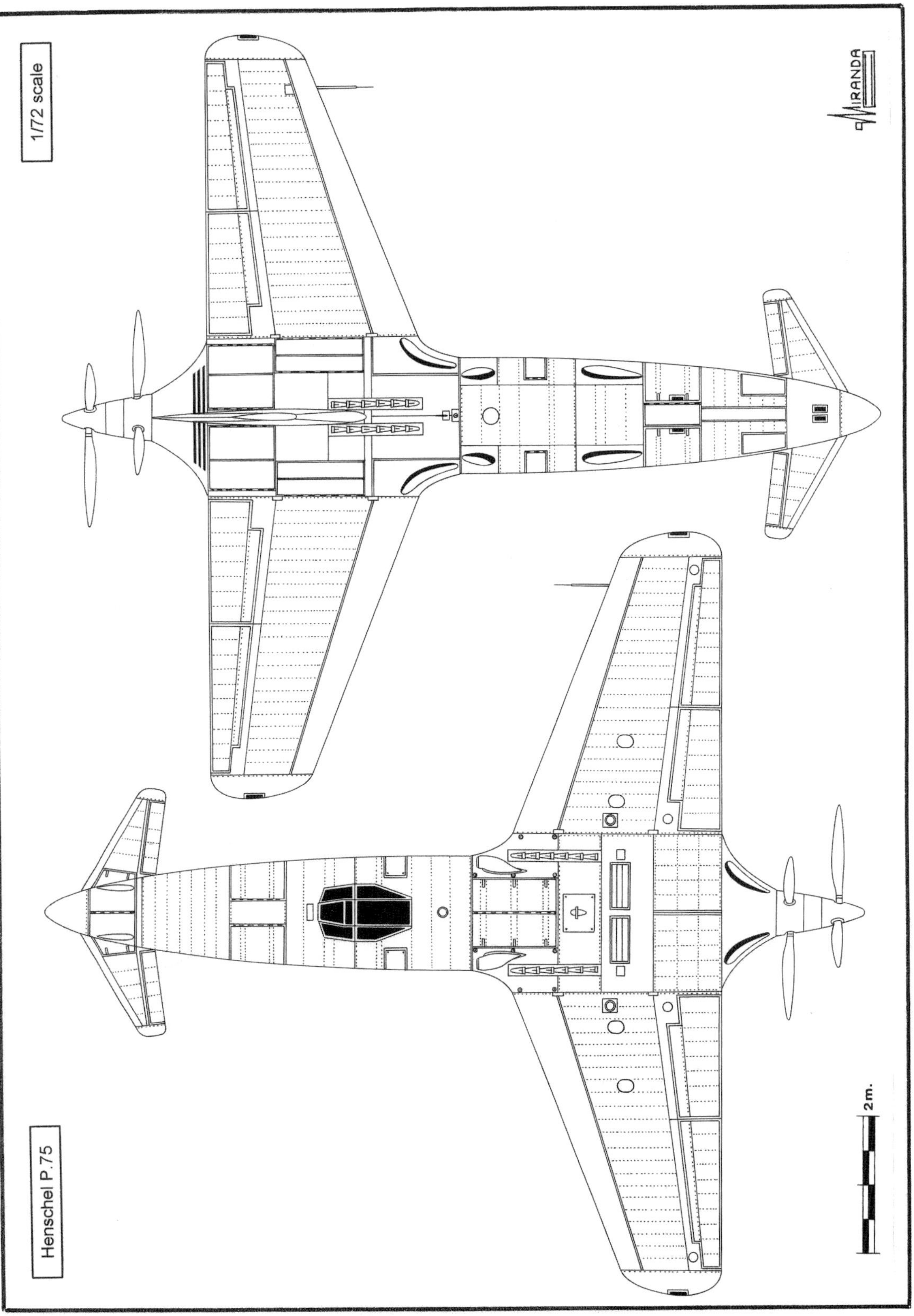
1/72 scale
Henschel P.75
MIRANDA
2m.

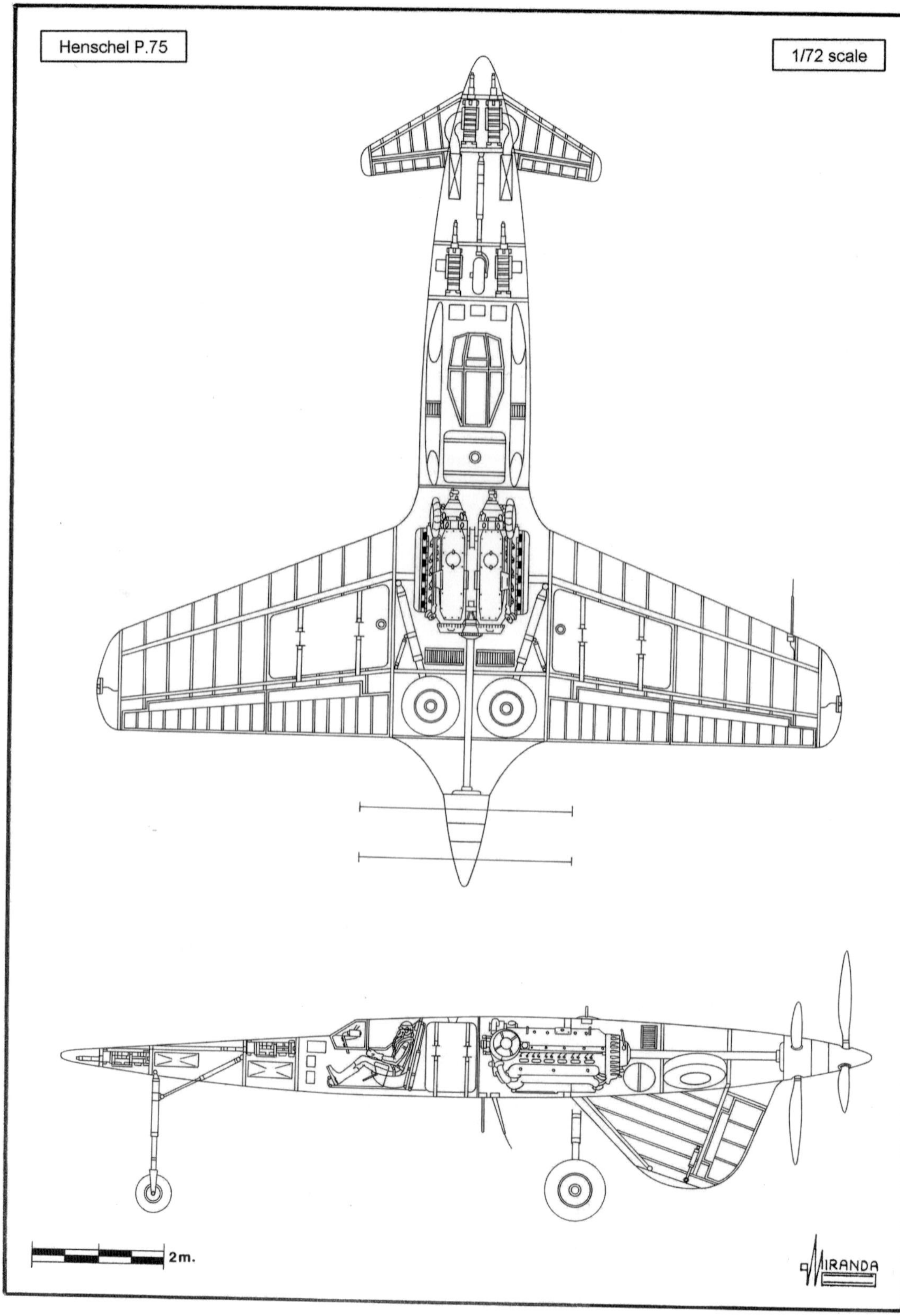
Henschel P.75
1/72 scale
2 m.
MIRANDA

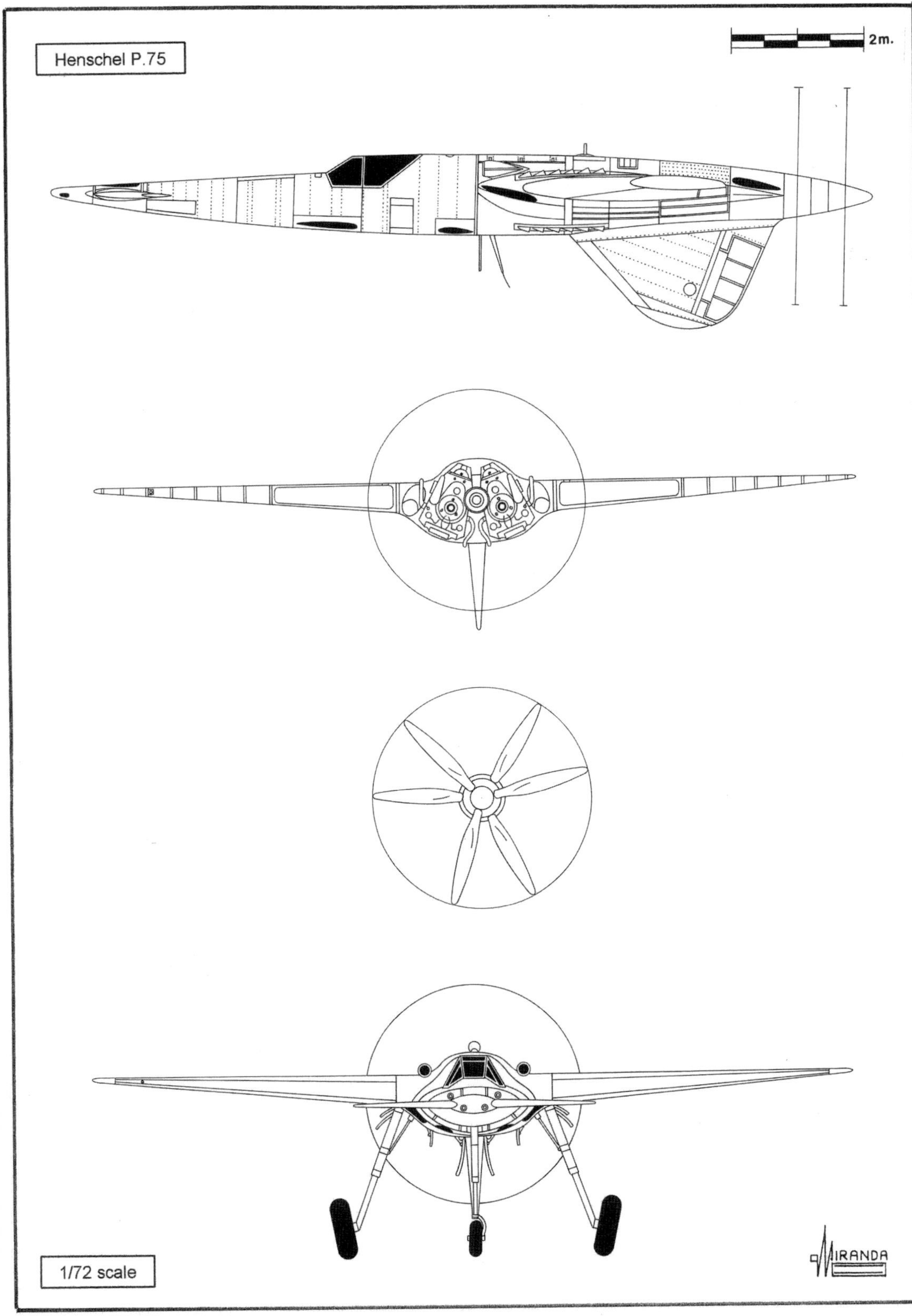
Henschel P.75
2m.
1/72 scale
MIRANDA

Chapter 30

Henschel P. 130

The interest of the Henschel firm in tail-less airplanes was initiated at the end of 1943, during their cooperation with Dr Alexander Lippisch on the design of the Delta VI.

In 1944, the team led by Dipl. Ing. Nicolaus proposed the building of the P.130, a tail-less heavy fighter powered by a DB 603 pusher engine that was expected to achieve a higher performance.

On 15 March 1945, the P.130 was modified to be powered by a HeS 011A turbojet, under the denomination P.135. As there was no hope of obtaining turbojets, the project underwent a final modification to install a Walter HWK 509C rocket engine.

Technical Data	
Type	Single-seat interceptor fighter.
Wings	Built of wood, in five sections, with a double cranked leading edge and 42-degree/38-degree/15-degree compound sweep. It had leading edge slats to improve stall characteristics and split flaps ahead of the rudders. Inner rudders acted as ailerons and outboard rudders as elevons. Thickness of 12 per cent at the root and 10 per cent outboard.
Fuselage	Light alloy structure, housing the armament, undercarriage, fuel tanks and engine.
Cockpit	Pressurised, control heating, frontal armour against 12.7 mm shelling and from the rear against 20 mm, Heinkel kartusche ejector seat.
Tailfin	Light alloy structure and cladding.
Undercarriage	Tricycle type, nosewheel would have retracted to the rear, rotating 90 degrees to lie flat in the wheel bay. The main wheels retracted forward into the fuselage
Engine	A Daimler Benz DB 603 of 1,900 hp, twelve-cylinder, inverted-V, liquid cooled engine, driving a 3 m diameter pusher propeller through an extension shaft.
Fuel tank	Two, behind and under the cockpit.
Armament	Four Mk 108/30 cannons in the nose.
Electronics	EZ 42 gyrogunsight, FuG 16ZY VHF transmitter/receiver, FuG 25a IFF radio set.
Wingspan	9.2 m
Length	9 m
Height	4.3 m
Wing area	20 sq m

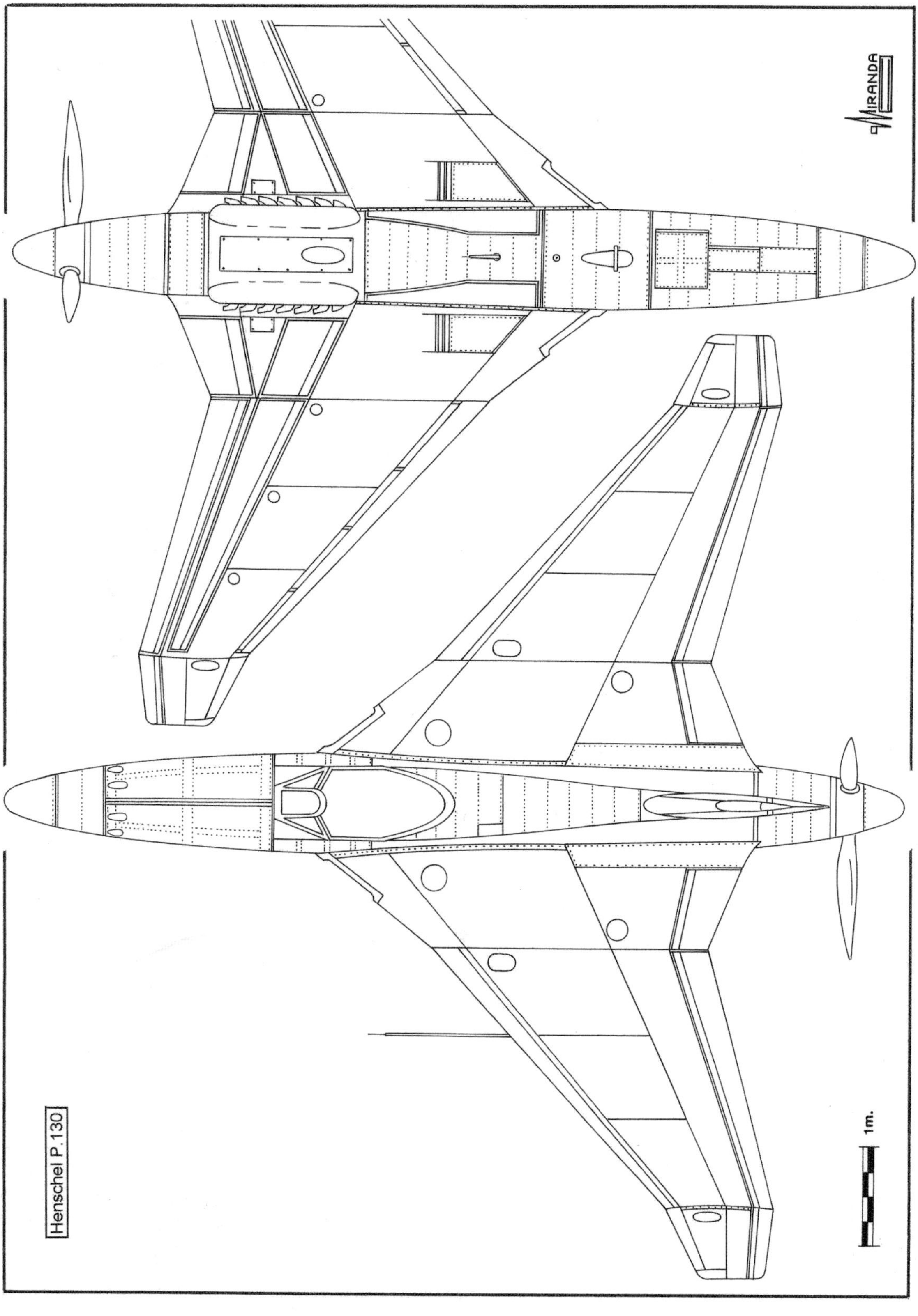
Henschel P.130
1m.

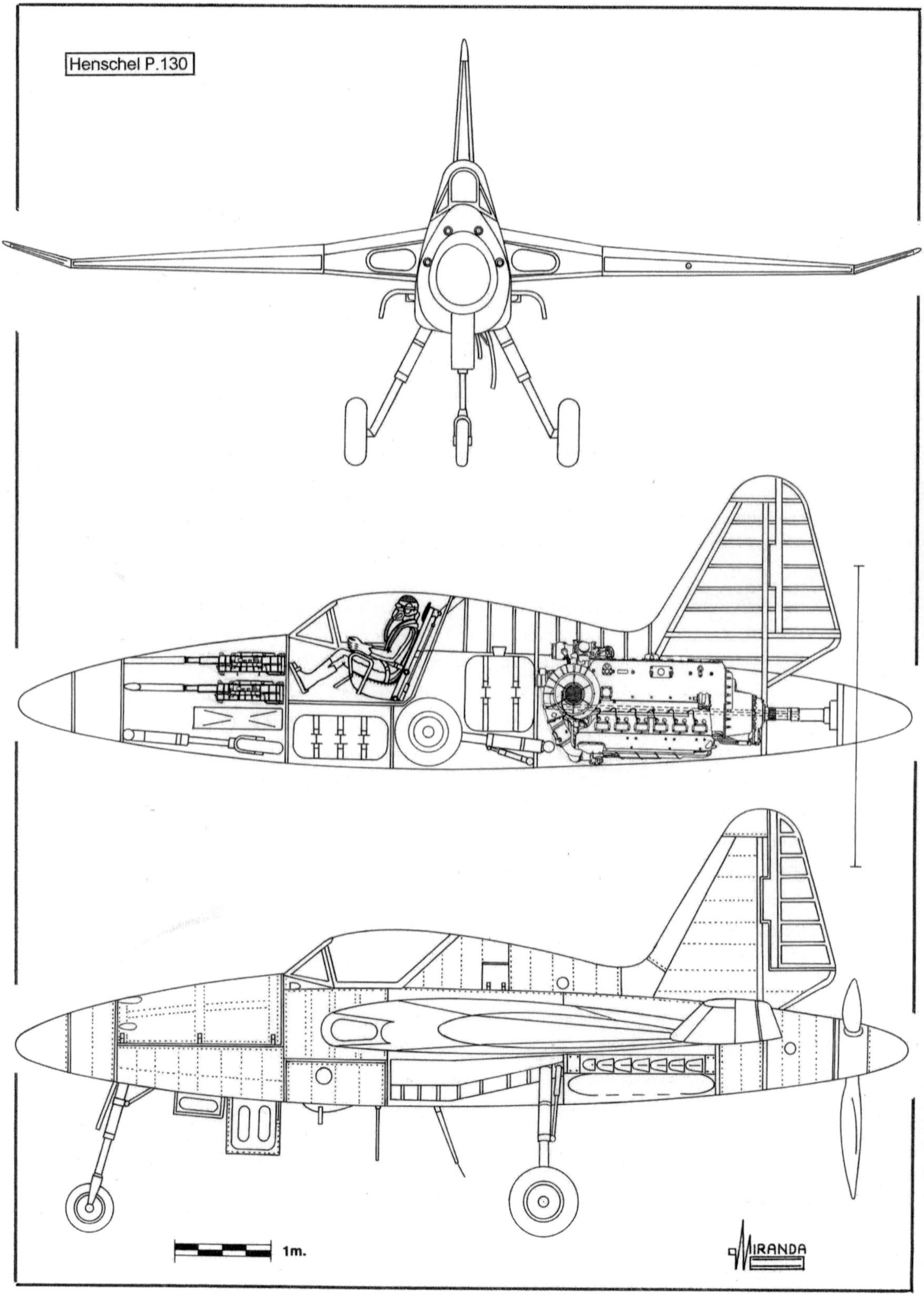
Henschel P.130
1m.
MIRANDA

Chapter 31

Lippisch 8-334 (Me-334)

At the beginning of 1943 the OKL had serious doubts abut the viability of the Me-163. As well as several crashes which occurred during the flight testing, there were concerns over the availability of the HWK RII-211 rocket engine; the first approved samples for flying – still far from being safe – would not arrive at Peenemünde until July.

The Allies bombing offensive increased every day. Their escort fighters repelled the Bf 109 and Fw 190 and more devastating incursions were expected with the arrival of good weather.

The Me 262 did not seem the best solution. Its performances in dog fighting were not brilliant, its combat ceiling was insufficient, its engines were not safe and its airframe suffered from compressibility buffeting. The Komet – whose first seventy airframes were uselessly expecting their engines at Regensburg factory – was urgently needed in combat.

The Lippisch design office Abteilung L proposed the building of two alternative versions (Parallelenwürfe) in April. The first project was named Lippisch P.20, on 16 April 1943. Essentially, it was a Me 163 with a Jumo 004 turbojet installed under the pilot and tricycle type undercarriage. The second project (Lippisch 8-334) never received an RLM official designation as, due to the strong personal disagreements between Lippisch and Messerschmitt, the Abteilung L was dissolved on 28 April and Lippisch himself left the company on 1 May.

The 8-334 was to be propelled by a Daimler Benz DB 603 or 605 conventional 12-cylinder piston engine located at the nose and driving a pusher propeller through an extension shaft.

Technical Data	
Type	Single-seat interceptor fighter.
Wings	Wooden structure, plywood cladding with 23.4-degree swept-back
Fuselage	light alloy structure and cladding.
Cockpit	Pressurised, control heating, frontal armour against 12.7 mm shelling and from the rear against 20 mm, Heinkel kartusche ejector seat.
Tailfin	Light alloy structure and cladding with tail bumper.
Undercarriage	Tricycle type. The main legs inwards retractable and the front gear retractable to the rear after switching 90 degrees to fold under the engine.

Engine	A Daimler Benz DB 605 of 1,475 hp or a DB 603 of 1,900 hp, both 12-cylinder, inverted-V, liquid cooled engines, driving a 3 m diameter pusher propeller through an extension shaft.
Fuel tank	Behind the pilot.
Armament	Two Mk 108/30 cannons in the wing roots and two MK 131/13 machine guns on top of the engine cowl.
Electronics	One EZ 42 gyrogunsight, FuG 16 ZY VHF transmitter/receiver, FuG 2a IFF radio set.
Wingspan	9.3 m
Length	7,0 m
Height	3.72 m
Wing area	17.3 sq m
Aspect ratio	5.0
Max. weight	3,000 kg
Max. speed	(with DB 605) Slightly better than a Me 109 G
Service ceiling	(with DB 605) Slightly better than a Me 109 G

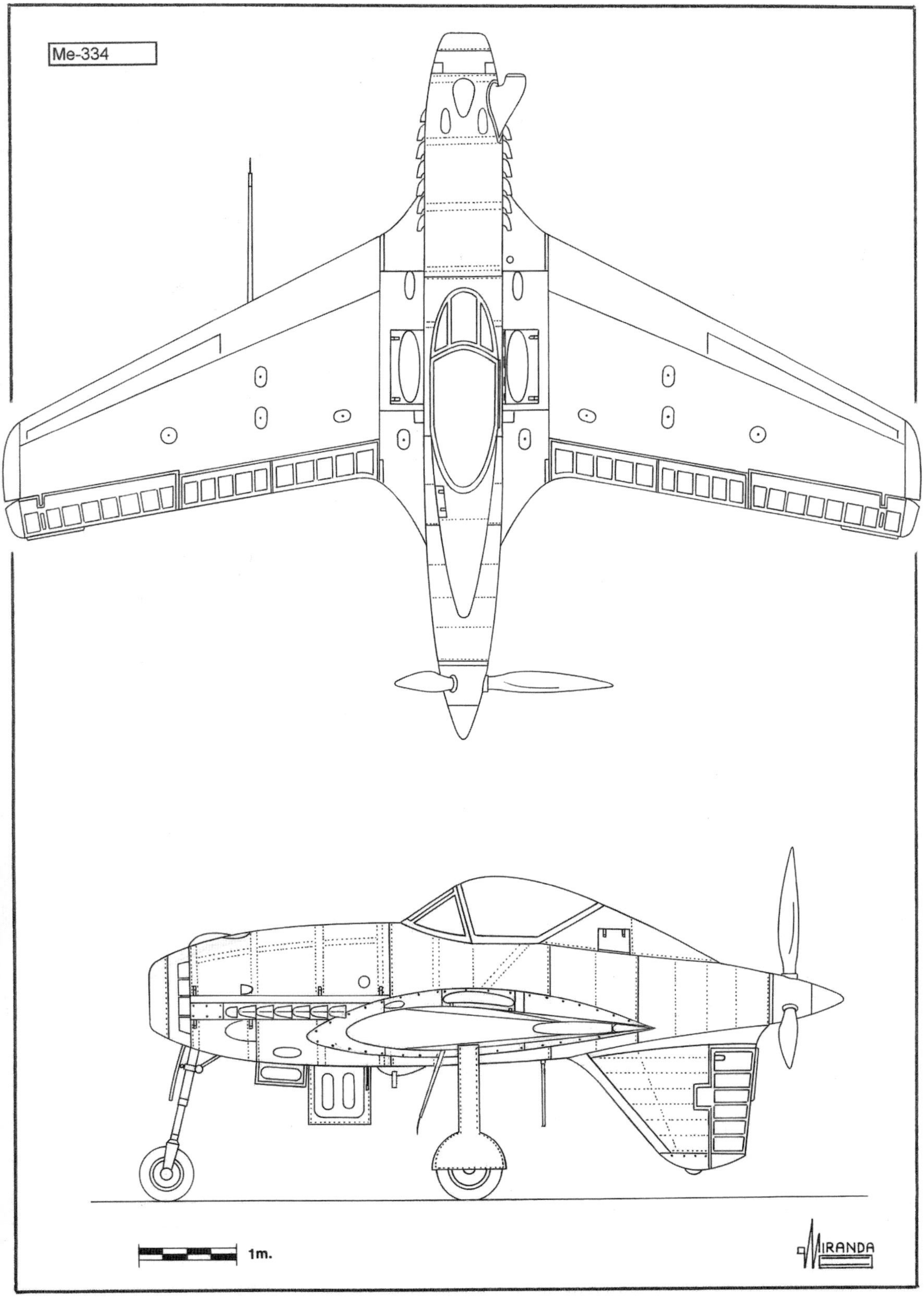
Me-334
1m.
MIRANDA

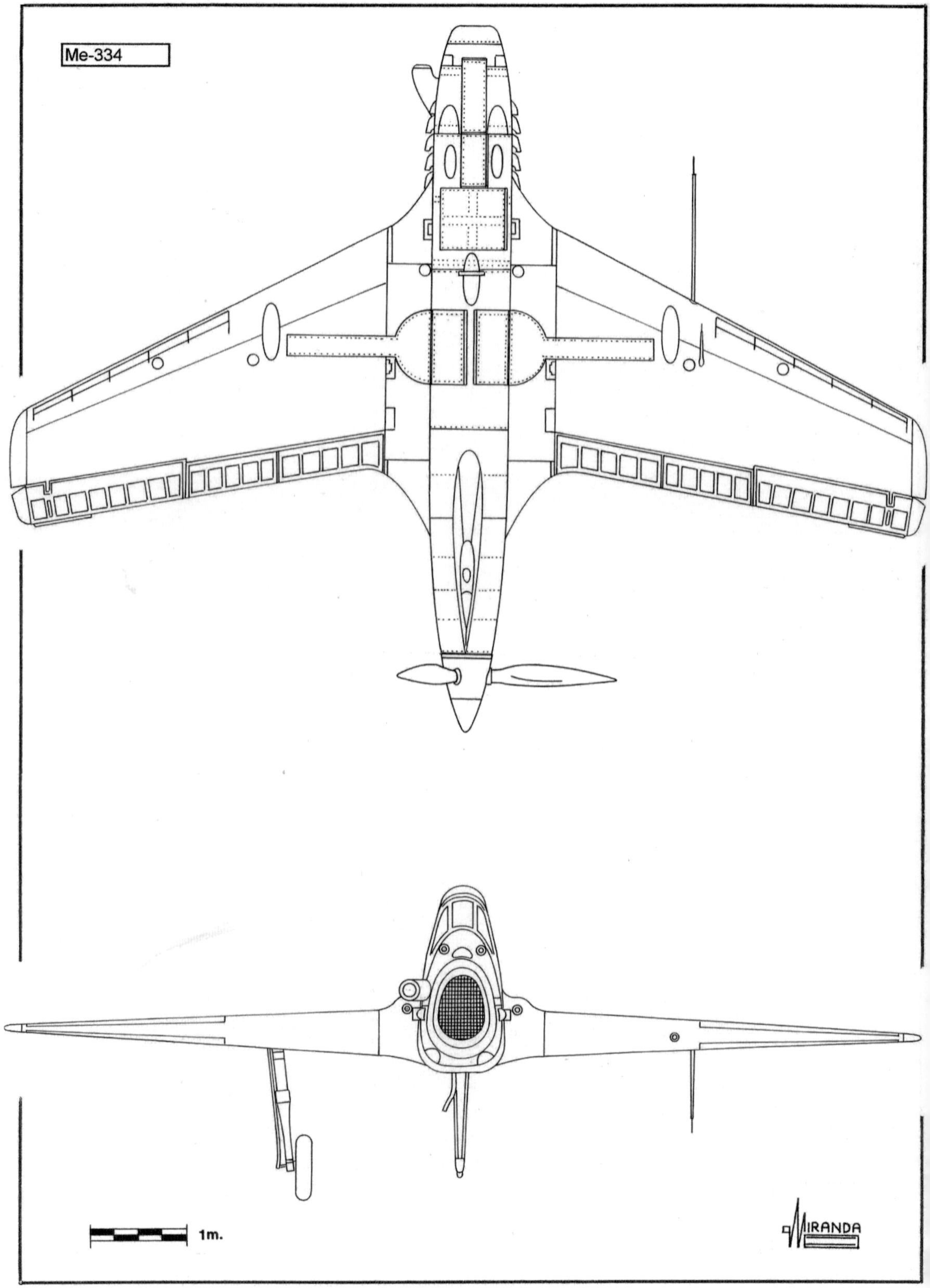
Me-334
1m.
MIRANDA

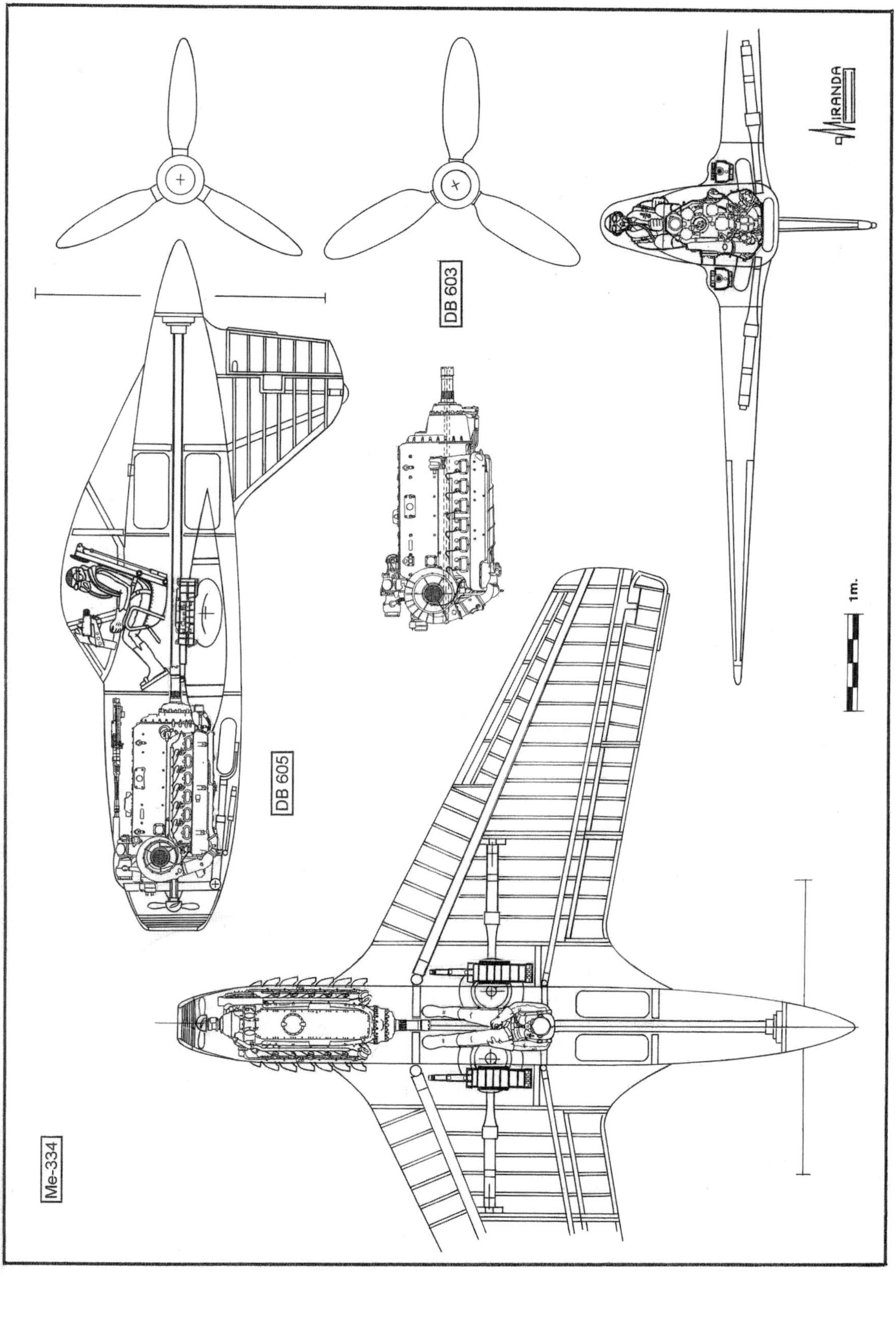
DB 603
DB 605
1m.
Me-334
MIRANDA

Chapter 32

Skoda-Kauba V5

After the annexation of Czechoslovakia in 1939, the old Skoda aviation factories were transformed into the Skoda-Kauba Werke Gmbh that, together with Avia, integrated the Hermann Göring Werke industrial complex.

The first project of the company was an unmanned flying bomb similar to the Miles Hoop-la British missile. It was a series of little airplanes powered by an in-line cylinder engine, guided by an automatic pilot and able to transport an explosive load of 500 kg.

Two different manned prototypes, the V1 and V2, were built to refine the design before the whole project was cancelled in favour of the more advanced Fieseler Fi 103 Vergelstungswaffe Ein. The V3 was a small training airplane based on the V2. The V4 was the prototype of the excellent training airplane Sk-257 that was mass manufactured since 1943.

In 1944 the Luftwaffe needed a high-altitude interceptor able to operate higher than the Me 262. Skoda proposed the manufacturing of the V5, based on the Sk-257, using their revolutionary manufacturing technique based on conic shape spars of steel and plywood cladding. It was a formidable machine in the line of the Me 209 H and Ta 152 H, though the latest was eventually chosen to be manufactured as it was a version of the Dora-9, already in production.

The V5 was basically a scaled-up version of the Sk-257 with a DB 603 engine, four guns of 20 mm, pressurised cockpit and a four-bladed propeller. Its building was simpler than that of its competitors and required less strategic materials

Skoda-Kuba V5 Technical Data	
Type	High-altitude interceptor fighter.
Phase	Design.
Wings	Trapezoid section with a unique conic shaped spar of steel to which the sixteen ribs of each wing were fixed. Cladding of plywood and of fabric in the control surfaces.
Fuselage	Structure of welded steel tubes, plywood cladding and pressurised cockpit.
Landing Gear	Similar to the one in the Fw 190. The main wheels were fixed to the wing spar by means of a welded tube at 90 degrees through which the gun barrel located nearest the fuselage passed. The tail wheel was not retractable.

Engine	A Daimler Benz DB-603 of 12 cylinders in inverted-V, liquid cooled and 1,756 hp driving a four-bladed VDM propeller of 3.38 m of diameter contra-prop in the October 44 version.
Fuel tank	One behind the pilot and another under the seat .
Armament	Four MG 151/20 guns of 20 mm in the wings.
Wingspan	12.2 m
Length	10 m
Height	3.1 m
Wing area	23 sq m
Empty weight	4,500 kg
Max. speed	765 km/h (October 1944)

P.603 No. 1 Technical Data

Type	Single-seat interceptor fighter.
Engine	One Daimler Benz DB 603N of 12 cylinders, inverted-V, liquid-cooled, with 2,830 hp, emergency power.
Cockpit	Pressurised, control heating, armoured front and rear, ejector seat.
Armament	One Mk 103/30 and two MG 213C/30 cannons in the nose.
Wingspan	11.00 m
Length	11.70 m
Height	3.13 m
Wing area	26 sq m
Max. weight	6,000 kg
Max. speed	703 km/h
Ceiling	12,600 m
Electronics	FuG 16 ZY, FuG 25, FuG 125

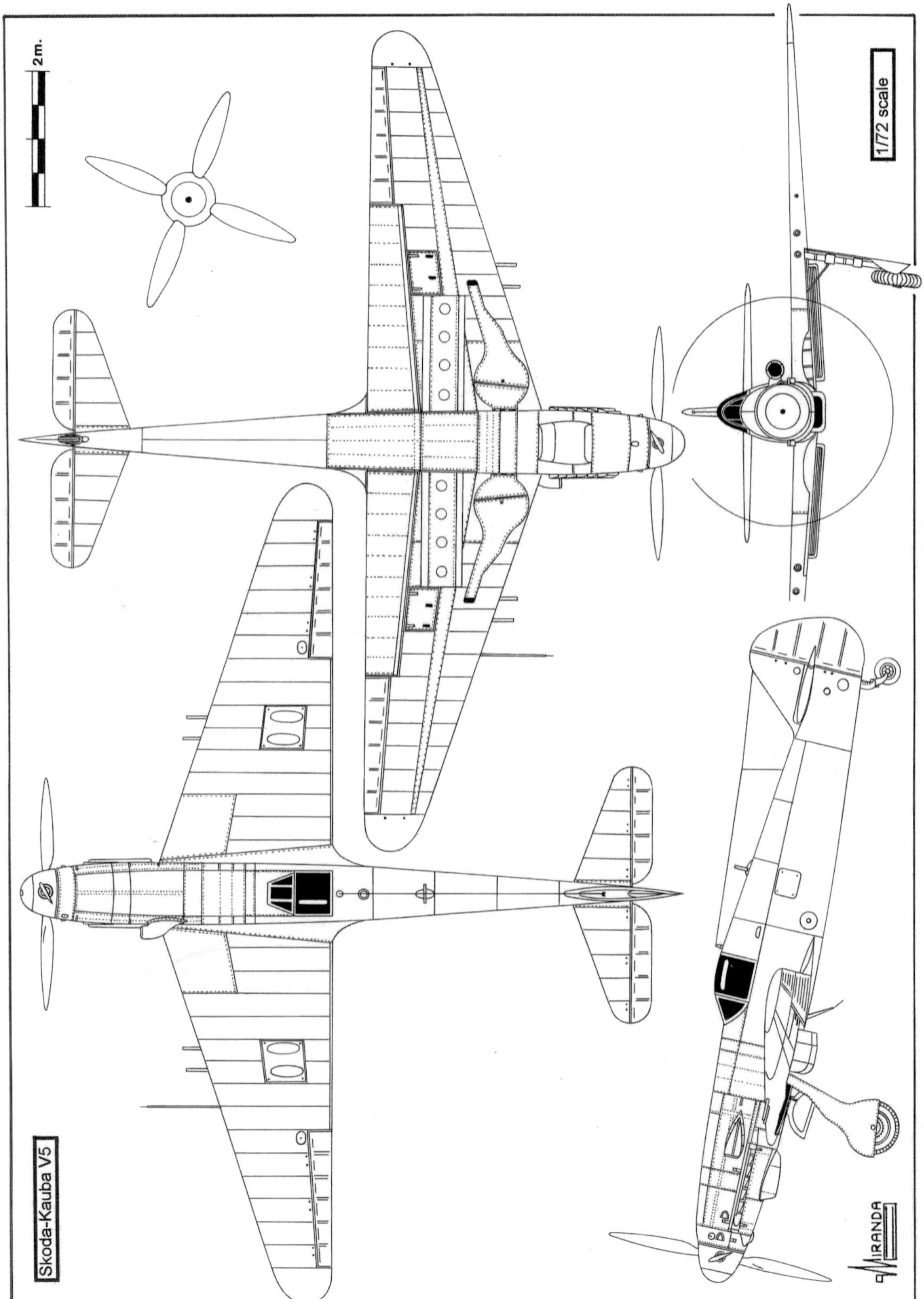
Skoda-Kauba V5
2m.
1/72 scale
MIRANDA

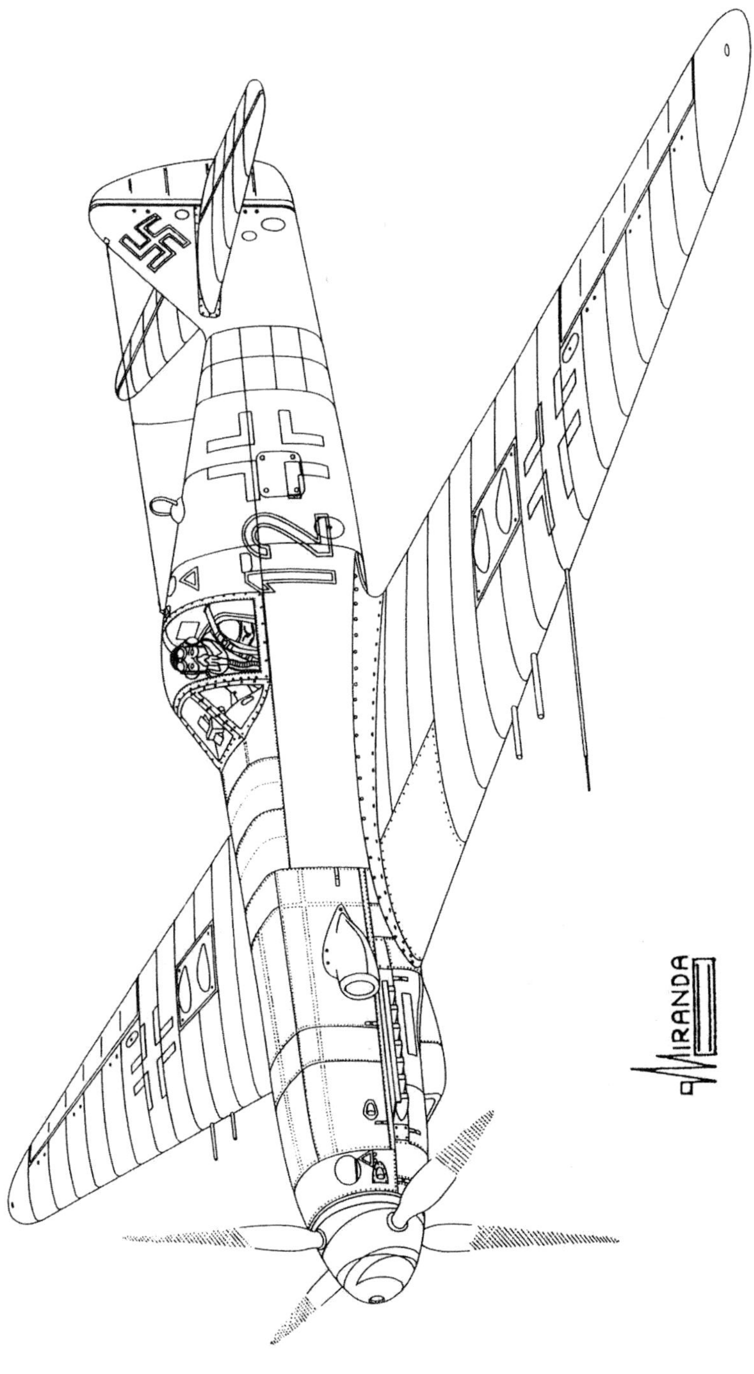
MIRANDA

Chapter 33

Ejector Seats

On 19 April 1945, a flight of Tempests of the 222nd Squadron on a patrol mission over the German aerodrome of Husum saw a type of airplane unknown up to then. It was one of the Heinkel 162 of the I./JG1 coming back to it Schleswig-Holstein base. Its pilot, Lieutenant Schmitt, worried by the low level of fuel, never knew who had shot him. He just found himself suddenly trapped in his cockpit while the small fighter twisted in a crazy spin, after losing one wing. Like many other pilots shot down during that terrible winter, Schmitt started to count the seconds until his death... but this time something different happened: his left hand pulled a lever and, with a low explosion, the seat was launched far from the fireball that was now his airplane.

Since 1939 the Luftwaffe Aviation Medicine branch had been actively experimenting with ejection systems. The physiological tests performed showed that a sitting human body could stand a vertical acceleration of +20 G during 0.1 seconds without major damage. During the war, Heinkel developed three different ejector seats and, by the end of 1942, all the experimental airplanes tested by the Luftwaffe were equipped with any of them. The first tests took place in 1939 and 1940 using sandbags and anthropomorphic dummies in a ground rig at Heinkel's plant in Rechlin.

The first launch with human beings was at the end of 1941, in Erprobungsstelle-Rechlin, when the trained parachutist Wilhelm Buss ejected from the back seat of a Ju 87B using a catapult device with spring mechanism. This type of seat was very heavy and difficult to maintain, not being appropriate to use in combat. It was used in flight tests with the new prototypes of airplanes like the Me 262 V2 and the Me 163B V1.

The second system developed by Heinkel used bottles of compressed air at very high pressure (1700 psi) and was able to launch a seat of 120 kg, with a pilot of 80 kg, at 6 m above the fuselage of the airplane. The ejection speed was of 17 m/s at 27G. The auxiliary equipment was very heavy and presented considerable maintenance problems to be kept successfully operational. It was tested during the flight tests of the He 280, being used for the first time in an emergency by the test pilot Schenk during a flight with the He 280 V1 (DL+AS), on 13 January 1943. Three test launches were performed with this seat in 1944 from the back seat of the He 219 (DV+DI) with a view to the installation of the new night fighter.

After the success of the testing, a double seat for the pilot and the radar operator, seated back to back, was designed. It was used in combat until the end of the war, working successfully in at least four different occasions:

when the He 219 of NJG 1, crewed by the Uffz. Herter and the Gefr. Perbix suffered mechanical failure on 11 April 1944;
when the He 219 (G9+GK) of NJG 1, crewed by litres Otto Fries and Fw. Alfred Staffa, was shot down by a Mosquito night fighter on 19 May 1944;
when the He 219 (G9+EK) of NJG1, with same crew as the previous one, was shot down by a Mosquito night fighter on 16 January 1945;
when the He 219 (G9+HH) of the NJG1, crewed by Hptm. Wilhelm Modrow and the Fw Alfred Staffa, was shot down by a Mosquito night fighter on 1 February 1945.

The third system, Schleudersitz Heinkel-Kartusche, was developed in cooperation with Dornier. It used an explosive cartridge with 30 g of powder and a catapult tube fixed to the upper end of the seat and at the lower end of the aircraft frame. The ejection speed was 11 m/s at only 12G, but the system was light, easy to maintain, could be installed in small airplanes and used at speeds of up to 700 km/h. It was installed on Dornier Do 335 and Heinkel He 162 of operational series and in some Me 262, Go 229 and Ar 234B. A He 162 of I/JG1, crewed by litres Rudolf Schmidt, used it during combat on 20/04/1945. The seat was fitted with a Sutton-type harness and the seat-type parachute pack included emergency oxygen equipment in the seat cavity.

The Focke Wulf company developed two types of explosive ejector seats.

The first one was very similar to the Heinkel design and it was tested in a Fw 190 A-O/U4 in Rechlin Roggenthin at the end of 1941 using an anthropomorphic dummy. Its installation was planned in the last series of the Fw 190 D and in the Ta 154 C night fighter.

The Fw 190 A-O/U4 of Rechlin was also used to test an explosive system to eject the cockpit canopy at speeds above 250 mph, at which it is not possible to do so manually due to the air pressure. It consisted of two standard 20 mm cartridges located to both sides of the armoured windshield in a similar disposition to those used by the Lockheed F-104 in the 60s.

The second type was a downward-operating ejector seat designed for the suicidal variant 'pulk- Zerstörer' of the Ta 154 A-1 from which at least six copies were built. By the end of the war, sixty aircrew had used ejection seats in combat.

Heinkel "Kartusche" Ejector seat

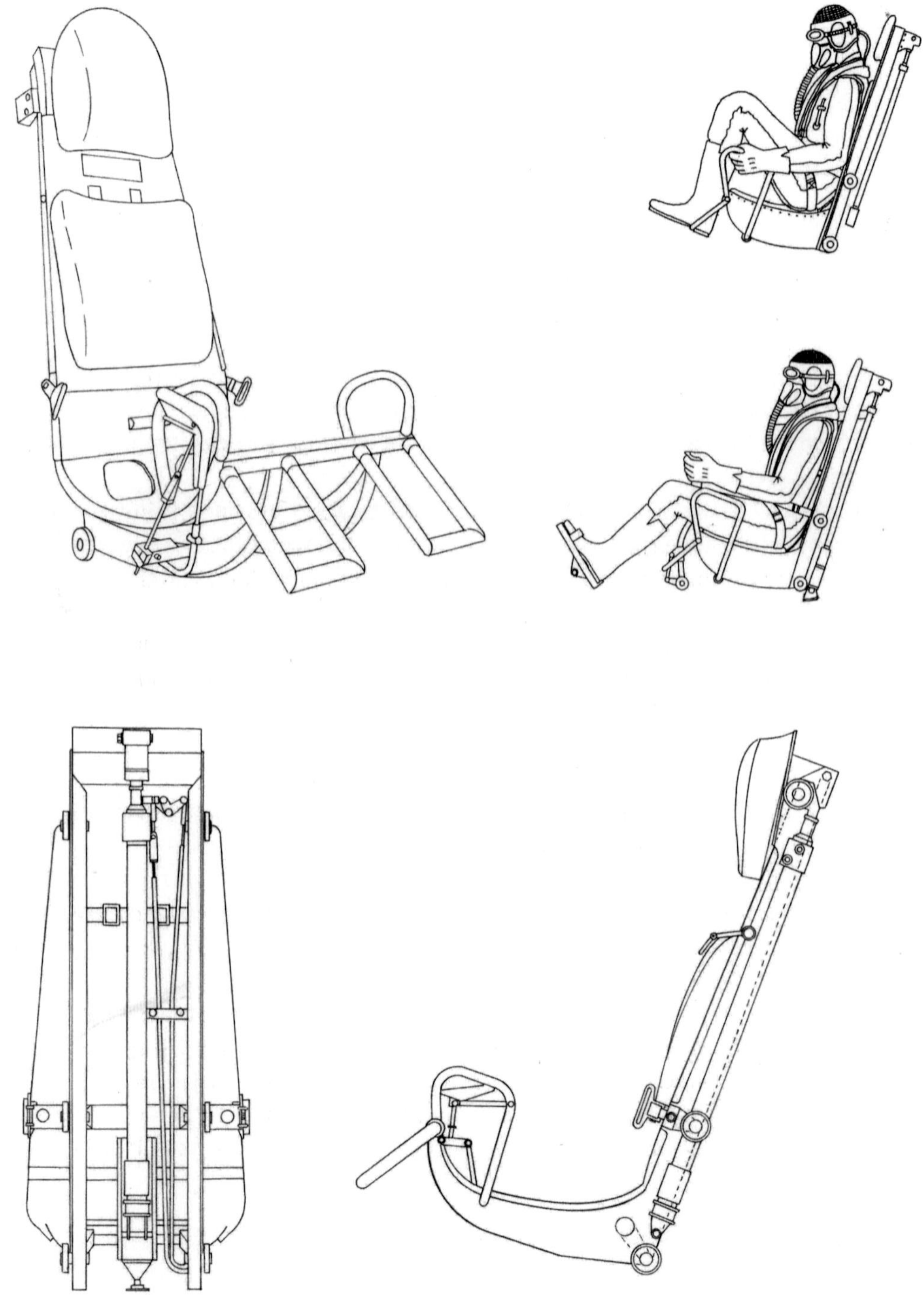

Chapter 34

Bordwaffen

Rheinmetall-Borsig MG-17. Belt-fed 7.92 mm machine gun with a rate of fire of 1,160 rpm and 13 kg weight. Equipped with synchronisation device, it was positioned above the engine of all Fw 190, from A-0 to A-7 series, and on the Fw 190 F-1.

Rheinmetall-Borsig MG-131. Belt-fed 13 mm machine gun with a rate of fire of 930 rpm and 16 kg weight. Equipped with synchronisation device, it was positioned above the engine of all the Fw 190, from A-7 to D-12 series, on the Fw 190 A-5 and on the F and G series.

Mauser MG-151/15. Belt-fed 15 mm machine gun with a rate of fire of 900 rpm and 43 kg weight. It was installed on the Fw 190 A-2 and A-4 and, with synchronisation device, above the engines of the Ta 152 A and B.

Mauser MG-151/20. Belt-fed 20 mm cannon with a rate of fire of 800 rpm and 43 kg weight. Used by the Fw 190, from the A-3/U7 to the D11, the F-1 and F-8 series and the Ta 152. Also as motor-cannon by the D-12.

Ikaria MG FF. Drum-fed 20 mm cannon with a rate of fire of 520 rpm and 28 kg weight. Used by the Fw 190 V12, A-1, Aa-3, A-4, A-5/U10 and A5/U16.

Rheinmetall-Borsig MK 108. It was a low velocity weapon for single-seat fighters, much lighter than the MK 103 and cheaper, because it used many stamped parts. The very short gun barrel and the low muzzle velocity allowed a higher rate of fire. The MK 108 was a blow-back operated, rear-seated, belt-fed 30 mm cannon with electric priming. It was electro-pneumatically operated by 8 x 21 compressed-air cylinders.

Caliber: 30 mm
Weight: 58 kg
Length: 1057 mm
Muzzle velocity: 505/530 m/sec
Rate of fire: 600/660 rpm
Effective range: 400 m

It shot low-velocity 30 x 90 RB ammunition of two types:

Minengeschoss of 312 grams each shell, self-destructing tracer.
Flamm incendiary shells of 330 grams each with hydrodynamic fuse.

The weapon was highly lethal, requiring one hit on fighters and five hits on heavy bombers. It was not the right weapon for use in daylight against heavy bombers due to its short range. It was expected that the Gotha P.60 would use it against the enemy fighters in air superiority missions and against the night heavy bombers in Schräge Musik configuration.

There was a project in 1945 for version MK 108 A with 900 rpm but its manufacturing was left aside in favour of the Mauser MK 213/30.

Used by the Fw 190 A-5/U16, A-6/R2, A-7/R2, A-8/R2, A9/R8, A-10, F-8/R2, D-1, D11, V20/U1, V58, V60 and Ta 152 A. It was also used as motor-cannon on the Fw 190 V21/U1, E-1, D-12/R11 and Ta 152 C-0, E-0 and Hu-E.

Rheinmetall-Borsig MK 103. Adapted from an airborne anti-tank MK 101 for an air-air usage but lighter, with a higher rate of fire, fed by belts and with electric priming. Its design was to be used mainly by Zerstörer and heavy fighters as its powerful recoil could cause structural problems to the single-engined fighters. Nevertheless, version MK 103M (Motoren) was specifically designed for mounting on the V-12 engine of the Bf 109 K-10.

Calibre: 30 mm L/38
Weight: 145 kg
Length: 2335 mm
Muzzle velocity (HE/AP tracer): 940 m/sec
Muzzle velocity (Minengeschoss): 860 m/sec
Muzzle velocity (Incendiary/tracer): 900 m/sec
Rate of fire (HE/AP tracer): 380 rpm
Rate of fire (Minengeschoss): 420 rpm
Penetration (HE/AP tracer): 110 mm armour plate at 90 degrees up to 300 m, 70 mm armour plate at 60 degrees up to 300 m

The MK 103 shot high-velocity 30 x 184B ammunition to attack bombers from a security distance. This might be of three different types:

1. Hartkern: Armour-piercing with tungsten-carbide core, tracer with additional incendiary effect, not self-destructive. Length: 296.6 mm. Diameter of cartridge: 39.5 mm.
2. Flamm: Incendiary/tracer shell, not self-destructive, fuse AZ 1587. Length: 298 mm. Diameter of cartridge: 39.5 mm.
3. Minengeschoss: A thin-drawn shell with a large explosive load. Weight of shell: 330 grams. Additional incendiary effect.

Trajectory range (HE/AP tracer)

Range	Elapsed time	Gravity drop	Shell velocity
500 m	0.66 sec	1.9 m	676 m/sec
1000 m	1.50 sec	9.4 m	519 m/sec
1500 m	2.60 sec	26.3 m	400 m/sec
2000 m	4.01 sec	58.2 m	323 m/sec

High lethality RLM specifications required one hit on fighters and five hits on heavy bombers. Statistically, a four-engined bomber could be shot down.

from	500 m	1000 m	1500 m	
with	40 rds	140 rds	308 rds	with 50 per cent certainty
	76 rds	203 rds	650 rds	with 95 per cent certainty

Used on the Fw 190 V19, A5/U11, A-5/U17, A-6/R3, A-8/R3, F-4, F-8/R3 and as motor-cannon on the Fw 190 V27, Ta 152 A, B and C.

Rheinmetall-Borsig MK 112. Basically a scaled-up Mk 108, 55 mm cannon with 300 rpm and 275 kg weight. Used by the Fw 190 A-8 works no. 170002 as suicide ramming aircraft prototype for the Selbstopfermänner units.

AIRBORNE GUNS

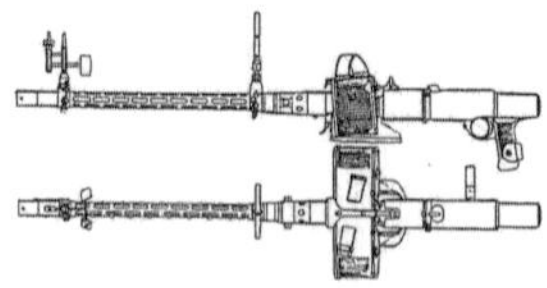

Rheinmetall-Borsig MG 15 / 7.92 mm

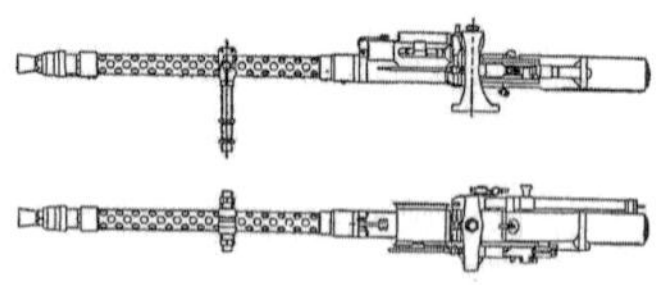

Rheinmetall-Borsig MG 17 / 7.92 mm

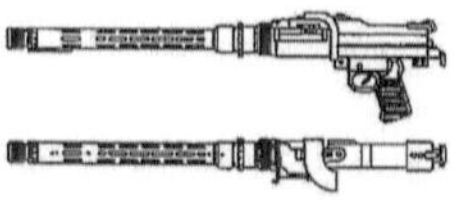

Waffenfabrik Mauser MG 81 / 7.92 mm

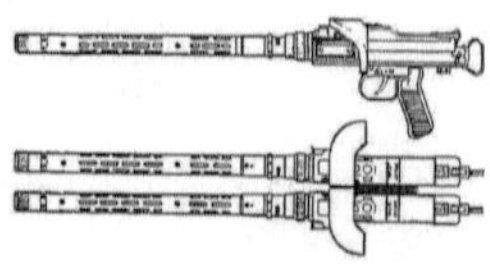

Waffenfabrik Mauser MG 81Z / 7.92 mm

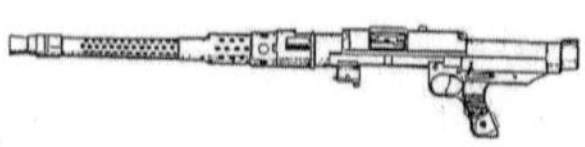

Rheinmetall-Borsig MG 131 / 13 mm

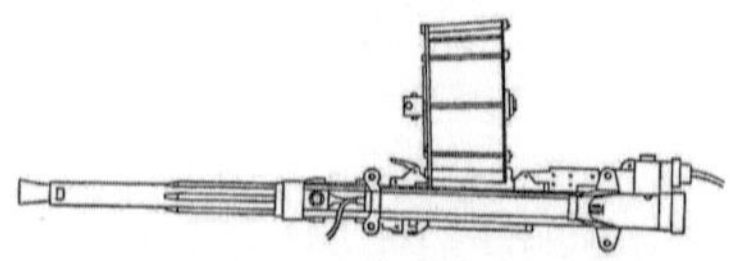

Ikaria Werke Berlin MG FF / 20 mm.

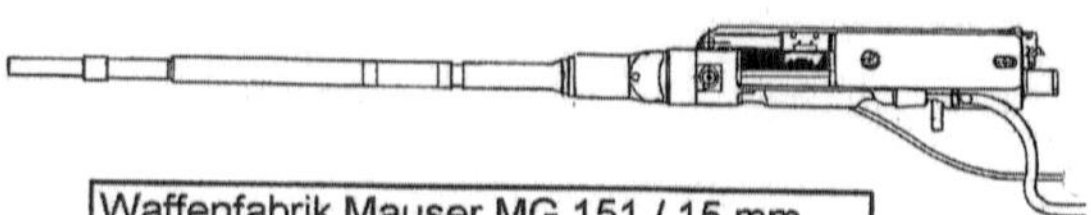

Waffenfabrik Mauser MG 151 / 15 mm

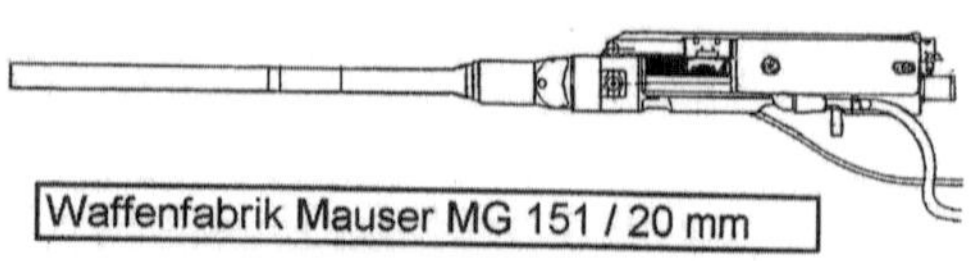

Waffenfabrik Mauser MG 151 / 20 mm

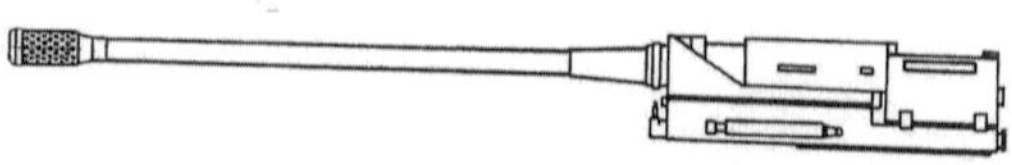

Waffenfabrik Mauser MK 213 C / 20 mm

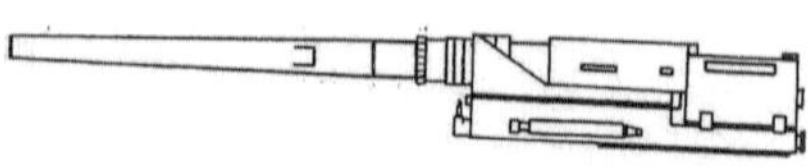

Waffenfabrik Mauser MK 213 C / 30 mm

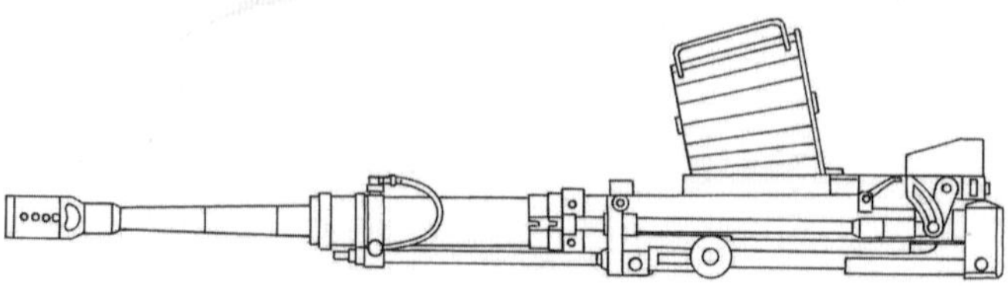

Rheinmetall-Borsig MK 101 / 30 mm

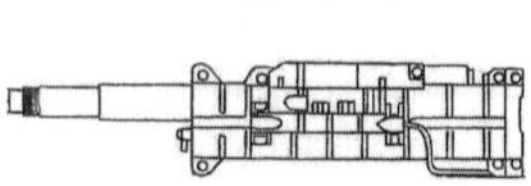

Rheinmetall-Borsig MK 108 / 30 mm

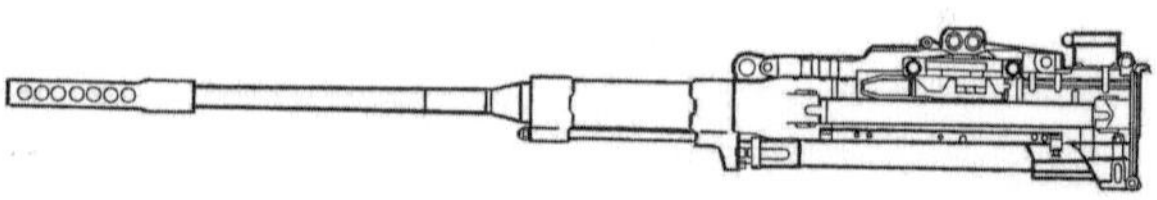

Rheinmetall-Borsig MK 103 / 30 mm

1/24 SCALE

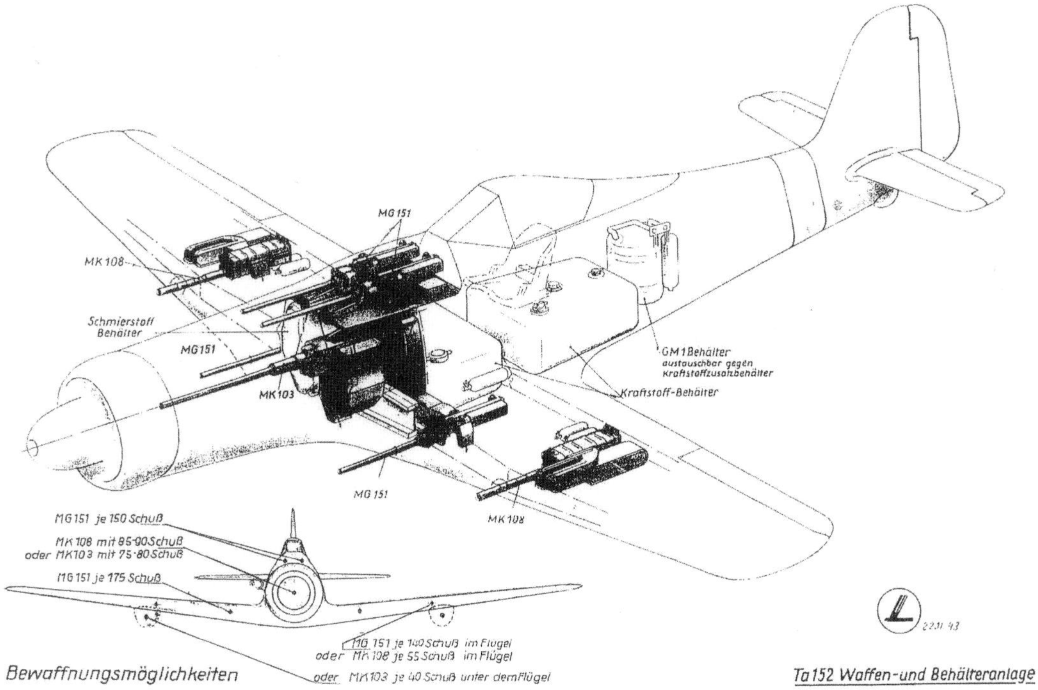

Ta 152 Waffen-und Behälteranlage

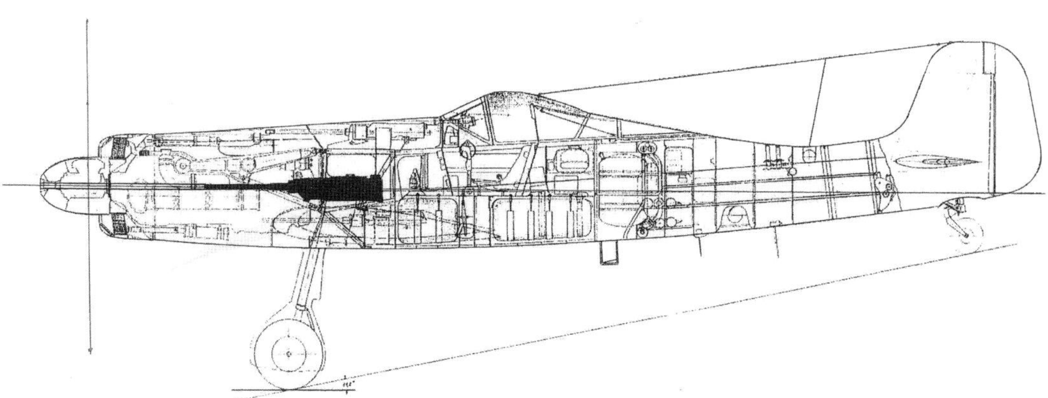

Jagdflugzeug Ta 152 A (Längsschnitt)
mit Jumo 213 A ETW und GM1-Anlage,
und Fla.V. Anlage

6.12.43

Chapter 35

Gustloff HF 15 Hohe Feurfolge

An extremely high rate of fire gun conceived in the early 1940s by the Hungarian Artillery officer Major Zettle, the development of the weapon was made in the Gustloff Werke Suhl-Thüringen between August 1944 and the beginning of 1945.

The HF 15 was a highly unusual gun using a MG 151/15 barrel and a cartridge that held seven HE/INC projectiles of 15 mm calibre and one single charge. The barrel was closed by a breach screw that chambered the cartridge of 75 mm calibre and electrical primer.

When fired, the central bullet was driven through the barrel and the gas pressure in the cartridge pressed another projectile into the central position, which was fired instantly. The process was repeated until the projectile chamber was emptied, in 11/1000 second. This would be an increase of twenty times over any other aircraft gun in service.

These weapons needed a special powder positioning to create saw teeth at gas pressure. The propellant would be loaded in seven wafer discs with six interposed inhibitor discs.

The weapon was fully developed and a small number produced. Nothing is known about combat use.

The HF 16 weighted 20 kg ready to fire and measured 1,575 mm of length. An Fw 190 F-8 could transport ten HF 15s in two Fluegelmontage groups of 112 kg, under each wing. Its rate of fire was of 38,000 rpm.

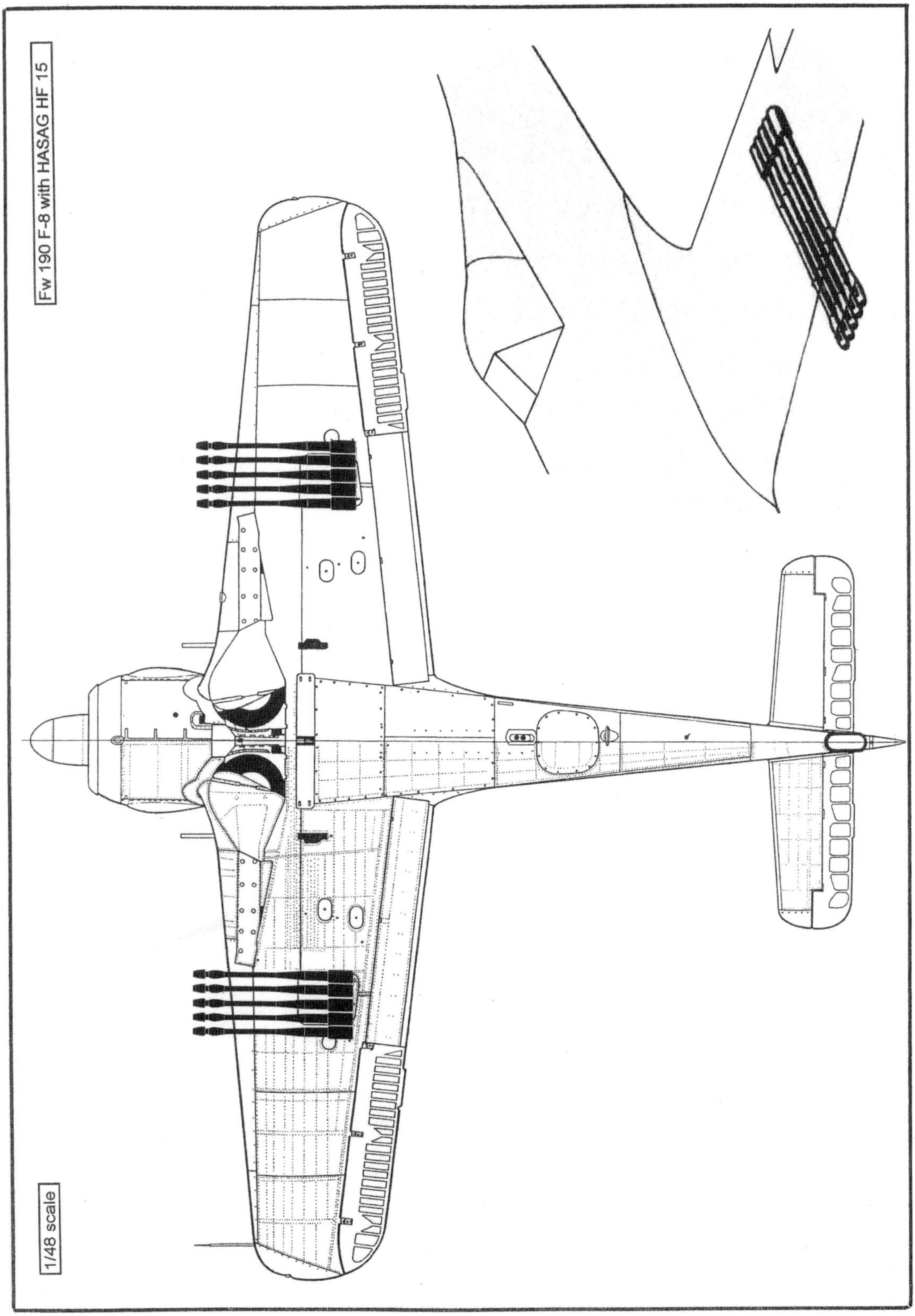
Fw 190 F-8 with HASAG HF 15
1/48 scale

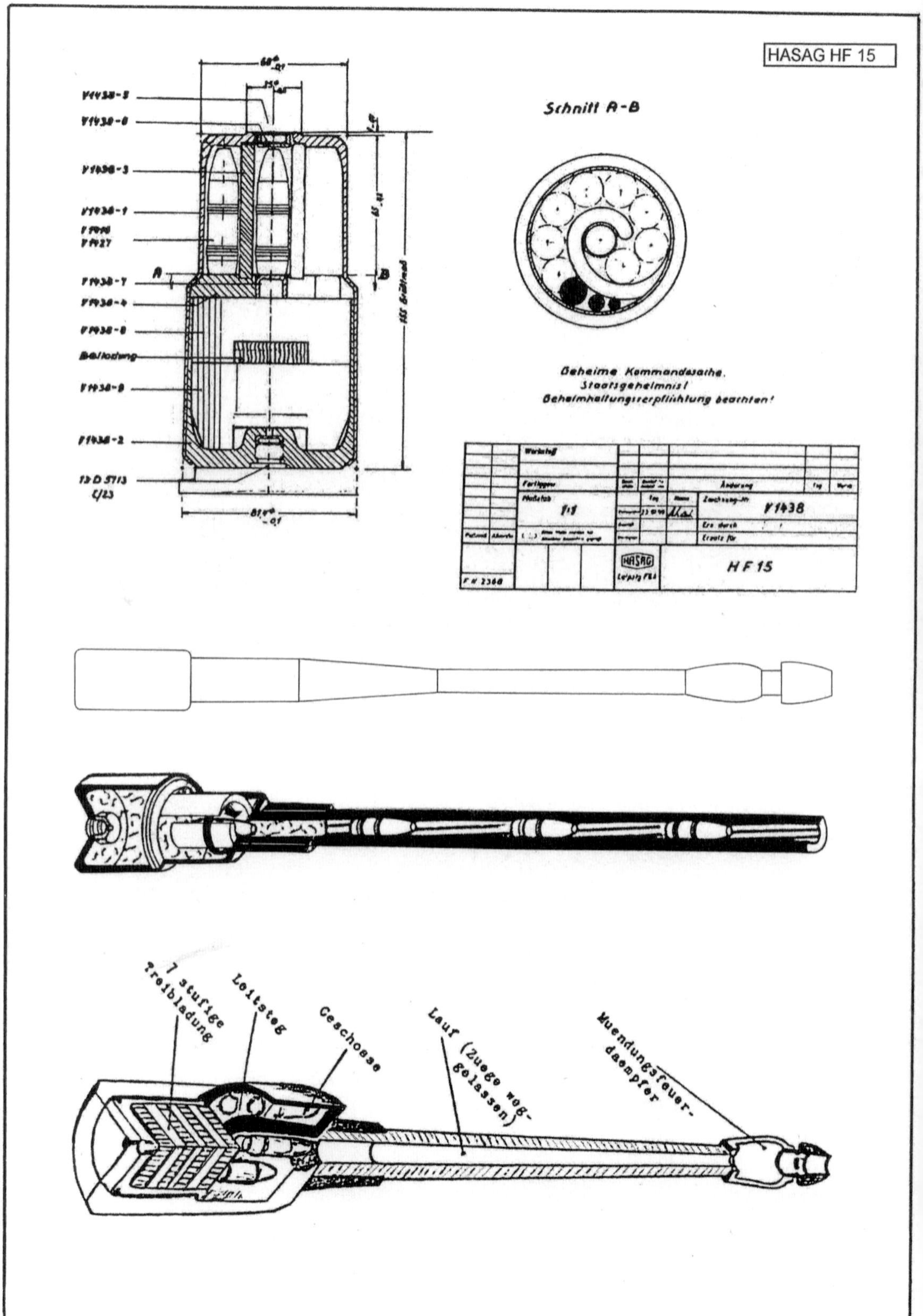
HASAG HF 15
Schnitt A-B
Geheime Kommandosache.
Staatsgeheimnis!
Geheimhaltungsverpflichtung beachten!
V1438
HF 15
7 stufige Treibladung
Leitsteg
Geschosse
Lauf (Zuege weggelassen)
Muendungsfeuer-daempfer

Chapter 36

Vertikalbordwaffen

The success achieved with the heavy fighters equipped with Schräge Musik devices, favoured the design of new weapons capable of being used by single engine fighters.

The Fw 190 was chosen to test four vertical-recoilless weapons actioned by photo-electrical cells:

The 25 mm Harfe – manufactured by Hasag-Schneider KG – consisted of single-shot RCL barrels, using the gas jet principle, firing fin-stabilised 135 gr shells at 320 m/s. The 1,250 mm long barrels weighed 2.3 kg and were electrically shot by means of the Fotozellenfühler optical sensor manufactured by Opta-radio. It was activated by the shadow of the attacked aircraft when the fighter flew by underneath.

The Harfe was developed by the Stabsingenieur Poppendick and tested by the E4/5 Gruppe in Travemünde in June 1942.

In Summer 1944, the system was tested in a Fw 190 F-8, fitted with a battery of fifteen Harfe in the port side of the fuselage. The operational version was to consist of two batteries of twelve barrels each, positioned to both sides of the fuselage, behind the pilot.

The Sondergerät SG 116 Zellendusche of 30 mm – manufactured by Rheinmetall Borsig – used the barrel of the Mk 103 high velocity (825 m/sec) cannon. It fired counterweight rearwards at 170 m/sec to cancel the recoil. Each barrel was a single-shot weapon with minor modifications in the chamber and a 3 cm Minenprojectile with powder in a cardboard tube.

The primers were electrically fired, converted from the 21 cm rockets. The photoelectric trigger, Fotozellenfühler, was a 90 mm selenium tube sensor that workedv similarly to a photographic exposure meter. It reacted to light/absence of light.

In December 1944. a Fw 190 A-8 was fitted with three SG 116 in the port side of the fuselage. The foremost barrel was set at an angle of 74 degrees the central barrel at 73 degrees and rearmost barrel at 72.5 degrees The trio of shells being fired at intervals of 0.03 seconds at a distance of approximately 50 m below the target.

It was tested by the VJG 10 in Parchim, using a Fw 58 and a remote controlled He 177 as targets.

The SG 116 was 1,620 mm long and weighted 32 kg ready to fire.

The Sondergerät SG 500 Jagdfaust of 50 mm was manufactured by Hasag and developed by Dr Langweiler to produce a recoil-free weapon by firing a counterweight from the back of the gun. In the Jagdfaust, the counterweight was the cartridge case, which was also extended upwards to act as the barrel and was held in place by a pair of frangible pins. The barrel was rifled, for greater stability in flight for the 50 mm Minengranate shell that weighted 1 kg, out of which 513 grams were HE. The muzzle velocity was of 400 m/sec, the range of 100 m.

Its release was photo-electric by means of either the Zossen selenium cell manufactured by AEG or the Selenzelle manufactured by Auge.

Tests were carried out between August and October of 1944 using the Fw 190 piloted by Lt Gustav Hachtel at the Brandis-Waldpohlenz airfield and in Tarnewitz by the EK 25 Gruppe. The Fw 190 was fitted with five SG 500s and a sensor in each wing. Barrage balloons were used for testing, achieving seven hits.

Another possible configuration consisted of six SG 500s installed in two groups of three on each side of the fuselage.

The SG 500 was operationally used by the Me 163 B-O of the EK16 and the JG.400 in 1945. Its installation was planned in the Ta 152 (five on each wing) in the Me 262 (twelve in the nose) and in the Me P.1101 project – August 22, 1944 – (eight in the nose).

The SG 500 measured 648 mm of length and weighted 8kg ready to fire.

The Sondergerät SG 117 Rohrblock 108 of 30 mm – manufactured by Rheinmetall Borsig – consisted of seven Mk 108 low velocity barrels (each loaded with a single Minengranate) which were clustered together for firing upwards at bombers. The barrels were fixed with concrete within a 130 mm diameter metallic cylinder that slid downwards out the aircraft during firing, sequentially triggering the shots as it did so (10,000 – 12,000 rpm) and simultaneously absorbing the recoil

The SG 117 was triggered by a AEG Zossen photocell that actioned seven spring-loaded firing pins mounted on a 20 mm thick plate. They were fired by an automatic electrical system at intervals of three milliseconds.

A Rohrblock 108 was 600 mm long and weighted 28 kg ready to fire

On 26 January 1945 the Fw 190 V74 (works no. 733713) performed its flying tests in the EK 25 of Tarnewitz, with two SG 117 installed one behind the other at the rearwards of the fuselage. The operational version planned for the Fw 190 and Ta 152 consisted of two SG 117s and a sensor, installed on each wing. Six Fw 190s equipped in this way were tested in combat, but the results were not satisfactory.

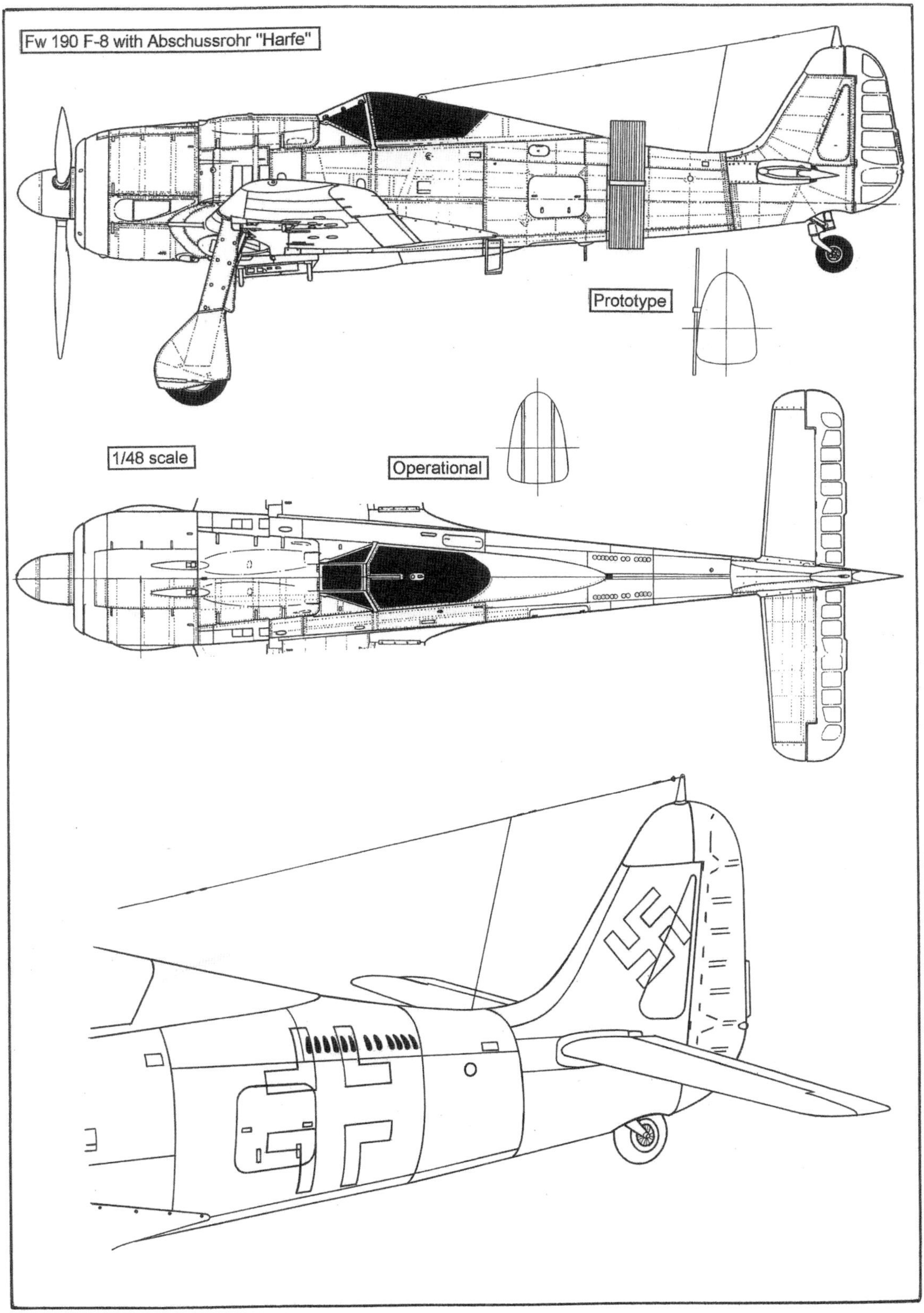
Fw 190 F-8 with Abschussrohr "Harfe"
Prototype
1/48 scale
Operational

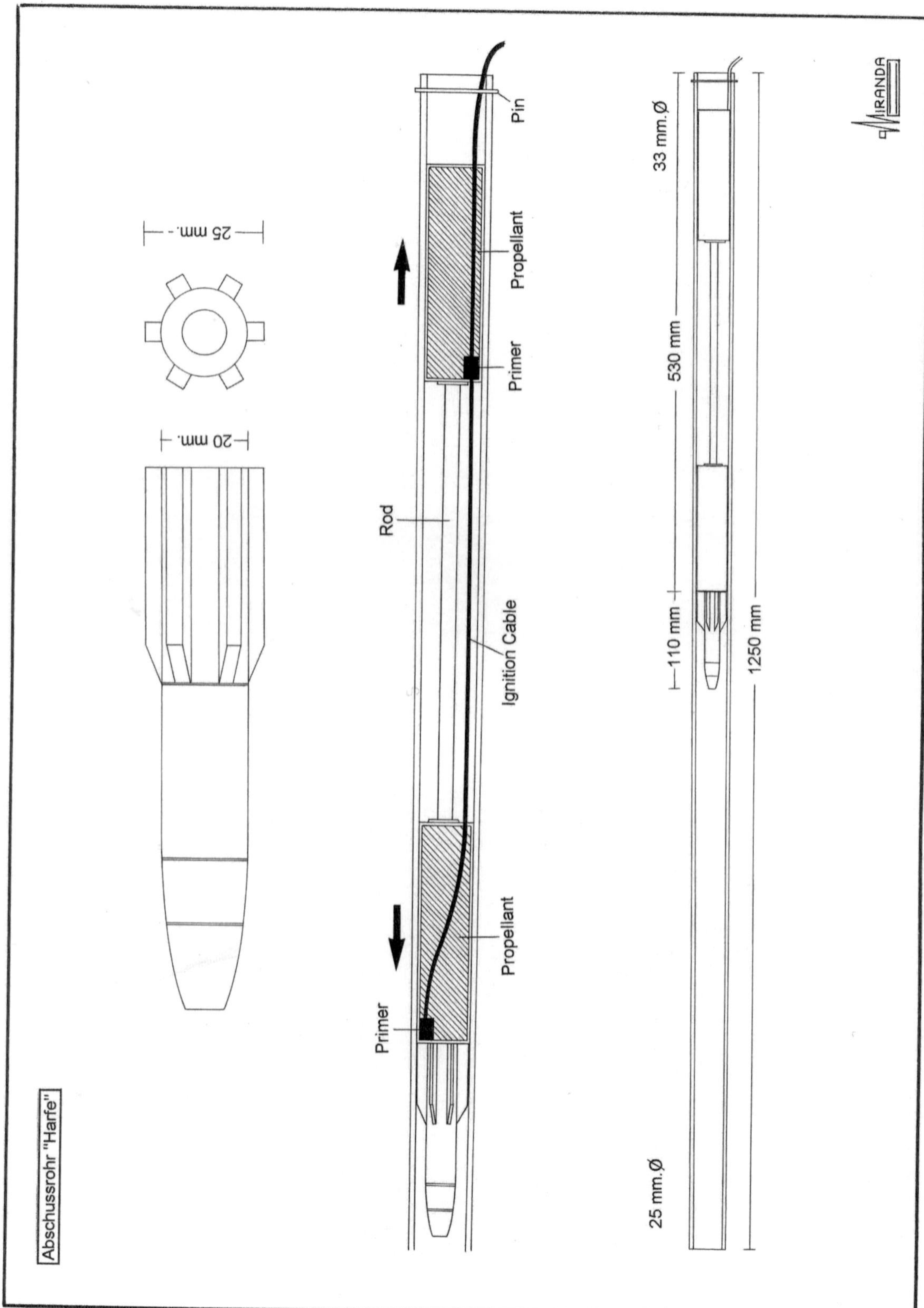
Abschussrohr "Harfe"
20 mm.
25 mm.
Primer
Propellant
Rod
Ignition Cable
Primer
Propellant
Pin
25 mm.Ø
110 mm
530 mm
33 mm.Ø
1250 mm

SG 116 "Zellendusche"

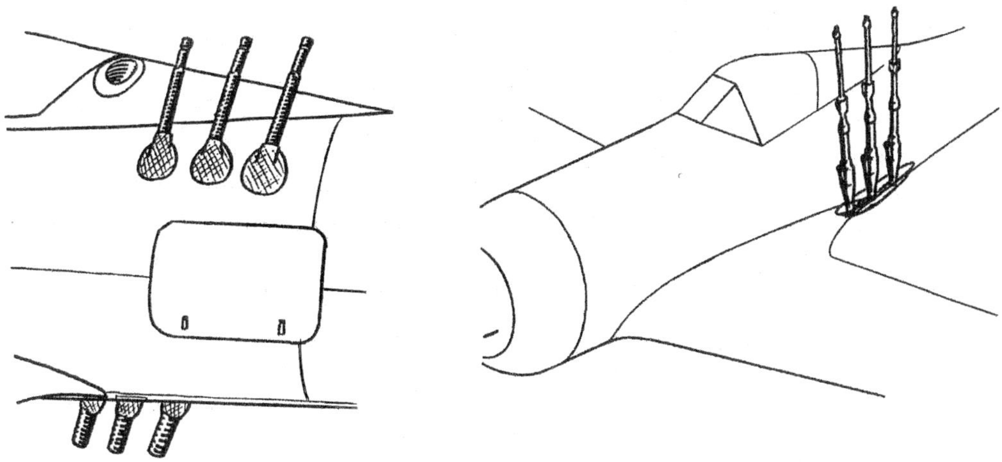

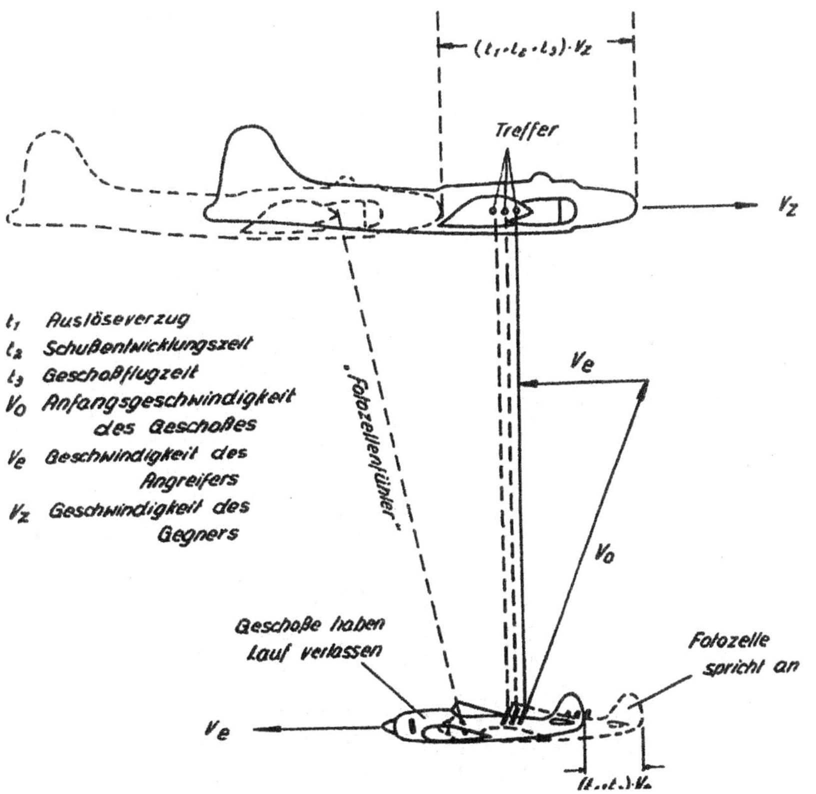

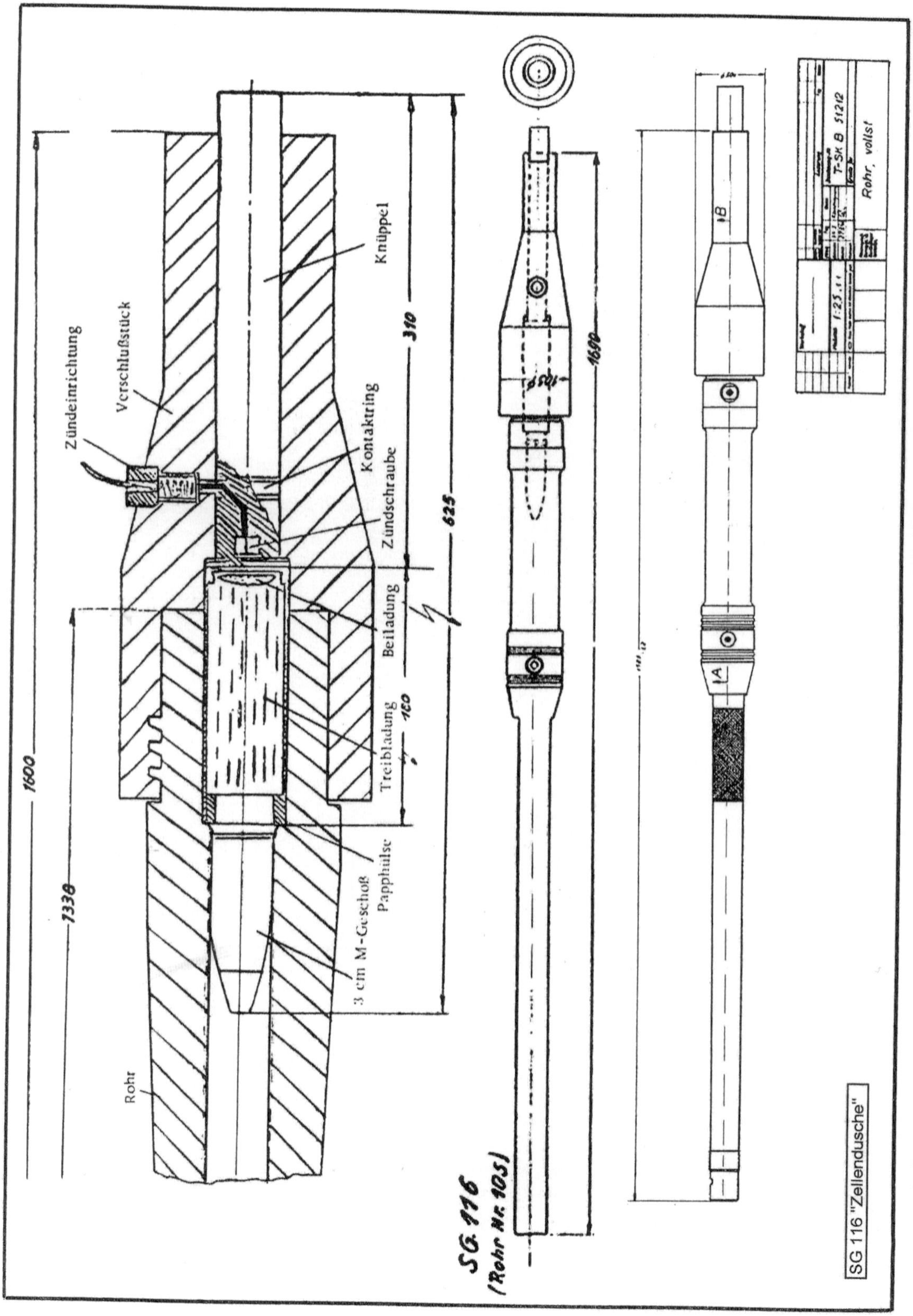

SG 116 "Zellendusche"

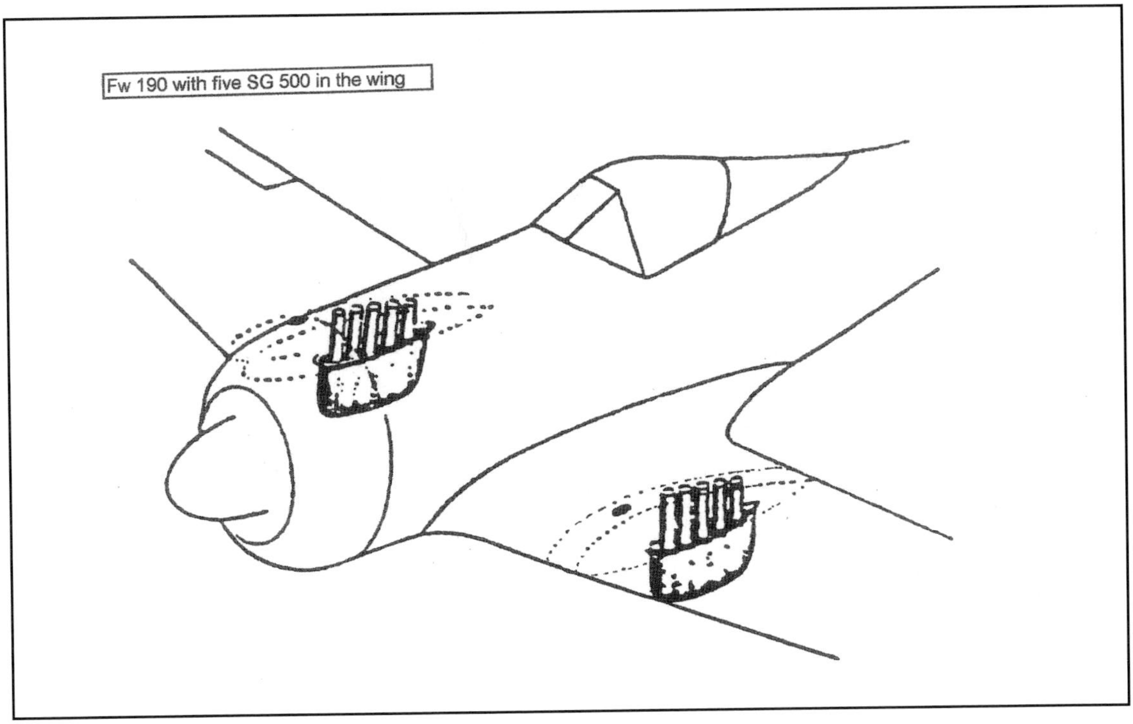
Fw 190 with five SG 500 in the wing

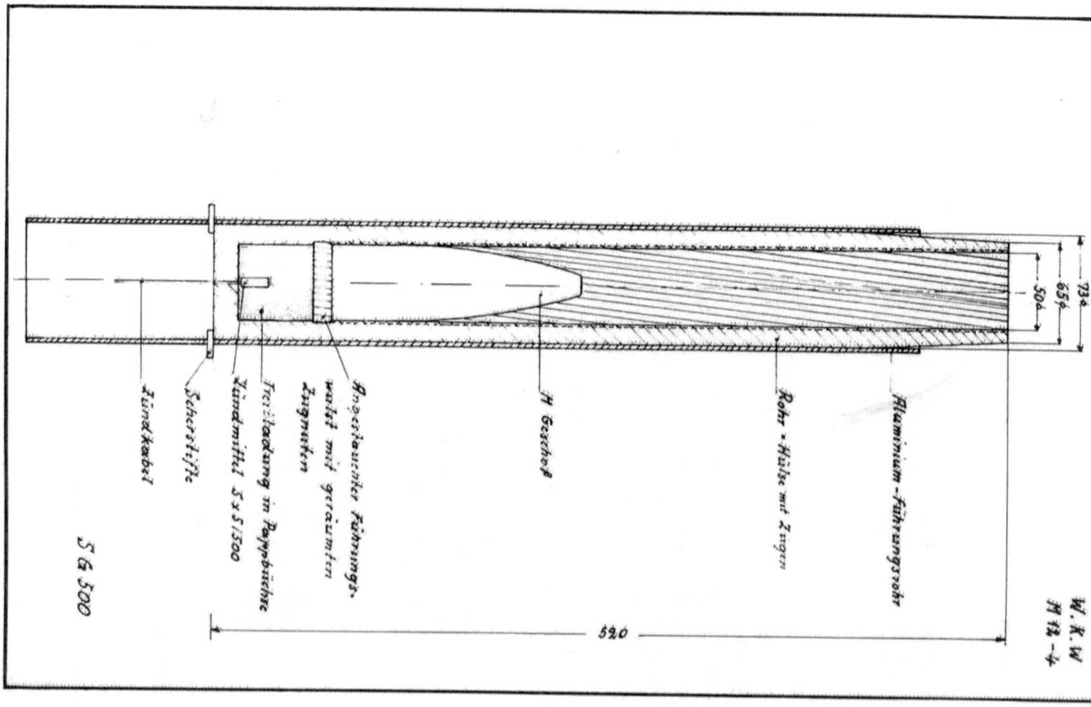

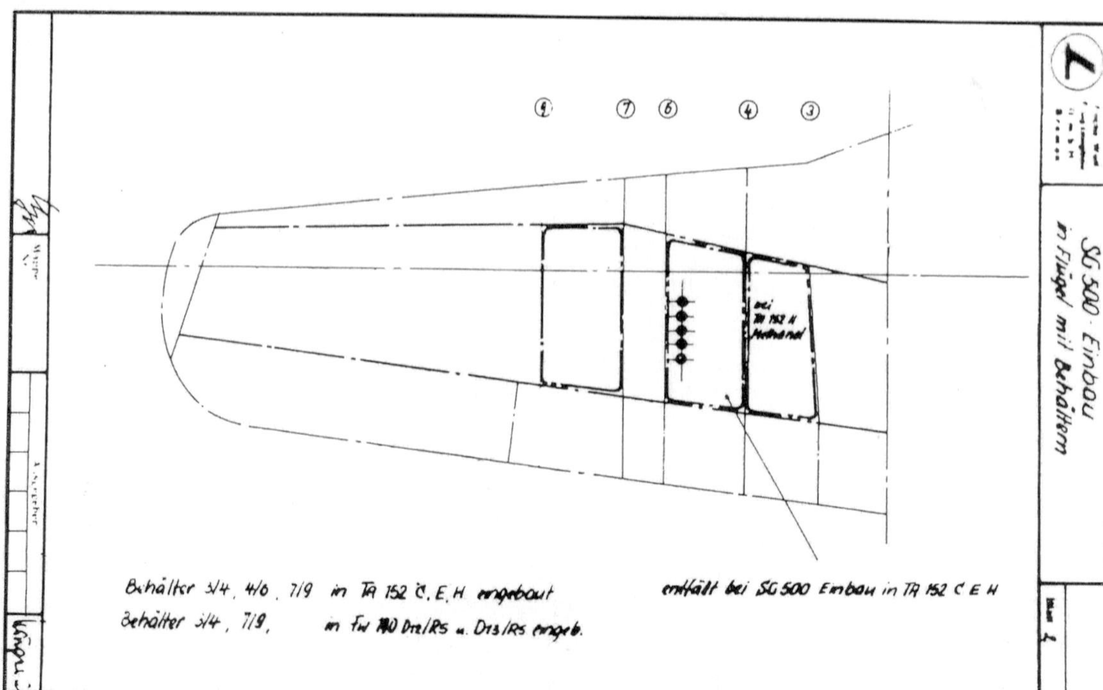

Focke-Wulf Flugzeugbau G. m. b. H. Nr. 26 a

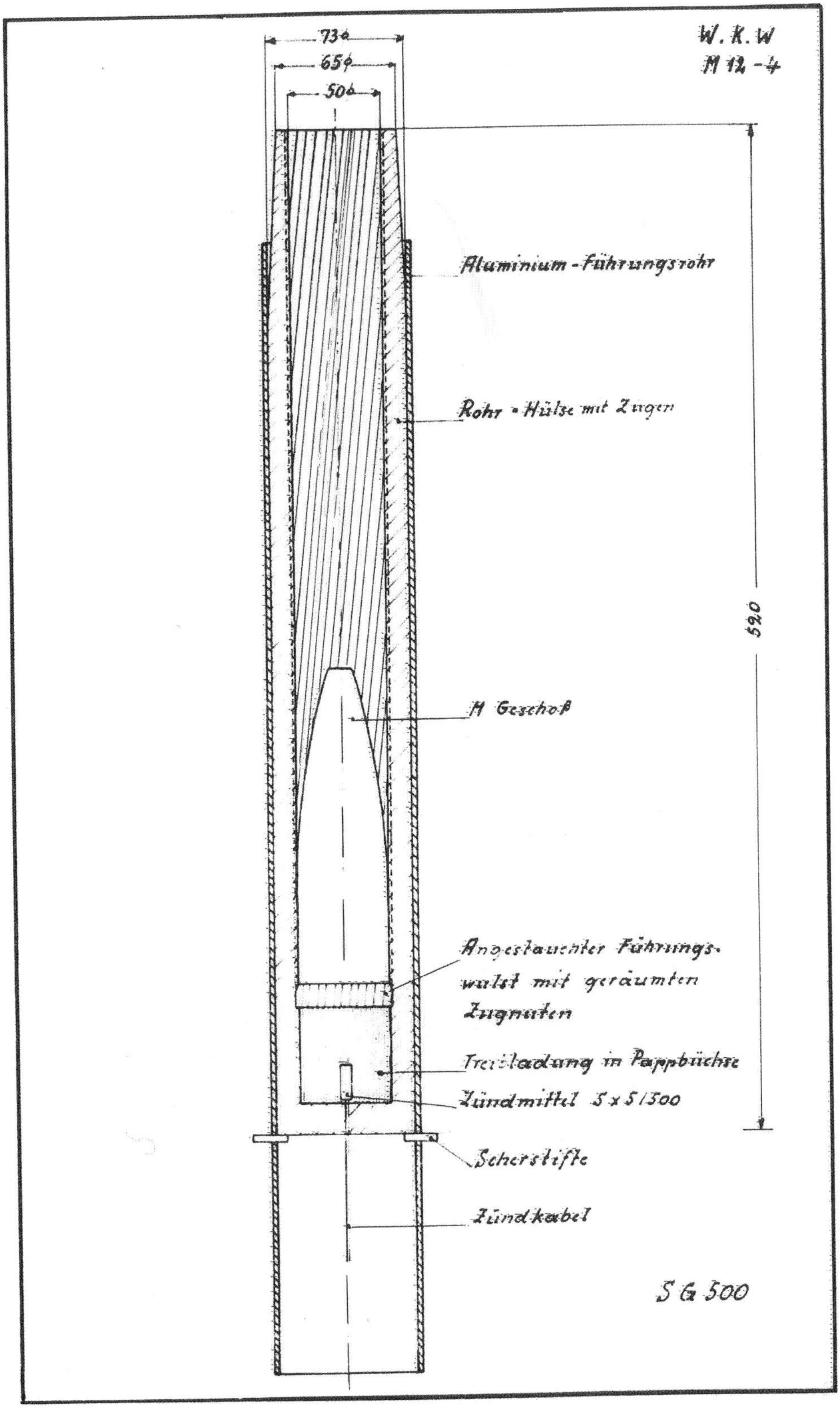
W. K. W
M 12 -4
73ϕ
65ϕ
50ϕ
520
Aluminium - Führungsrohr
Rohr - Hülse mit Zügen
M Geschoß
Angestauchter Führungs-
wulst mit geräumten
Zugnuten
Treibladung in Pappbüchse
Zündmittel 5 x 5/500
Scherstifte
Zündkabel
S G 500

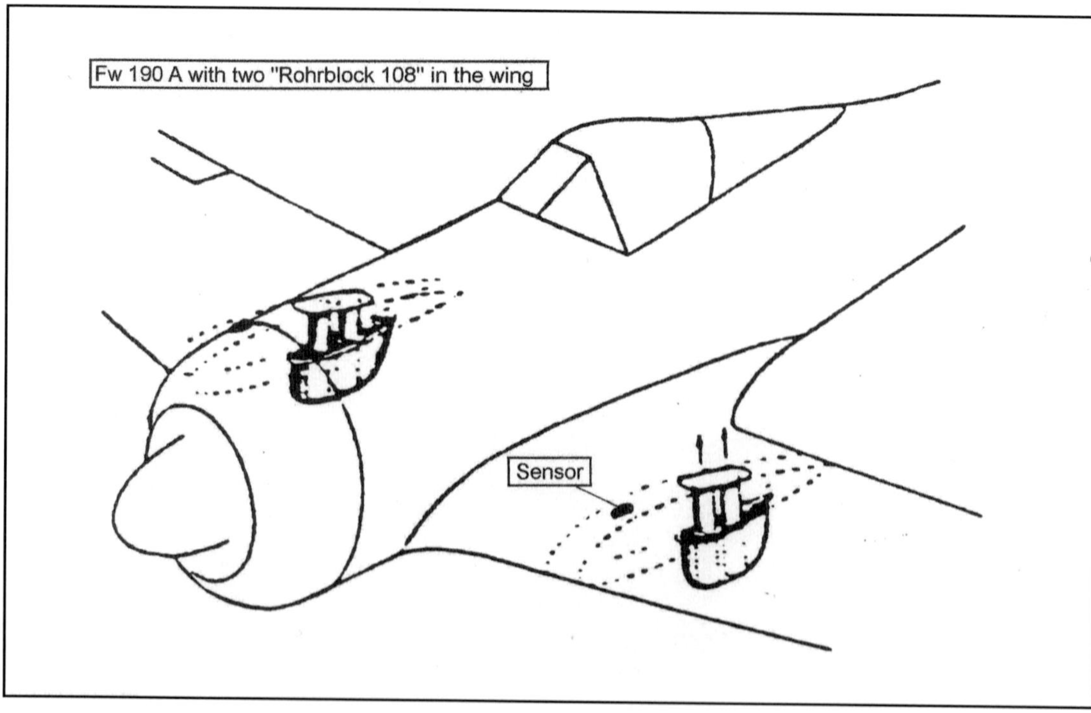
Fw 190 A with two "Rohrblock 108" in the wing
Sensor

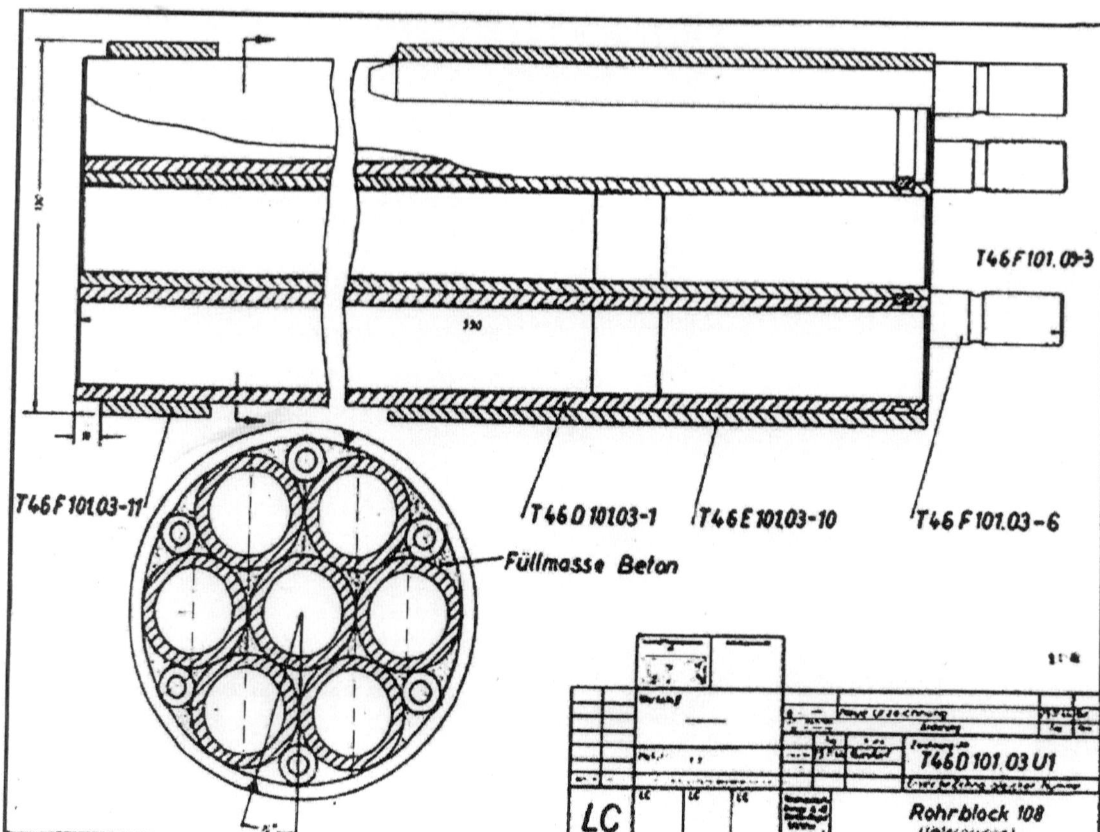
T46F101.03-3
T46F101.03-11
T46D10103-1
T46E101.03-10
T46F101.03-6
Füllmasse Beton
T46D 101.03 U1
LC
Rohrblock 108

Fw 190 A with two "Rohrblock 108" in the fuselage

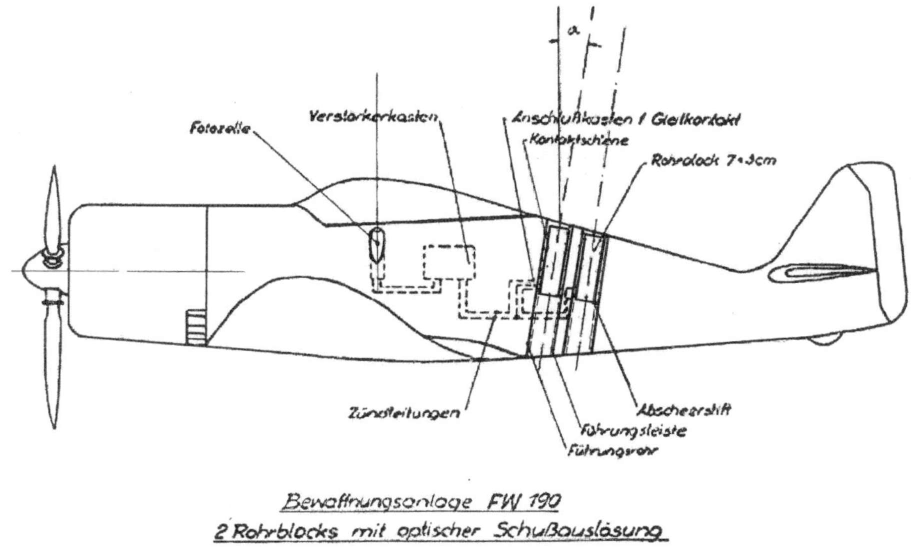

Ta 152 C with two "Rohrblock 108" in the wing

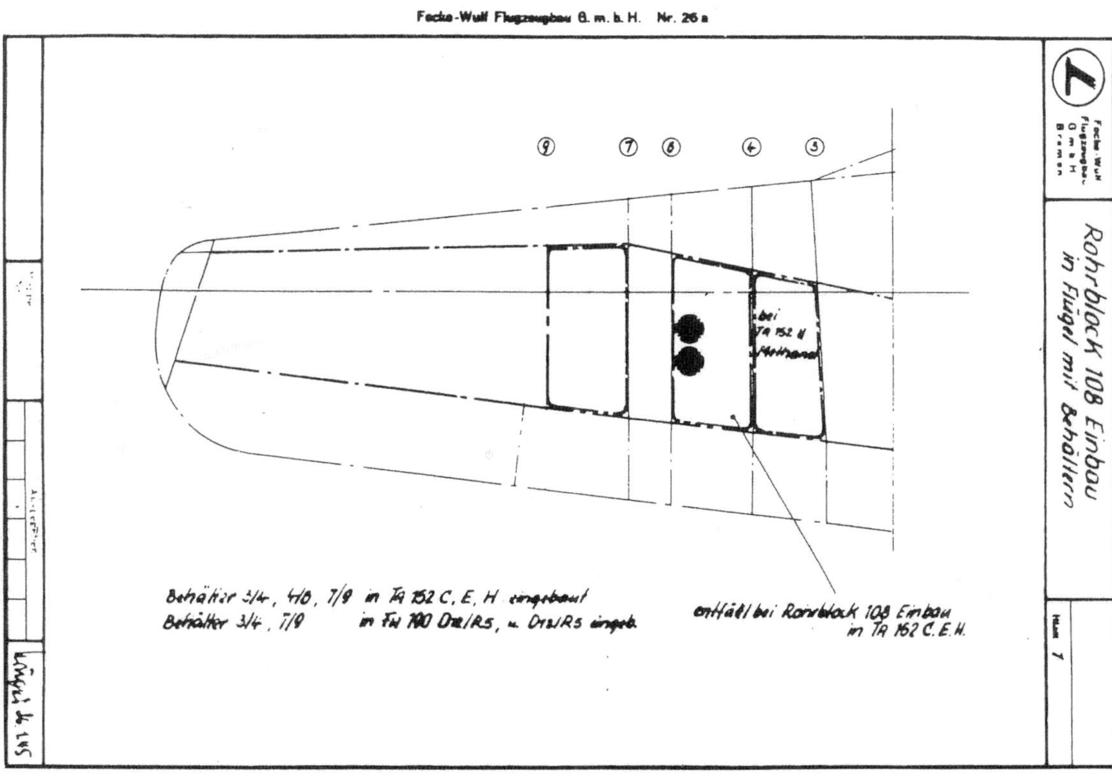

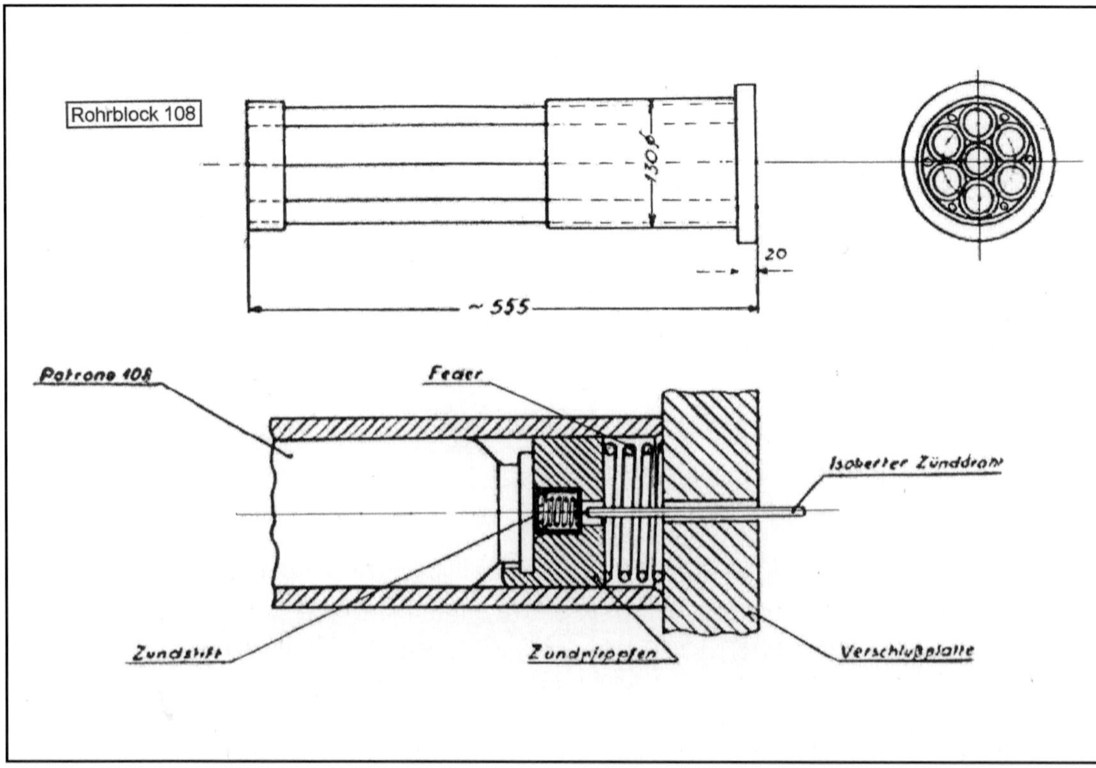
Rohrblock 108
130 ϕ
20
~555
Patrone 108
Feder
Isolierter Zünddraht
Zündstift
Zündpfropfen
Verschlußplatte

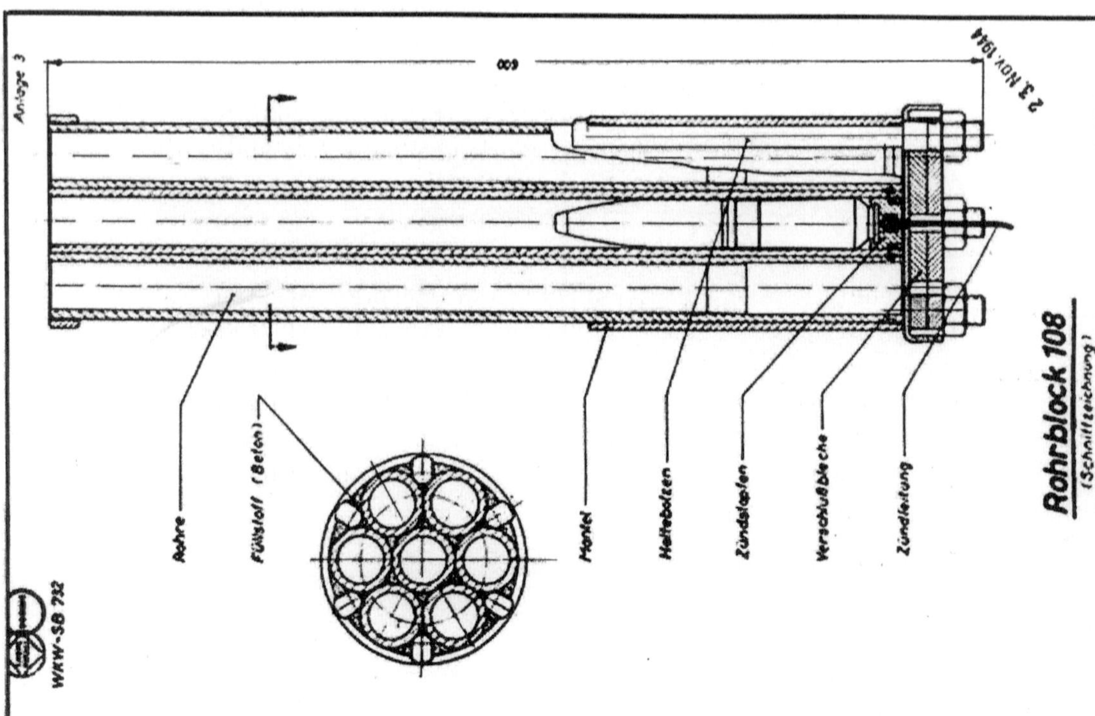
Anlage 3
600
23. Nov. 1944
Rohre
Füllstoff (Beton)
Mantel
Haltebolzen
Zündstopfen
Verschlußbleche
Zündleitung
Rohrblock 108
(Schnittzeichnung)
WKW-SB 732

Chapter 37

Rheinmetall-Borsig Sondergerät SG 113a Förstersonde

The SG113a was an anti-tank recoilless one-shot 77 mm cannon. Mounted vertically in the wings of an Fw 190 with 15-degree rearward slant, it shot automatically when flying over a tank, launching downwards at 650 m/s one saboted 45 mm armour-piercing projectile. It was once again balanced by a Davis-type counterweight.

The gun was triggered by the electrical impulse caused by the magnetic trigger PB 3a Isegrim developed in the Ernst Orlich Institute by Drs. Hackermann and Schwetzke. The Isegrim could detect the magnetic field generated by the metal of a tank, at between 9 and 50 m of altitude, using two T-shaped magnetic anomaly sensors.

The flight tests were made with three Hs 129 B and three Fw 190, at the FZG in Stuttgart, Lüneburg Heath, Rechlin, Volkenrode, Wolfersdorf-Jena and Tarnewitz (EKdo 26), between October 1944 and January 1945.

The Fw 190 F-8 works nos. 586586 and 933452 were used in October 1944 and the Fw 190 V75 works no. 5782071 (DR+MH) between September and November of the same year. The Kuhglocke electrostatic trigger developed in Braunschweig Volkenrode was also tested.

The SG 113a measured 1,600 m length and weighted 67 kg in its full version. Its projectile could pierce 40 mm armour with 60-degree impact angle and 50 mm with 75-degree impact angle. Tests were performed in Wolfersdorf with a Pz.Kw.V Panther and with an American Sherman. A Russian tank was used in Tarnewitz.

The 113a should shoot while flying at 300 km/h over flat land and without trees. It could be used by night and in fog. The pilot could choose whether to fire one, two or all four guns. For forced down landings, the SG 113a could be ejected by means of a small explosive charge below 300 km/h.

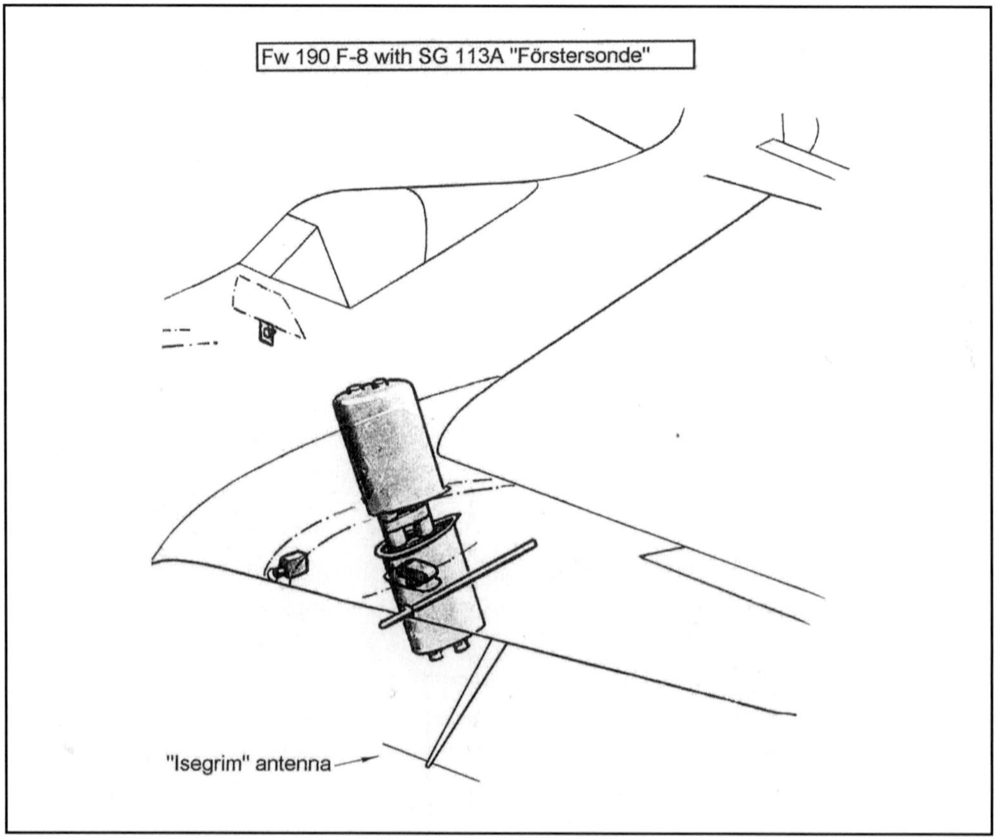
Fw 190 F-8 with SG 113A "Förstersonde"
"Isegrim" antenna

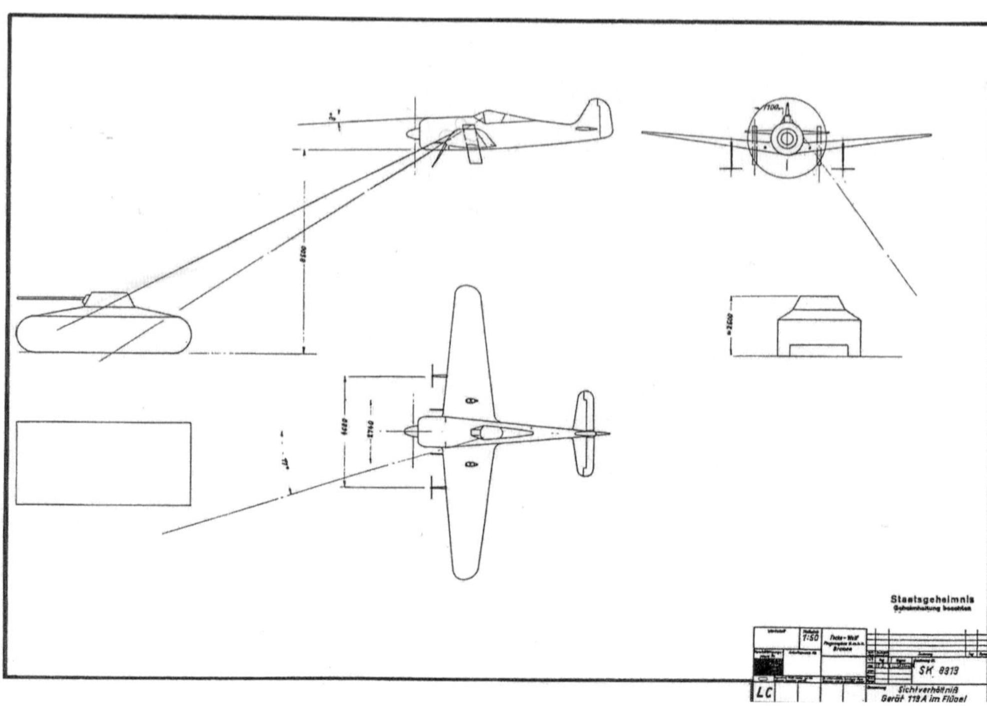
Staatsgeheimnis
1:50
SK 8313
LC
Sichtverhältniß
Gerät 113A im Flügel

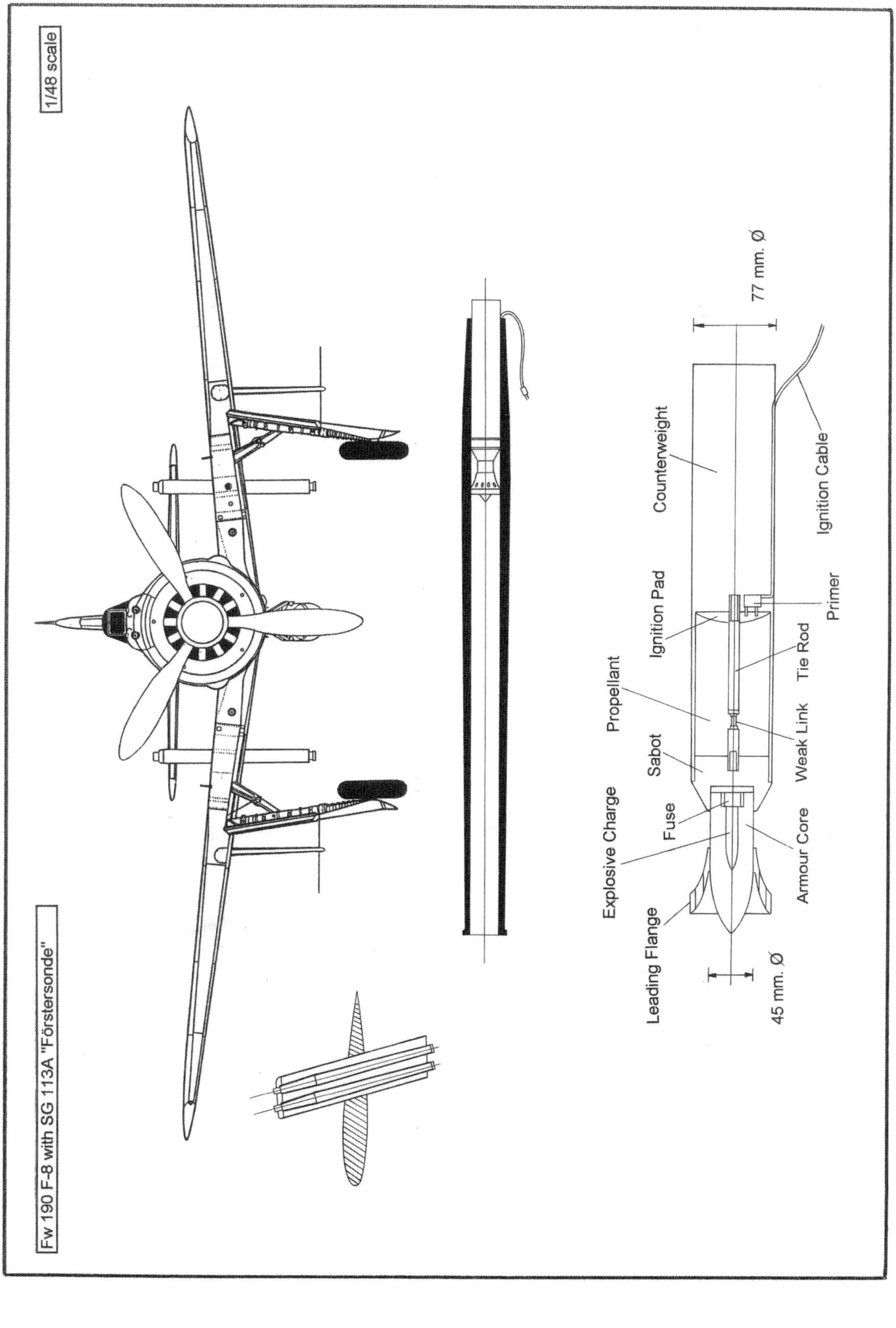
1/48 scale
Fw 190 F-8 with SG 113A "Förstersonde"
77 mm. Ø
45 mm. Ø
Counterweight
Ignition Cable
Ignition Pad
Primer
Propellant
Tie Rod
Sabot
Weak Link
Explosive Charge
Fuse
Armour Core
Leading Flange

Chapter 38

Spin-Stabilised Rockets

In 1936, research was started to provide the Luftwaffe with a 'Bordrakete' unguided rocket capable of being launched from any airplane. After the testing performed at the research centre in Tarnewitz in 1937, it was decided to manufacture the RZ 65 (Rauch Zylinder) model presented by the Rheinmetall-Borsig company.

This was a spin-stabilised rocket of 73 mm calibre fitted with a Ra Z51 (Raketenaufschlag zünder) nose percussion fuse and a powerful explosive charge of 280 g of RDX/TNT able, in theory, to shoot down a heavy bomber in just one impact.

The rotation was achieved with six inclined exhaust venturis located at the base of the cylinder, following the Baron von Unge system, improved by Krupp in 1909. It was a practical design, easy to store, that could be shot from a tube (Einzelschussrohr) by means of an electrically activated percussion mechanism. The launcher had a slightly higher calibre (75 mm) and the rocket was kept at the centre of the tube thanks to the three longitudinal fins fixed to its inner walls to allow the gases to be expelled with the minimum friction.

On the other hand, its use from airplanes proved to be a failure for different reasons.

The process of drilling the venturis at the rocket base was a costly operation that did not adapt well to German methods of mass production. The result was not very accurate, affecting the rocket flying path, making it unpredictable. During further tests performed in November 1941, it was proved that after 544 launches only 15 per cent had hit a target the size of a bomber. In comparison, the MG/FF guns of 20 mm considered an average transition design in 1940, had a 26 per cent rate of good shots.

The low quality of the DEGN powder as propellant provided the RZ 65 a practical range of just 250 m. This meant that the launching airplane had to fly well into the 100 yards area covered by the artillery of the B-17.

The Luftwaffe did many tests in 1941 trying to adapt the RZ 65 to the design of the airplanes in service at the time. Multiple launchers of four tubes were installed under the wings of a Messerschmitt Bf 109 F-2 and a F-4/R1 and of six tubes in a Focke Wulf Fw 190 A-3/U2, works no. 135386, leading to the conclusion that a salvo of eight to twelve rockets had no possibility of hitting a bomber at more than 100 m. The installation of twelve tubes grouped together under the fuselage of the Bf 110 V19 and of sixteen tubes under the wings of a Ju 88 P-4 did not achieve better results.

After the failure in the development of their own rockets, the Luftwaffe tried to adapt some of the Heeresartillerie designs for the air to air use. The first was the Wurfgranate Wgr.42 with a calibre of 210 mm. It was a spin-stabilised heavy rocket designed to be launched from a Nebelwerfer NbW 42 five-barrelled artillery weapon. The base was closed by a venturi block with twenty-two nozzles, each angled at 16 degrees.

The Luftwaffe version, 'Bordsprengrakete 1943', was named W.Gr 21 (Wurfgranate 21 cm) with a length of 1250 mm and a weight of 109.55 kg of which 10.17 were of Hexogen explosive and 18.27 of Diglycol propellant. Its speed was 320 m/sec and the range 2,200 m. It was fitted with a RaZ 51 impact fuse and a S/30 time fuse, the warhead being detonated at a pre-set distance between 600 and 1200 m with high lethality zone of 30 m.

During the first half of 1943, the Erprobungsstelle testing of adaptation to the airplanes in service started at Tarnewitz. 'Werferrohr' tubes with a single rocket were installed under the wings of three Fw 190 F-8 followed by successful ground launches. It became clear during the flight shooting tests that the W.Gr 21 suffered considerable deviations on its path. Starting from 1000 m onwards, it fell below 50 m under the launch level. To correct that flaw the tubes were installed with a +7 degree pitch, calculated to make the rockets to converge at 1400 m. They were electrically shot by means of an ERZ 38 low-tension detonator. Although not very accurate, they achieved some success during the second half of 1943 and 1944 when aimed with a Revi 16F gunsight shooting from Fw 190, Bf 109 and Bf 110. The last of these carried two Werferrohr tubes under each wing.

The AG 40 assembly (Abschussgerät), consisting of two Werferrohr set in a vertical configuration, one above the other, were also installed in some Fw 190. When two AG 40 were installed together, the assembly was named Vierersätz. They were tested at least in a Ju 88 A-4. Two lines of six Werferrohr tubes with a pitch of +67 degrees were experimentally installed in the fuselage, behind the cabin, of a Ju 88. This setting of armament was named Reaktiver Bewaffnung and was shot like the Schräge Musik of the night fighter, aimed with a Revi 16B gunsight.

Krebs-Gerät

Some operational tests were conducted with a single aft-firing W.Gr.21 rocket. The Werferrohr was mounted at +7 degrees beneath the fuselage of several Fw 190 A-8 of the JG 3 to be shot rearwards against the bomber 'boxes' after conventional attack with guns. The device was named 'Parthian shot' by the Allies due to its similarity to the last arrow that the old Scythian horsemen launched backwards when retreating after an attack. The W.Gr.21 was used in combat by the Bf 109 G-5/R2, G-6/R2 and G-10/R2, by the Bf 110 F-2 and G-2/R3, by the Fw 190 A-4/R6 and A-8/R6 and by the Me 262 A-1a of JG 7.

By the beginning of 1944, several launches of the powerful W.Gr. 28/32 rockets of Rheinmetall-Borsig, performed from airplanes, tested its potential use as anti-tank weapon. They had been designed as front-line artillery that could be shot from their own packing boxes – 'Packkiste' – from a Schweres Wurfgerät 40 improvised ramp, the Nebelwerfer 41 launcher, SdKfz 251 half-track vehicle 'Stuka-zu-Fuss', or the deck of an immersed Type IX C U-Boat Do 38 Gerät. In spite of its versatility the use of these

rockets for air to ground purposes turned out to be impossible due to the low accuracy of its flight path.
Some testing was done at Tarnewitz of double launchers installed under the wings of a Fw 190 A-5/R6 and under the fuselage of a Henschel 129 B. There was also a project involving an automatic launcher of six tubes, similar to the Do Werfer, to be installed in a Ju 88 C.

The W.Gr.28 (WurfGranateSpreng 28 cm) was a high explosive demolition rocket of 280 mm calibre, 1190 mm of length and 83 kg of weight. The warhead contained 50 kg of Amatol/TNT 40/60. The propellant charge was 6.6 kg of Diglycol. There were twenty-six venturis with a pitch of 12 degrees in the rocket base and it had a range of 1925 m.

The W.Gr.32 (WurfGranateFlamm 50) was an incendiary rocket of 320 mm calibre with the same engine as the W.Gr.28 and a warhead filled with 50 litres of Flammöl Nr. 19, an inflammable fluid made up of kerosene and diesel oil with magnesium fuse. Its length was 1289 mm and weighted 79 kg. Its range was 2200 m.

In an attempt to improve the accurateness of the rockets, the Kurt-Osterrode company modified the W.Gr. 28 to convert it from a spin-stabilised to a fin-stabilised weapon. To that end, the rocket base was replaced by another in which the venturis were drilled with a 0 degree pitch, and four forward-swept fins with a span of 290 mm were fixed to the outer part of the engine.

The new 14WK BS (Wurfkörper Brandschrapnelrakete) rocket was launched by means of AG 200 rails in triple mountings and weighted 80 kg. The plan was to use it for the Ar 234 Werfer Zerstörer ground-attack-specialised version, which could transport nine rockets under the engines and the fuselage.

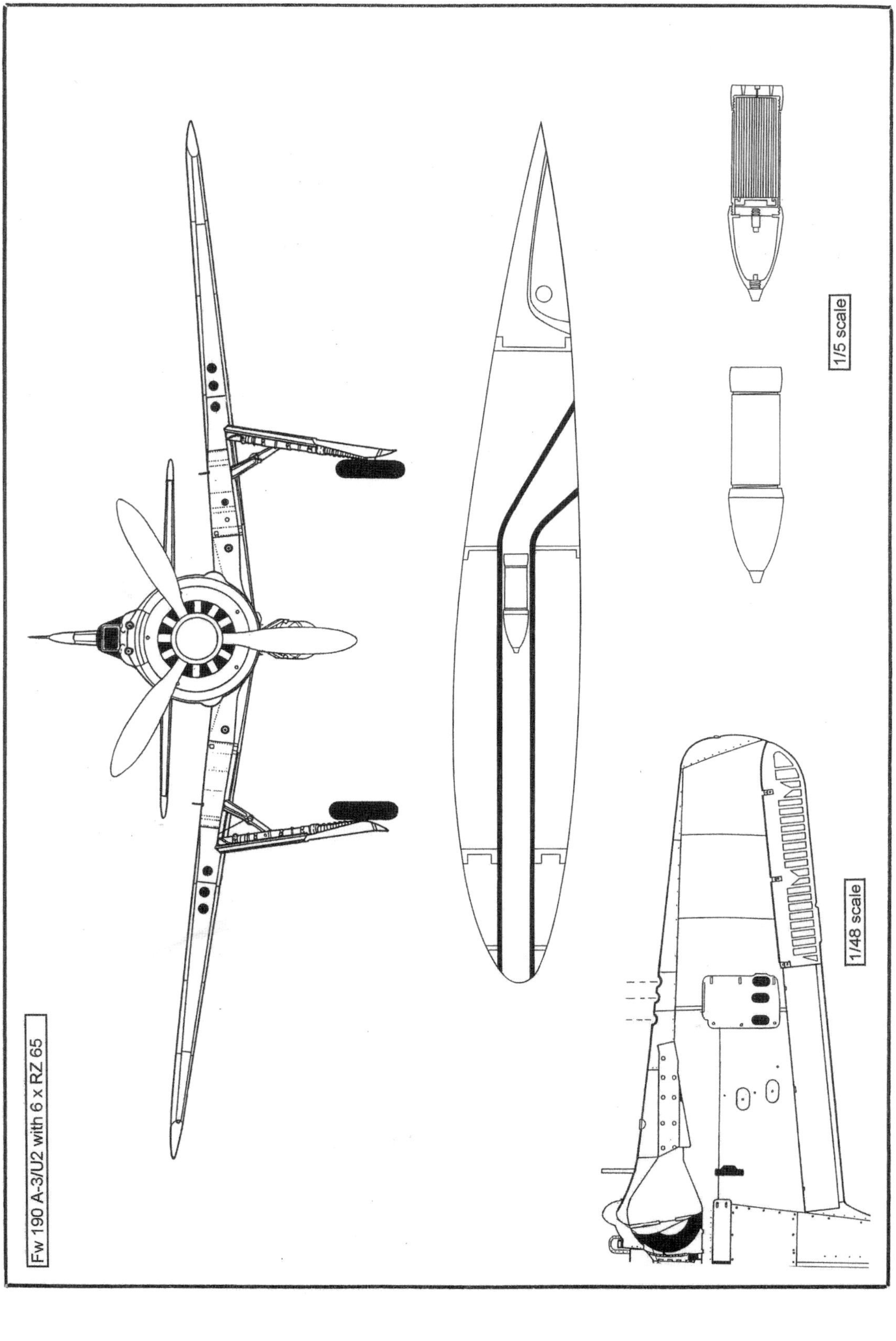
Fw 190 A-3/U2 with 6 x RZ 65
1/5 scale
1/48 scale

Fw 190 F-8 with four W.Gr.28 rockets

1/48 scale

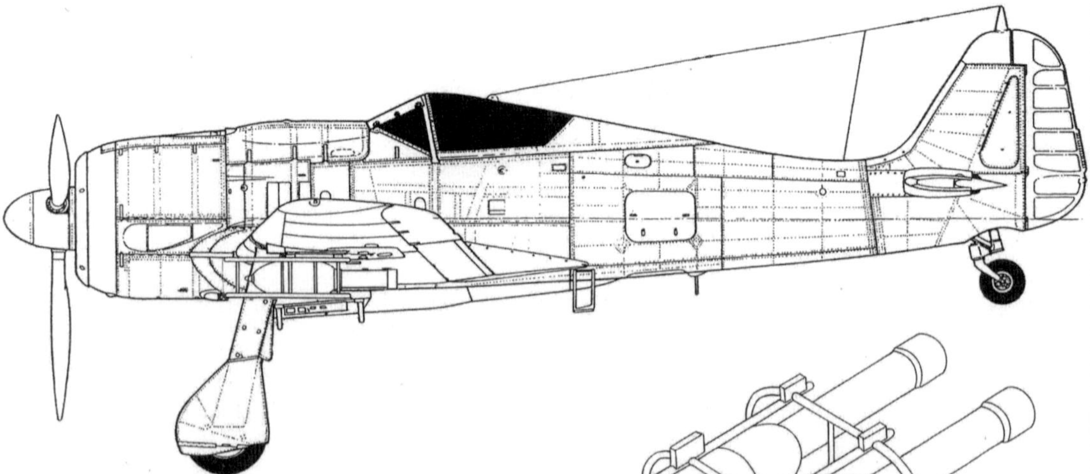

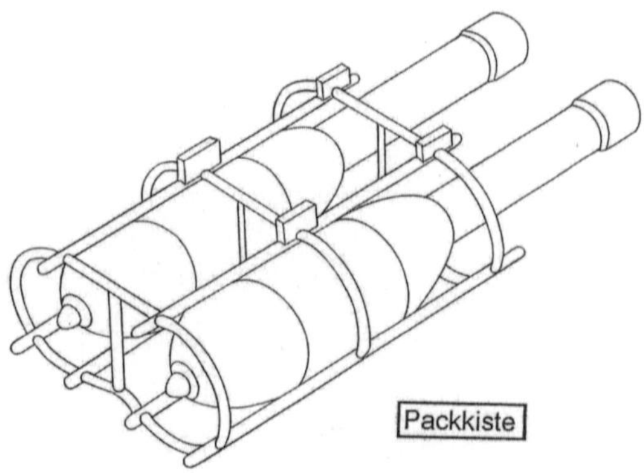

Packkiste

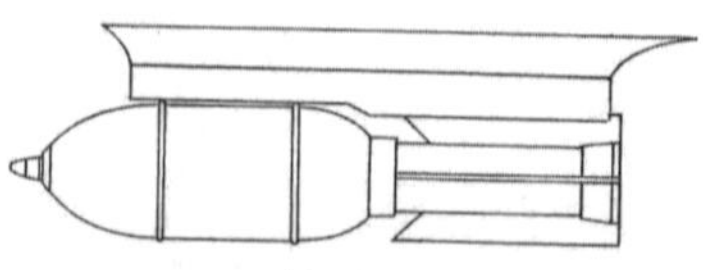

WK 14 BS Abschussgerät

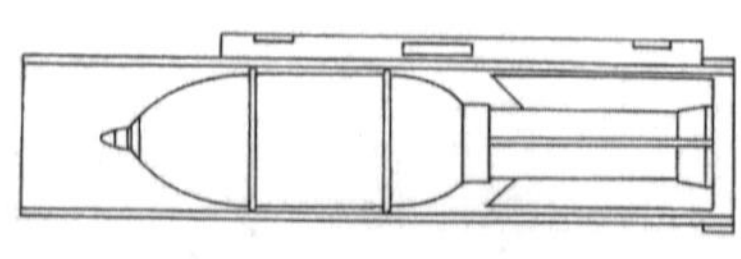

WK 14 BS Abschussrohr

28 cm Wurfkörper (Spr.)

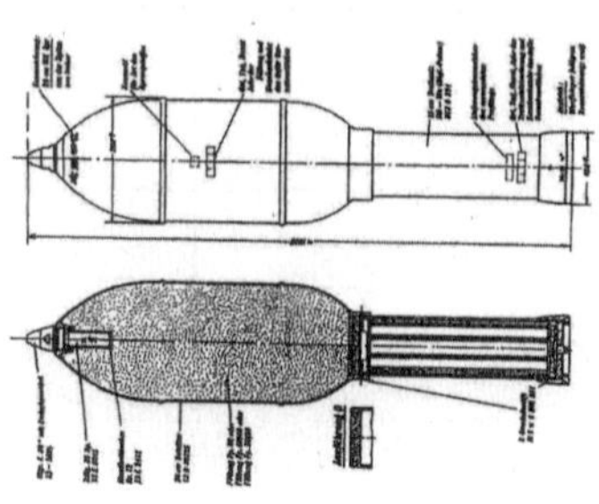

32 cm Wurfkörper (Fl.)

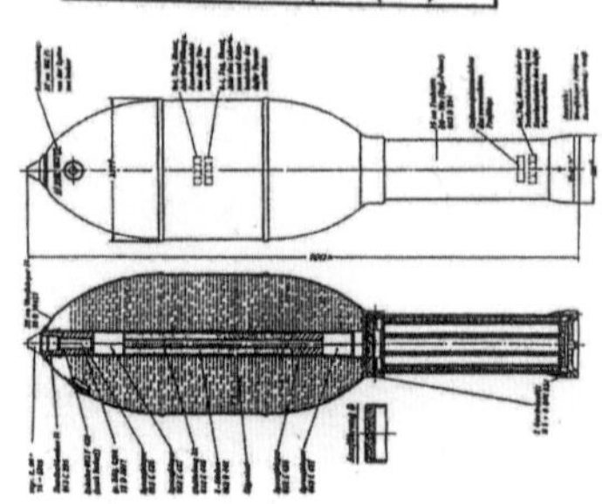

1/24 scale

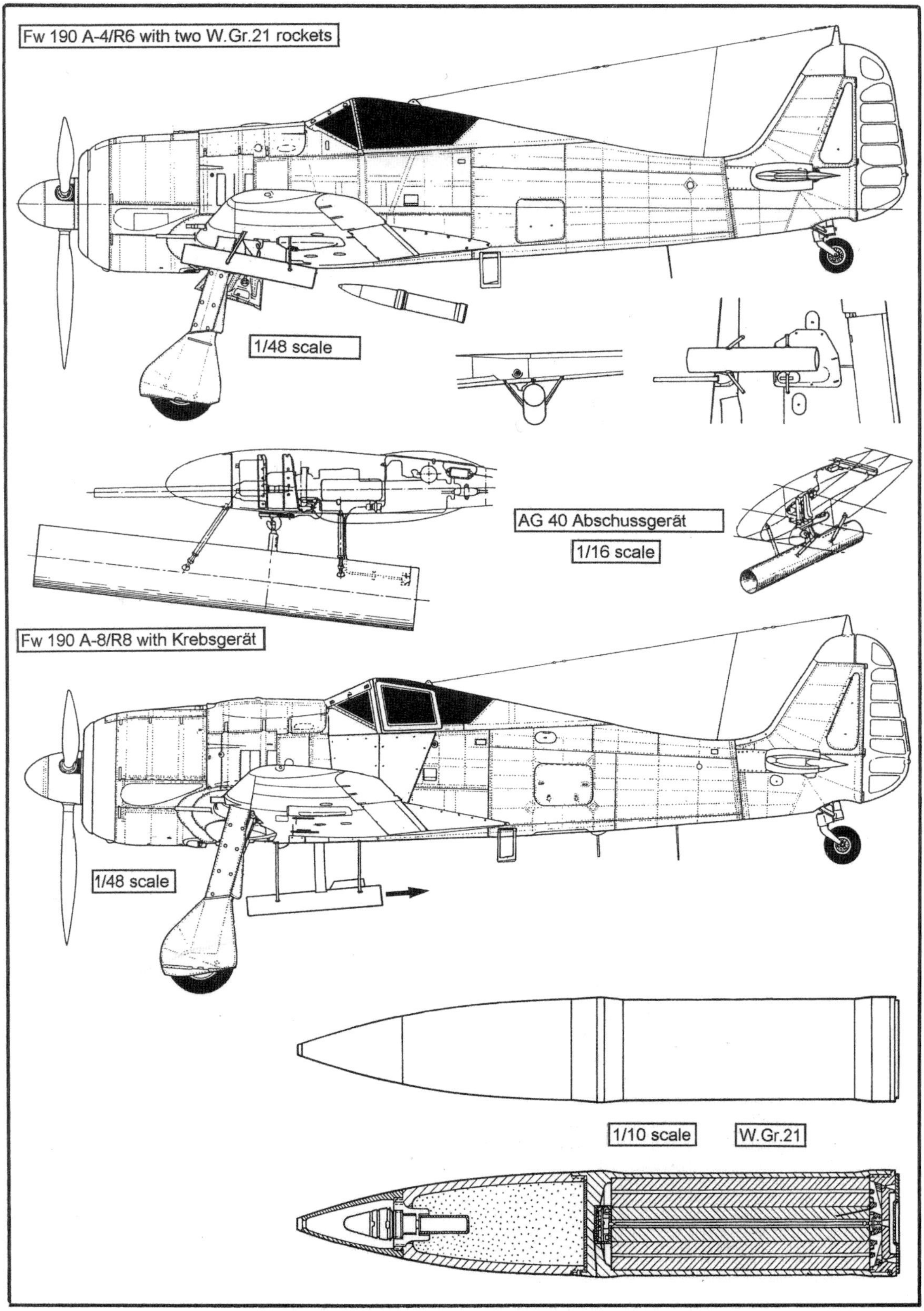
Fw 190 A-4/R6 with two W.Gr.21 rockets
1/48 scale
AG 40 Abschussgerät
1/16 scale
Fw 190 A-8/R8 with Krebsgerät
1/48 scale
1/10 scale
W.Gr.21

Chapter 39

Fin-Stabilised Rockets (Air-to-Air)

After the lack success achieved in air combat by the spin-stabilised rockets, the Rheinmetall Borsig company designed the R100 (Rakete, 100 kg) under the direction of doctors Lambrich and Vüllers.

It was a big air-to-air fin-stabilised rocket, able to transport a payload of HE equivalent to that of the 8.8 cm shells of the Flakartillerie into a bomber formation and, once there, explode causing the greatest possible damage (Pulk Zerstörer).

Its production was proposed in five different versions:

R100 M Minenkopf/Minengeschoss with conventional HE warhead and RaZ 51 impact fuse.

R100 BS/I Brandsplitter, derived from the R100 M, with incendiary pellets warhead and Doppz device (time fuse and impact fuse).

R100 BS-KLW Brandsplitter-Klappleitwerk, derived from the BS/I, with folding fins to be launched from a tube like the W.Gr21.

R100 BS/II, an improved version of the BS/I with one-third more propellant and a warhead containing 400 BR/44 submunitions. They were made of incendiary thermite, 20 mm long cylinders of 55 g in weight that deployed in a conical pattern in front of the missile with a lethal radius of 80-100 m.

The explosion was regulated by a ZZ9B Zündanlage (time fuse and impact fuse).

R100 MS Minensplitter-Minen Schrapnelrakete, derived from the R100 BS/II, the warhead of which contained six submunitions with a length of 220 mm and a diameter of 50 mm, stabilised by four 8 mm long small fins. Each submunition contained 1 kg of Hexogen and an impact fuse or a hollow charge for anti-armour attacks.

The explosion of the warhead was regulated by a ZZ9b Zündanlage or by an electro-optic proximity fuse.

	Length	Diameter	Span	Warhead
R100 M	1,462 mm	210 mm	428 mm	Hexogen
R100 BS/I	1,722 mm	210 mm	428 mm	He + incendiary pellets
R100 BS/KLW	1,830 mm	210 mm	663 mm	He + incendiary pellets
R100 BS/II	2,080 mm	210 mm	428 mm	He + incendiary pellets
R100 MS	1,825 mm	210 mm	406 m	6 x 50 mm submunitions

The R100 could be shot at distances of between 600 and 2000 m from the target, using the automatic triggering system, Oberon. This consisted of a combination of the EZ 42 Adler gyroscopic gunsight with the EG3 navigation system Elfe 3 and a radiotelemeter of the FuG 218 or FuG 248 Eule types.

The rocket was launched from an 800 mm rail of the AG 140 type. The combination of the two AG 140 was named Rüstsätz W, and of three of them Rüstsätz W1. The plan was to use the R100 in the Werfer-Zerstörer versions of the Ar 234 and Me 262. The R100 M was first fired successfully in December 1944 without an explosive charge.

In January 1945, 500 R100 BS were ordered for initial tests.

The first R100 BS test took place at Tarnewitz (E2 Abteilung), in February 1945, using the Me 262 A-1a works no. 111994 and the Fw 190 A-6 works no. 550214, equipped with a FuG 217 J Neptun Liliput, Elfe EG3 device and EZ 42 gyro-reflex sight.

By 28 February 1945, only twenty-five R100 BS missiles had been built, ten of which had been released automatically using the Oberon system without problem. An R100 fitted with infra-red equipment and acoustic fuse was reported to be close to operational readiness in May 1945.

Although being a very accurate and efficient weapon, its production was very costly and both the weight and the required electronic equipment for the launch prevented its use in single-engined fighters.

As an alternative to the R100, Dr Fritz Heber (Kurt Heber-Osterrode) received the order to design the smallest rocket with pop-open fins that could be launched in salvos with the help of a Revi 16 B gunsight.

To achieve this, a Diglykol engine was used, able to accelerate it up to 550 m/sec, thus having the same ballistic characteristics of the 30 mm shells of the Mk 108 gun.

The original specification required that a single rocket should be enough to destroy a heavy bomber. Extensive study of battle casualties indicated that 400 g of Hexogen penetrating any part of the B.17 bomber would result in their destruction. Foreseeing that the Allies would enter into combat with heavier airplanes of the B-29 type, it was decided to increase the explosive load up to 500 g.

The final result was a rocket with a diameter of 5.4 cm and 71 cm of length with eight spring-out fins and an AzRz2 impact fuse. It was named R4M Orkan (Rakete, 4Kg, Minenkopf/Minengeschoss) rocket of 4 kg with high explosive, thin-walled warhead.

The R4M had a range of 1800 m and it was estimated that, from such a distance, a salvo of twenty-four rockets had a field of fire of 30 x 14 m, approximately the size of a B-17.

From the 20,000 units ordered to the DMW-Lübeck, Siemens LGW-Görlitz, LGW Hakenfelde, Schneider KG, and Kratzau Werke-Sudetenland at the end of 1944, around 12,000 rockets were finished before the end of the war in Europe. Circa 10,000 units were used in combat achieving the destruction of around five hundred enemy planes.

The flight testing was done with a Me163 A-0 rocket plane. Under its wings, two launchers of twelve rails each known as Abschussrosten were installed. The R4M were electrically fired by means of the automatic Schaltwalze sequencer at 50 milliseconds intervals.

The Me 262 A-1a of the Jagdverband 44 were equipped with Abschussrosten in March 1945.

Some testing was done in February with launchers of seventeen and twenty-four rails using six Me 262 A-1b in the Messerschmitt experimental plant at Oberammergau. These airplanes were also tested in combat with great success.

The installation of the Abschussrosten was also envisaged under the wings of the Fw 190 D-9 interceptors of the I./JG 301 and of the new Ta 152 C-1/R31 and Ta 152 H-1/R11. The hollow-charge principle was applied to the air-to-air rockets, foreseeing that they would be necessary to fight against the great B-29 bombers that would soon enter into service.

In addition to the work at TAL and Waffen F, some research was done at the high-explosive research Institute at Kempten and at DWM-Lübeck. DWM designed a hollow-charge of 55 mm using an aluminised explosive filler and copper conical liner.

The R4HL (Rakete 4Kg Hollandungskopf) was produced by adapting the new warhead to the body of an R4M. This was also known as a Jägerfaust. The plan was to use it together with the R4M in multiple launches, but it was never mass produced.

The R4HL was tested in combat by some Fw 190 A-8/9 of the JG 301.

R4M Technical Data (R4HL) (Schlange)	
Length	812 mm (790 mm)
Diameter	55 mm (55 mm) (55 mm)
Wingspan	215 mm (215 mm)
Total weight	3.85 kg (-) (3.5 kg)
Maximum speed	525 m/sec (525 m/sec) (450 m/sec)
Range	1,500 m (1,500 m)

R-100 M (Minenkopf)

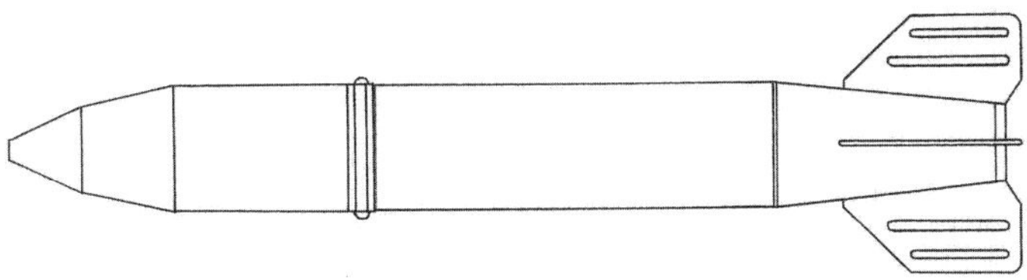

R-100 BS (Brandsplitter) Early type

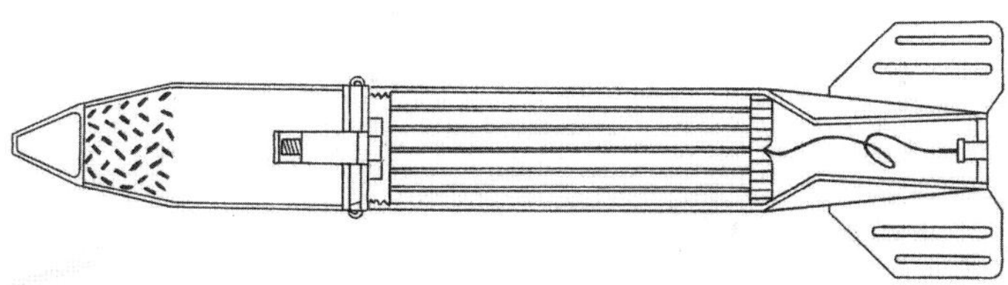

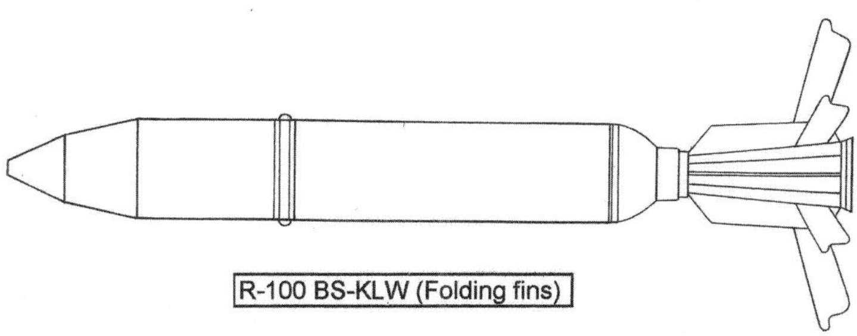

R-100 BS-KLW (Folding fins)

1/15 scale

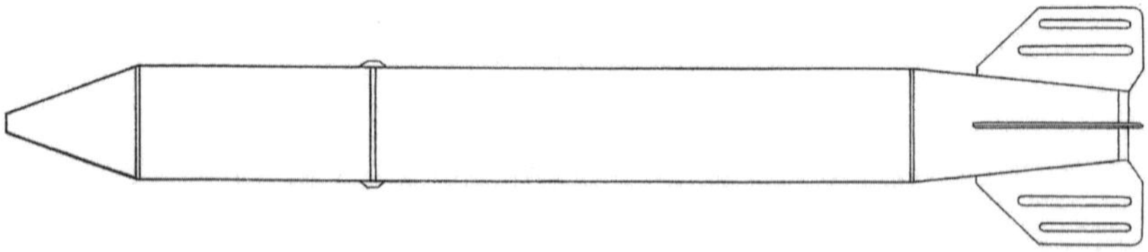

R-100 BS (Brandsplitter) Late type

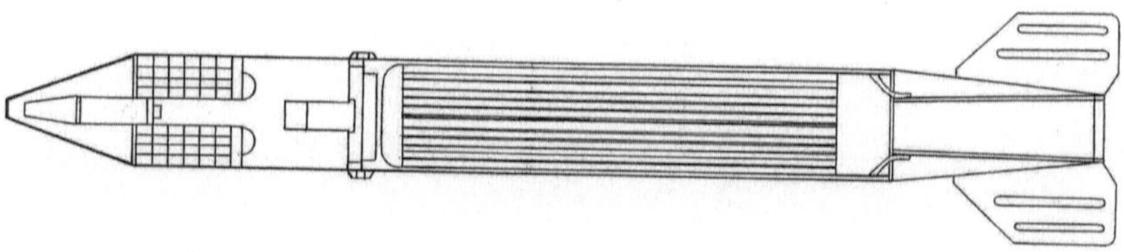

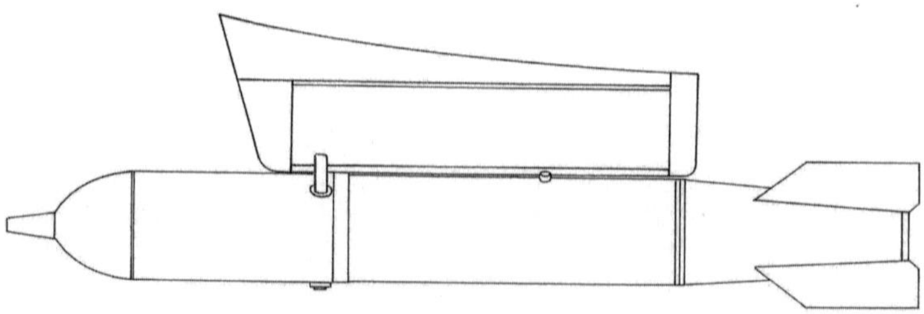

R-100 MS (Minensplitter)

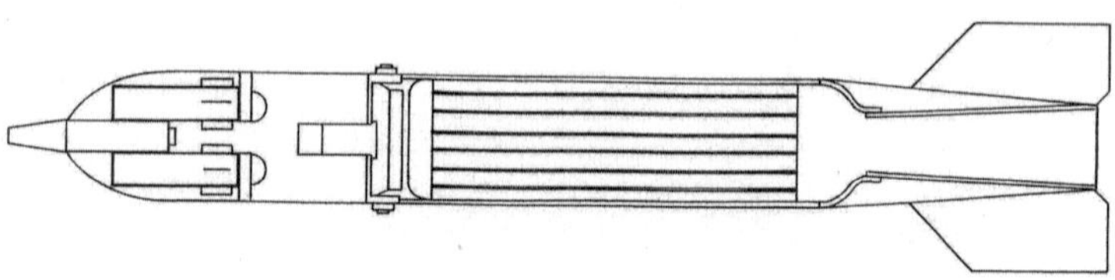

1/15 scale

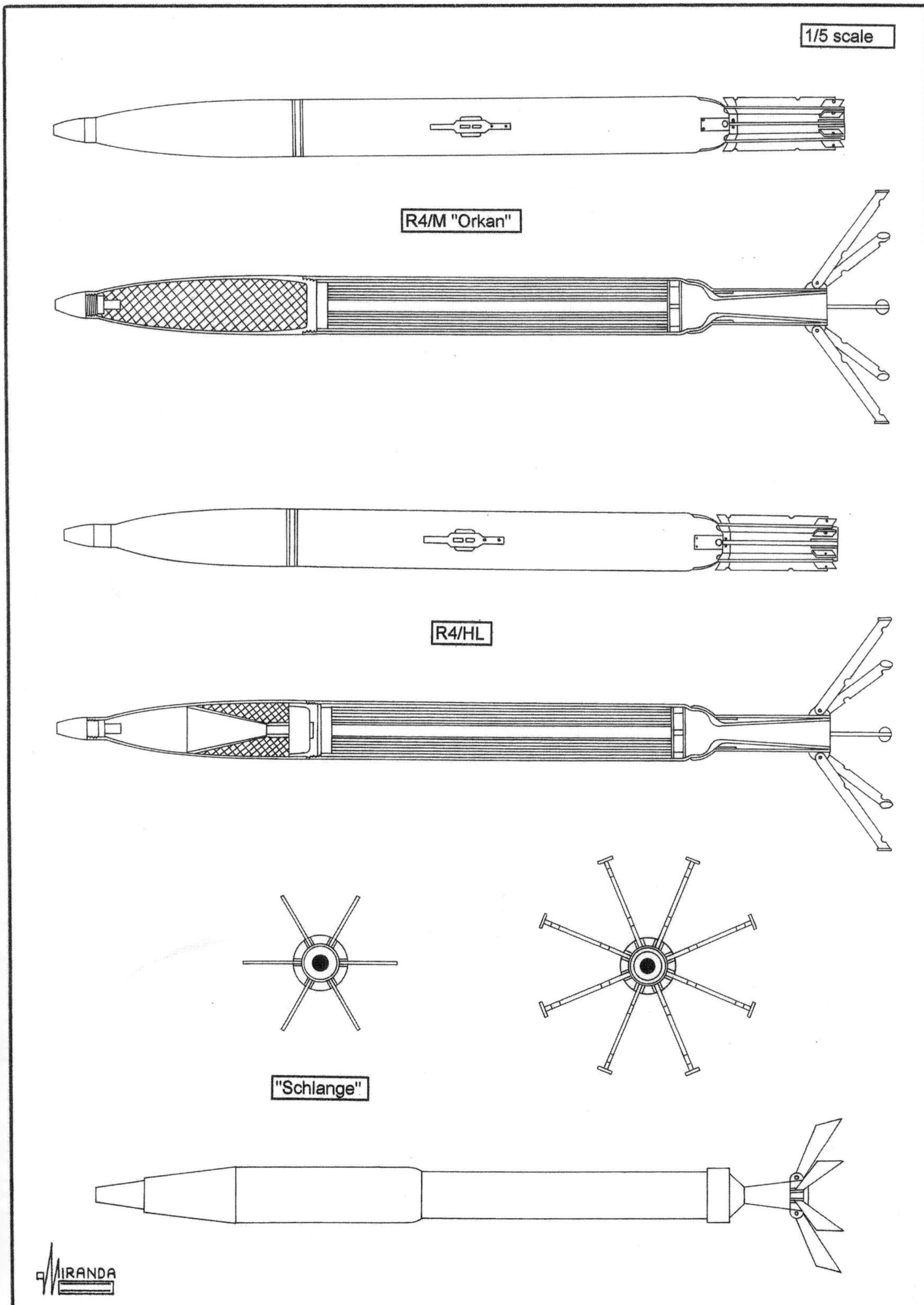
1/5 scale
R4/M "Orkan"
R4/HL
"Schlange"
MIRANDA

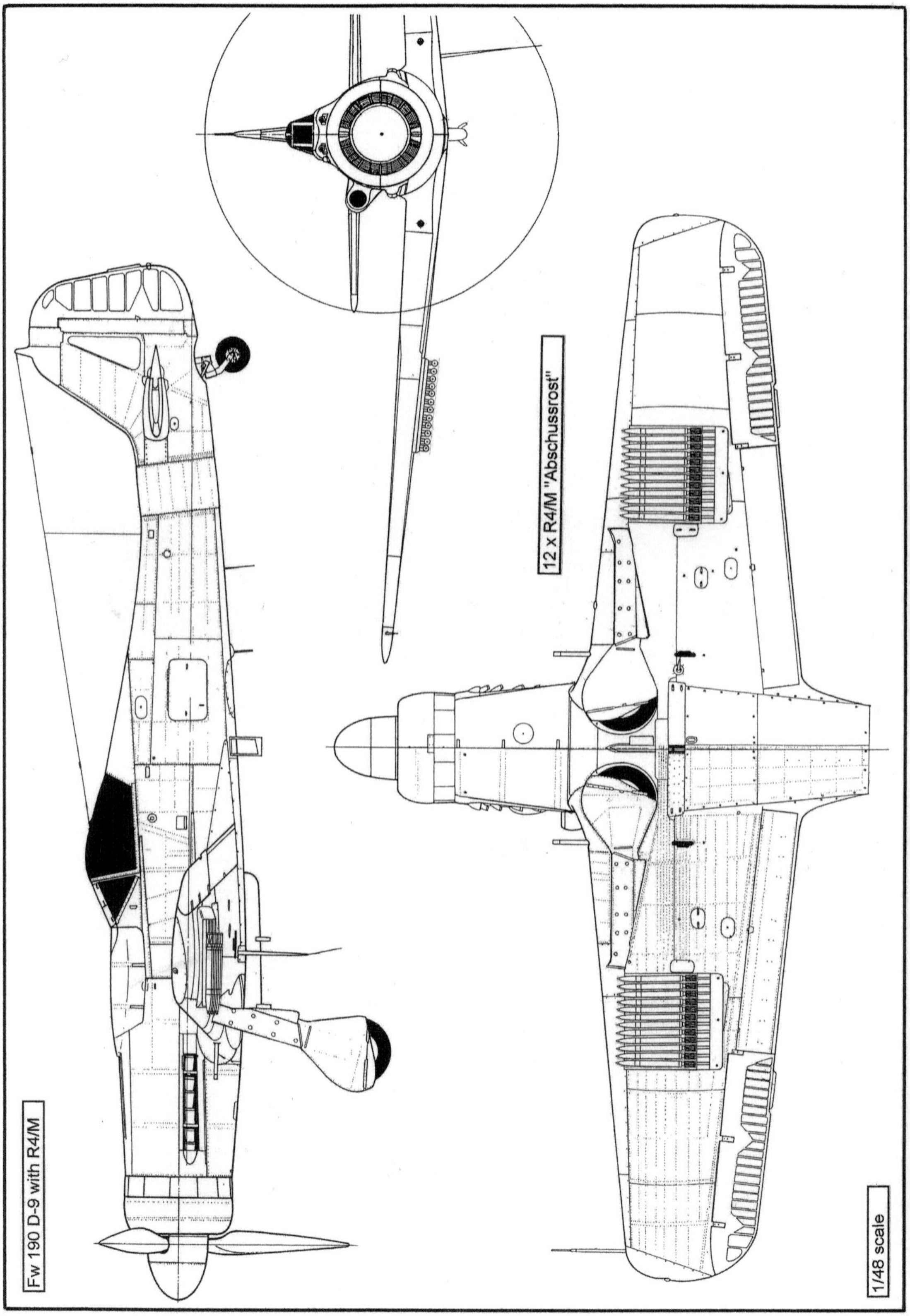
Fw 190 D-9 with R4/M
12 x R4/M "Abschussrost"
1/48 scale

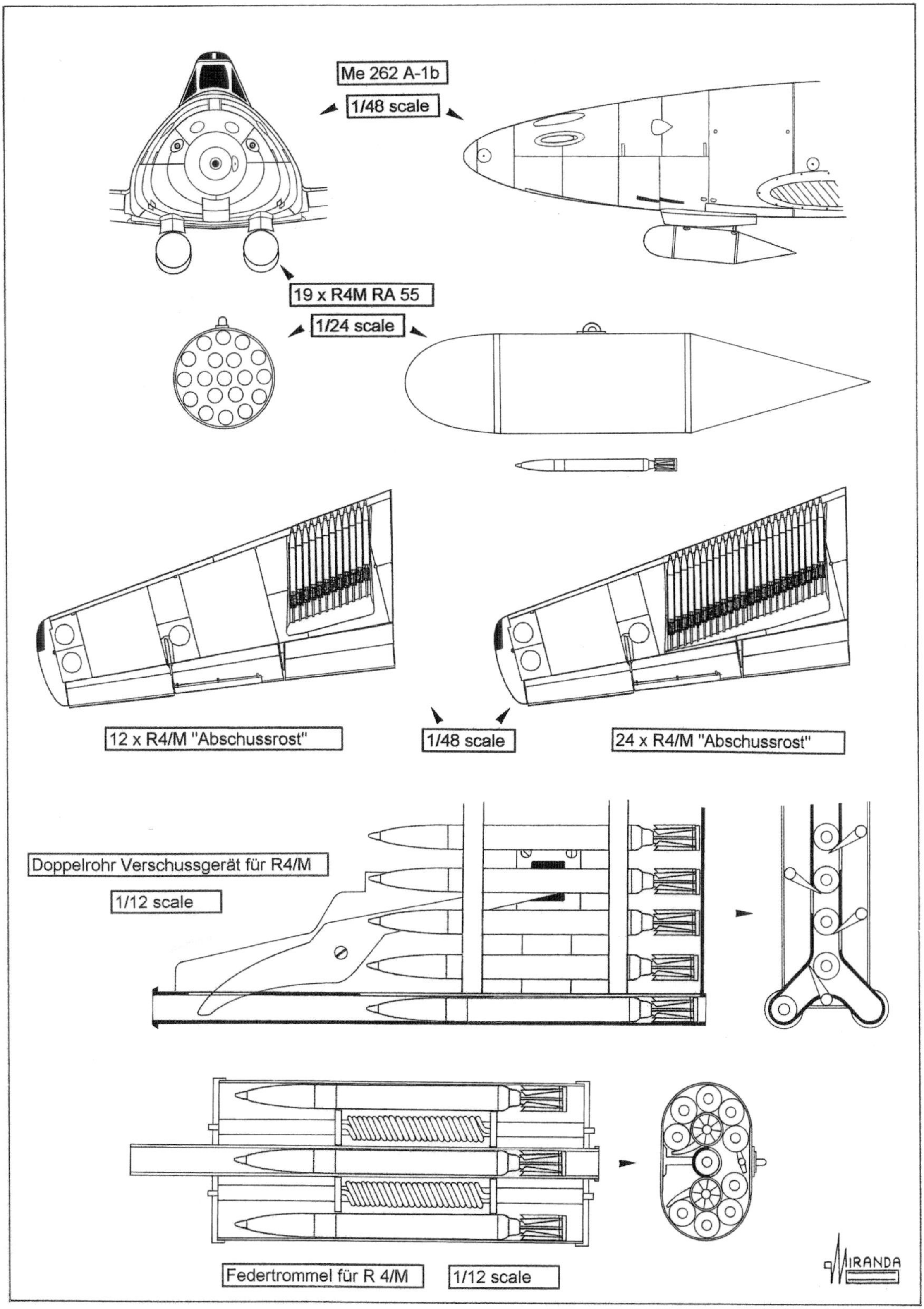
Me 262 A-1b
1/48 scale
19 x R4M RA 55
1/24 scale
12 x R4/M "Abschussrost"
1/48 scale
24 x R4/M "Abschussrost"
Doppelrohr Verschussgerät für R4/M
1/12 scale
Federtrommel für R 4/M
1/12 scale
MIRANDA

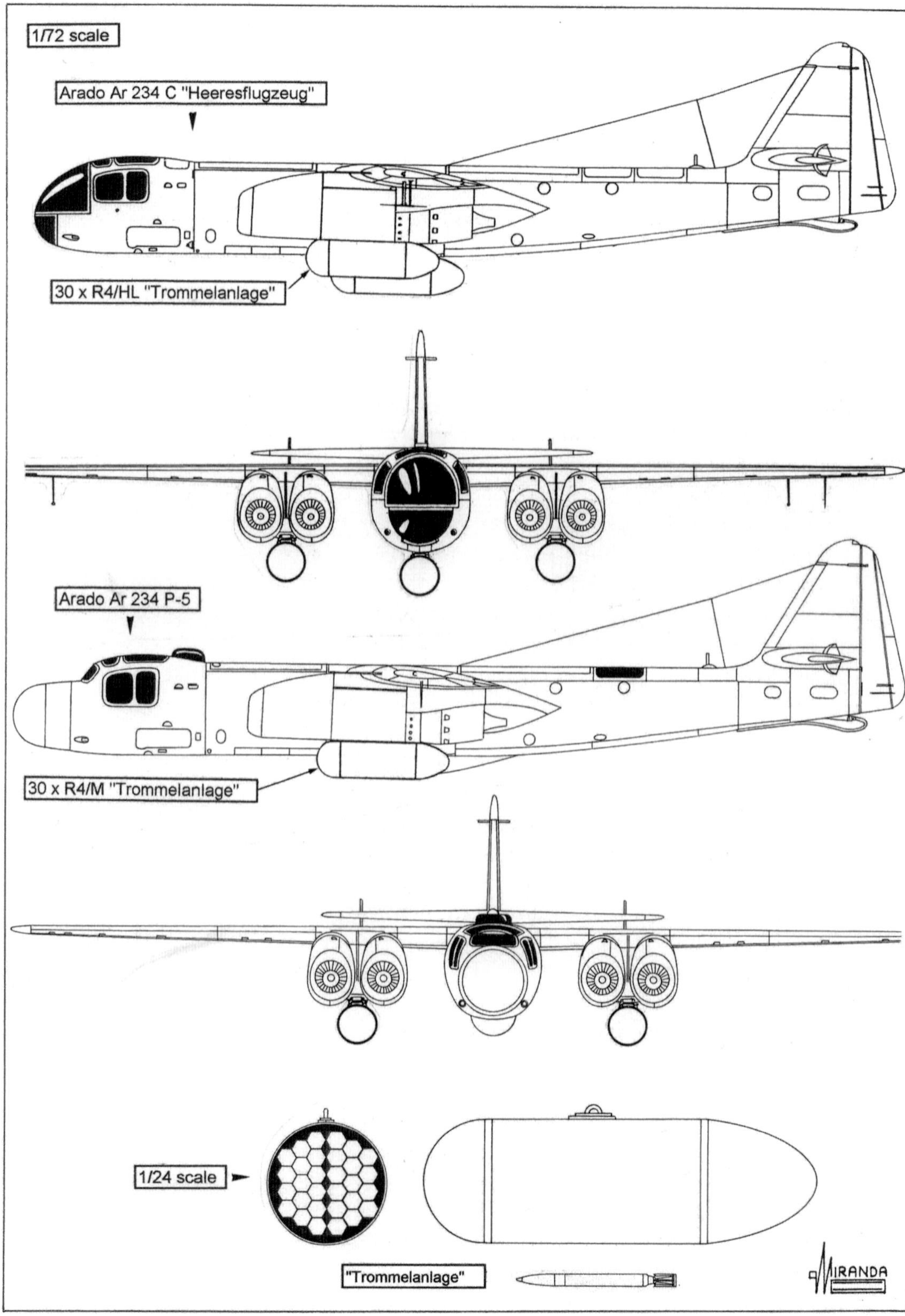
1/72 scale
Arado Ar 234 C "Heeresflugzeug"
30 x R4/HL "Trommelanlage"
Arado Ar 234 P-5
30 x R4/M "Trommelanlage"
1/24 scale
"Trommelanlage"
MIRANDA

Chapter 40

Fin-Stabilised Rockets (Anti-Tank)

During the tests performed with different types of anti-tank ammunition by the Wehrmacht in 1939, the conclusion was reached that the shaped charges did not work well when used in conventional spin-stabilised shells. The reason was that the centrifugal forces acting on the jet dispersed it, losing most of its drilling power. To avoid this, a fin-stabilised hollow-charge shell known as 8 cm Raketenpanzerbüsche Granate 4992 was built and equipped with a powerful rocket with a range of 180 m.

The 4992 grenade was 65 cm in length, and the 8.8 cm hollow-charge warhead contained 0.667 kg of Cyclotol (41.2 per cent TNT, 58.8 per cent cyclonite) and the AZ 5095 impact fuse had a 0.0002 seconds delay. The propellant charge was formed by seven sticks (64 per cent nitrocellulose, 34.5 per cent DEGN, and 1 per cent stabiliser).

The unofficial denomination of these weapons was Panzerschreck ('tank terror'). They were shot from a Bazooka style tube named Raketenkpanzerbüsche 43 Ofenrohr. A flak version, known as Fliegerschreck ('airplane terror') was also manufactured. It consisted of a new 8.8 cm grenade with a warhead length of 174 mm, especially designed for use against airplanes. It contained 144 Brandschrapnel incendiary pellets of phosphorus, of 1.4 g each, and automatically exploded after running 320 m by means of a time fuse and a charge of Nitropenta. The lethal range was 30 m. It was shot from an R.Pz.B.54 fitted with a special gunsight calculated for airplanes with a wingspan of 12 m flying at low altitude. The DWM firm manufactured five hundred Fliegerschreck sets in 1945.

The increasing number of Soviet armoured vehicles forced the creation of new air units specialised for the anti-tank fight. New versions of airplanes were built to perform this task and new "wonder weapons" were designed to be transported by them.

Some of the best anti-tank guns of the Wehrmacht were modified for airborne use, with poor results. Those with a low calibre would fly too low and slowly to destroy the tanks whereas the heavier ones caused damage to the structure of the airplane when being shot.

While the wonder weapons of SG series and the new recoilless guns were still being developed, it was decided to adapt some of the infantry weapons to the available Fw 190s as a provisional measure, Notlösung. The Panzerschreck was adapted by means of several designs known as Fliegende Panzerschreck and used in combat by the Fw

190 F-8. The Fliegende Panzerschreck I consisted of a cluster of three tubes with a C-section and 164 cm in length, joined to a semi-cylindrical holder that could hang under the ETC 50 racks. The cluster weighted 50 kg including the electrical connections and could shoot three anti-tank R.Pz.BGr.4322 grenades.

The Fliegende Panzerschreck II was formed by three tubes of R.Pz.B.54/1 with a length of 135 cm, joined together in a bunch of triangular section. It was used in combat suspended under the wings of the Me 210 Ca-1 in October 1944.

The Fliegende Panzerschreck III was formed from two overlapping tubes of R.Pz.B.54/1 with a length of 135 cm hanging under the ETC 50 racks, four of which could be carried by each

Fw 190. The official name was PD 8.8 Ausführung 1. The system contained two R.Pz.B.Gr 4992 grenades and weighed 25 kg when loaded, producing less drag than the previous model. In case of emergency, it could be dropped like a bomb. The four-tube mounting was PD 8.8 Ausführung 2.

The final design was the PD 8.8 cm Pz Büchsenrohr, or PD 8.8 Ausführung 3. It was a cluster of four tubes specially designed for aerial use. Their length was 99.5 cm only and they were joined to a central wooden structure containing the electrical contacts and the fixing mechanism joining them to the ETC 50 racks. The cluster had quadrangular section, a width of 18.8 cm and weighed around 45 kg. It could shoot both the R.Pz.BGr. 4992 grenades and the Fliegerschreck designed to be used against airplanes. To reduce the air drag, the wooden structure was cut in angles on its forward section and the tube opening was covered by a frangible plastic seal. The Fw 190 F-8 only transported two Büchsenrohr because they considerably decreased the speed of the airplane.

In August 1944, several Fw 190 F-8 armed with Parzerschreck I performed operational tests with the EK 26. In October of the same year, the Fw 190 F-8 of the I./SG 51 performed the operational tests of the Panzerschreck II in Hungary. In January 1945, the Buchsenröhr was flight tested in Udetfeld E-Stelle with the Fw 190 F-8 (W.Nr.580383) coded CM+WL. Other units using the Panzerschreck devices were 5./SG77, 8/SG1 and 6./SG3.

Impressed by the efficiency of the Soviet rocket launchers, or Katyusha, the Germans decided to manufacture their own version of the Russian rockets, the M-8, 82 mm, at the beginning of 1942. It was named 8 cm Raketen Sprenggranate and had a length of 744 mm, a diameter of 78 mm and a fragmentation warhead with 0.6 kg of HE. The Soviets had used their own version of the M-8 since 1937. It was known as RS-82 (Raketnij Snarjad 82 mm) and was launched from RO (Reaktivnoe Orudie) rails installed under the wings of the airplanes. The RBS 82 variant, equipped with an armour piercing warhead and a more powerful rocket (ROFS) to destroy tanks and concrete bunkers, entered into service in 1942.

The Luftwaffe adopted the idea installing rail launchers on the Henschel Hs 129 B-2 and Focke Wulf Fw 190 F-8 and F-9 airplanes, specialising in anti-tank fighting. They had six rails of 1430 mm under each wing.

The Wehrmacht rocket 8 cm RSp. Gr. was renamed Panzerblitz RSp.Gr. by the Luftwaffe and operationally tested by the Hs 129 B-2 of the EKdo 26 in January 1944. It was used in combat by the Fw 190 F-8 of II./SG1, II./SG2, III./SG3, II./SG4 and I./SG10 with little success due to the low accuracy of the weapon, which was shot with the help of a Revi 16 B gunsight.

Following the Soviet example, an armour piercing version was manufactured, equipped with a warhead of 323 mm of length and an AzRz2 impact fuse. It was a longer and heavier rocket than previous one and, although having a more powerful engine, it was inaccurate when firing against targets located at more than 200 m distance. To obtain good results, the pilots of the Schlacht units were forced to fly low and slow, thus suffering heavy losses from the Soviet DCA.

The armour piercing version, with a length of 970 mm, was named Panzerblitz Pz (Panzerabwehrrakete) and could be launched from short rails of just 705 mm. Both versions, afterwards known as Panzerblitz 1, were developed by the technical team of the Waffernwerke Brünn firm in Czechoslovakia and shared its manufacturing with DWM Lübeck.

The Panzerblitz Pz was tested on the Fw 190 A-8 W.Nr.733705 in the E-Stelle Tarnowitz, at the end of 1944, being used in combat by the units 7./SG4, 8./SG4, 9./SG4, 3.(Pz)/SG9, I.(Pz)/SG9, 9./SG9, 3./SG1, 6./SG1, 9./SG2, 9./SG77, 13./SG9 and 13./SG151. The poor performance in combat by Buchsenrohr and Panzerblitz 1 was a consequence of their low flying speed. The rockets were not powerful enough to follow a straight trajectory and could not be accurately aimed.

It was decided to match the most powerful engine available (that of the R4M) to the best hollow-charge warhead of 8.8 cm Raketenpanzerbüchse Granate 4992. The result was the R4MP (Rakete 4 Kg Minenkopf Panzerbüchsengranate) anti-tank rocket of 4 kg with armour piercing warhead and a speed of 370 m/s. Developed and manufactured in small series by Waffenwerke Brünn, it was tested by the Luftwaffe under the name Panzerblitz Pb2.

The higher diameter of the 4992 grenade decreased the range of the weapon due to the drag.

To improve the design, a new rocket named Panzerblitz Pb 3 was built, with a more powerful engine and an aerodynamic ovoid coverage in the forward area of the grenade. The AZ 5095 fuse was replaced by the Az Rz 2 impact fuse of the R4M.

Test launches were performed with the Pb3 before the end of the war obtaining speeds of 480/570 m/sec. The Pb 4 variant was being studied using the same warhead and a speed of 600 m/sec. The bigger diameter of the 4992 grenade prevented the launch of the Pb2 from the same devices as the R4M and it was necessary to modify the Abschussrost launcher of twelve rails into one of seven units known as the AG 150.

	Calib.	Length	Weight	Max. speed	Warhead type
RS 82	82 mm	560 mm	6.8 Kg	315 m/sec	Fragmentation
RBS 82	82 mm	607 mm	15 Kg	-	Armour piercing
8 cm RSpGr	78 mm	724 mm	6.9 Kg	290 m/sec	Fragmentation
Panzerblitz RSp Gr	78 mm	915 mm	-	290 m/sec	Fragmentation
Panzerblitz Pz	80 mm	705 mm	6.54 Kg	374 m/sec	Armour piercing

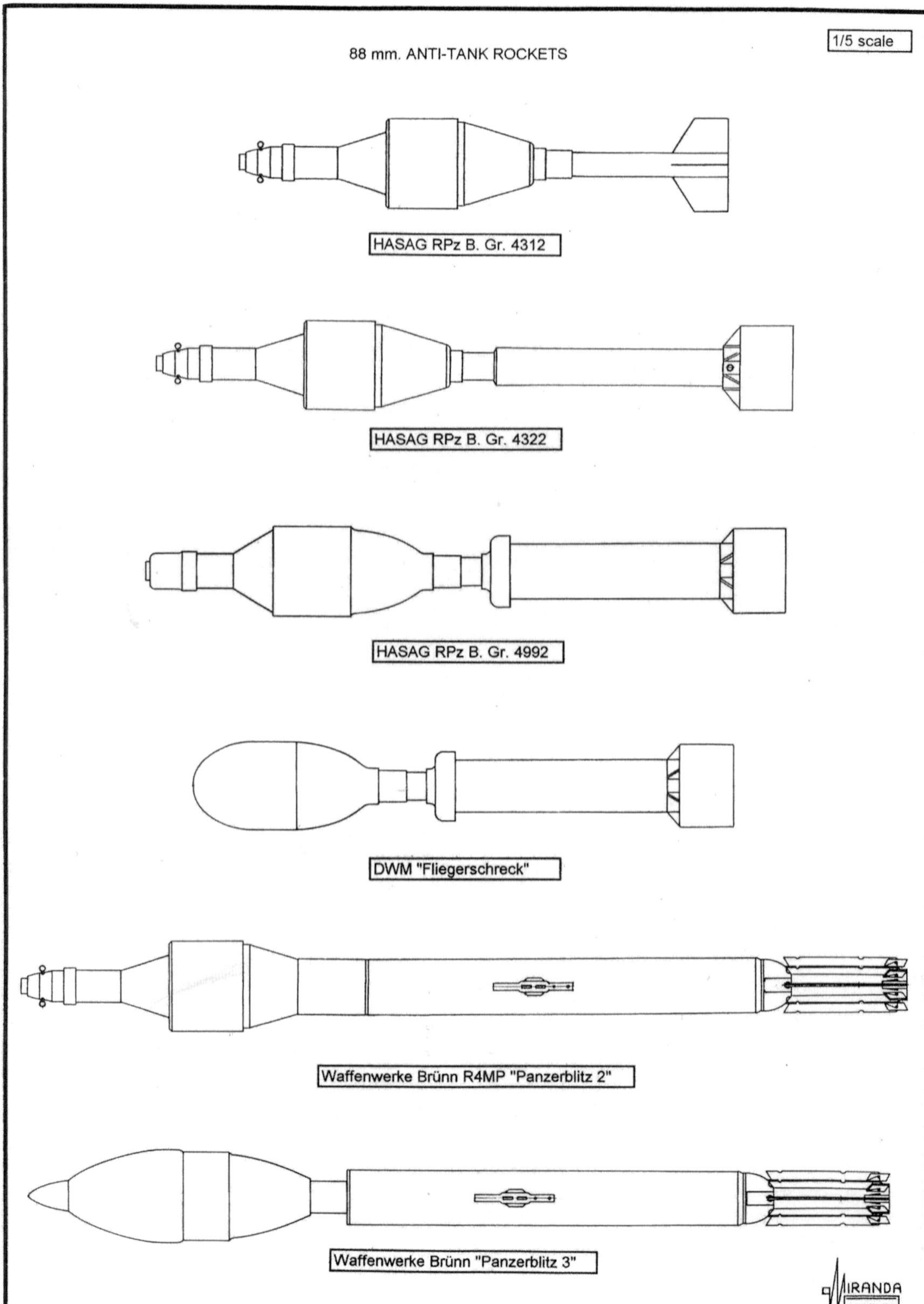
1/5 scale
88 mm. ANTI-TANK ROCKETS
HASAG RPz B. Gr. 4312
HASAG RPz B. Gr. 4322
HASAG RPz B. Gr. 4992
DWM "Fliegerschreck"
Waffenwerke Brünn R4MP "Panzerblitz 2"
Waffenwerke Brünn "Panzerblitz 3"
MIRANDA

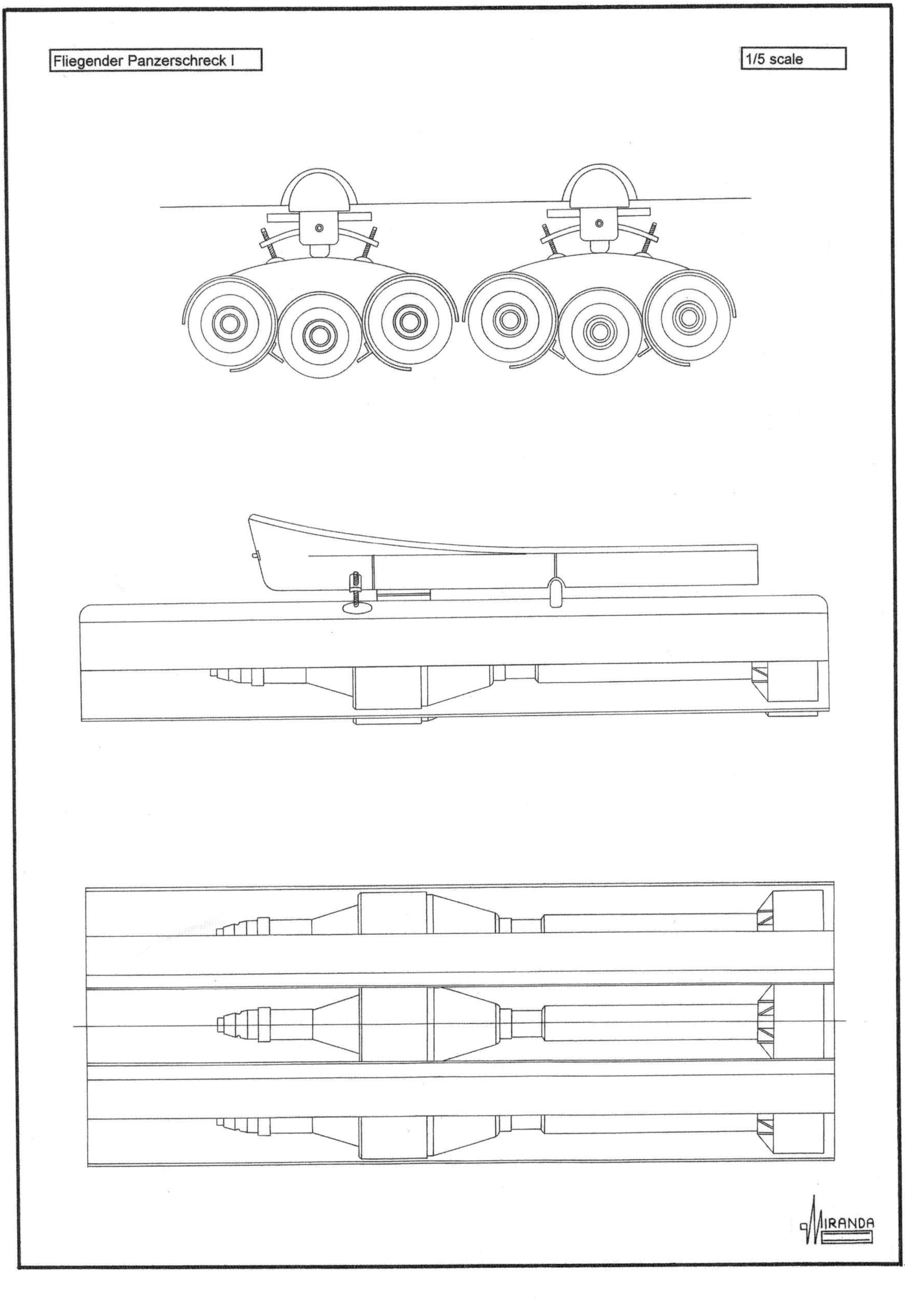
Fliegender Panzerschreck I
1/5 scale
MIRANDA

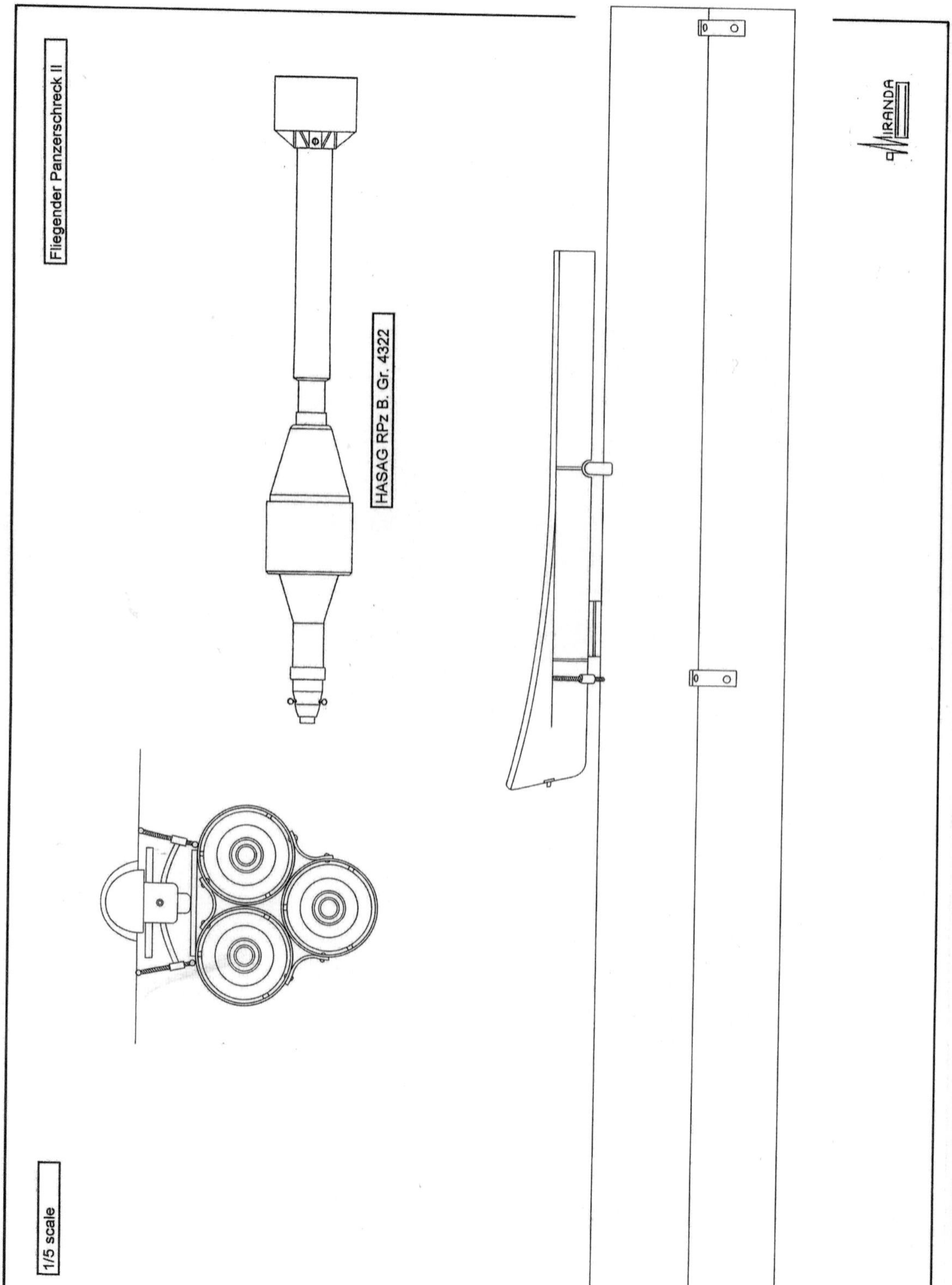
Fliegender Panzerschreck II
HASAG RPz B. Gr. 4322
1/5 scale

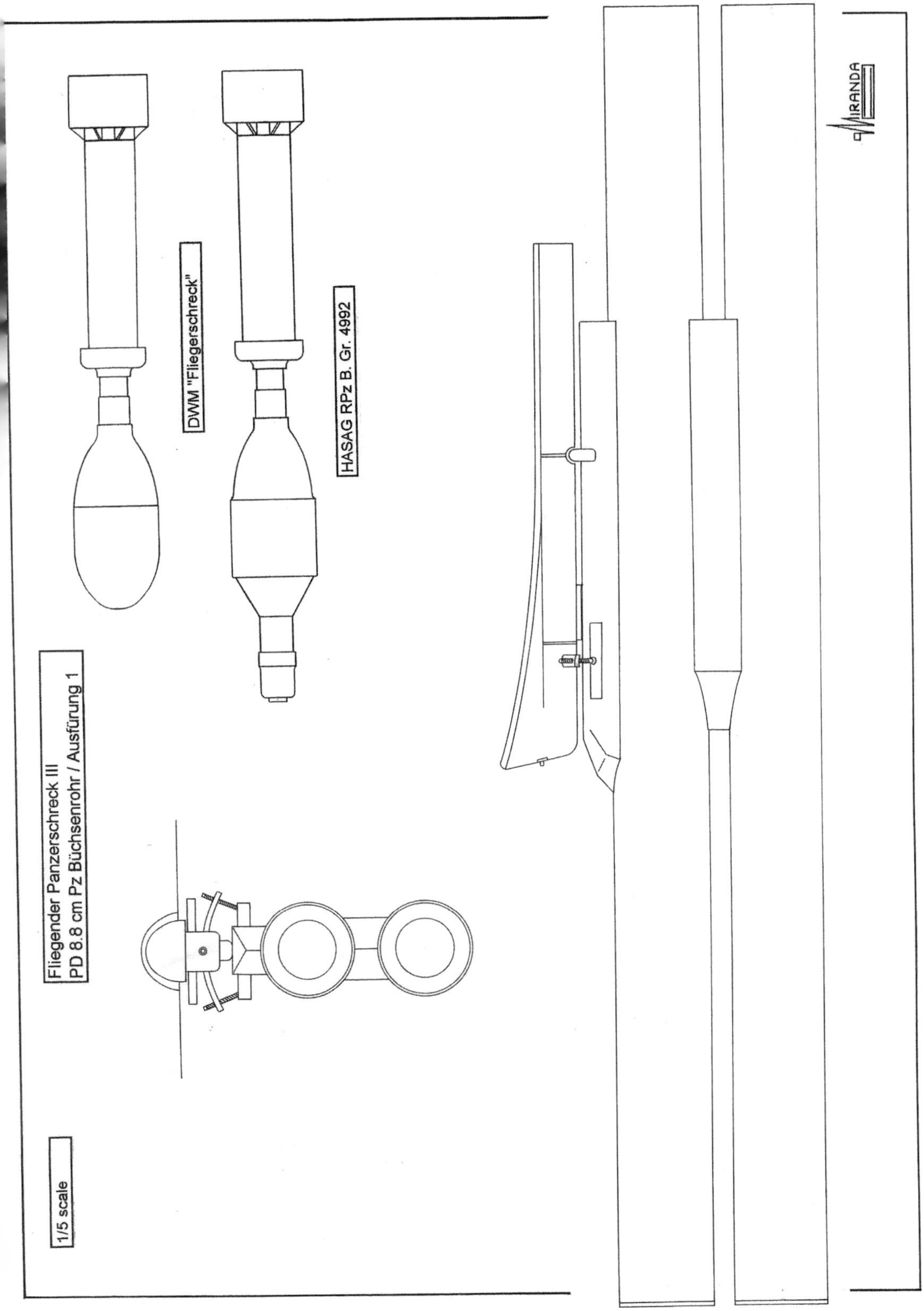
DWM "Fliegerschreck"
HASAG RPz B. Gr. 4992
Fliegender Panzerschreck III
PD 8.8 cm Pz Büchsenrohr / Ausfürung 1
1/5 scale
MIRANDA

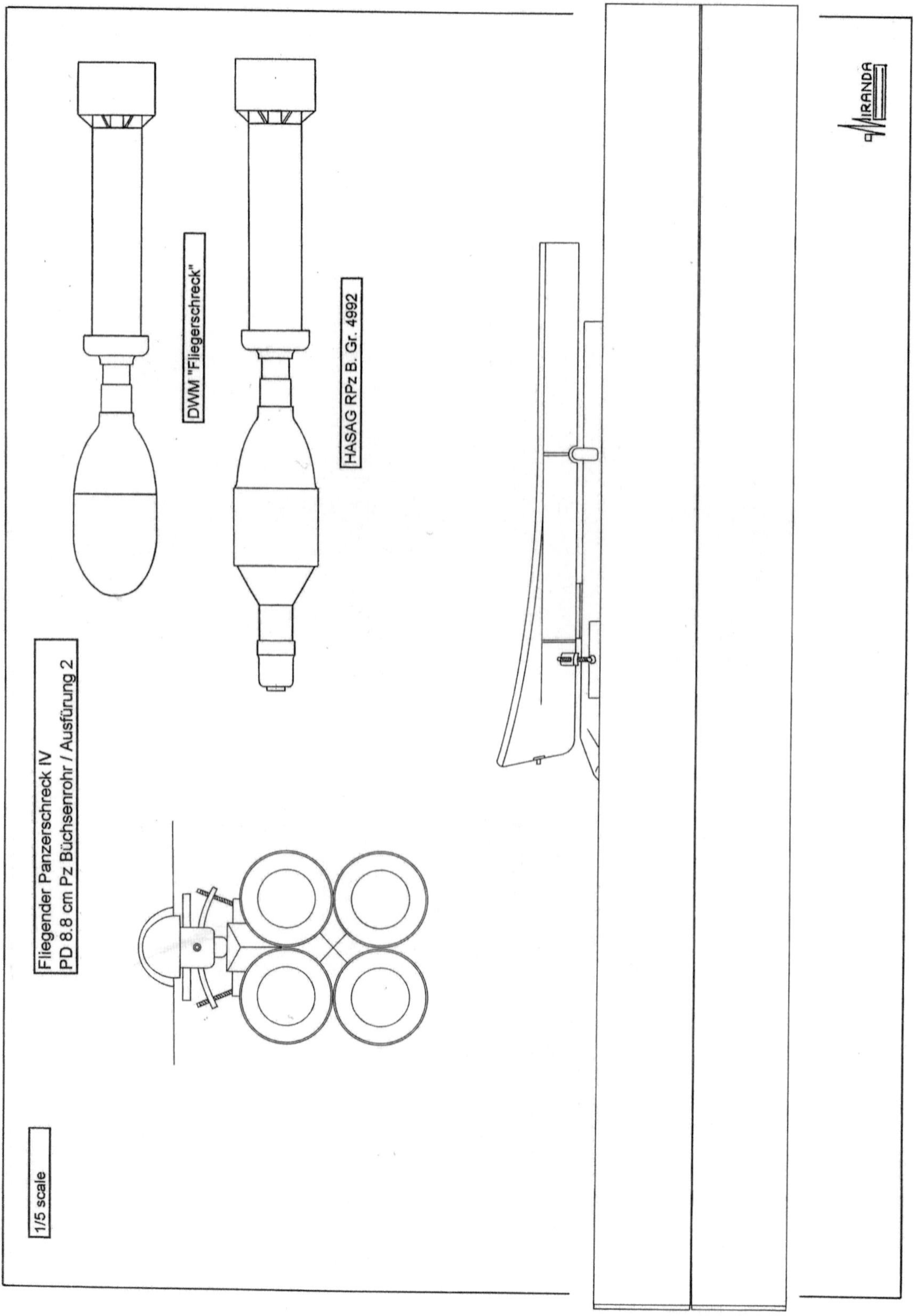
Fliegender Panzerschreck IV
PD 8.8 cm Pz Büchsenrohr / Ausfürung 2
DWM "Fliegerschreck"
HASAG RPz B. Gr. 4992
1/5 scale

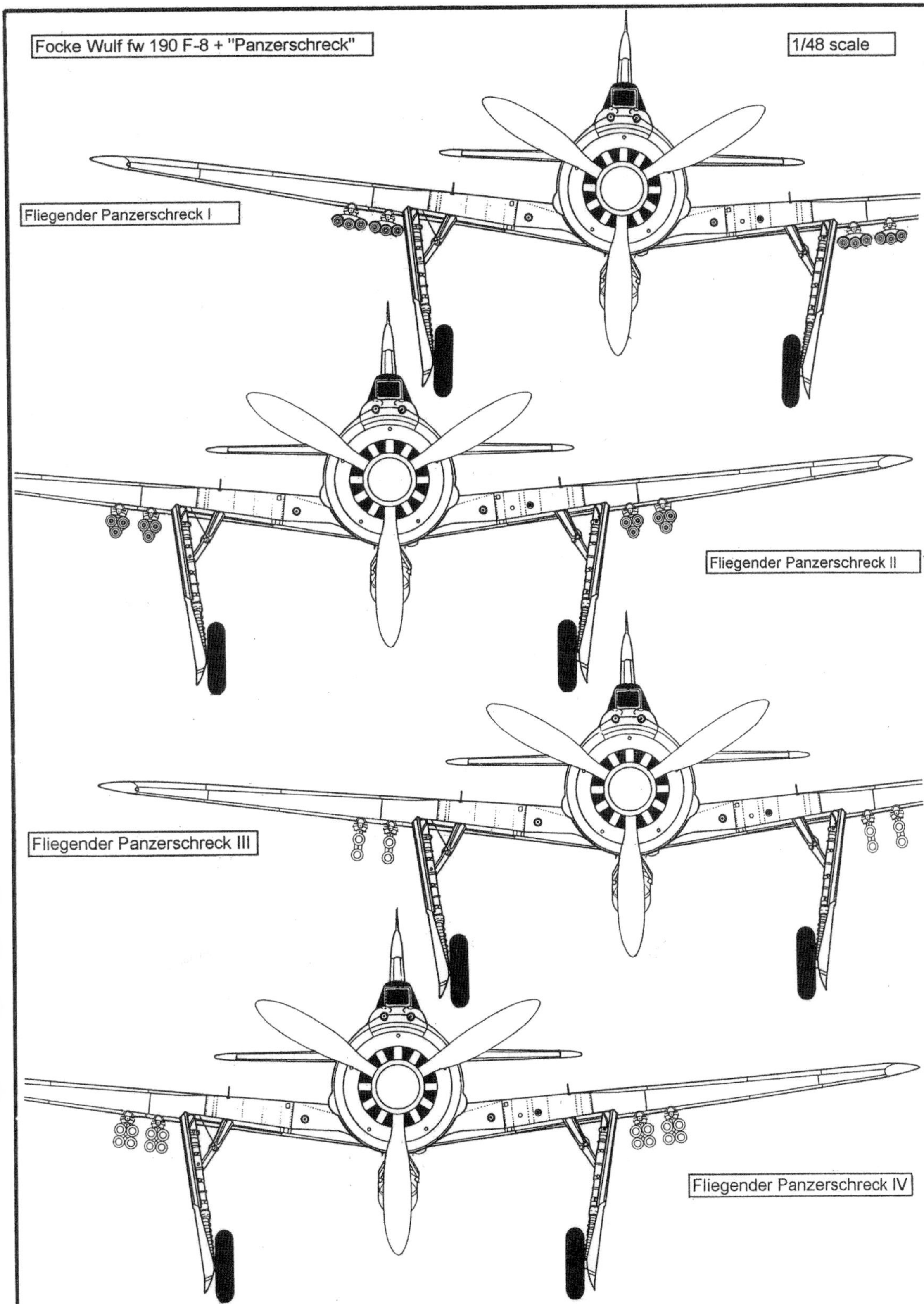
Focke Wulf fw 190 F-8 + "Panzerschreck"
1/48 scale
Fliegender Panzerschreck I
Fliegender Panzerschreck II
Fliegender Panzerschreck III
Fliegender Panzerschreck IV

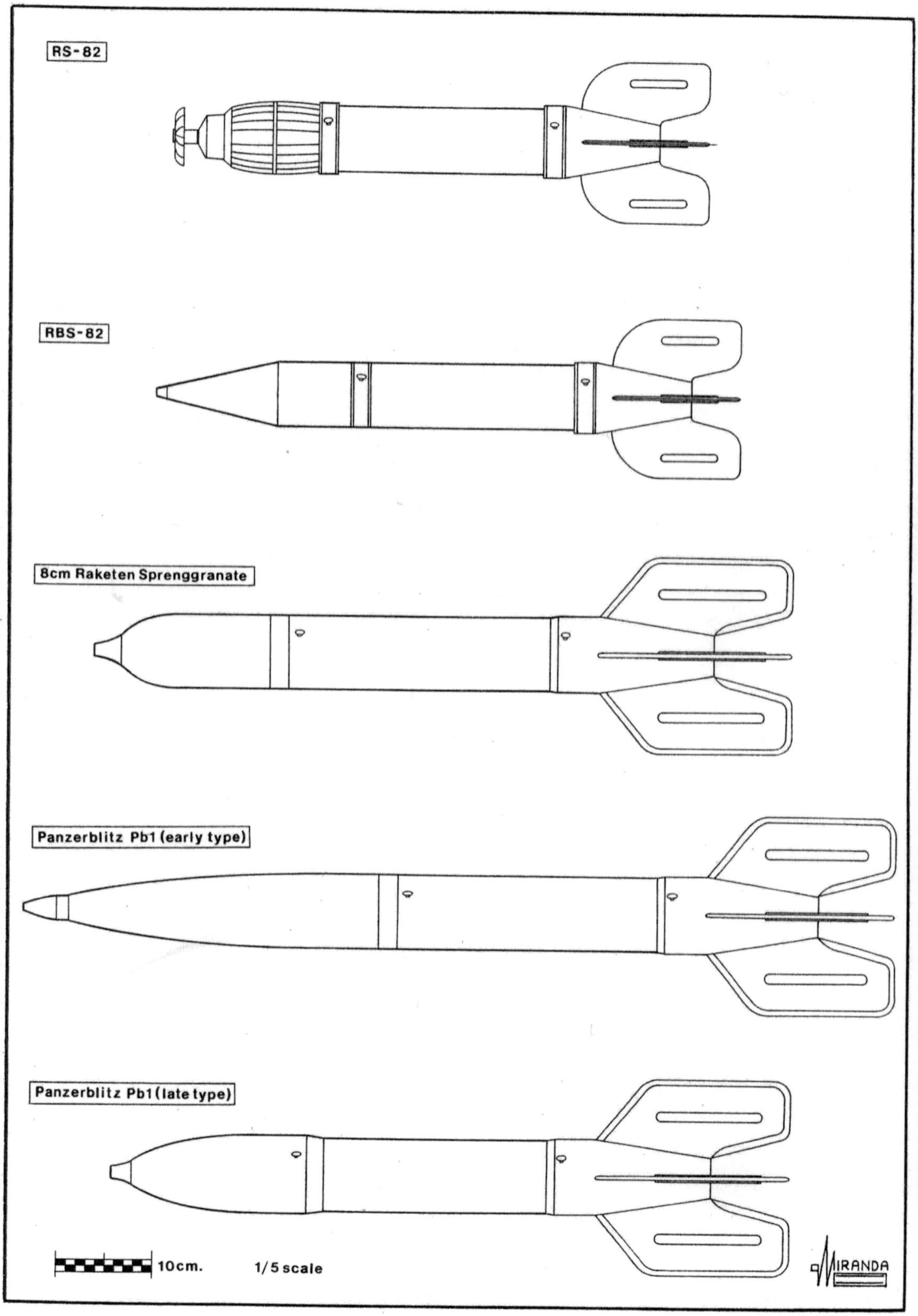
RS-82
RBS-82
8cm Raketen Sprenggranate
Panzerblitz Pb1 (early type)
Panzerblitz Pb1 (late type)
10cm.
1/5 scale
MIRANDA

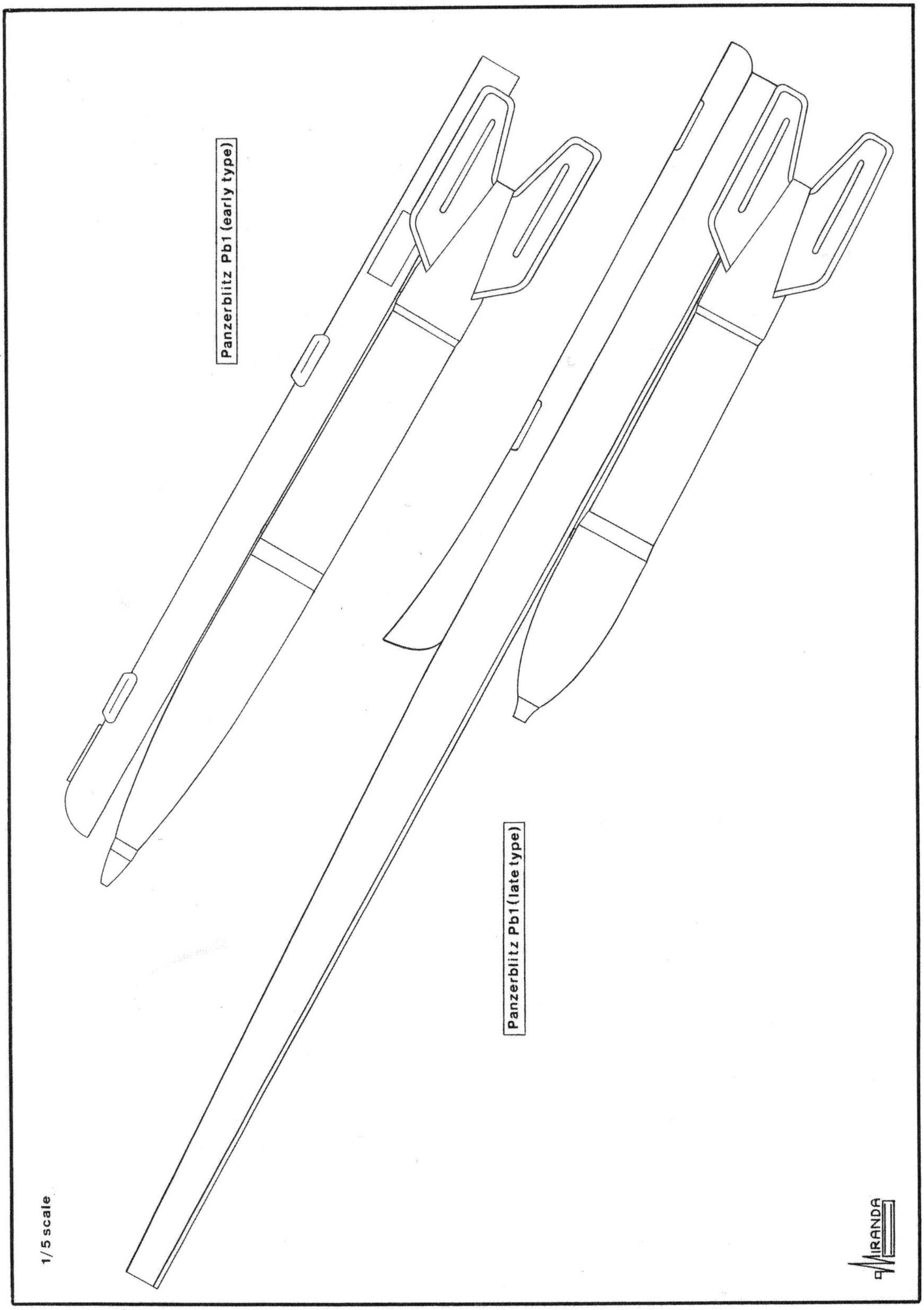
Panzerblitz Pb1 (early type)
Panzerblitz Pb1 (late type)
1/5 scale

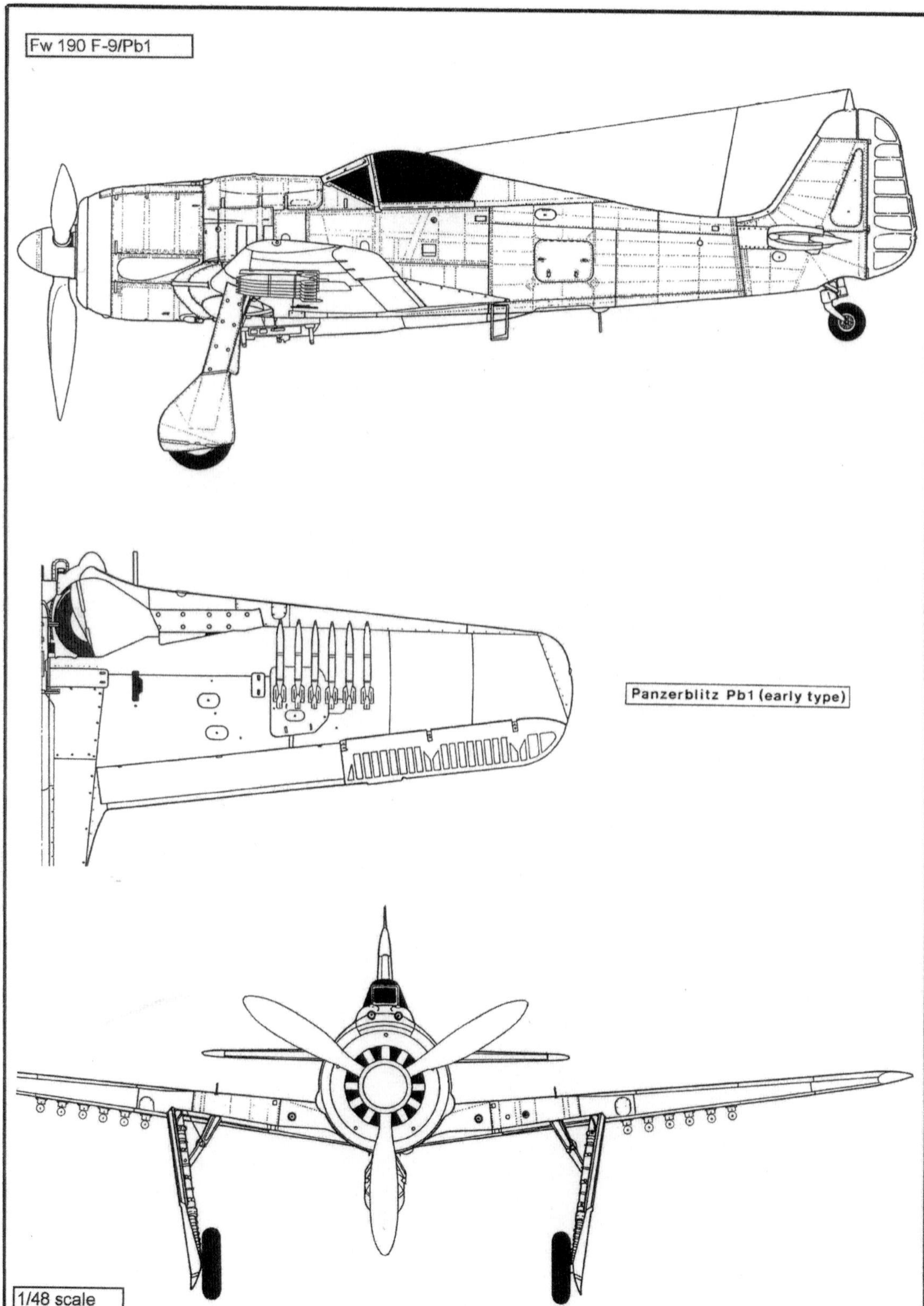
Fw 190 F-9/Pb1
Panzerblitz Pb1 (early type)
1/48 scale

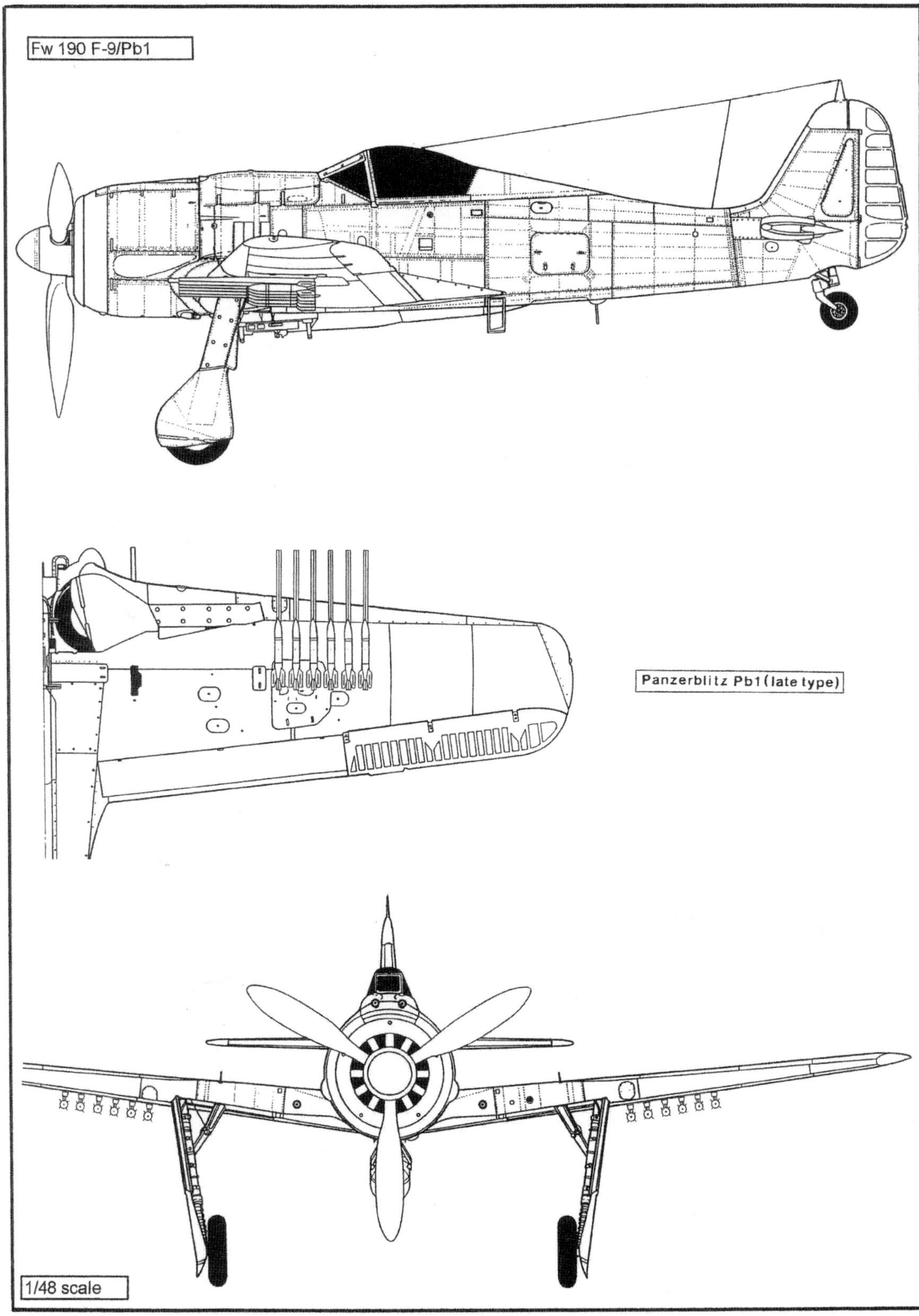
Fw 190 F-9/Pb1
Panzerblitz Pb1 (late type)
1/48 scale

Chapter 41

Blohm und Voss BV246 B Hägelkorn

The BV246 B was an anti-ship glide bomb designed by Dr Richard Vogt in 1943. Originally designated BV 226, the plan was that it was to be wireless-guided from a launch aircraft. The initial production version, named BV 246 A, used the radio link system, Y-Verfahren.

The BV 246 B had a gyroscopic stabilisation system. Models C and D were projects only.

The E-1 was an antiaircraft missile with Wasserfall guidance system.

The F-3 had a ZSG Netzhaut infrared seeker device.

The F-4 was fitted with a Tonne-Seedorf TV guidance system.

The F-5 had a ZSG Radieschen radar passive seeker against Loran navigational radio systems.

The F-6 was fitted with a Höhenführung radiocontrol device.

The BV 246 B had a length of 3,525 mm, 6,408 mm span, and 542 mm diameter. The fuselage was of wood and the wings were made of steel and concrete, manufactured by Magnesit-Zement. Total weight was 730 kg.

It was to be launched from 7,000 m of altitude and, thanks to its glide ratio of 25:1, had a range of 210 km at 450 km/h. The warhead contained 435 kg of HE Amatol 39 and an impact fuse. Flight tests were performed in Unterlüss and Karlshagen using a He 111 H-6 of KG 101, a Ju 188 E-1, a Fw 190 V2 with ETC 2000 bomb rack, a Fw 190 F-8 and a Fw 190 G-8.

The planned operational version was the Fw 190 A-5/U15. By the beginning of 1944, 1,100 units had been built. After ten test launches and eight failures, the program was cancelled on 26 February 1944.

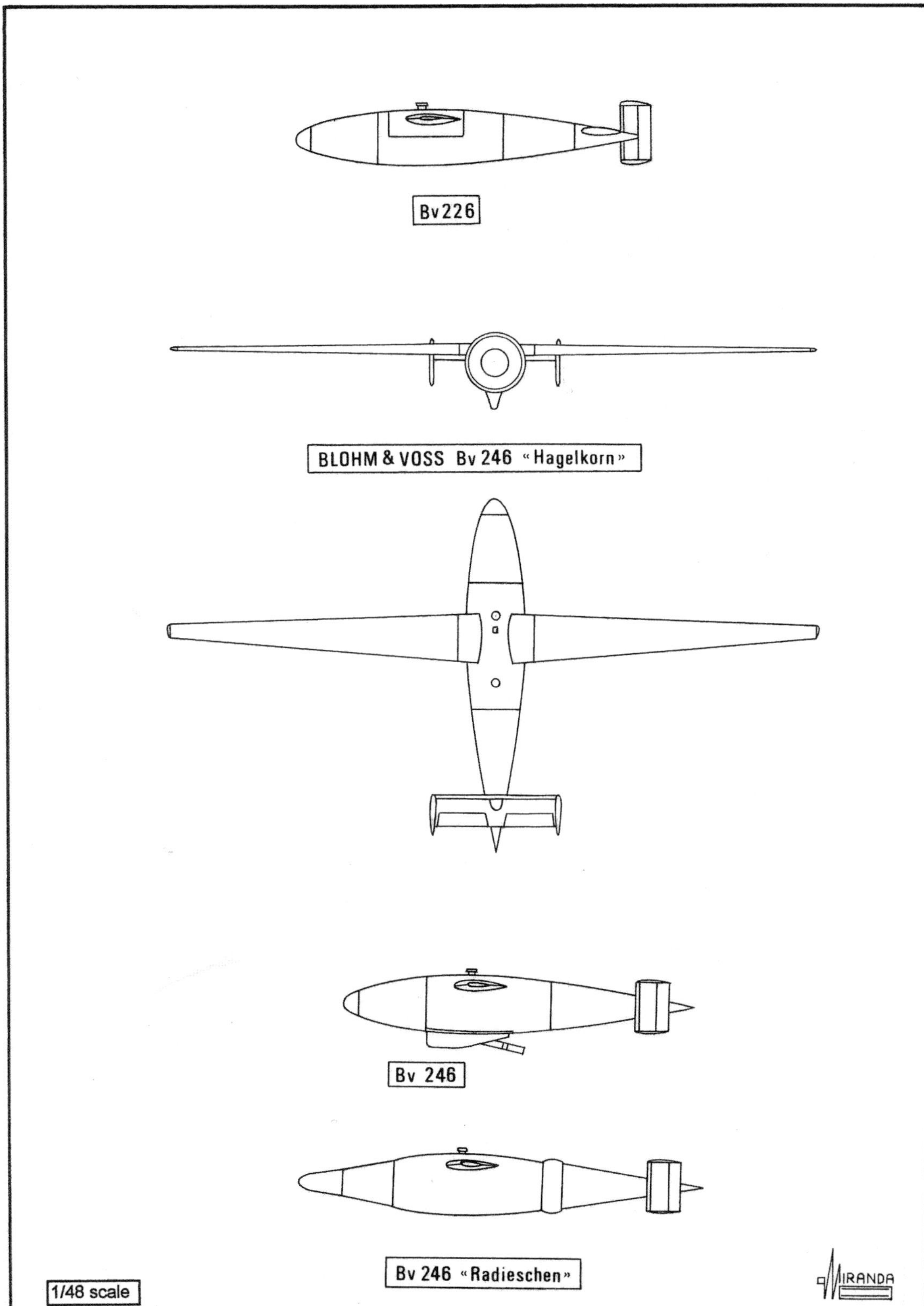
Bv226
BLOHM & VOSS Bv 246 «Hagelkorn»
Bv 246
Bv 246 «Radieschen»
1/48 scale
MIRANDA

Chapter 42

Gotha P.56 & 57

Gotha P.56

The Gotha P.56 was a small aircraft designed by DFS to be towed by a Fw 190 A-5, attached by two wires of 6.6 mm in length. The Gothaer Waggonfabrik firm had planned its manufacturing in three versions: parasite fighter, fuel tank and glider bomb, all of them with 'V' tail and 5.18 m span.

There were several accidents during the tests performed by DFS with a Fw 190 B due to the glider's tendency to fly above the Fw 190, and the project had to be abandoned.

Gotha P.57

The P.57 was a 500 kg glider bomb project designed to be towed by a Ta 152 C.

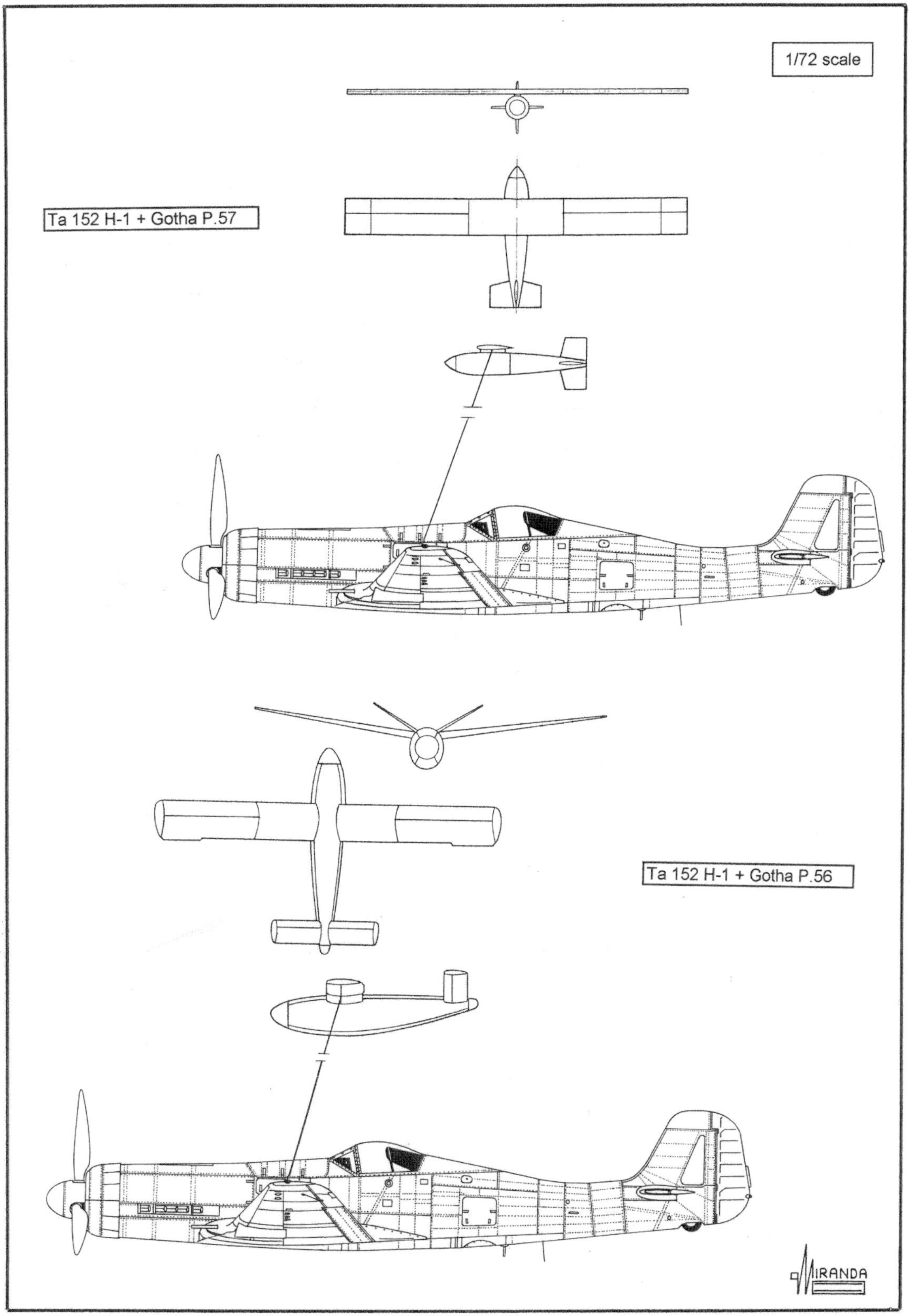
1/72 scale
Ta 152 H-1 + Gotha P.57
Ta 152 H-1 + Gotha P.56
MIRANDA

Chapter 43

Hs 298 Luftkampfrakete

This was the world's first air-to-air missile, developed by Henschel und Sohn in 1944 under the leadership of Dr Ing. Herbert Alois Wagner. It was a small metallic airplane propelled by rockets and equipped with a proximity fuse that activated the warhead.

Two different versions were built. The V1 was 2,003 m long and was fitted with a 30-degree swept-back wing with a span of 1,290 m. It carried a 25 kg HE warhead and a Fuchs radio-fuse manufactured by AEG. The engine was a Schmidding 109-543 (SG 32) solid fuel rocket with 150 kp thrust. The guidance system was a FuG 203 Kehl/FuG 230 Strassburg. Two controllers were required to guide it to its target and it could be launched only from big airplanes of the Ju 88 G, Ju 388 L and Do 217 N type. Its maximum speed was 234 m/sec and had a range of 1,600 m.

The V2 had a length of 2,680 m with a 38-degree swept-back wing with a span of 1,274 m. The warhead contained 48 kg of HE and the proximity fuse (acoustic) was a Kranich, manufactured by Ruhstahl AG. Its maximum speed was of 175 m/sec and its range of 2,000 m. The guidance system, which required a single operator, was a FuG 512 Kogge/FuG 530 Brigg and could be used from single-seat fighters.

More than three hundred missiles of both models were fired during extensive testing at Karlshagen between December 1944 and February 1945. It was established that the attack had to be within a cone of about 30 degrees semi-angle astern of the target. They were launched from Focke Wulf 190 V69 (works no. 582072), V70 (works no. 80029) and F-8 (works no. 583431, 583438 and 584221).

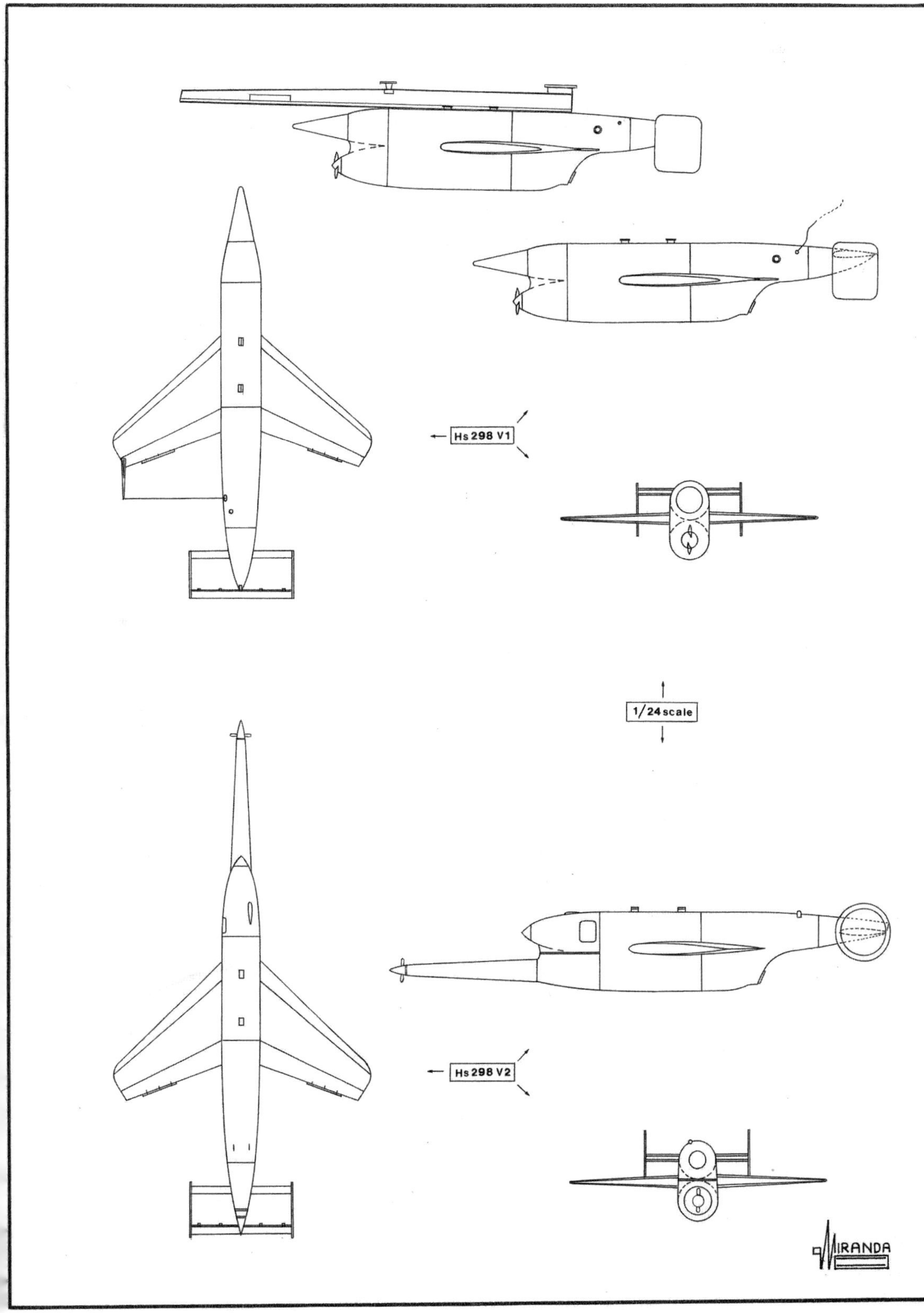
Hs 298 V1
1/24 scale
Hs 298 V2
MIRANDA

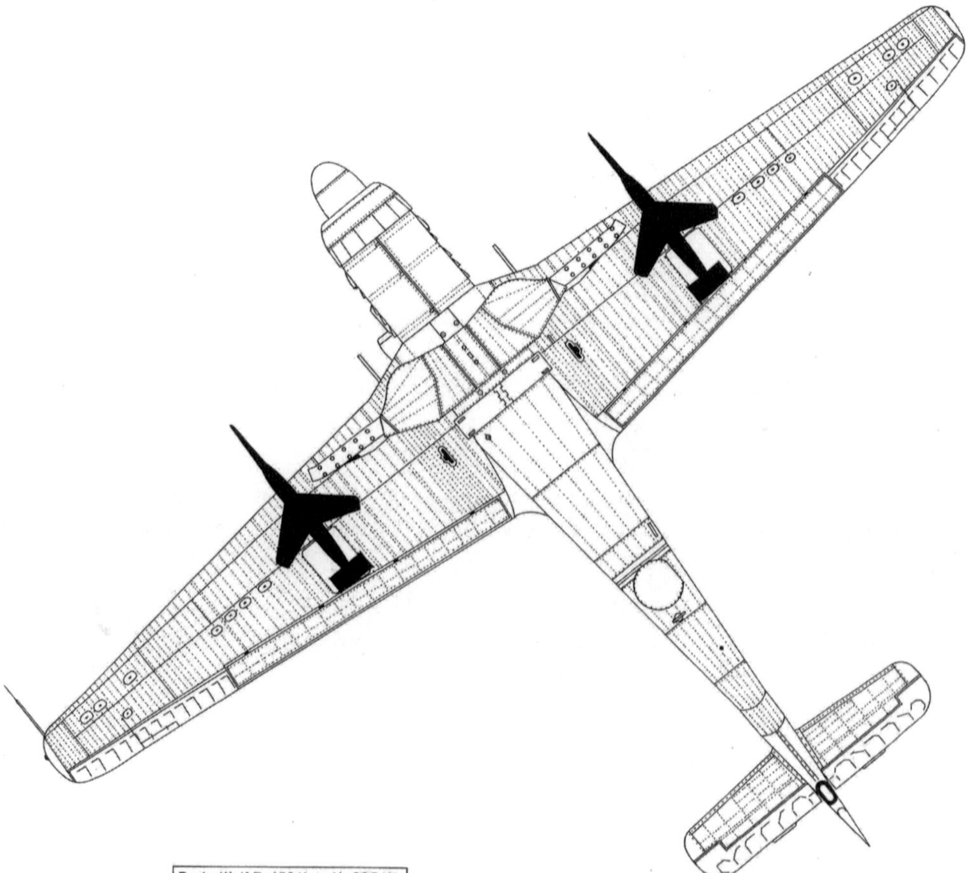

Focke Wulf Ta 152 H-1 + Hs 298 V2

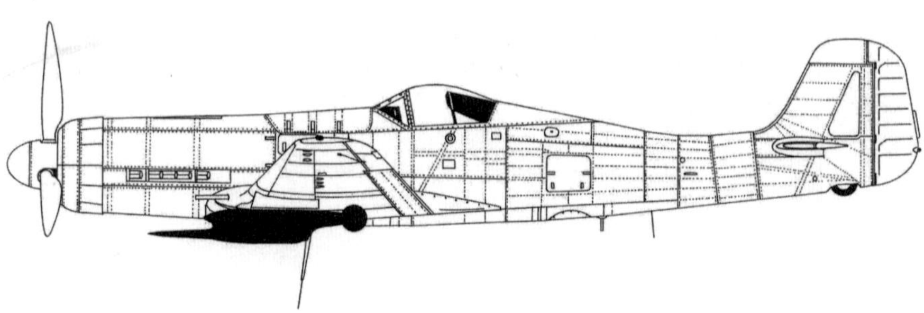

MIRANDA

1/72 scale

Chapter 44

Ruhrstahl 8-344 (X-4) Jägerrakete

The long-range X-4 air-to-air missile was a wire-guided rocket based on the work of Dr Max Kramer from the DVL. It was mass produced at the Ruhr Stahlwerke AG in Brackwede until the end of 1944.

Designed to be launched from smaller daytime fighters, it was fitted with a 20 kg warhead of HE and a wire and joystick guidance system FuG 228 Detmold/FuG 510 Düsseldorf.

The engine was a BMW 548 bifuel rocket of 140 kp thrust, which provided a range of 3,500 m. The warhead detonation, with a lethal radius of 15 m, was produced by an acoustic proximity fuse, an impact fuse or a self-destroying fuse.

In November 1944 it was decided to examine the use of the X-4 as an anti-tank weapon with an impact fuse and a solid fuel rocket engine Schmidding 109-543 of 150 kp thrust.

Between 1,300 and 1,500 units of both types were built between August and December 1944. The flying tests were performed at Karlshagen test centre between November 1944 and February 1945, using Ju 88 G-1, Ju 388 and several Fw 190 airplanes, two prototypes – the V69 and V70 (works nos. 582072 and 530025) – and three F-8 (works nos. 583431, 583438 and 584221) with underwing racks of the ETC 503, ETC 70 AI and ETC 71 CI types.

The air-to-air version measured 2,001 mm of length and 725 mm of span, weighted 60.5 kg and reached a maximum speed of 248 m/sec. The anti-tank version was fitted with a 88 mm hollow-charge R.Pz.BGr 4992 warhead

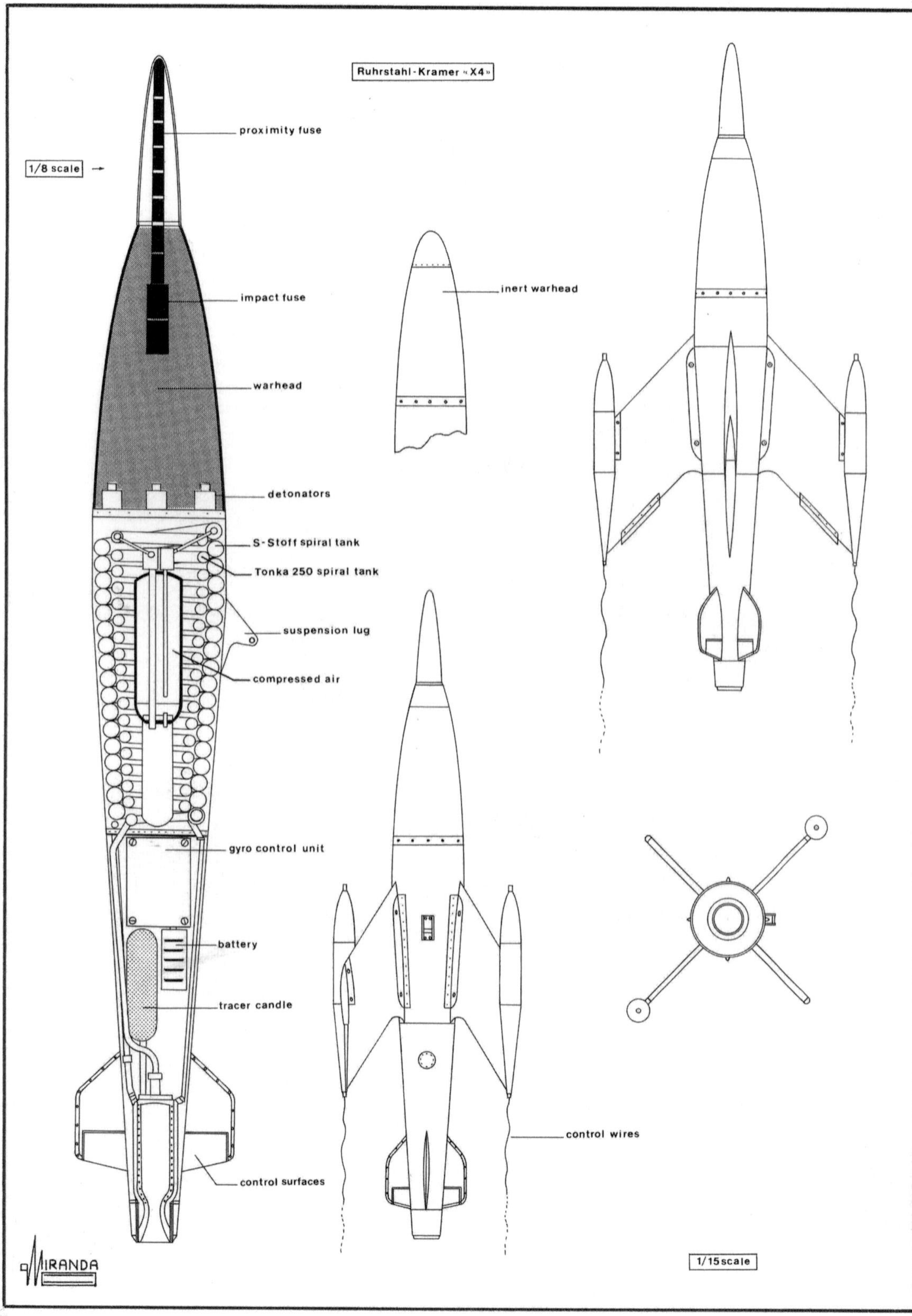
Ruhrstahl-Kramer «X4»
1/8 scale
proximity fuse
impact fuse
warhead
detonators
S-Stoff spiral tank
Tonka 250 spiral tank
suspension lug
compressed air
gyro control unit
battery
tracer candle
control surfaces
inert warhead
control wires
1/15scale
MIRANDA

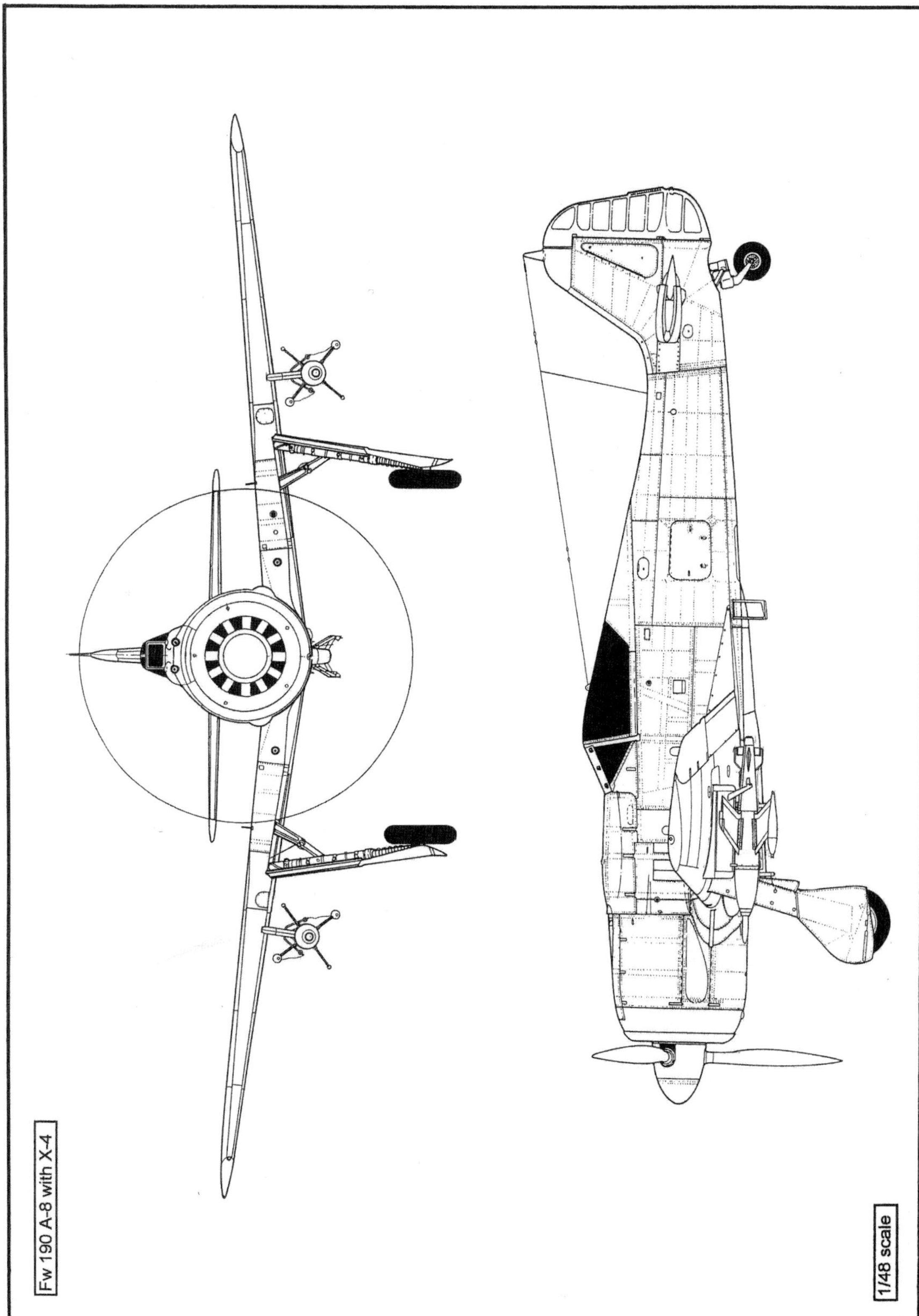
Fw 190 A-8 with X-4
1/48 scale

Index